☀ INSIGHT GUIDES

THAILAND

Discovery
CHANNEL

APA PUBLICATIONS
Part of the Langenscheidt Publishing Group

INSIGHT GUIDE
THAILAND

ABOUT THIS BOOK

Editorial

Project Editor
Scott Rutherford
Editorial Director
Brian Bell

Distribution

UK & Ireland
GeoCenter International Ltd
The Viables Centre, Harrow Way
Basingstoke, Hants RG22 4BJ
Fax: (44) 1256 817988

United States
Langenscheidt Publishers, Inc.
36-36 33rd Street, 4th Floor
Long Island City, NY 11106
Fax: (1 718) 784 0640

Canada
Thomas Allen & Son Ltd
390 Steelcase Road East
Markham, Ontario L3R 1G2
Fax: (1 905) 475 6747

Australia
Universal Publishers
1 Waterloo Road
Macquarie Park, NSW 2113
Fax: (61 2) 9888 9074

New Zealand
Hema Maps New Zealand Ltd (HNZ)
Unit D, 24 Ra ORA Drive
East Tamaki, Auckland
Fax: (64 9) 273 6479

Worldwide
**Apa Publications GmbH & Co.
Verlag KG (Singapore branch)**
38 Joo Koon Road, Singapore 628990
Tel: (65) 6865 1600. Fax: (65) 6861 6438

Printing

Insight Print Services (Pte) Ltd
38 Joo Koon Road, Singapore 628990
Tel: (65) 6865 1600. Fax: (65) 6861 6438

©2005 Apa Publications GmbH & Co.
Verlag KG (Singapore branch)
All Rights Reserved
First Edition 1978
Thirteenth Edition 1998
Updated 2005

CONTACTING THE EDITORS
We would appreciate it if readers
would alert us to errors or out-
dated information by writing to:
**Insight Guides, P.O. Box 7910,
London SE1 1WE, England.
Fax: (44) 20 7403 0290.
insight@apaguide.co.uk**
NO part of this book may be reproduced,
stored in a retrieval system or transmitted
in any form or means electronic, mechan-
ical, photocopying, recording or otherwise, without prior written permission of
Apa Publications. Brief text quotations
with use of photographs are exempted for
book review purposes only. Information
has been obtained from sources believed
to be reliable, but its accuracy and
completeness, and the opinions based
thereon, are not guaranteed.

www.insightguides.com

This guidebook combines the interests and enthusiasms of two of the world's best-known information providers: Insight Guides, whose titles have set the standard for visual travel guides since 1970, and Discovery Channel, the world's premier source of non-fiction television programming. Editors of Insight Guides provide both practical advice and general understanding about a destination's history, institutions, culture and people. Discovery Channel and its website, www.discovery.com, help millions of viewers explore their world from the comfort of their own home, at the same time encouraging them to reach out and experience it first-hand.

This 13th edition of *Insight Guide: Thailand* journeys to one of Asia's most accessible nations and long-lived kingdoms. Our writers and photographers will help reveal it all – epic history, exquisite food, Buddhist foundations, and the rich and varied destinations, from the chaotic boulevards of Bangkok to the often serene solitude of Thailand's beaches and villages.

Using this book

The book is carefully structured to convey an understanding of Thailand and its culture, and to complete information on travel, accommodation, restaurants and other practical aspects of the country. Information is located quickly using the index printed on the back-cover flap, which also serves as a handy bookmark.

The contributors
This edition was supervised by **Scott Rutherford**. A considerable amount of the updating was done by three associates of CPA in Chiang Mai: **Andrew Forbes**, with a doctorate in Asian history; **Simon Robson**, who lives in Mae Sa; and **David Henley**, who has lived in Thailand for well over a decade. Bangkok was updated by **Susan Cunningham** – who also updated Ko Samui and Nan – along with **Paul Hicks**.

Jerry Hopkins, a best-selling author, wrote about arts, architecture and the *Rama-kien*. **Ken Scott** updated Phuket and Krabi, and Bangkok-based **Sandy Barron** covered the Gulf Coast and the west of Thailand. Over-hauling the extensive Travel Tips was **Katja Thomas**, who also updated areas just outside of Bangkok. The *Insight On* picture stories were written by **Clare Griffiths**. This revised edition was updated by **Suksawat Sabaijai** in 2004 and was edited by **Clare Griffiths** in Insight Guides' London office.

In 2005, this guide was again updated with the help of Suksawat Sabaijai, under the supervision of **Jocelyn Lau** in Insight Guide's Singapore office.

Wat Sri Mongkran, Mukdahan.

expertly guide the reader through its sights and attractions:
◆ The Features section covers the country's history and culture in lively authoritative essays written by specialists.
◆ The Places section provides full details of all the sights and areas worth seeing. The chief places of interest are coordinated by number with specially drawn maps.
◆ The Travel Tips listings section at the back of the book offers you a convenient point of reference for

Map Legend

──‧‧──	International Boundary
⊖	Border Crossing
─‧─‧─	National Park
─ ─ ─ ─	Ferry Route
✈	Airport
🚌	Bus Station
Ⓟ	Parking
❶	Tourist Information
✉	Post Office
⁘	Archaeological Site
∩	Cave
🛉	Statue/Monument
★	Place of Interest

The main places of interest in the **Places** section are coordinated by number with a full-colour map (e.g. ❶), and a symbol at the top of every right-hand page tells you where to find the map.

INSIGHT GUIDE
THAILAND

CONTENTS

Limestone formations, Phuket area.

Insight on....

Information panels

Places

Travel Tips

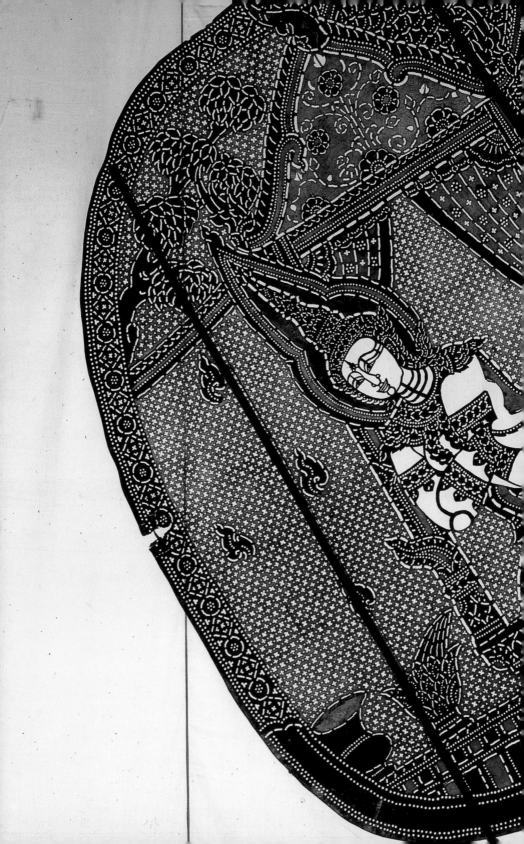

KINGDOM OF THAILAND

Imagine a place that defines graciousness, tolerance
and aesthetic ideals. You've just imagined Thailand

Land of the free, land of smiles. The former is a literal translation of *Thailand*, while the latter is a promotional slogan that carries considerable truth. Both define the Thai people. Beneath their graciousness, the Thai have a strong sense of self and a humanity without subservience. It is this pride in themselves, and in their monarchy, that underlies the Thai sense of identity and an ability to smile at the vicissitudes of life.

The Kingdom of Thailand is ruled by an elected government but is inspired by the world's longest-reigning monarch, who celebrated 50 years on the throne in 1996. It has a population of over 64 million and is about the same size as France – twice that of Britain. Its climate is tropical, with three seasons: the hot season (March–May), the wet or monsoonal season (June–November) and the cool season (December–February). The capital city of Bangkok, called Krung Thep in Thai, has at least 10 million people (accurate estimates are by definition dubious) and lies at the same latitude as Khartoum, Guatemala City and Manila.

Just inland from the apex of the Gulf of Thailand, Bangkok is the country's international gateway, and its seat of government, business and the royalty. It is almost a city-state unto itself and bears little similarity to the rest of the nation. When a Thai says that "I'm heading upcountry tomorrow," she or he could mean anywhere outside of Bangkok's city limits. Anywhere is upcountry. Indeed, the second-largest city in Thailand (Udon Thani) is perhaps one-fortieth the population of Bangkok. Most of Thailand is rural, a patchwork of rice fields, villages, plantations and forests.

Thailand is commonly divided into four regions: the central plains, of which Bangkok is a part; the north, including Chiang Mai and Chiang Rai; the northeast; and the south, extending from Chumphon down to the Malaysian border. Each region has its own culture and appeal.

Since the East first encountered Siam a millennium ago and the West began trickling in during the 16th century, Thailand has been a powerful magnet for adventurers and entrepreneurs. An abundance of resources, a wealth of natural beauty, a stunning cultural tradition revealed in dazzling architecture and art, and a warm, hospitable people have proved irresistible lures.

Thailand's traditional charms form only one side of the picture, of course. It is a country in transition, rapidly changing from a developing to a developed country in a roller-coaster of a ride. In the

PRECEDING PAGES: centuries-old illustration of elephants from a temple mural; architectural detail from Bangkok's Grand Palace; *nang yai*, the shadow-puppet; daughter and her father, protected from evil and misfortune by body tattoos and amulets.
LEFT: Buddha images of Wat Mahathat, in Phetchburi, south of Bangkok.

1990s, it went from being one of the fiercest of Asian economic tigers to nearly becoming an economic disaster, a precursor of the economic doldrums that hit Asia in mid-1997. But true to the people's spirit, consistent throughout the country's history, Thailand reversed course quickly, regained stability, and recovery is underway.

Throughout its history, Thailand has shown a stubborn maverick streak and a sense of pragmatism, both of which have created a determination to chart its own course. The result is a country that has never been colonised by a foreign power, has never sought to conquer a neighbour, and one that has intentionally retained its past while moving ahead into the future.

It is hard to ignore the changes taking place, yet there is much that sets Thailand apart from nations on similar paths. The natural beauty is still there in superb beaches, seas of green rice, and forested hills, somewhat safe now that logging is illegal (although it still happens). And even in the most modern towns, the past continues to shine through as temples, palaces and cultural presentations. This uniqueness is not always apparent, especially in a chaotic city like Bangkok that pounds on the senses unceasingly. *This is not the exotic Thailand I was promised,* the visitor whines. *This is a nightmare.* True, it is a city that is vibrantly alive, but it is also a repository of some of the world's most exquisite architecture and historical artefacts.

The Thais enjoy life. Something that fails to give personal satisfaction, whether in work or in play, is not worth doing. Any activity must have something of this quality within it, something that gives value to life. Part of this is distilled from holding on to one's traditions. This may change in Thailand, but for the moment, it is firmly intact. The traveller can't help but notice it.

About spellings of place names

The transliteration of Thai pronunciation into a Roman alphabet has proved to be a quagmire of phonemes and good intentions. The traveller will encounter several, not just one or two, possible spellings for a single place name. Leaps of linguistic creativity are in order as one negotiates street signs (often Romanised), maps and guide books, including this one. As much as possible, this book has sided with common sense and common usage, along with a dose of consistency.

When the letter *h* follows a consonant, it makes the consonant's sound less explosive, softer. Just as Thailand is pronounced *tai-land,* not *thigh-land*, so too with the *ph* sound. The pronunciation of *Wat Po* is the same as *Wat Pho*, and, in fact, they are the same temple in Bangkok. Similarly, the wonderful island of *Phuket* is always spelled with *ph*, but it is pronounced, always, like *poo-ket,* not *foo-ket* or in other less gracious ways. Other common variations of place-name spellings include *ratcha* and *raja*, and *chom* and *jom.*

The rule of thumb regarding spellings is to be like a Thai when in Thailand: adaptable and tolerant, and with a sense of humour. ❏

RIGHT: the canals in and around Bangkok still teem with life and are vital to the city's commerce. **OVERLEAF:** detail of mural.

Decisive Dates

PRE-THAI CIVILISATION

3600–250 BC: Ban Chiang culture flourishes in north-eastern Thailand.

circa **250 BC:** Suvannabhumi trading with India.

4th–8th century AD: influence of Mon and Khmer empires spreads into Thailand.

9th–13th century: Khmer Empire founded at Angkor. Thai peoples migrate south from Yunnan Province of China into northern Thailand, Burma, and Laos. Lopburi becomes an important provincial capital in Khmer Empire, and later tries to become independent.

SUKHOTHAI ERA

1238: Khmer power wanes. Kingdom of Sukhothai founded under Intaradit.

1281: Chiang Saen kingdom founded in north.

1296: Lanna Kingdom founded at Chiang Mai. Mangrai controls much of northern Thailand and Laos.

1280–1318: Reign of Ramkamhaeng in Sukhothai. Often called Thailand's "Golden Age," the period saw the first attempts to unify the Thai people, the first use of the Thai script, and flourishing of the arts.

1317–1347: Lo Thai reigns at Sukhothai. The slow decline of the Sukhothai kingdom starts.

1438: Sukhothai is now virtually deserted; power shifts to the Kingdom of Ayutthaya, to the south and along the Chao Phraya River.

KINGDOM OF AYUTTHAYA

14th century: Area around Ayutthaya settled by representatives of the Chiang Saen kingdom.

1350: City of Ayutthaya founded by Phaya U-Thong, who proclaims himself Ramathibodi I. Within a few years he controls the areas encompassed by the kingdoms of Sukhothai and the Khmer empire.

1369: Ramesuen, son of Ramathibodi, becomes king.

1390: Ramesuen captures Chiang Mai.

1393: Ramesuen captures Angkor in Cambodia.

1448–1488: Reign of King Trailok, who finally unites the Lanna (Chiang Mai) and Ayutthaya kingdoms.

1491–1529: Reign of King Ramathibodi II.

1549: First major warfare with Mon Kingdom of Bago.

1569: Burmese capture and destroy Ayutthaya.

1590: Naresuen becomes king and throws off Burmese suzerainty. Under Naresuen, Ayutthaya expands rapidly at the expense of Burmese and Khmer empires and flourishes as a major city.

1605–1610: Ekatotsarot reigns and begins significant economic ties with European traders and adventurers.

1610–1628: Reign of King Songtham. The British arrive and obtain land for a trading factory.

1628–1655: Reign of Prasat Thong. Trading concessions expand and regular trade with China and Europe is established.

1656–1688: Reign of King Narai. British influence expands. Reputation of Ayutthaya as a magnificent city and a remarkable royal court spreads in Europe.

1678: Constantine Phaulkon arrives at Narai's court and gains great influence; French presence expands.

1688: Narai dies, Phaulkon executed.

1733–1758: Reign of King Boromakot. Ayutthaya enters a period of peace, and of arts and literature.

1767: Burmese King Alaungpaya captures and sacks Ayutthaya. Seven months later General Phaya Taksin returns and expels the Burmese occupiers. He moves the capital from Ayutthaya to Thonburi, near Bangkok.

BEGINNING OF THE CHAKRI DYNASTY

1767: Phaya Taksin crowned as King Taksin.

1779: Generals Chao Phaya Chakri and his brother Chao Phaya Sarasin conquer Chiang Mai, expel the Burmese from what is now Thailand, adding most of the Khmer and Lao kingdoms to the Thai kingdom. The Emerald Buddha is brought from Vientiane, Laos, to Thonburi.

1782: The now-erratic Taksin deposed and executed, and Chao Phaya Chakri is offered the throne, founding the Chakri dynasty and assuming the name Ramathibodi and later Rama I. Capital is moved across the river to Bangkok. Under Rama I, the Siamese Kingdom consolidates and expands its strength. Rama I revives Thai art, religion, and culture.

1809–1824: Reign of Rama II, best known for construction of Wat Arun and many other temples and monasteries. Rama II reopens relations with the West, suspended since the time of Narai.

1824–1851: Reign of Rama III, who left as his trademark the technique of embedding Chinese porcelain fragments as decorations on temples.

1851: King Mongkut (Rama IV) ascends the throne. He is the first Thai king to understand Western culture and technology. Before becoming king he spends 27 years as a monk, studying Western science.

1868: Chulalongkorn (Rama V) ascends the throne, reigning for the next four decades, the second-longest reign of any Thai king. Chulalongkorn ends the custom of prostration in royal presence, abolishes slavery, and replaces corvée labour with direct taxation. Schools, infrastructure, military and government modernised.

1910–1925: Reign of Vajiravudh (Rama VI), Oxford-educated and thoroughly Westernised.

1925–1932: Reign of Prajadhipok (Rama VII). Pressures from the Great Depression encourage discontent.

END OF THE ABSOLUTE MONARCHY

1932: A coup d'état ends the absolute monarchy and ushers in a constitutional monarchy.

1939: The name of the country is officially changed from Siam to Thailand, "Land of the Free." King Ananda (Rama VIII) ascends the throne.

1942: Japan invades, with the acquiescence of the military government, but a resistance movement thrives.

1946: King Ananda is killed by a mysterious gunshot, and Bhumibol Adulyadej (Rama IX) ascends the throne. The royal family becomes a symbol of national spirit.

1973–1991: Bloody clashes between army and demonstrating students bring down the military government; political and economic blunders bring down the resulting civilian government just three years later. Various military-backed and civilian governments come and go for almost 20 years.

1992: Another clash between military forces and civilian demonstrators brings the leaders of both factions kneeling in contrition in front of the king; the military leaves government to the civilian politicians. Thailand begins five years of unprecedented economic growth. The face of Bangkok modernises dramatically.

1996: King Bhumibol Adulyadej celebrates his golden jubilee of 50 years on the throne.

1997: Thailand's banking system and economy begins a free-fall as the baht loses half of its value.

1998: While other Asian economies wallow in crisis, Thailand follows guidelines established by the International Monetary Fund to resuscitate its economy.

1999: The government institutes a series of legal, finance sector and economic reforms. The Thai economy returns to growth.

2000: Senators for the Upper House are democratically elected for the first time under a new constitution.

2001: Thaksin Shinawatra and his Thai Rak Thai party win the national polls for the Lower House.

2002: Unhappy with PM Thaksin's hardline policies in the south, Thai Muslim nationalists step up terror operations in Yala, Pattani and Narathiwat provinces.

2004: Indian Ocean earthquake-generated tsunami claims 8,000 lives along Thailand's Andaman coast.❑

CHAKRI MONARCHY

Since 1782, a single royal dynasty – known as Chakri – has lorded over Thailand.

Rama I (Chakri)	1782–1809
Rama II (Phutthalaetia)	1809–1824
Rama III (Nangklao)	1824–1851
Rama IV (Mongkut)	1851–1868
Rama V (Chulalongkorn)	1868–1910
Rama VI (Vajiravudh)	1910–1925
Rama VII (Prajadhipok)	1925–1935
Rama VIII (Ananda)	1935–1946
Rama IX (Bhumibol)	1946–

LEFT: elephant on an old temple mural. **RIGHT:** portrait of King Chulalongkorn, or Rama V.

THE RISE OF SUKHOTHAI

Sukhothai, the "dawn of happiness," was the first independent Thai kingdom.
Many consider it to be the golden era of Thai history, and of Thai culture

The Thai people have fiercely defended their country's independence for more than 800 years, and can boast the distinction of being the only country in Southeast Asia never to have been a European colony. Nor has the country been divided by serious civil war, as tumultuous as modern Thai politics can be. Indeed, Thai shrewdness in international diplomacy has won them the admiration of nations far more powerful and influential.

The name *Thai* means "free." Although the country was called *Siam* by foreigners from the 12th to the 20th centuries, to its citizens it always carried the name of its capital – Sukhothai and Ayutthaya, for example. In the l9th century, Siam was adopted as the official name of the kingdom, but this was changed to Thailand in 1939.

In the beginning

The origin of the ethnic Thai has been hotly debated for decades. Popular tradition claims that the first people fled to Siam from China to escape the depredations of Kublai Khan's hordes sweeping southward out of Mongolia. The theory might explain Thai empathy with later immigrants. Other theories suggest they originated in Thailand a millennium or two ago; Thais found in today's China are said to have emigrated north from Thailand about 1,000 years ago. Whichever conjecture is correct, it is accepted that the Thais' first home in Thailand was in the northern hills. As the centuries passed, they shared the country with ethnic Laotians, who populated the northeast, bringing a similar language and culture. The southern isthmus linking Thailand (from Bangkok south) with the Malay Peninsula became the home of Muslims. Over the centuries, the population was augmented by Hindu and Sikh Indians, who arrived as merchants, and by Chinese.

PRECEDING PAGE: two terracotta figures from the Sukhothai period. **LEFT:** sculpture from Sukhothai of a Hindu deity. **RIGHT:** illustration of two early indigenous Thai men.

Ban Chiang culture

But long before the Thai people migrated into today's Thailand, the Chao Phraya valley was inhabited by a high civilisation. The first discovery of their prehistoric relics was made during World War II, by a Dutch prisoner of war forced to work on the Siam–Burma "Death

Railway." He uncovered Stone Age implements at Ban Kao, in the western province of Kanchanaburi, which led to the discovery of Paleolithic and Neolithic caves, and to cemeteries containing pottery, tools and other artefacts.

The most important site, however, is the tiny village of Ban Chiang, near Udon Thani in the northeast. Excavations have uncovered painted pottery, jewellery, and bronze and iron tools. If thermoluminescent dating is correct, the Bronze Age in Thailand corresponds to – and according to some, may even predate – that of the Tigris-Euphrates Valley civilisation, which preceded the Bronze Age in Europe. The idea remains controversial, however.

The identity of the Ban Chiang people is a mystery. According to archaeological timetables, the existence of pottery normally suggests a culture already 2,000 years along the road to civilisation; Ban Chiang's pottery dates from about 3600 BC. Settlement seems to have lasted until 250 BC, after which the people mysteriously faded from history. While they thrived, they farmed rice, domesticated various animals, and developed highly original pottery-decorating skills, with each design unique to that pot alone and not repeated in others. Their red-painted jars, decorated with fingerprint whorl patterns, were buried in funeral mounds as offerings. Glass beads and semiprecious stones were also included in the mounds.

OTHER ORIGINS

The Ban Chiang findings illustrate a high level of culture and technology. It also suggests, but not without debate, that China may not be the sole origin of East Asian civilisation.

fied as Southeast Asia. By the beginning of the Christian era, maritime trading between India and the south of Thailand had begun. Hindu statues found at settlements in southern Thailand suggest habitation from about the 4th century. In later centuries, Buddhism and Hinduism – along with Indian ceremonial rites, iconography, law codes, and cosmological and architectural treatises – were adopted *en bloc* by the Southeast Asian ruling elite and modified to suit local requirements and tastes. Sanskrit became the court lan-

guage, while Pali was the language of the Buddhist canons. Native chiefs wanting to consolidate power and increase their prestige may have been responsible for this diffusion of culture, calling in Brahman priests (Indians of the priestly caste) to validate and consecrate their rule.

Indian influence

Archaeological evidence is scant, but ancient texts discuss the presence of people from India in the region around the 3rd century BC.

The Sinhalese Buddhist chronicle, the *Mahavamsa*, relates that India's great Emperor Ashoka (ruled 268 to 232 BC), the first royal patron of Buddhism, sent two missionaries to Suvannabhumi, the "land of gold" now identi-

This transmission at court level had a vital and permanent impact, especially in nearby Cambodia. The Mons and Khmers were the first Indianised peoples to form settlements in present-day Thailand. Mon influence is evident in the Buddhist art of the Dvaravati period (6th–11th century); the Khmers, famed as the builders of Cambodia's Angkor Wat, left many temples in Thailand's northeastern provinces. There is also archaeological evidence of Mon religious settlements at Lopburi and Nakhon Pathom, from the 7th century onwards.

Arrival of the Thais

As noted earlier, there are several theories to explain the early habitation of Thailand. The most persuasive one says that from perhaps as early as the 10th century, a people living in China's Yunnan region migrated down rivers and streams into the upper valleys of the Southeast Asian river system. There, they branched off. The Shans, also known as Thai Yai (Great

Mai, in 1296. Long after the main group of Thais moved further down the peninsula to establish more powerful states, Chiang Mai continued to rule more or less autonomously over the northern region, maintaining a distinctive culture of its own. By the 13th century, the Thais had begun to emerge as the dominant rulers of the region, slowly absorbing the weakened empires of the Mons and Khmers. Their rise to power culminated around 1238, when (according to inscriptions) the Khmers were expelled from Sukhothai.

The history of peninsular Thailand is lesser known than that of the north. It was once under

Thais), went to Upper Burma. The Ahom Thais established themselves in Assam. Another group settled in Laos, and yet another occupied the island of Hainan, off the Vietnamese coast.

The greatest number of Thai Noi (Little Thais) first settled in the north of modern Thailand, around Chiang Saen and valleys to the south. They formed themselves into principalities, some of which later became independent kingdoms. The first was in 1238, at Sukhothai, at the southernmost edge of Thai penetration. Then came Chiang Rai, in 1281, and Chiang

LEFT: perhaps from India, terracotta figures found in central Thailand. **ABOVE:** Sukhothai stone engraving.

the control of the mighty empire of Srivijaya, which existed from the 8th–13th century. Ancient chronicles state that in the Srivijayan capital, "a man at noon cast no shadow." This suggests an equatorial location, but there is serious disagreement where that might be. There are competing schools of thought, each claiming Palembang in Sumatra, or Chaiya in southern Thailand. A site in Borneo has also been postulated. The proof of claim forwarded for Chaiya is the discovery of an 8th-century inscription of a Srivijayan king, at Chaiya, near the Kra Isthmus. The empire disintegrated during the 13th century and its dependencies were absorbed by Sukhothai.

Dawn of Sukhothai

The name *Sukhothai* translates into "the dawn of happiness", and if early inscriptions are to be believed, its people enjoyed considerable freedom to pursue their livelihoods. This first independent Thai kingdom is considered the golden era of Thai history, and is often looked back upon with nostalgia as the ideal Thai state. It was a land of plenty, governed by just and paternal kings who ruled over peaceful, contented citizens. Sukhothai represented early Thai tribal society in its purest form.

Siamese tradition attributes the founding of the kingdom to Phra Ruang, a mythological containers, which arrived in Angkor intact. This success aroused the suspicion of the Khmer king. His chief astrologer said the ingenious Thai inventor was a person with supernatural powers who constituted a threat to the empire. The king at once dispatched a gifted general – who had the magic ability to travel swiftly underground – to eliminate the Thai menace.

Phra Ruang perceived the danger and went to Sukhothai, where he concealed himself at Wat Mahathat as a Buddhist monk. The Khmer general, who coincidentally surfaced in the middle of the *wat*, was turned into stone by Phra Ruang. From then on, Phra Ruang's fame spread far and

hero. Prior to his time, according to historical legend, the Thai people were forced to pay tribute to the Khmer rulers of Angkor. This tribute was exacted in the form of sacred water from a lake outside Lopburi; the Khmer god-king needed holy water from all corners of the empire for his ceremonial rites, a practice later adopted by Thai kings.

Every three years, the water tribute was sent by bullock carts in large earthenware jars. The jars inevitably cracked en route, compelling the tribute payers to make second and third journeys to fill the required quota. When Phra Ruang came of age, he devised a new system of transporting water in sealed woven bamboo wide. He left the monkhood, married the daughter of Sukhothai's ruler, and when that monarch died, he was invited to the throne by popular mandate. He assumed the title Sri Indraditya, sovereign of the newly independent Kingdom of Sukhothai. Fact and fiction are inseparable in this popular account.

Rule of Ramkamhaeng

The most famous king of Sukhothai was the founder's second son, Ramkamhaeng. He was the first Thai ruler to leave detailed epigraphical accounts of the Thai state, beginning with his own early life. He earned his title at age 19 on a campaign with his father against a neighbouring state, in which he defeated the enemy leader in a Thai form of medieval jousting: hand-to-hand combat on elephant-back. As a result, he was named Phra Ramkamhaeng (Rama the Brave) by his father.

Around the time of Ramkamhaeng's accession, the Sukhothai kingdom was quite small, consisting only of the city and surrounding areas. By the end of his reign, he had increased its size tenfold – from Luang Prabang in the east, in modern-day Laos, through Thailand's central plains to the

> **BUDDHIST BEDROCK**
>
> Since the ancient days of Sukhothai, Buddhism has been deeply rooted in the Thai way of life. Together with the monarchy, it provides a continuity lasting to the present day.

bition of slavery and guaranteed inheritance. However, some experts now doubt its authenticity and believe the inscription to be a much later work.

The king was a devout and conscientious Buddhist of the Theravada school that was practised in Sukhothai. Exchanges were initiated with Sri Lankan monks that resulted in a purification of texts and an adoption of Sinhalese influences in *chedi* design. There remained, however, a trace of animism in Thai Buddhism. Ramkamhaeng wrote about a

southern peninsula. The Mon state in lower Burma also accepted his control.

Ramkamhaeng was noted as an administrator, legislator and statesman – and sometimes as an amorous king. He is credited with the invention of Thai script, which he achieved by systematising the Khmer alphabet with Thai words. A stone inscription bearing the date 1292 and employing the new script has been attributed to Ramkamhaeng. In the inscription, he depicted the idyllic conditions of his kingdom: fertile land and plentiful food, free trade, prohi-

Left: detail of Khmer ruins, Prasat Phanom Rung.
Above: Wat Mahathat, in old Sukhothai.

mountain-dwelling ghost named Phra Khapung Phi, a spirit "above all others in the land."

If correctly propitiated, he would bring prosperity to the country. The idea of a superior spirit looking after the Thai nation survives today, in the image of Phra Siam Devadhiraj, Siam's guardian angel.

One of the keys to Ramkamhaeng's success lay in his diplomatic relations with China. The Mongol court in northern China pursued a "divide-and-rule" policy and supported the Thais' rise, but at the expense of the Khmers. Ramkamhaeng was said to have gone to China himself in 1299, and the *History of the Yuan* records seven missions from Sien (Siam, or

Sukhothai) between 1282 and 1323. Chinese craftsmen came to teach the Thais their secrets of glazing pottery, resulting in the production of the famous ceramic ware of Sawankhalok, whose kilns still remain and whose products were shipped to China aboard Siamese junks.

In the same year, 1287, that Bagan fell to the armies of Kublai Khan, Ramkamhaeng formed a pact with two northern Thai princes, Mangrai of Chiang Rai and Ngam Muang of Phayo. The three agreed not to transgress, but instead to protect each others' borders against common enemies. The alliance was maintained throughout their lifetimes.

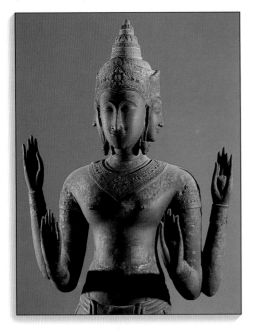

Founding of Chiang Mai

Mangrai completed Thai political ascendancy in the north by annexing the last Mon kingdom of Hariphunchai, in about 1292. He first sent an agent provocateur to sow discord, and when the time was right, his army "plucked the town like a ripe fruit."

Wishing to found a new capital, Mangrai invited his two allies to help him select a site. The location they agreed upon as truly auspicious was one where two white sambars, two white barking deer, and a family of five white mice were seen together. On that spot by the river Ping, Mangrai laid the foundation of Chiang Mai (New Town) in 1296, supplanting his

former capital at Chiang Rai and giving him a more centralised location from which to administer the southern portion of his newly expanded kingdom. Thus, Chiang Mai became the capital of the Kingdom of Lanna, which translates as "Land of the Million Rice Fields."

Tradition says Ramkamhaeng drowned in the rapids of the Yom River at Sawankhalok. His son, Lo Thai (ruled 1318–1347), preferring religion to war, lost the feudatory states as fast as he had gained them. He was called Dharmaraja, the Pious King, an epithet his successors also bore. The relationship between Sukhothai and Sri Lanka, the centre of orthodox Buddhism, intensified during his rule; Lo Thai recorded that he built many monuments to house sacred relics of the Buddha obtained from Sri Lanka.

Lo Thai's son, Li Thai, was as pious as his father. As heir to the throne, he composed a famous treatise on Buddhist cosmology, the *Traibhumikatha,* or *Tales of the Three Worlds*. When he became king in 1347, he ruled according to the ten royal precepts of Buddha. He pardoned criminals, for example, as he wanted to become a Buddha "to lead all creatures beyond the oceans of sorrow and transmigration."

The prioritising of religion over military affairs might have permitted the meteoric rise of one of Sukhothai's former vassal states, Ayutthaya. This kingdom expanded rapidly, extending its control over the Chao Phraya valley, until Li Thai was forced to acknowledge its hegemony. Deprived of his independence, the pious king took deeper refuge in religion, eventually assuming the yellow robe.

His family ruled for three more generations, but in 1378, power shifted to Phitsanulok, and Sukhothai's population followed. By 1438, Sukhothai was nearly deserted.

The Sukhothai period saw the Thai people, for the first time, develop a distinctive civilisation with their own administrative institutions, art and architecture.

Sukhothai Buddha images, characterised by refined facial features, linear fluidity, and harmony of form, are perhaps the most beautiful and the most original of Thai artistic expressions. Many authorities and Thais say that the Sukhothai aesthetic has been the high point of Thai civilisation. ❏

LEFT: Sukhothai Hindu deity. **RIGHT:** ruins of Wat Chetupon, Sukhothai.

AYUTTHAYA

Ayutthayan kings adopted Khmer cultural influences from the very beginning. Unlike those of Sukhothai, the rulers of Ayutthaya were absolute and inaccessible monarchs

History is ignorant regarding the ancestry of Ayutthaya's founder. But Thai folklore fills the lacuna. The king of Traitrung unhappily discovered that his unmarried daughter had given birth to a child after eating an aubergine, which a vegetable gardener had fertilised with his own urine. The culprit – Nai Saen Pom, or Man With a

kings. During the reign of Phaya U-Thong, a cholera outbreak forced the ruler to evacuate his people to the site of Ayodhya (Ayutthaya), an ancient Indianised settlement named after Rama's legendary kingdom in India.

The location of Phaya U-Thong's new capital was blessed with several advantages. Situ-

Hundred Thousand Warts – was summoned and promptly banished from the city, along with the princess and her new son.

The god Indra, with his divine eye, saw the misery of the trio and decided to grant the gardener three magic wishes. Saen Pom first asked for his warts to disappear. Next, he prayed for a kingdom to rule over. And lastly, he wanted a cradle of gold for his son. The child was known as Phaya U-Thong, Prince of the Golden Crib.

Rise of Ayutthaya

Historically, U-Thong was an independent principality in today's Suphanburi. Its rulers were members of the prestigious line of Chiang Saen

ated on an island at the confluence of the Chao Phraya, Lopburi and Pasak rivers, not far from the sea and surrounded by fertile rice plains, it was an ideal centre of administration and communications. Phaya U-Thong officially established the city in 1350, after three years of preparation, when he assumed the title Ramathibodi I, King of Dvaravati Sri Ayodhya. Within a few years, the king united the whole of central Siam – including Sukhothai – under his rule, and extended control to the Malay Peninsula and lower Burma. He and his successors pursued expansionist campaigns against Chiang Mai and the Khmers in Cambodia. No longer the paternal and accessible rulers that the kings of Sukhothai had been, Ayutthaya's sovereigns were absolute monarchs whose positions were enhanced by trappings of royalty reflective of a Khmer *devaraja* (god-king).

The *devaraja* concept was, however, tempered by the tenets of Theravada Buddhism, wherein the king was not actually divine, but was the protector and supreme head of the religion. Nevertheless, Khmer court rituals and language were emulated at the Ayutthaya court. Brahman priests officiated with Buddhist monks at state ceremonies.

KHMER INFLUENCES

Although the Thais were responsible for the decline and eventual collapse of the Angkor empire, the Ayutthaya kings adopted Khmer cultural and artistic influences from the very beginning.

Angkor three years later, and according to the *Pongsawadan*, the Annals of Ayutthaya, some 90,000 prisoners of war were taken. Given the economics of the time, labourers were more precious than gold.

The death blow to the Khmer capital was delivered in 1431 when forces entered Angkor. The Khmer king abandoned his ancient capital in favour of Phnom Penh. The Siamese army returned from the campaign with booty and many prisoners, including artists and Brahman priests.

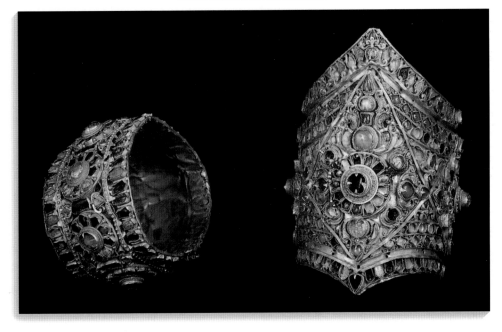

Ramathibodi I divided his administration into ministries of royal household, finance, interior and agriculture. This, and his subsequent legislation, provided a strong foundation for the kingdom, which survived for 417 years, with Ayutthaya as its capital.

Ramathibodi died in 1369. His son, Ramesuen, captured Chiang Mai in 1390, reportedly with the use of cannon, the first recorded use of this weapon in Siam. Ramesuen's army sacked

PRECEDING PAGE: 17th-century adventurers immortalised on a lacquer cabinet. **LEFT:** crypt mural detail, Wat Ratchaburana, Ayutthaya. **ABOVE:** Ayutthayan royal jewellery found at Wat Ratchaburana.

Reign of King Trailok

Two centuries of wars between Chiang Mai and Ayutthaya reached a climax during the reign of King Borom Trailokanath, more popularly known as Trailok, who ruled from 1448 until 1488. In his campaigns against Maharaja Sutham Tilok, guile and the occult complemented military might.

Envoys sent from Ayutthaya to Tilok were discovered to have buried seven jars containing ingredients which, it was feared, would magically bring doom upon Chiang Mai. The jars were cast into the river, followed by the envoys themselves, their feet tied to rocks. The fighting between these rival kingdoms led to the transfer of Ayutthayan power, from the capital to Phit-sanulok during the last 25 years of Trailok's reign. The war, however, ended in a stalemate.

Trailok is important for having introduced reforms that shaped the administrative and social structures of Siam, up until the 19th century. He brought Ayutthaya's loosely controlled provinces under centralised rule, and regulated *sakdi na*, an ancient system of land ownership that stratified society, dictated responsibilities of both overlord and tenants, and determined salary levels of the official hierarchy.

Trailok also defined a system of corvée labour, under which all able-bodied men were required to contribute labour during part of each working year to the state. This system indirectly heightened the status of women, who were responsible for the welfare of their families in the absence of the men.

Portuguese and Burmese

The 16th century was marked by the first arrival of Europeans, and by continual conflict with the Burmese. The Portuguese had conquered Malacca in 1511, and soon thereafter their ships sailed to Siam. King Ramathibodi II (ruled 1491–1529) granted the Portuguese permission to reside and trade within the kingdom in return

PALACE PROTOCOL

Trailok's Palace Law of 1450 spelled out the relative ranks of members of the royal family, prescribed the functions of the various grades of officials, and regulated official ceremonies.

It also fixed punishments: death for "introducing amatory poems" into the palace, for whispering during a royal audience, and amputation of the foot of anyone kicking a palace door.

The royal family was not spared punishment either, although the Palace Law stipulated that no menial hands were allowed to touch royal flesh. It was therefore the executioner's responsibility to beat the condemned royal personage at the nape of the neck with a sandalwood club.

for arms and ammunition. Portuguese mercenaries fought alongside the king in campaigns against Chiang Mai and taught the Thais the arts of cannon foundry and musketry.

But this did nothing to stem the rising tide of Burmese aggression against Ayutthaya, already weakened by wars with Chiang Mai. In 1549, the Burmese laid siege to Ayutthaya. The Ayutthayan king, Mahachakrapat, led a sortie against them. Not only his sons, but his wife and daughter accompanied him into battle mounted on elephants. The queen, disguised as a warrior, galloped her mount between the king and his Burmese foe when she saw her husband in trouble, saving his life, but losing her own.

The Burmese invasion of 1549 was doomed to failure. They withdrew, and Ayutthaya's defences were fortified with Portuguese help. Three hundred wild elephants were captured and trained for further wars against Burma.

Seven of the new war elephants were white ones. When Burma's new king heard about this, he launched another invasion of Ayutthaya.

In 1569, Ayutthaya fell to Burmese forces. The invading Burmese thoroughly ransacked and plundered the city, and forcibly removed much of Ayut-

WHITE ELEPHANTS

Buddhist kings of Southeast Asia treasured white elephants, considered to be auspicious, thus enhancing royal prestige and ensuring the country's prosperity.

Naresuen had gained an insight into Burmese armed strength and strategies during his formative years in Burma. He trained his troops in the art of guerrilla warfare; their hit-and-run tactics earned them the nicknames of Wild Tigers and Peeping Cats. Naresuen's opportunity to restore Siamese independence came following the death of the Burmese king in 1581. Revolts in the Burmese empire were tying down the new king at home when Naresuen declared Ayutthaya's freedom, in 1584. During the following nine years,

thaya's population to Burma. The king was among the captives of the Burmese; he died before arriving in Pegu.

The defeated king's leading deputy was appointed by the Burmese to rule Siam as a vassal state. His eldest son, Naresuen, was brought to Burma by the Burmese king as a guarantee for the new vassal's good conduct. Naresuen was repatriated to Siam at the age of 15. Together with his younger brother, Naresuen began to gather armed followers.

***

LEFT: mural image of a 17th-century European adventurer. **ABOVE:** European impression of Ayutthaya in the 17th century.

the Burmese made several attempts to resubjugate Siam, but Naresuen had taken thorough defensive measures and repulsed all invasions. On one of these occasions, he killed the Burmese king in single combat, both of them mounted on elephants.

Naresuen assumed full kingship upon his father's death in 1590. He reconsolidated the Siamese kingdom, then turned the tables on Burma with repeated attacks that contributed to the disintegration of the Burmese empire. The Khmers, who had been whittling away at Siam's eastern boundary during Ayutthaya's period of weakness, were also subdued. Under Naresuen, Ayutthaya prospered.

Door to the east

The reign of Naresuen's brother, Ekatotsarot, between 1605 and 1610, coincided with the arrival of the Dutch in Siam. Ekatotsarot was not interested in pursuing Naresuen's militaristic policies. Instead, he sought to develop Ayutthaya's economy. To these ends, he decreed several measures to increase state revenue, among them the introduction of taxes on commerce. This gave him a reputation as a "covetous man" among Europeans.

The Dutch opened their first trading station at Ayutthaya, in 1608. Keen to promote commercial relations, Ekatotsarot sent emissaries to

a demand in Thai society for luxury items like porcelain and silk. The Japanese, who already had established a sizeable community of traders at Ayutthaya, paid in silver for local Siamese products such as hides, teak, tin and sugar.

The Dutch established maritime dominance in the Far East when they drove the Portuguese out of Malacca, in 1641. Seven years later, they made a show of naval force in the Gulf of Siam, thereby persuading the Thai court to agree to certain trade concessions and giving the Dutch virtual economic control in Siam. A new king, Narai (ruled 1656–1688), despised the Dutch and welcomed the English as a European ally to

The Hague, the first recorded appearance of Thais in Europe. During the reign of Songtham (1610–1628), the English arrived bearing a letter from King James I. Like the Dutch, they were welcomed and allotted a plot of land on which to build.

Europeans were primarily attracted to Siam as a door to the China trade. The nature of seasonal monsoons made direct sailing to China impossible, so Ayutthaya and its ports became entrepôts for goods travelling between Europe, India and the East Indies, and China and Japan.

The Siamese home market was also quite substantial. The peace initiated by Naresuen had given rise to a surplus of wealth, which created

JAPANESE MERCENARIES

Under the Japanese adventurer Yamada Nagamasa (born 1590), who earned himself an official rank in the Thai court, many Japanese gained employment as the king's guards.

In 1628 they used their positions to help the future king Prasat Thong establish himself as regent to a boy-king, and subsequently to depose the rightful ruler. Unfortunately, the shogun in Edo (modern-day Tokyo) refused to recognise him as the Thai monarch, prompting Prasat Thong to wreak his revenge on the Japanese settlement in Ayutthaya. Several of the Japanese residents were killed in the incident, while the remainder made their escape into Cambodia.

counter Holland's influence. But another Dutch blockade, in 1664, this time at the mouth of the Chao Phraya River, won them a monopoly on the hide trade and, for the first time in Thai history, extraterritorial privileges.

Greek favourite

It was the French who gained greatest favour in King Narai's court. Their story is interwoven with that of a fascinating character, a Greek adventurer named Constantine Phaulkon.

French Jesuit missionaries first arrived at the court of Ayutthaya in 1665. The king's friendliness and religious tolerance were taken by the bishops as a sign of his imminent conversion. Their exaggerated accounts excited the imagination of Louis XIV, who hoped that the salvation of Siamese heathens could be combined with French territorial acquisition. Narai was delighted to receive a personal letter from the Sun King in 1673.

Enter Phaulkon. Son of a Greek innkeeper, he began his career with the East India Company as a cabin boy. He worked his way east with the British, arriving in Siam in 1678. A talented linguist, he learned the Thai language in just two years, and with the help of his English benefactors, he was hired as interpreter within the court. Within five years, Phaulkon had risen through Thai society to the rank of *Phaya Vijayendra*. In this powerful position, he had continual access to the king, whose confidence he slowly and surely cultivated.

The previous year, Phaulkon had fallen out of favour with the East India Company. As Phaulkon moved firmly into the French camp, so did Narai. He sent two ambassadors to Louis's court, and the French reciprocated with a visit to Ayutthaya in 1685. Phaulkon, of course, served as interpreter during the French visit. He secretly outlined to visiting Jesuit priests his plans to convert the entire country of Siam to Catholicism. To effect this, he said, he would need civilians and troops from France. Following another exchange of embassies between the courts of Louis and Narai, a French squadron accompanied French and Thai delegations aboard warships to Siam. The small, but disciplined and well-equipped, French force of 500 soldiers was given landing rights by Narai,

under Phaulkon's advice. For his pains, Phaulkon was created a Count of France and a Knight of the Order of St Michael.

Then the tables began to turn against Phaulkon. A number of high-ranking Siamese officials had become increasingly alarmed by the influence of the "Greek Favourite" on the king. Phaulkon's extravagant lifestyle was considered proof of his blatant robbery of the country. His unpopularity was fuelled not only by the ominous French military presence, but also by a rumour that Phaulkon had converted King Narai's adopted son to Christianity, intending to secure succession to the throne.

When Narai fell gravely ill in 1688, a nationalistic, anti-French faction took immediate action. Led by Phra Phetracha, a commander of the Royal Regiment of Elephants, the rebels confined the ailing king to his palace. Phaulkon was arrested for treason, and in June was executed. Narai died the following month, and Phra Phetracha mounted the throne, declaring as his top priority the immediate withdrawal of French troops. The French eventually removed their soldiers from Thailand.

The presence of Europeans throughout Narai's reign gave the West most of its early knowledge of Siam. Voluminous literature was generated by Western visitors to Narai's court.

LEFT: Naresuen engages the Burmese in a sea battle.
RIGHT: Thai manuscript showing royal parade, 1600s.

Their attempts at cartography left a record of Ayutthaya's appearance, though few maps exist today. Royal palaces and hundreds of temples crowded the area within the walls around the island on which the capital stood. Some Western visitors called it "the most beautiful city in the east."

The kings who succeeded Narai ended his open-door policy. A modest amount of trade was maintained and missionaries were permitted to remain, but Ayutthaya embarked on a course of isolation that lasted about 150 years. This left the rulers free to concentrate mainly on religious and cultural affairs.

second Burmese invasion succeeded in capturing Ayutthaya after a siege of 14 months.

The Burmese killed, looted and set fire to the whole city, thereby expunging four centuries of Thai civilisation. Showing complete disregard for their common religion, the Buddhist Burmese plundered Ayutthaya's rich temples, melting down all the available gold from Buddha images. Members of the royal family, along with 90,000 captives and the accumulated booty, were taken to Burma.

Despite their overwhelming victory, the Burmese didn't retain control of Siam for long. Attacks on Burma's northern borders compelled

Ayutthaya's golden age

The reign of King Boromakot (1733–1758) began with a particularly violent struggle for power, but Boromakot's 25-year term was an unusually peaceful one and became known as Ayutthaya's Golden Age. Poets and artists abounded at his court, enabling literature and the arts to flourish as never before.

The tranquil days proved to be the calm before the storm. Boromakot's son Ekatat ascended to the throne in 1758 and surrounded himself with female company to ensure his pleasure. Meanwhile, the Burmese empire had regrouped, although invading Burmese armies were repelled in 1760. But seven years later, a

the Burmese to withdraw most of their forces, and Thai tenacity shortened the period of Burmese domination.

Giving meaning to an ancient proverb that "Ayutthaya never lacks good men," a young general named Phaya Taksin gathered a small band of followers during the final Burmese siege of the Thai capital. He broke through the Burmese encirclement and escaped to Chanthaburi, on the southeast coast of the Gulf of Thailand. There, Phaya Taksin assembled a large army and navy. Seven months after the fall of Ayutthaya, the general and his forces sailed up the Chao Phraya to Ayutthaya and expelled the Burmese occupiers.

Move to Bangkok

Taksin, as Phaya Taksin is popularly known, immediately moved the capital. A site nearer to the sea would facilitate foreign trade, ensure the procurement of arms, and make defence and withdrawal easier.

In the 17th century, a small fishing village downstream had become an important trade and defence outpost for Ayutthaya. Known as Bangkok, or "village of hog plums", it contained fortifications built by the French. The settlement straddled both

> ### DREAMY ORDERS
>
> Taksin told his troops that the old kings had appeared in a dream and told him to move the capital. However, strategic considerations were probably more significant in his decision than those of the supernatural sort.

Taksin ruled until 1782. In the last seven years of his reign, he relied heavily on two trusted generals, the brothers Chao Phaya Chakri and Chao Phaya Sarasin, who were given absolute command in military campaigns. They liberated Chiang Mai and the rest of northern Thailand from Burmese rule, and brought Cambodia and most of present-day Laos under Thai suzerainty. It was from the victorious Laotian campaign that the Thai kingdom obtained the famous Emerald Buddha.

banks of the Chao Phraya, at a place where a short-cut canal had widened into the main stream. On the west side of the river, called Thonburi, Taksin officially established his new capital and was proclaimed king.

Taksin's reign was not an easy one. The lack of central authority after the fall of Ayutthaya had led to the rapid disintegration of the kingdom, and it fell upon Taksin to reunite the provinces. At the same time, he contended with a number of Burmese invasions that he resolutely repulsed.

At Thonburi, Taksin's personality underwent a slow metamorphosis from strong and just to cruel and unpredictable. He came to consider himself a *bodhisattva* or future Buddha, and flogged monks who refused to pay obeisance to him. He tortured his officials, his children, and even his wife to make them confess to imaginary crimes. When a revolt broke out in 1782, Taksin abdicated and entered a monastery. A minor official who engineered the revolt offered the throne to Chao Phaya Chakri, who assumed the kingship on 6 April and established the still-reigning Chakri dynasty. Taksin, regarded by a council of generals as a threat to stability, was executed in a royal manner. ❑

LEFT: King Narai, and Constantine Phaulkon.
ABOVE: wat mural of foreigners.

ERA OF THE CHAKRI MONARCHY

For a century and a half, Thailand was under the rule of an absolute monarchy.

A coup d'état ended it in 1932 while the king was at the royal beach in Hua Hin

Upon assuming the throne, General Chakri took the name of Ramathibodi. Later known as Rama I, he ruled from 1782 until 1809. His first action as king was to transfer his administrative headquarters from the marshy confines of Thonburi to the more spacious Bangkok, east across the river.

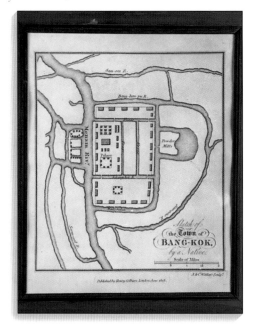

Understanding the value of traditions and symbols, he set about restoring the confidence of his war-shattered people. Buddha images were transported to Bangkok from Sukhothai and Ayutthaya, architects were instructed to design buildings in the Ayutthayan mode, and even bricks from ruined Ayutthaya were floated by barge to Bangkok for the city's new wall.

He assembled surviving master craftsmen from the old city and had them design the first permanent building in the new capital: Wat Phra Kaew, constructed to house the Emerald Buddha. An elaborate ceremony marked the movement of the Buddha image from Thonburi to the new temple.

One of Rama I's chief concerns was to secure the borders of his kingdom. Early in his reign, King Bodawpaya of Burma had launched a series of military expeditions involving the largest number of troops in the history of Thai-Burmese wars. Siamese troops boldly counter-attacked the invaders at strategic border points, routing the Burmese before they could do serious harm. After Bodawpaya, Burma became embroiled in British colonial conflicts and Thailand was left more or less in peace.

Modern Thailand is indebted to Rama I for his assiduous cultural revival programme. He appointed experts to review and assemble fragments of historical and religious treatises, few of which had survived the destruction of Ayutthaya in 1767.

Rama I perpetuated another Ayutthaya tradition by appointing his brother as *Maha Uparaja*, a "second" or deputy king, with powers almost equal to his own. His home, the Wang Na or Palace at the Front, now houses the National Museum and once extended across the northern half of Sanam Luang.

Because the royal regalia had been destroyed with everything else during the siege of Ayutthaya, Rama I had a new crown and robes commissioned for his coronation. Similarly, in his old age, he commissioned a golden urn to be prepared for his body, in accordance with ancient court protocol prescribing that the bodies of high-ranking royalty be placed in urns between the times of death and cremation.

Rama II and Rama III

Rama I's successors, Rama II and Rama III, completed the consolidation of the Siamese kingdom and the revival of Ayutthaya's arts and culture. Best remembered as an artist, Rama II (ruled 1809–1824) was responsible for building and repairing numerous Bangkok monasteries. His most famous construction was Wat Arun, the Temple of Dawn on the opposite bank from the Grand Palace, and which was later enlarged to its present height by Rama IV. He is said to have carved the great doors of Wat Suthat, throwing away the special chisels so his work could never be replicated.

During his father's reign, Rama II had gained renown as a great poet. His classic version of the *Ramakien*, the Thai interpretation of the Indian classical saga, *Ramayana*, was completed during his reign, with large sections composed by the king himself. At his court, Rama II employed *khon* and *lakhon* dance-drama troupes to enact his compositions, just as in the courts of Ayutthaya. Rama II reopened relations with the West, and allowed the Por-

PORCELAIN LEGACY

Virtually any temple with porcelain-decorated gables, such as Wat Arun, can immediately be ascribed to the reign of Rama III.

Mongkut (Rama IV)

With the help of Hollywood, Rama IV (ruled 1851–1868) became the most famous king of Siam. Commonly known as Mongkut, he was portrayed in *The King and I* as a frivolous, bald-headed despot. But nothing could have been further from the truth. He was the first Thai king to understand Western culture and technology, and his reign has been described as the bridge spanning the new and the old.

The younger brother of Rama III, Mongkut spent 27 years as a Buddhist monk prior to his

tuguese to open the first Western embassy in the Bangkok capital.

Rama III, who ruled from 1824 to 1851, continued to open Siam's doors to foreigners. The ready availability of Chinese porcelain led him to decorate many temples, including Wat Arun, with ceramic fragments. This vogue did not survive his lifetime. An extremely pious Buddhist, Rama III was considered to be "austere and reactionary" by Europeans. But he encouraged missionaries to introduce Western medicine.

accession to the throne. This gave him a unique opportunity to roam as a commoner among the populace. He learned to read Buddhist scriptures in the Pali language; missionaries taught him Latin and English, thus enabling him to read European texts. As a monk, Mongkut delved into many subjects: history, geography and the sciences, especially astronomy.

Even as an abbot, he established himself as a reformer, ridding the Buddhist scriptures of their superstitious elements and founding a sect, the *Dhammayutika*, which stressed strict adherence to Buddhist tenets. Today, these monks can be recognised by their brown robes. Mongkut realised that traditional Thai values would not

PRECEDING PAGE: procession of royal barges at Prajadhipok's 1925 coronation. **LEFT:** early map of Bangkok. **ABOVE:** Bangkok khlong, late 19th century.

save his country from Western encroachment. On the contrary, he believed that modernisation would bring Siam in line with the West and reduce hostilities with foreigners.

Britain was the first European country to benefit from this policy, when an 1855 treaty – not gained entirely without coercion by the British – granted extraterritorial privileges: a duty of only three percent on imports, and permission to import Indian opium duty-free. Other Western nations, including France and the United States, followed suit with similar treaties. And when Mongkut lifted the state monopoly on rice, that crop rapidly became

Siam's leading export. Mongkut wanted his children to gain the same benefits from the English language as himself. For this purpose, he engaged Anna Leonowens as an English teacher. The self-elevated governess greatly exaggerated her role in the Thai court in her autobiographical writings, misrepresenting the king as a cruel autocrat permanently involved in harem intrigues.

In fact, her five years in Siam are hardly mentioned in Thai chronicles. The book, as well as the movie and play based on it, are regarded as insulting to the deeply revered institution of the monarchy and are seldom mentioned by most Thais nowadays.

Mongkut's beloved hobby, astronomy, was the indirect cause of his death. From observatories at his favourite palaces, the Summer Palace at Bang Pa-in and the Palace on the Hill, at Phetchburi, he successfully calculated and predicted a total eclipse of the sun in 1868.

European and Asian sceptics joined him on the southeastern coast of the Gulf of Thailand to await the event. As the moon blocked the sun's light, both the Europeans and the scoffers among the royal astrologers raised an exclamation of admiration, raising the king's esteem among both parties.

But his triumph was short-lived. The king contracted malaria during the trip, and died two weeks later from it.

Chulalongkorn (Rama V)

Mongkut's son, Chulalongkorn, was only 15 years old when he ascended the throne. But he reigned over Siam as Rama V for over four decades – longer than any Thai king until the present King Bhumibol, who has been on the throne for over half a century.

The farsighted Chulalongkorn immediately revolutionised his court by ending the ancient custom of prostration, and by allowing officials to sit on chairs during royal audiences. He abolished serfdom in stages, giving owners and serfs time to readjust to the new order, and replaced corvée labour with direct taxation.

His reign was truly a revolution from the throne. When Chulalongkorn assumed power, Siam had no schools, and few roads, railways, hospitals, or well-equipped military forces.

To achieve the enormous task of modernisation, he brought in foreign advisors and sent his sons and other young men abroad for education. He also founded a palace school for children of the aristocracy, following this with other schools and vocational centres for the common people. Until then, the only previous schools in Siam had been the monasteries.

Chulalongkorn's brothers were leading figures in his government, especially Prince Deva-wongse, the foreign minister, and Prince Damrong, the first interior minister and a historian who has come to be known as the father of Thai history. Chulalongkorn's elder children returned home from their European schools in the 1890s, contributing to the modernisation of the army and navy. The first hospital, Siriraj, was opened in 1886 after years of unrelenting opposition. Most of the Thai common people preferred herbal remedies to *farang* (foreign) medicine. Besides, there was a shortage of doctors. Eventually, the obstacles were overcome.

In foreign relations, Rama V had to compromise and give up parts of his kingdom to protect Siam from foreign colonisation. When France conquered Annam in 1883 and Britain annexed upper Burma in 1886, Siam found itself sandwiched uncomfortably between two rival expansionist powers. Border conflicts and gunboat diplomacy forced Siam to surrender

WESTERN-FREE ZONE
Thailand is the only nation in Southeast Asia that has never been subjected to Western colonial rule.

during his reign, in 1897 and 1907. These led him to seek more spacious surroundings than those of the Grand Palace, so he built a palace on the site of a fruit orchard to the north, in Dusit. It was directly connected to the Grand Palace by the wide Thanon Ratchadamnoen. At the Dusit palace, he held parties and even fancy-dress balls, often cooking the food himself.

The many reforms of Chulalongkorn bore fruit within his lifetime. The economy of the country flourished, and Thai peasantry – by comparison with its counterparts in French

to France its claims to Laos and the western part of Cambodia. Similarly, certain territories on the Malay Peninsula further south were ceded to Great Britain in exchange for renunciation of British extraterritorial rights in Siam.

By the end of Chulalongkorn's reign, Siam had given up 120,000 sq km (50,000 sq miles) of fringe territory. But to the Thais, this concession seemed a small price to pay for maintaining the peace and independence of Siam.

Chulalongkorn made two European tours

Indochina and British Burma – were very well-off. It is no wonder that Chulalongkorn was posthumously named *Phaya Maharaj*, the Beloved Great King.

As Rama V, Chulalongkorn was conscious of worldwide democratic trends, not to mention the implications of technology, but he judged his country as yet unprepared for such rapid change. It is said that he brought progress to Siam through the judicious exercise of his absolute power.

Today, there is considerable adulation for King Chulalongkorn and his efforts at reform and innovation, not to mention his down-to-earth attitude.

LEFT: Rama IV (Mongkut) and his queen. **ABOVE LEFT:** Rama V (Chulalongkorn) and his entourage in Europe. **ABOVE RIGHT:** a son of Chulalongkorn.

Vajiravudh (Rama VI)

King Chulalongkorn's successor, Vajiravudh, began his reign (1910–1925) with a lavish coronation. Oxford-educated and thoroughly anglicised, his Western-inspired reforms to modernise Siam affected modern Thai society.

One of the first changes was a 1913 edict commanding his subjects to adopt surnames. In the absence of a clan or caste system, genealogy was virtually unheard of in Siam. The law generated much initial bewilderment, especially in rural areas, and King Vaji-

FIND ANOTHER NAME

Before the reign of Rama VI, Vajiravudh, most Thai people had used only first names, a practice that the king considered to be uncivilised.

Under a pseudonym, he also wrote essays extolling the virtues of the nation.

At the outbreak of World War I, Siam remained neutral, but late in the war, Vajiravudh joined the Allies in 1917 by sending a small expeditionary force to fight in France, thereby securing Siam's admittance to the League of Nations. The then flag of Thailand, a white elephant against a red background, was flown with others at Versailles, but the pachyderm was unfortunately mistaken for a small domestic animal. The incident greatly dis-

ravudh personally coined patronymics for hundreds of families. To simplify his forebears' lengthy titles for foreigners, he invented the Chakri dynastic name, Rama, to be followed by the proper reign number.

Primary education was made compulsory throughout the kingdom; Chulalongkorn University, in Bangkok and the first in Siam, was founded, and schools for both sexes flourished during his reign.

Rama VI's most significant political contribution was to promote the concept of nationalism. An accomplished author, he used literature and drama to foster nationalism by glorifying Thai legends and historical heroes in plays.

comfited the king, who then changed the flag to red, white and blue stripes to represent the nation, the religion and the monarchy – elements regarded by Thais as essential to the structure of modern Thailand.

Vajiravudh preferred individual ministerial consultations to summoning his appointed cabinet. His regime was therefore criticised as autocratic and lacking in coordination. Members of his family were dissatisfied because he rarely saw them, enjoying more the company of his courtiers. His extravagance soon emptied the treasury built up by Chulalongkorn. Towards the end of his reign, the national treasury met deficits caused by the ruler's personal expenses.

Vajiravudh married late. His only daughter was born one day before he died in 1925. He was succeeded by his youngest brother, Prajadhipok, who reaped the consequences of his brother's brilliant but controversial reign.

Prajadhipok (Rama VII)

The early death of his elder brother propelled Prajadhipok to royal succession, although being an old Etonian, he would have preferred a soldier's career to that of a ruler. Once king, however, he stressed economy and efficiency within the government. Unlike his brother, he tried to cut public expenditure by drastically reducing

the civil service and royal household expenses. Prajadhipok's economic policies, combined with the blessings of increased revenue from foreign trade, amply paid off for the kingdom.

In the early years of his reign, communications were improved by a wireless service, and the Don Muang Airport began to operate as an international air centre. It was also during his reign that Siam saw the establishment of the Fine Arts Department, the National Library and the National Museum, institutions that continue

today as important preservers of Thai culture.

Hard-working and conscientious, Prajadhipok was personally concerned with improving the welfare of his subjects. He was aware of the rising demand for greater participation in government by a small foreign-educated faction, but felt that the Thais were, on the whole, not ready for democracy. In 1927, he publicly commented that the people must first be taught political consciousness before democracy could effectively be introduced.

The worldwide economic crisis of 1931 affected Siam's rice export. By the time Prajadhipok dropped the gold standard, linking the Thai *baht* to the pound sterling, it was too late to stem the financial crisis. The government was forced to implement further economies by cutting the salary of junior personnel, and by resorting to a retrenchment of the armed services. Discontent brewed among army officials and bureaucrats, who felt promotions were due.

Coup d'état

Rumours and speculation were rampant during the 150th anniversary celebrations of the Chakri dynasty in 1932. Prajadhipok was the last regal representative of traditional Thai kingship to preside over grand pageantry, which featured a royal barge procession.

Two months later, a coup d'état ended the absolute rule of the Thai monarchs. The coup was staged by the People's Party, a military and civilian group masterminded by foreign-educated Thais. The chief ideologist was Pridi Panomyong, a young lawyer trained in France. On the military side, Capt. Luang Pibulsongram was responsible for gaining the support of important army colonels. With a few tanks, the 70 conspirators sparked off their "revolution" by occupying strategic areas and holding the senior princes hostage. Other army officers stood by as the public watched.

At the time, the king was in Hua Hin, a royal beach retreat to the south. Acknowledging the writing on the wall and to avoid bloodshed, he accepted a provisional constitution by which he "ceased to rule but continued to reign."

Since then, the Thai constitutional monarchy has nevertheless become a beloved institution and a symbol of continuity and stability, not to mention a moral anchor, while civilian and military governments have come and gone with great frequency. ❑

LEFT: Chulalongkorn's widow and family; Vajiravudh and Prajadhipok are at centre top and lower right.
ABOVE: Prajadhipok delivers the new constitution.

CONTEMPORARY THAILAND

Thailand's modern history has been peppered with intrigue and punctuated with violence. The monarchy, however, has provided a stabilising anchor

Originally motivated by idealism, the People's Party soon succumbed to internal conflicts. A National Assembly was appointed, but universal suffrage was postponed while the public was to be tutored in the rudiments of representative democracy. The Thai people didn't show much interest, however, and they wouldn't voluntarily attend the party's educational rallies. Other parties were outlawed.

The party's military factions quickly outmanoeuvred the civilian factions. They had greater cohesion and more extensive connections with traditional royal power brokers. The officers exercised their influence when Pridi presented a vague and utopian economic plan in 1933. It called for the nationalisation of land and for the creation of peasant cooperatives. When his opponents attacked the plan as communistic, Pridi slipped into his first overseas exile. The power of Pibul and the army was further strengthened in October of 1933 by the decisive defeat of a rebellion led by Prince Boworadet, who had been Prajadhipok's war minister.

The king had no part in the rebellion, but he had become increasingly dismayed by quarrels within the new government. He moved to England in 1934 and abdicated in 1935. In a farewell message, he said that he had wished to turn over power to the entire people and not to "any individual or any group to use in an autocratic manner." Sadly, a subsequent history of coups, aborted coups and blood baths has caused the king's words to be often quoted.

Ananda Mahidol (Rama VIII), a 10-year-old half-nephew, agreed to ascend the throne, but he remained for some time in Switzerland to complete his schooling.

The governments of the 1930s had some achievements. Most notably, public primary education, totalling four years, was extended to many rural areas. Indirect and, later, direct elec-

PRECEDING PAGE: Royal Barges on Bangkok's Chao Phraya
LEFT: King Bhumibol's coronation in 1950.
RIGHT: book showing coup d'état leaders.

tions, to the lower house meant that for the first time representatives from provincial areas had a voice at national level. After a series of crises and an election in 1938, Pibul became prime minister. His rule grew authoritarian.

While some Thai officers favoured the model of the Japanese military regime, Pibul admired

and sought to emulate Hitler and Mussolini. Borrowing many ideas from European fascism, he attempted to instil a sense of mass nationalism. With tight control over the media and a creative propaganda department, Pibul whipped up sentiment against Thailand's Chinese residents. Chinese immigration was restricted, Chinese were barred from certain occupations, and state enterprises were set up to compete in industries dominated by Chinese firms.

By changing the country's name from Siam to Thailand in 1939, Pibul intended to emphasise that it belonged to Thai (or Tai) ethnic groups and not to Chinese, Malays, Mons or any other minorities.

World War II

When Hitler invaded France in 1940, French hold over its Indochinese colonies was seriously weakened. Anticipating that Japan might make a claim, Thailand made its own by invading southern Laos and parts of western Cambodia, in November 1940. Then on 7 December 1941, the Japanese bombed Pearl Harbor and launched invasions throughout Southeast Asia. Thailand was invaded at nine points. Resistance lasted less than a day. Pibul acceded to Japan's request

> ### DEMOCRATIC FOCUS
>
> The Democracy Monument in central Bangkok was built in 1939 to commemorate the 1932 revolution. In the 1970s, 1980s and 1990s, it was the focus of numerous pro-democracy demonstrations, and the scene of much bloodshed.

By 1944, Thailand's initial enthusiasm for its Japanese partners had evaporated. The country faced runaway inflation, food shortages, rationing, and black markets. The assembly forced Pibul from office. When the war ended in 1945, Britain demanded reparations and the right to station troops in Thailand. The Thais argued that due to the work of Seri Thai, they were in fact allies. The United States supported the Thai position, partly because it was then trying to blunt British and

for "passage rights," but Thailand was allowed to retain its army and political administration.

Popular anecdote has it that the Thai ambassador to Washington, Seni Pramoj, single-handedly prevented war between Thailand and the United States by hiding the declaration in a desk drawer. Thailand in fact declared war against the Allies. But it is also true that Seni immediately offered his services in Washington to set up an underground resistance movement, Seri Thai. Starting with overseas Thai students, Seri Thai linked up with a network in Thailand headed by Pridi. The resistance supplied Allied forces with intelligence, but it never quite reached the stage of operating a guerrilla army.

French efforts to repossess their Asian colonies.

The next three years were marked by a series of democratic civilian governments. Pridi served behind the scenes, drafting a constitution, and briefly served as prime minister. In 1948, under threat of military force, Pibul took over once again. In the early years, his power was contested. Two coup attempts, supported by the navy, resulted in fierce battles on the streets of Bangkok and along the Chao Phraya River. In the 1950s, Pibul's grip grew tighter. Police power was abused, newspaper editors were beaten, critics disappeared. Pibul had also rid himself of Pridi. After attempting a coup in 1949, Pridi fled into exile. (After years in China, he died in France in 1983.) Pibul sealed Pridi's fate by convening an inquiry that implicated him in the death of King Ananda.

In 1946, on a visit to Thailand from school in Europe, the young king was found dead of a gunshot in his palace bedroom. Pridi believed that the king accidentally shot himself. The charge now seems absurd. Ananda was succeeded by his younger brother, Bhumibol Adulyadej (Rama IX), the present monarch. However, he returned to Switzerland to complete law studies and did not take up active duties as monarch until the 1950s.

enterprises. Private firms were also encouraged to appoint officers to their boards of directors.

In 1957, a clique of former proteges overthrew Pibul. These generals ran the government until 1973. While Pibul had retained some trappings of democracy, such as a constitution and legislature, the generals employed martial law.

Unadorned dictatorship did not hinder official relations with the United States. By the end of the 1960s, the war in Vietnam was raging and Thailand was America's staunchest ally. American funds built the first roads in the northeast of the country, where air bases and other military facilities proliferated. From here, US aircraft

Vietnam War

In addition to renewed anti-Chinese campaigns, Pibul vigorously hunted out communists. Many of the leaders of the small, outlawed Communist Party of Thailand were Sino-Thais. Pibul's anti-communist credentials helped win both economic and military aid from the United States. The resulting American largesse, with too few strings, has been blamed as cause for the corruption that permeates the police and military to this day. Another cause was Pibul's practice of placing military officers to run state

LEFT: 1947 coronation of King Bhumibol Adulyadej.
ABOVE: Bhumibol at crown prince's investiture.

ROYAL SUCCESSION

In the 15th century, King Trailok decreed that a king's eldest son, then brother, is heir apparent. The current king and queen have three daughters and one son. Thus, Crown Prince Maha Vajiralongkorn, born in 1952, is heir to the throne. If for some reason he cannot ascend the throne, the eldest daughter, Princess Ubol Ratana, born in 1951, is technically next in line. However, after marrying an American and settling down in the US, it is doubtful that she would rule.

The popular choice among the Thai people is Princess Sirindhom, born in 1955, a woman of considerable academic and social accomplishments, who is very highly respected.

bombed Vietnam and Laos. The northeast was also the Thai base for forays into Laos.

Meanwhile, Thai communists had turned to armed conflict in 1965. The original strongholds were in the impoverished northeast, but by the early 1970s, there were communist areas throughout, including the Muslim south, and especially along the northern frontiers. It would be some time before they were not a threat.

The ruling generals used their power to accrue enormous personal fortunes, but they also improved health standards. Construction boomed, while the business sector expanded. A middle class began to emerge.

The October revolution

In a mystifying burst of generosity, Prime Minister Thanom issued a constitution and held elections, in 1969. His party naturally won most seats, but the general nonetheless quickly bored of slow parliamentary processes. In November 1971, parliament was dissolved and the generals reverted to their old ruling habits. Many Thais felt betrayed, but only students kept up low-key protests, despite grave personal risk.

With reasonable demands for a constitution and popular elections, students were able to harness public support. The final straw against the government was the arrest of 13 student leaders and professors who had made demands for popular elections. On 13 October 1973, a demonstration to protest the arrests attracted 400,000 people to Bangkok's Democracy Monument. The next day, the protest turned violent and at least 100 students were shot by riot police. Discovering that their army had deserted them, the ruling generals fled to the United States.

Political parties, labour unions and farming organisations sprang to life with very specific grievances. Right-wing and paramilitary organisations sprang up in response. The middle class was originally strongly supportive of the student revolution, as were parts of the upper class. But they came to fear that total chaos or a communist takeover was at hand. The 1976 return of one of the previously exiled generals, ostensibly to become a monk, sparked student protests.

On 6 October, police and paramilitary thugs stormed Thammasat University in Bangkok, just north of the Grand Palace. Students were lynched and their bodies burned on the spot. A faction of army officers seized power. Self-government had lasted three years.

The civilian judge appointed to be prime minister, Thanin Kraivichien, outlawed political parties, unions and strikes, and he ordered arrests of anyone "endangering society." A curfew was strictly enforced. Teachers suspected of left-wing leanings were required to attend anti-communism indoctrination. Many students and other dissidents joined the communists in the countryside. Yet another military coup took control in 1977. For the next decade, two comparatively moderate generals headed government, endorsing amnesties for communists.

Fragile democracy

A former general was elected in 1989, but deposed two years later in a bloodless military coup. The junta, the self-dubbed National Peacekeeping Council, installed a businessman and ex-diplomat as a caretaker premier, Anand Panyacharun, who made several important reforms in the government, and earned the Thais' lasting affection for running the cleanest government in memory.

As expected, the junta's new party won the most parliamentary seats in the 1992 elections. Unexpected, however, was the public discontent when the coup leader, Gen. Suchinda Krapayoon, assumed the prime minister's post without having stood for election. In the following weeks, students, professors, social workers, and the curious public convened in a series of outdoor rallies.

On 17 May, more than 70,000 had gathered at Sanam Luang, where later on the same evening soldiers fired on them. Shootings, beatings, riots, arson and mass arrests continued sporadically for three days. The crisis ended when King Bhumibol summoned Prime Minister Suchinda and Chamlong Srimuang, the leader of the pro-democracy movement, to a meeting at the Royal Palace. Entering the room on hands and knees, the two leaders were told by the king to end the violence

THE KING'S POWER

While distancing himself from the free-for-all of Thai politics, the king of Thailand retains an immense amount of moral authority, and power. Even the most ruthless of bickering generals and politicians yield to his authority, as in 1992.

He can be credited with diluting the power of military officers in many state enterprises, such as Thai Airways and the Tobacco Monopoly. But for many, he was too passive a leader. No one was held responsible for the 1992 crackdown, and the numbers and identity of those who died or disappeared are still in dispute. Most disappointing, Chuan failed to push through a law that would have relegated more power to local governments. The coalition finally collapsed in 1995 when wealthy members of Chuan's

and work together. The event was broadcast around the world.

The next day, the violence subsided, and life returned to normal. A little later, an unrepentant Suchinda stepped down and left the country.

The Democrat Party and other prominent junta critics prevailed in the September elections. A rarity in Thai politics, the newly elected Prime Minister Chuan Leekpai was not personally corrupt and lived modestly. He prevailed for three years, setting a record for a civilian, elected government.

LEFT: remembering pro-democracy protesters killed by the army, 1992. ABOVE: waiting for national election results in Bangkok.

own party were discovered profiting from the latest land reform programme.

Two subsequent elections brought a provincial businessman, Banharn Silpa-archa, and a former general, Chavalit Yongchaiyudh, to the highest office. Both had unsavoury reputations for their business dealings and campaign expenditures, and were lambasted by the public and the press for their incompetent handling of the economy. In fact, the rot had set in earlier. Kick-started by a massive influx of Japanese assembly plants in the late 1980s, Thailand had been one of the fastest growing economies in the world, with per capita GNP increasing by an average of 8.2 percent per year. More than 4 million rural people migrated to urban jobs.

Even as economic growth was slowing down, liberalisation of the financial sector in the early 1990s enabled Thai companies to borrow cheaply. Property firms in particular went on a borrowing binge. Visitors today can readily spot the empty hotels, office blocks and abandoned construction sites that stand as monuments to profligacy.

The first cracks opened in mid-1996 when two officials at the Bangkok Bank of Commerce fled after embezzling more than US$ 2 billion. The central bank stepped in with bail-outs that eventually extended to cash-strapped finance companies. More than US$ 16 billion later, the central bank

had covertly carried out the biggest bank bail-out in world history. There was no end in sight.

The road to recovery

In the summer of 1997, faced with capital flight, currency speculation and a deteriorating balance of payments, Thailand floated the baht from its dollar-weighted peg. It quickly dropped 25 percent in value. The government sought the help of the International Monetary Fund, and reluctantly agreed to halt bail-outs of shareholders, raise income tax and VAT, cut the state budget, and privatise a number of state enterprises.

The economy ground to a halt. Expensive European cars were pawned at bargain prices;

bankers and corporate managers found themselves driving taxis and waiting in restaurants; and public works projects were cancelled.

Late in 1997, Chavalit resigned under pressure and former Prime Minister Chuan Leekpai returned to power, bringing with him an internationally respected economic team, which followed through on the IMF programme. By early 1999, the economy was back in the black.

The year 2000 saw Senators to the Upper House elected for the first time, rather than nominated as under the previous Constitution. The voting, however, was marred by widespread fraud, and many candidates were either disqualified or forced into a re-election.

Prime Minister Chuan dissolved the Lower House of Representatives, calling an election on 6 January 2001. The result was a victory for Thaksin Shinawatra and his Thai Rak Thai (Thais love Thais) party. Thaksin campaigned on a populist ticket, offering virtually free medical treatment for the poor, cheap loans for small businesses and a moratorium on farmers' debts.

He also pledged sweeping changes to the economy, with more focus on developing self-reliance. The biggest thorn in the side of the Thaksin administration has been increasing violence in the southern Thai provinces of Yala, Pattani and Narathiwat, where Thai Muslim nationalists have renewed their 45-year struggle for a separate Muslim nation, Pattani. The violence intensified in March 2004 when Thai police killed 112 Muslim militants taking refuge in a Pattani mosque. During a crackdown on demonstrations against police brutality later that year, 78 Thai Muslims suffocated to death while being transported to jail in overcrowded lorries.

A bad year ended even worse when a massive tsunami swept Thailand's Andaman coast, claiming 8,000 lives in Thailand and temporarily displacing tens of thousands of residents. With the help of local, national and international efforts, most tourist destinations in Thailand's six Andaman provinces were back to near-normal conditions within six months.

When general elections were held in February 2005, Thaksin was re-elected by an overwhelming majority, no doubt a mandate rewarding the government's speedy and authoritative response to the tsunami. ❏

LEFT: Bangkok's Skytrain has helped alleviate the city's traffic snarls. **RIGHT:** the king and queen at a ceremony.

The King

In a cynical world, it is difficult to imagine the depth of respect that the Thai people have for their monarch, King Bhumibol – Rama IX in the Chakri line. Sceptical outsiders may think it contrived or quaint, but Thais have a profound respect for the king – no mere ceremonial figurehead – and for his moral authority that has offered sanctuary during Thailand's turbulent past 50 years.

Originating in the distant past, in the ancient city of Sukhothai, the royal symbol has endured through wars, revolutions, the fall of dynasties, the smashing of traditions and governments – both dictatorial and democratic – and through times of tribulation and prosperity. During the political turmoil in 1992, Bhumibol ended a political crisis between the prime minister and his chief political opponent, which had threatened civil war. The two men prostrated themselves at the king's feet, on live television, where they stayed silent as the king instructed them on how to bring the country back to peace. Violence in the streets, which killed dozens, ceased, and there were free elections.

King Bhumibol was born in Cambridge, Massachusetts, in 1927, where his father, Prince Mahidol of Songkhla, was studying medicine at Harvard University, and his mother, nursing. His father, a son of King Rama V and later regarded as the father of modern medicine in Thailand, was a minor member of the royal family. At his birth, there seemed little chance of Prince Bhumibol becoming king. Between him and the throne, according to the laws of succession, stood Bhumibol's own father, and Bhumibol's elder brother, Prince Ananda. (Rama VII had borne no sons to take the throne.)

Bhumibol came to the throne in 1946, the latest monarch in the Chakri dynasty, which has produced several enlightened monarchs in the 19th and 20th centuries. The abolition of the absolute monarchy in 1932 had exerted unprecedented strain on the system; royalty seemed to lose contact with the people, along with their confidence. There were doubts if the monarchy could survive the turmoil of World War II, when 18-year-old Bhumibol ascended the throne unexpectedly after the fatal shooting of his elder brother, King Ananda, in the Grand Palace, in Bangkok. The king's death was never fully explained publicly, but much later, two royal servants were executed.

In the 50-plus years since his coronation, the king has proved himself a worthy successor to his celebrated ancestors. With Queen Sirikit, he has travelled to every part of Thailand, the first monarch to visit some parts of the country. He rarely travels outside of Thailand.

He has also turned over his palace grounds to agricultural purposes. Behind the walls of Chitralada Palace, where the king lives (the Grand Palace is for ceremonial and state occasions), the king has transformed gardens into an agricultural research station, with a dairy farm, rice fields, and orchards. His involvement with agriculture began with a concerted effort to find new crops for the hill tribes, in order to wean them from opium cultivation. He then applied this experience to farm programmes.

The monarchy costs the Thai treasury nothing, at least directly, since the royal family pays its own way with income from vast property holdings and investments. The king's mother, who died in 1995, founded the Flying Doctors programme to provide medical and dental services in remote areas. Queen Sirikit works to preserve the arts and crafts, and the techniques of the ancient crafts, and to provide skills and income for rural people.

In addition, the king and queen take part in the numerous royal ceremonies that punctuate the year – the seasonal robing of the Emerald Buddha, the various Buddhist holy days, the opening of Parliament. A skilful musician, King Bhumibol plays jazz on clarinet and saxophone. ❏

NATURAL HISTORY

Although Thailand's wild lands have diminished from excessive logging before 1989, it is still endowed with some unique flora and fauna

Thailand's biological treasures and diverse landforms derive from its geographical position as the crossroads of Southeast Asia. Just as the nation has accommodated many peoples and cultures, so it has served as a conduit dispersing plant and animal life.

Roughly the size of France, Thailand covers 513,115 sq km (198,115 sq miles). The overall shape resembles an elephant's head with the southern peninsula forming the trunk. The most conspicuous landscape features are striated mountains enclosing cultivated valleys, but there are great contrasts in six geographical regions. In the north, extending along the borders of Burma and Laos, parallel mountains run north to south, generally reaching over 2,000 metres (6,500 ft) in height. The valleys have been cultivated for centuries, but until 50 years ago – with the proliferation of slash-and-burn farming – there was considerable forest cover in the higher altitudes.

To the south, the vast valley called the Central Plain stretches 450 km (280 miles) to the Gulf of Thailand. The overflowing tributaries traditionally deposited rich silt that created an agricultural rice bowl. The farms nowadays are supported by intensive irrigation, courtesy of a network of highly controversial big dams. The western region consists mostly of mountain ranges, the source of tributaries of the Mekong, Chao Phraya and Salween rivers. Sparsely populated by humans, this region is the richest repository of wildlife.

The northeast encompasses the broad shallow Khorat Plateau, which lies less than 200 metres (656 ft) above sea level. This is a land of poor soils, little rain, too many people, and a bit of grass and shrub. The sandstone base has weathered into strange shapes. The small, hilly southeast coast is bordered on the north by the Cardomom Range, which protrudes from Cambodia. It includes 80 rocky, forested islands.

PRECEDING PAGES: bats take flight as a setting sun ends the day. **LEFT:** yellow bittern fishing from a lotus leaf. **RIGHT:** waterfall in Khao Yai National Park.

Intense heat and violent underground pressures created the rubies and sapphires mined here.

Endowed with the heaviest rainfall and humidity, the south covers the isthmus down to the Malay peninsula. The coastal forests were cleared to make way for rubber and palm plantations. But 275 islands, especially in the western

Andaman Sea, support unique species and are surrounded by coral reefs. The tsunami that struck in December 2004 damaged about 5 percent of Thailand's Andaman reefs.

The limestone rock so common in the western region was once seabed. Soft and easily eroded, it is limestone that is the basis of the crumbly mountains and jutting islets. Underground streams in limestone also created the many spectacular caves.

Flora

Sixty years ago, forests covered about 70 percent of Thailand's land area. In 1960, the figure had dropped to 50 percent. Today, probably only about 15 percent of undisturbed forest remains, although perhaps another 15 percent of it has been replanted, often with non-indigenous species, or else turned into plantations growing the likes of palm-oil trees or eucalyptus. Aside from tiny Singapore, the scale and rate of forest loss in Thailand is the greatest in Southeast Asia. Following fatal landslides, logging was finally outlawed in 1989.

The nation's forests can be classified as either evergreen or deciduous; the latter shed leaves seasonally. There are many sub-categories and a single habitat may contain both types of trees. Evergreen forests, of course, are green all year

round. They are most abundant in the uplands of both the south and southeast, where rainfall is plentiful and the dry season brief. Rainforests are among the evergreens.

Contrary to many preconceptions, all tropical forests are not evergreen, and all evergreen forest is not rainforest. A rainforest is a four-layered forest harbouring the world's densest concentration of species. Herbs, shrubs, ferns and fungi form the bottom layer. A relatively open layer of palms, bamboos and shrubs is above ground level. Mid-level trees, festooned with vines, mosses and orchids, create a 25-metre (82-ft) high canopy. The well-spaced trees of the uppermost canopy soar as high as 60 metres

(200 ft). Healthy rainforests can be found in the Khao Luang, Koh Surin, Tarutao and Thale Ban national parks, all in the south.

More common than rainforest is the broad-leaved evergreen forest, which is found at higher elevations. Here are found temperate-zone laurels, oaks and chestnuts, along with ferns, rhododendrons and the yew-like podocarps. Varieties of orchids proliferate. Usually the ground level consists of shrubs and grasses that attract larger mammals. The leaves of the taller dipterocarps turn yellow and red before shedding in the dry season. A few weeks later, they burst into purple, pink, orange and red flowers.

One hundred years ago, deciduous forests of the north were thick with teak trees, but virtually all were cut long ago.

Fauna

Of the world's 4,000 species of mammals, 287 can be found in Thailand: 13 species of primates, 18 hoofed species, nine of wild cats (including tigers and clouded leopards), two of bear, two of wild dogs and eight of dolphins. Bats are abundant, with 107 species identified so far. Tigers and the larger deer could soon join the list of mammals that have vanished since 1900: rhinoceros, several species of deer, two otter species, and the kouprey – wild cattle that was discovered in Thailand in the 1930s.

Declared the country's first protected species back in 1921, the Asian elephant is the national mascot, but nonetheless perilously close to extinction. From well above 20,000 a century ago, fewer than 8,000 survive in Thailand today, and most of these are domesticated. Khao Yai National Park offers the best chance of observing some of the few thousand remaining wild elephants.

Thailand also harbours four types of reptiles and three types of amphibians. Among 175 species of snakes are deadly cobras, kraits and vipers. No doubt most of the insect species haven't been identified yet, but there are 1,200 variegated butterflies. Beetle species may number in the tens of thousands, but have been so little studied that amateurs occasionally discover a new one.

Visitors of national parks and sanctuaries may not see any large animals, but they will be compensated with sightings of birds. There are around 900 species that are permanent residents of the region. In the north are the colourful montane birds with Sino-Himalayan affinities. The birds of the south are similar to those of Malaysia. There are also about 240 wintering and non-breeding migrants that pass through.

Marine life

Off the west coast, the flora and fauna of the Andaman Sea are characteristic of the Indian Ocean. Off the east coast, in the Gulf of Thailand, they are characteristic of Indo-Pacific seas. Coral reefs off both coastlines have been little surveyed, but they support at least 400 species of fish and 30 of sea snakes. The corals them-

LITTLE ENFORCEMENT

The country in fact does have environmental and wildlife protection laws, but they are irregularly enforced.

habitats, be they forests or coral reefs, many more species of flora and fauna could disappear, not only from Thailand, but from the world.

The Forestry Department, which includes the Parks Service, is underfunded and understaffed. In the past few decades, at least 40 rangers have been murdered in the line of duty. Earning less than a factory worker, many rangers also collude with poachers of logs and animals. The country's poorest people inadvertently contribute to the degradation by farming on protected lands. The demands of Chinese-Thais and Chinese vis-

selves consist of almost 300 species, with the Andaman Sea boasting a far greater diversity. Intact reefs survive only in areas far from human habitation, such as the vicinity of the Surin and Similan islands.

Environment at risk

As many of the aforementioned remarks concerning habitats and wildlife indicate, Thailand's is an environment in danger of irreversible damage. With the destruction of

LEFT: *Burmannia disticha*, a flower endemic to Khao Yai National Park. **ABOVE:** decreasing in numbers, the Asian elephant, such as this youth, can still be seen.

itors, for both medicinal purposes and gourmet "jungle" dining, further threaten the endangered populations of tigers, bears and deer.

Tourism undoubtedly plays a part in the degradation of Thailand's ecosystems, most visibly when seaside hotels spew untreated sewage. There are also signs that tourism might conceivably become a positive force in the preservation of what remains of Thailand's ecology. There are encouraging signs that a few Thais – among them trekking guides and local green groups, and even a few progressive politicians – are becoming aware that environmental caretaking will sustain tourism longer than continued destruction. ❏

PEOPLE

It will be readily apparent that the Thai people expect life and its experiences, large or small, to be fun and comfortable. Otherwise, what's the point?

Travellers to Thailand are generally struck by the ubiquity of smiles, warmth and friendliness. There are always amiable questions – not to be interpreted as nosiness – and an openness seldom found elsewhere. The standard greeting is *pai nai*, or "Where are you going?" But this is not meant to be interpreted literally, but rather it is the approximate equivalent of "Hello" or "How are you?"

The key focus for understanding the Thai is *sanuk*, a word that can be translated as "fun" or "enjoyable." Indeed, the quantity – and quality – of sanuk, whether in work or play, determines if something is worth pursuing. Almost as important is the concept of *sabai*, best translated as "comfortable" or "contented". As far as Thai people are concerned, in the best of all possible worlds life should be both sanuk and sabai – for visitors to the kingdom as much as for its inhabitants. The antithesis of sanuk is *seriat* – a borrowing from the English word serious. Life just isn't meant to be taken too seriously.

Background

Thailand's lifestyle traditionally has been centred on agriculture, an activity that nurtures a sense of community, especially during planting and harvest. All over the country, ethnic Thais inhabit lowland valleys or plains, growing rice in irrigated paddy fields. They leave the hills and mountains to other peoples – the *chao khao*, or hill tribes, like the Akha and Hmong.

Today, most Thais still live in the country or in small towns, although Bangkok, the archetypal primal city, is now home to more than 10 million people, nearly 20 percent of the national population. The demands of city life have changed much of the countryside's casual ways, but even in Bangkok it is a rare Thai who does not enjoy getting together with friends. Indeed, the notion that one might go off solo to a dinner or on a holiday is considered *mai sanuk*, or not

PRECEDING PAGES: a net fisherman on Ko Lanta, south of Krabi and Phuket. **LEFT:** a woman working on a farm in Thailand's northeast. **RIGHT:** Thai sailor, Chanthaburi.

fun. Similarly, office life must contain a certain amount of chatting and passing around of snacks for it to avoid being mai sanuk.

Generally speaking, Thais hate to be alone, and most are puzzled by the average foreigner's need for occasional solitude. There is a sense of family about Thai activities, a gathering that

does not exclude outsiders. For the visitor invited to join, there is no automatic expectation of reciprocation, although it would always be much appreciated. It is not unusual for a visitor to stray into a small city lane and be invited to join a partying group. Such activities are usually accompanied by music, alcoholic drinks and small snacks. Drunkenness is frowned upon, but a certain tipsiness is acceptable in such circumstances.

When a visitor encounters a tense situation, it is usually because of differences of language and custom. In such instances, it is best to adopt another Thai attitude, *jai yen*, or cool heart, to deal calmly with the problem. It is difficult to stir a Thai to real anger. A smile and an apology should deflate almost any tense situation. Anger, demonstrated by physical violence or raised voices, can provoke serious hostility, however, and an angry Thai can be aggressive indeed. For example, touching a Thai (especially on the top of the head), shouting, or threatening the strong sense of independence that Thais have may effect an immediate and often hostile response. Visitors should also avoid pointing their feet at Thais, for example, when crossing their legs. The foot is considered unclean,

MISTAKEN IDENTITY

The original Thai flag was changed by the king when Europeans, during a royal visit to Europe, mistook the elephant for a rodent.

without breaking, then snapping back into place and swaying in the breeze.

The flag and royalty

At eight o'clock each morning, the Thai national flag is ceremoniously raised in every Thai town and city. The modern flag – introduced in 1917 to replace an earlier red flag emblazoned with a white elephant, the flag of the absolute monarchy – is composed of five horizontal bands of white, red, and blue. The white symbolises the purity of

and pointing it at someone is thought to be a great insult.

Closely allied with jai yen is a concept that provides the answer to all of life's vicissitudes: *mai pen rai,* a phrase best translated as "never mind." Most Thai would rather shrug their shoulders in the face of adversity than risk escalating a difficult situation. Solutions that contribute to restoring or maintaining calm are welcomed. In fact, one reason the Thais have survived intact as a sovereign nation is by adopting a superb sense of compromise, putting trifling or trivial matters in perspective, or else ignoring them. Truly, this aspect of the Thai character may be likened to a bamboo, bending

Buddhism; red, the land and its people; and blue, the monarchy as the force that binds the other two together. The central elements of the Thai polity – what makes Thailand Thai – have traditionally been perceived as the Buddhist religion, the Thai language and the monarchy. In recent years, this has changed somewhat, as recognition of other constituent elements of the Thai people, most notably the Malay-speaking Muslims of the deep south, have been brought into the equation. Still, to most Thai people, religion, language and king still constitute a unique definition of being Thai.

The three colours, and the flag, are revered as symbols of enduring qualities amidst changes, values evoked in 1992 when Thais rose up against the military's grip on political power. For the first time, Thailand's burgeoning middle class exerted their influence on political issues; extensive civil unrest, if not civil war, loomed. Using the moral authority that the monarchy possesses in Thailand, King Bhumibol lectured the prime minister and his primary opponent on live television, as the two men prostrated themselves at the king's feet. The crisis immediately evaporated. Since then, the changes in government and politics have been enormous, and are continuing.

Since the constitutional revolution of 1932, the king does not govern the country, but he retains considerable influence in government and in society, serving as a beacon of high moral standards and a bell-wether in troubled times.

Thais regard the royal family with a reverence unmatched in other countries, and people will react strongly if they consider any member of royalty to have been insulted. Ill-considered remarks or refusing to stand in a cinema for the royal anthem before the start of a movie will earn some very hard stares, or even knocks.

A similar degree of respect is accorded the second pillar of society, Buddhism. Disrespect towards Buddha images, temples or monks is not taken lightly. Such insults may be unintentional – for example, climbing or clambering about on Buddha images for purposes of photography – so visitors should exercise discretion at all times, removing shoes before entering temples (or mosques in the south), and behaving politely.

Monks observe vows of chastity that prohibit their being touched by women, even their mother. When in the vicinity of a monk, a woman should try to stay clear to avoid accidentally brushing against him. When visiting a temple, it is acceptable for both sexes to wear long pants but not shorts. Unkempt persons are frequently turned away from major temples.

From the Hindu religion has come the belief that the head is the fount of wisdom and the feet are unclean. For this reason, it is insulting to touch another person on the head, or to point one's feet at or step over another person. Kicking in anger is worse than spitting. When wishing to pass someone who is seated on the floor,

bow slightly while walking and point an arm down to indicate the path to be taken. It is also believed that spirits dwell in the raised doorsills of temples and traditional Thai houses, and that when one steps on them, the spirits become angry and curse the building with bad luck.

Military

For the first time in recent memory, the elected parliament has moved to the peak of political power in Thailand. After the turmoil of 1992, the constitution was changed to make it mandatory for the prime minister to be an elected member of parliament. Previously, Thailand had

mainly been governed by generals, who had seized power by force or had been appointed to office by their peers.

Changes in the constitution have weakened the political role of the armed forces, but how the military will accept its diminished status over the long run has yet to be seen.

Its role is vastly different from that in the West, but it is a role that has its roots in Thai history, when rulers and leaders rose out of the ranks of the military. In fact, it has been the traditional avenue for advancement in all sectors of society. The Thai soldier, like the civil servant, belongs to a sprawling and complex organisation whose activities have typically

LEFT: expressway toll-booth workers, north of Bangkok.
RIGHT: Thai trainer factory, near Bangkok.

gone beyond national defence. Thai conscripts serving obligatory two-year terms fill most of the lower ranks and perform duties of defending borders. The upper ranks, however, have been intimately involved in the business and government of Thailand.

High-ranking military officers sit on the boards of banks, own hotels, and take part in business even as they actively pursue military careers. It is one of the few occupations in which a bright but poor young man can achieve advancement on merit. The military establishment is

> **UBIQUITOUS UNIFORMS**
>
> The wild card in modern Thai politics has always been the military, which is involved in business and banking as well.

prime minister and the parliament might seem far removed from the population, except perhaps at election time, they are, in fact, usually quite responsive to the electorate. It is not unusual for a delegation of disgruntled citizens to rent a fleet of buses to personally lodge a noisy protest in front of the parliament building or local government office against officials or a decree with which they disagree.

Ministers, even the prime minister, often talk with these delegations to remedy problems, although with the clamour generated by the surprisingly vocal

now such an integral part of Thai society that it is difficult to imagine life without it. Its meddling in government, however, has been problematic, and increasingly unpopular with the Thai people. Since General Suchinda was forced to resign following the violence in 1992, the military has increasingly removed itself from politics and has refused to intervene, even during the 1997 financial crisis.

Government

Executive power is wielded by a prime minister selected by the majority party or a coalition of parties. He or she formulates and executes policies through a cabinet of ministers. While the

and independent local press, it would be difficult for leaders to ignore their protests. In part, it reflects the sense of family that constantly appears in Thai conversations, and in exhortations to stand together against common enemies. Although Thai leaders are regarded paternalistically, they are increasingly held accountable for their actions.

Provincial governors are still appointed by the government in Bangkok, but most other local officials must now be elected for a fixed term. Previously, they were elected for life, or else obtained posts through dubious means. Most of the changes were embodied in the amended constitution, in 1997.

Women

The constitutional changes of 1997 also spelled out the equality of men and women. (The constitution also says that a woman may now be the monarch, previously a forbidden possibility.) As in any society, true equality is by no means the norm in daily life, but the improved status of women, and their greater share of power in society, has been one of the most remarkable changes of the past few decades. Women obtained the vote at the same time as men, in 1932, but it was not until 1999 that discriminatory laws relating to women's citizenship and right to own land were amended.

In many ways, though, Thai women have always been powerful and influential behind the scenes. A 15th-century Chinese visitor reported that "it is their custom that all affairs are managed by their wives, both the king and the common people. If they have matters that require thought and deliberation... all trading transactions great and small, they all follow the decision of their wives." In big business, women have been at the top for generations, as it has been customary for men to go into government and the military.

Today, women are particularly prominent in the hotel business, tourism, real estate, advertising, the export trade, banking, medicine and law. Women are at the helm of major companies and own several of the largest hotels in Bangkok. Women head villages and occupy top positions in the civil service and in medicine. The university population is almost equally male and female, while the bureaucracy attracts large numbers of women.

In Thailand, lower-class women have less power but often control the family purse-strings and moral upbringing of the children. Women with lower levels of education can be found on construction sites, cleaning offices, running small businesses, and driving buses. On the other hand, however, lapses in enforcement combined with years of tradition have contributed to the exploitation of women in the sex industry.

Sexual attitudes

Thailand has acquired something of a reputation as a sexual playground in the West. Much emphasis has been placed on the exploitation

and degradation of women and, especially, children. To be sure, prostitution exists and, while it does attract some unsavoury foreign tourists, most of the clients are in fact Thais. Estimates of how many of the female population are involved in adult and child prostitution vary between 0.5 and 3 percent. Outside of a few outrageous urban areas like Bangkok's Patpong, Soi Cowboy and Nana Plaza, or the tawdry bar scene of Pattaya, prostitution in Thailand is similar to elsewhere: brothels exist on the margins of almost every medium-sized town, but the rest of society is usually fairly conservative where sex is concerned.

This said, Thai people are generally open-minded and sympathetic in their attitude towards people's sexuality. Sex is seen as a normal human function and, if practised between consenting or married adults, it is definitely sanuk – who could doubt it? Attitudes towards consensual adult homosexuality are sympathetic, and this extends to a peculiarly Thai (or Southeast Asian) phenomenon: transvestism. Thailand has more than its share of katoeys, or "lady men" – transvestite men who are accepted for what they are, treated with understanding and respect, and generally addressed as women. In fact, one of the most popular and successful kick boxers in 1998 was a transvestite.

LEFT: walking under an elephant for good luck.
RIGHT: amulets protect from misfortune and evil.

The differing Thais

Whilst all Thai-speaking, Buddhist inhabitants of Thailand consider themselves part of the Thai family, considerable regional differences exist. Basically, Thailand can be divided into four regions – Central Plains, North, Northeast and Peninsular South. All educated Thais – and literacy is estimated to run as high as 96 percent – can speak and understand Central Thai, the language of Bangkok, and of the radio and television. Yet Central Thai is far from being the mother tongue of the other three regions. In the Northeast, people speak *Isaan* at home, whilst in the North the people speak *kham muang*, or

world – generally serve Central Thai cuisine, which has become justly famous internationally.

Northeastern cuisine, by contrast, favours "sticky rice" *(khao niaw)* instead of the more common long-grain rice, which is eaten with the fingers rather than a spoon or chopsticks. Northerners are unique in Thailand in serving cooked tomatoes. The cuisine of Chiang Mai owes much to the culinary influence of neighbouring Burma and Yunnan. Southerners like to use the ubiquitous coconut in their dishes, and the creamy effect of coconut milk helps to tame the otherwise fiery heat of the dishes found in the deep south.

"the language of the Principalities". Southern Thai is closer to the Central variant, but spoken much faster and with an economy of terms. Thus, the simple word "tasty" or "delicious" is pronounced *aroi* in Central Thai, *roi* in the snappy southern dialect, *sep* in Northeastern Isaan, and *lam* in the kham muang of the North. In Central Thai, "Do you speak Thai" emerges as *khun phut phasa thai dai mai?* In kham muang it's *oo kham muang jang ko?* Quite a difference, but the visitor has no need to worry, as Central Thai is universally spoken.

There are also considerable differences in regional cuisine. The Thai restaurants of London and Los Angeles – indeed all over the

The population

Thailand's population is around 65 million. Most people (about 95 percent) are Theravada Buddhists. About 80 percent of the population are ethnic Thai.

There is a small percentage of Thai Malays living in the south who are Muslim. Islam is Thailand's second religion, accounting for perhaps 5 percent of the population, and Thai-speaking Muslims may be found in every province of the country, from Chiang Rai in the north to Yasothon in the far northeast. The 2 percent of the population who are Confucianist or Mahayana Buddhist are mainly urban, living in the Chinatown areas of cities like Bangkok,

Khorat, Hat Yai and Nakhon Sawan. Some 12 percent of Thailand's total population are of Chinese descent.

Hill-tribe people living in the north and west total about half a million, and many of the tiny group of Christians in Thailand are concentrated among them. Catholicism made some inroads in Chanthaburi in the south-east, due mainly to French influence. Christians in the north have been strongly influenced by the Protestantism of American Presbyterian missionaries. The main hill-tribe groups include Lisu, Lahu,

GETTING ALONG

Although there is a significant Chinese population, not to mention the hill tribes, Thailand has little racial tension.

The Chinese

Like every country in Southeast Asia, Chinese merchants have been active in Thailand since the earliest days of commerce. When King Rama I selected Bangkok as his new capital, the site on which he wanted to build the Grand Palace was occupied by Chinese shops. He asked the owners to move a kilometre down the riverbank to Sampeng, where they settled in what is today Bangkok's Chinatown.

Throughout the 19th century and the first half of the 20th, immigrants from China poured

Akha, Karen, Hmong and Mien. The smallest and least-known peoples living in Thailand are the Mlabri, or "Spirits of the Yellow Leaves", about 250 of whom survive in the Phrae-Nan borderlands, and the Moken, or sea gypsies, who live on islands in the Andaman Sea between Phuket and Ranong.

Bangkok's population is thought to exceed 10 million; an accurate census is virtually impossible due to the semi-permanent migrant population. The city functions as the epicentre of the country's political, business and religious life.

LEFT: getting around on a set of modern wheels.
ABOVE: sisters beside a Bangkok canal, or *khlong*.

into the country. As in other Asian countries, these immigrants were denied ownership of land and participation in government, so they naturally drifted towards trade and commerce. One thing, however, has long distinguished the Thai Chinese from their counterparts in most other Asian countries: they have been assimilated to a remarkable degree into the life of their adopted land.

In part this has been due to deliberate government policy. All children, Chinese or otherwise, are required to learn the Thai language in primary school. (Chinese language was not even taught at university level until a few years ago.) Moreover, the Chinese were required to take Thai names when they wanted to apply for a passport, a government scholarship, or an official document.

As a result, Chinese and Thais have intermarried freely, so that today, especially in the cities, it is difficult to point to anyone and say with assurance that he or she is "pure" Thai or Chinese. Indeed, the odds are quite against it.

There is no deep-rooted anti-Chinese bias in Thailand, nor have there been any of the serious racial conflicts marring the recent histories of neighbouring countries. Only among the older

Public behaviour

The Thai greeting and farewell is "Sawadee", spoken while raising the hands in a *wai, a* prayer-like gesture, the fingertips touching the nose, and bowing the head slightly. It is an easy greeting to master and will win smiles.

Thais believe strongly in personal cleanliness. Even the poorest among them bathe daily and dress cleanly and neatly. They frown upon those who do not share this concern for hygiene, and are not impressed by grubby foreign travellers and their grimy backpacks.

SIZE MATTERS
Bangkok is estimated to be at least 40 times larger than the country's second-largest city, Udon Thani.

generation are there people who think and speak of themselves specifically as Chinese. The younger generation thinks of itself as Thai, speaks the language, voices loyalty to Thailand, and has only cursory interests in affairs in China – though pride in Chinese origins remains strong amongst Sino-Thais, and all Thais consider Chinese to be canny businessmen – not without reason. To be sure, there has been, and still is, some jealousy over the ethnic Chinese command of the Thai economy, but the Thai response has been to intermarry with, rather than to isolate, the Chinese. It's a policy that has worked, and which makes Thailand unique in Southeast Asia in the absence of racial tensions.

Thailand is a hot country, and the Thai people are fastidious. Shower and change often, for your own comfort and to receive respect. Toilet paper is not generally provided except in hotels, airports and other tourist-oriented institutions. Look for the tap and water bowl, or spray-hose which are more commonly used.

Twenty years ago, Thai couples showed no intimacy in public. That has changed due to Western influence on the young, but intimacy still does not extend beyond holding hands. As in many traditional societies, displaying open affection in public is a sign of bad manners.

Old people in Thailand are treated with great respect, as are teachers, doctors and other professionals. Mishaps or accidents – such as a small traffic crash – are best met with smiles and apologies. Violence or rude language should be avoided at all times. The average Thai driver will respond positively to a smiling apology which defuses the situation. The same person, met by harsh words or insults, may well reach for his gun.

Terms of address

Thais are addressed by their first, rather than their last, names. The name is usually preceded by the word *khun*, a term of respect. Thus, Silpachai Krishnamra would be addressed as Khun Silpachai when someone speaks to him. You will find some Thais referred to in newspapers with the letters M.C., M.R. or M.L. preceding their names. These are royal titles normally translated as "prince" or "princess." The five-tier system reserves the highest two titles for the immediate royal family. After that comes the nobility, remnants of the noble houses of old. The highest of these three ranks is Mom Chao (M.C.), followed by Mom Rachawong (M.R.) and Mom Luang (M.L.).

The title is not hereditary, thanks to a unique system that guarantees Thailand will never become top-heavy with princes and princesses. Each succeeding generation is born into the next rank down. Thus, the son or daughter of a Mom Chao is a Mom Rachawong.

Concepts

A few Thai concepts will give not only an indication of how Thais think, but will smooth a visitor's social interaction with them.

Thais strive to maintain equanimity in their lives and go to great lengths to avoid confrontation. The concept is called *kreng jai* and suggests an unwillingness to burden someone older or superior with one's problems. In many cases, it means not giving someone bad news until too late for fear it may upset the recipient.

Thais don't like saying "no" too directly for fear of causing offence. In a common manifestation of *kreng jai*, giving no answer to a question, or evading a direct answer, is a considerate but sometimes confusing way of saying "no."

As noted earlier, jai yen, or "cool heart," an attitude of remaining calm in stressful situations,

is a trait admired by Thais. Getting angry or exhibiting *jai ron* (hot heart) is a sign of immaturity and lack of self-control. Reacting to adversity or disappointment with a shrug of the shoulders and saying "mai pen rai" (never mind) is the accepted response to most situations.

Thais converse readily with any stranger who shows the least sign of willingness. They may be shy about their English language ability but they try nonetheless: speak a few words of Thai and they respond even more eagerly. Be prepared, however, for questions considered rather impolite in Western societies, such as: How old are you? How much money do you earn? How

much does that watch (camera, etc.) cost? Thais regard these questions as part of ordinary conversation and will not understand a reluctance to answer them.

If, however, one is reticent about divulging personal information, a joking answer delivered with a smile will usually suffice; for example, to the above question of "How old are you?", answer with "How old do you think?" Be warned, however, that Thai people can be extraordinary flatterers. Speak a few words of Thai, and you will likely be pronounced *keng*, or "excellent," not to mention handsome or pretty. Smile, enjoy, respond in kind. Remember that life is meant to be sanuk. ❑

LEFT: bargaining in a Nonthaburi market.
RIGHT: saffron-robed monk, near Surat Thani.

HILL TRIBES

One of Thailand's prime tourist draws, the hill tribes of the north – less than two percent of the population – have both benefited and suffered from this attention

The tribal people of Thailand make up less than two percent of the total population, but account for a significant degree of interest with visitors to Thailand. (This is in striking contrast to neighbouring Laos and Burma, where the shares are at least 30 percent and 15 percent, respectively, but without the

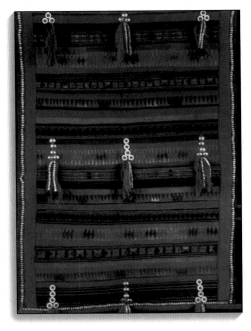

tourist obsessiveness.) Thousands of foreigners annually trek to the tribal people's mountain villages. The average Thai views tribal people as foreigners, if not illegal aliens, and thus not entitled to the same rights as Thais. Most tribal immigration – from Burma or Laos – has occurred only in the past 100 years. In fact, only relatively recently have significant numbers of tribal people been granted Thai citizenship. They cling to the bottom rung of the steep Thai economic and social ladder.

Thailand is home for up to 20 tribes, but there are six principal groups: Karen, Hmong, Mien, Lahu, Lisu and Akha. Living in villages at higher elevations, most hill-tribe farmers prac-

tise slash-and-burn *(swidden)* agriculture. In March, at the height of the dry season, they set massive fires to burn the undergrowth on the mountain sides. The ashes at first provide a rich fertiliser, but over the years the process depletes the soil. Villagers used to then move their villages to a new site, but there's no place to move nowadays. With poorer soil and less of it, villagers traditionally rely on the opium poppy as a cash crop. Nowadays opium cultivation in Thailand is quite scarce.

Karen

The 265,000 Karen form by far the largest tribe. In Thailand, they comprise two sub-groups, the Sgaw and Pwo, whose dialects are not mutually intelligible. (The Karennic language belongs to the Tibeto-Burman linguistic group.) The Karen have settled in Thailand since the 18th century and they are still (illegally) trickling in. In Burma, there are between 3 million and 4 million Karen, a Karen rebel state, and a Karen rebel army that has been fighting the Burmese government for almost five decades.

The Karen were early converts to Christianity when Burma was a British colony. Some Thai Karens are Baptists or Seventh-Day Adventists. But whether of Christian, Buddhist or animist beliefs, the Karen place a great emphasis on monogamy, look down on premarital sex, and can trace ancestry through the mother. Unlike other Thai tribes, they have long practised lowland wet-rice farming.

Opium use is somewhat common. Kinship is patrilineal and polygamy is permitted. Like Thai, Hmong is an Austroasiatic language, meaning that its roots have been traced to southern China. In fact, four million Hmong live today in China's Yunnan Province. The White Hmong and Blue Hmong can be identified by their dialects and clothing: Blue Hmong women wear indigo, pleated skirts and their hair in huge buns. White Hmong women wear white hemp skirts and black turbans.

> **NORTHERN HOMES**
>
> With the exception of the Karen, who extend down to Kanchanaburi and Tak provinces, most hill tribes live in the three northwestern provinces of Chiang Mai, Chiang Rai and Mae Hong Son.

Hmong

The most recent arrivals in Thailand, the Hmong are the second-largest hill tribe, numbering about 80,000. The majority immigrated in the 1950s and 1960s, fleeing from the long civil war in Laos. Ever on the alert for communists, the Thai military then regarded Hmong as subversives, and Hmong relations with Thai officialdom still remain edgy. Ironically, Hmong are renowned for their fierce independence and, in Laos, for anti-communism. Indeed, they were American allies during the Vietnam War.

LEFT: hill-tribe textile, and a White Hmong woman.
ABOVE: Hmong with clothing of heavy black cotton.

Mien

Like Hmong, most Mien (Yao) probably came to Thailand from Laos, but there are large numbers in Burma, Vietnam and China's Yunnan Province – as well as Laotian Mien refugee communities in San Francisco and Seattle. Many Chinese elements, such as ancestor worship and Daoism, are evident in their animist religious beliefs. Kinship is patrilineal and polygamy is practised. Mien place great emphasis on the peaceful resolution of conflict. Of all the hill tribes, they probably have the smoothest relations with Thais. Mien, including women, are often outgoing. Mien have also taken to the Thai dress of T-shirts, sarongs and jeans, but traditionally women wear black jackets and trousers, red fur-like collars and large blue or black turbans. Their dense, intricate embroideries are valued on bags and clothing. The language is Austroasiatic.

Lahu

Like the Karen, some of the 60,000 Lahu are Christian. Also like the Karen, traditional Lahu mix animism with millennial myths that have led them to be receptive to messianic movements; some hope for the return of a man-god called Geusha. Besides the usual opium, corn and rice, Lahu have successfully cultivated

chilli peppers as a cash crop. The traditional dress of the four groups – Red Lahu, Black Lahu, Yellow Lahu and Lahu Sheleh – is slightly different, but red and black jackets are common. Lahu are skilled makers of baskets and bags. Lahu languages are Tibeto-Burman.

Lahu are famed for their hunting prowess with both rifles and crossbows. Although leopards and tigers no longer roam the northern hills, Lahu continue to hunt bear, wild pigs, deer, squirrels, birds and snakes. Several hundred thousand Lahu live in Burma, where a small Lahu army, aligned with the Karen separatists, has fought the Burmese government since the 1970s.

Lisu

Although there are only about 25,000 Lisu, they are easily identified by their penchant for bright colours. Women wear long green or blue cotton dresses with striped yokes. Men wear baggy loose pants of the same colours. Lisu are good silversmiths and make jewellery for Akha and Lahu. Lisu are regarded by other tribal people as sharp businesspeople. Animist beliefs are combined with ancestor worship.

Lisu have a strong sense of self-esteem and will eagerly cite the reasons for the pre-eminence of their family, clan or village. Yet unlike other tribes, Lisu have an organisation that extends across villages. Lisu are a sub-group of the Kachin, a large minority group in the Kachin state in the far north of Burma. The Kachin languages are Tibeto-Burman.

Akha

Probably the poorest and the shyest of the hill tribes, the Akha have been the most resistant to assimilation by the Thais. Ironically, the 34,000 Akha are the people that most tourists want to see. The draw is the heavy ornate headdress worn by the women. It consists of silver discs festooned with old coins, beads and feathers. And unlike other tribal women, who save their finery for ceremonies, Akha wear this even while tending the fields. Animist beliefs are mixed with ancestor worship; Akha can recite their ancestry back 20 generations.

An Akha village is extended by one of two gateways, which separate the domain of people and rice from that of spirits and wild animals. Akha neither farm nor consume opium. The language is Tibeto-Burman.

Other minorities

Strictly speaking, they are not Thai hill tribes, but two other groups, the Shan and Kayan, deserve mention, as their villages are frequent stops on trekking tours.

In their settled communities, rice-growing practices and Theravada Buddhism, the Shan are very similar to Thais. In fact, they are an ethnic Tai (Thai) group, also known as Thai Yai (Big Thai). Their language is similar to the northern Thai dialect, although not intelligible to central Thai speakers. Many Shans have immigrated to Thailand in recent times to escape the upheavals in Burma, but Shans may have been the first Tai inhabitants of northern

Thailand, in the 9th or 10th century. In the large area of Burma bordering the northern tip of Thailand is the home of 4 million Shans and several armies battling for autonomy. One of these was headed by the notorious opium trafficker, Khun Sa.

The Kayan (Padaung) are a Karennic people residing in the southern Shan areas. Until a few years ago, tours from Mae Hong Son would ferry tourists across the border to view Kayan women whose necks had been elongated by a lengthy brass coil

DEADLY NECK COILS

The heavy coils around the necks of the "giraffe women" depress their collarbones, which make their necks look longer. However, contrary to popular belief, the women can remove them at will without consequence.

Loss of culture

The cultures of Thailand's hill tribes are very much in danger of extinction. The chief culprit is not tourism. Greater threats are posed by a shortage of land, loss of land, resettlement, lack of land rights and citizenship, illiteracy and poor medical care. Official Thai hill-tribe policies have been shaped by the desire to discourage swidden farming and the cultivation of opium. Some of the crop substitution programmes sponsored by the Thai government, the United

weighing up to 15 kilogrammes. Kayan leaders, many of them Catholic, had long discouraged the practice and it had virtually died out. But the money generated from tours to view the "Giraffe Women" was so great that Thai officials allowed three tourist villages to set up west of Mae Hong Son. Many Kayan women, forced by grinding poverty, have since donned the coils and initiated girls beginning at age five. This is one of the unfortunate ways in which tourism has been responsible for the revival of a barbaric practice.

Nations and foreign governments have been very successful. Tribal people are marketing coffee, tea and fruit. But as trekkers can observe, such projects have not penetrated to villages distant from roads and transport.

Some farmers have also resisted switching to non-opium cash crops because of the capital investment involved. They already know how quickly one can get into a crippling debt with (the usually Chinese) moneylenders. According to development experts, wiser policies would attempt to ensure that villagers could grow enough crops to feed themselves. If they could do that, they wouldn't need to grow and sell opium to buy rice. ❑

LEFT: distinctive headdress of an Akha woman, which are worn even in the fields. **ABOVE:** Mien women in their traditional – and daily – attire.

CUSTOMS AND FESTIVALS THROUGHOUT THAILAND

Many festivals and feasts are held throughout the year and visitors should be able to attend at least one celebration during their stay. Loy Krathong, Bun Bang Fai and Songkran are especially worth seeing.

Songkran, one of the most important festivals in the Thai calendar, comes from the Sanskrit and means the beginning of a new solar year. During this festival, people wear new clothes and visit their local *wat* to offer food to the monks. Housewives clean their homes on the eve of the festival and throw out anything old or broken so it will not bring bad luck. On the afternoon of April 13, Buddha images are bathed as part of the ceremony. Young people pour scented water into the hands of their elders and parents as a mark of respect and ask for their blessing. The Songkran custom of throwing water is thought to derive from a rain-making ceremony. According to myth, *naga* (mythical serpents) brought rain by spouting water from the seas. The more seawater they spouted, the more rain there would be, which is why, apart from it being good fun, Thai people throw water at this time of year.

Another custom during this time is the releasing of caged birds and live fish, which are sold in the markets for this occasion. This part of the festival remembers the time when the central plains of Thailand were flooded during the rainy season. After the earth had dried, little pools of water were left which often trapped young fish. Farmers caught the fish and then released them back into the water on Songkran, thereby gaining merit and preserving a food source.

FESTIVAL OF LIGHTS

Loy Krathong is one of the most beautiful Thai festivals. *Loy* means "to float" and a *krathong* is a leaf cup traditionally made of banana leaf. The festival is not strictly Buddhist, but the floating of krathongs is thought to bring good luck. When the full moon rises, the krathongs are taken to the banks of waterways, and small candles and incense sticks inside them are lit. A prayer is said as they are launched into the water. Children often swim out to collect coins that are put inside the krathongs.

PLANTING TIME▷
The Royal Ploughing Ceremony takes place in the Sanam Luang at the time of rice planting, in May. Monks bless rice seeds that are scattered over the fields.

◁ **WINTER FESTIVALS**
Nearly all of the country's temples and provinces have festival days, which tend to occur during the cool season.

◁ SPRING FLOWERS

The Chiang Mai flower festival takes place on the first weekend in February. The town has a parade of floral floats and marching bands, holds beauty contests, and produces beautiful displays of the town's cultivated flora.

▽ AUTUMN CANDLES

Loy Krathong is held on the night of the full moon in the 12th lunar month (usually mid November). Small leaf boats contain candle, incense, and often a coin.

WHEN THE MOON SHINES BRIGHT

As Thailand is a Buddhist country, several religious holidays are attached to the lunar calendar and held on nights of the full moon. Visakha Puja (above) is a nationwide public holiday. It falls on the 15th day of the waxing moon in the sixth lunar month, which is May. This is the date of Buddha's birth, enlightenment and entry into *nirvana*.

On this night, devout Thais and their families gather at *wat* to hear a sermon on the life of Buddha given by the chief monk. As the moon rises, they hold a candle, incense stick and flowers between their hands, which are placed in a position of prayer. The monks of the wat then lead a procession three times around the temple *bot* (ordination hall), and the candles and incense are placed in a tray at the front of the bot. It is a solemn and moving ceremony that only a few foreign visitors will be invited to attend.

Visakha Puja has been celebrated in Thailand since 1300 AD. The ceremony was revised in 1817 and its observance was strengthened by Rama IV. During his reign, three nights were devoted to reading the *Life of Buddha*. Today, reading from this text is limited to one evening; however, several temples hold religious ceremonies that last until the dawn of the following day.

◁ NEW YEAR SPLASH

Songkran is the Thai new year festival, celebrated from 13 to 16 April. It involves lots of good-natured water throwing - so be prepared to get rather wet, if not drenched.

MAY MAYHEM ▷

The Bun Bang Fai or rocket festival is celebrated in the northeast, especially in Yasothon. Rockets are fired into the sky to bring rain at the end of the dry season.

RELIGION

A sense of spirituality filters through almost every aspect of Thai daily life.
At its foundation is Buddhism, with a distinctly Thai texture

I*n the pale light of early morning, a young saffron-robed monk walks with grave dignity along a city street, a cloth bag over one arm, a metal alms bowl cradled in the other. Silently, he opens his alms bowl to receive the offerings – not handouts – of rice and curries placed in it by ordinary Thais, who have stood for a long while before their homes, awaiting his arrival. He says not a word of thanks, because, according to Buddhist tenets, he is doing them a favour, providing them a means to make merit so they can be reborn in the next life as higher beings. Turning, he continues to walk on bare feet to the next set of alms givers, following the steps of monks before him for 2,000 years.*

Buddhism – a philosophy, rather than a religion – has played a profound role in shaping the Thai character, particularly in the people's reactions to events.

The Buddhist concept of the impermanence of life and possessions, and of the necessity to avoid extremes of emotion or behaviour, has done much to create the relaxed, carefree charm that is one of the most appealing characteristics of the people. Tension, ulcers, nervous breakdowns and the like are not unknown in Thailand, at least not in places like Bangkok. But they are still fairly uncommon, in no small way due to the influence of Buddhism.

Buddhism first came to Southeast Asia from India as early as the 4th century, and was passed to the Thais by way of the Mon and Khmer kingdoms between the 10th and 12th centuries. King Ramkamhaeng introduced Theravada Buddhist influence to Thailand from Sri Lanka (Ceylon) in the 13th century, after he invited Ceylonese monks to reform the Khmer-influenced Buddhism then being practised in his Sukhothai kingdom.

The basic form of Buddhism now practised

in Thailand is *Theravada*. Originating in India, Theravada is also practised in neighbouring Burma, Cambodia and Laos, but even a casual visitor to temples in these countries will quickly perceive some differences among them.

As they have done with most important outside influences – Khmer temple decorations and

Chinese food, for instance – over the centuries the Thai people have evolved a form of Buddhism of their own.

In addition to Theravada Buddhism, there is the *Mahayana* (Greater Vehicle) tradition of Buddhism practised by those of Chinese descent. Their shrines can be found throughout Bangkok, and in most towns of Thailand. To the visitor stepping into a *sanjao,* or deity shrine, it is immediately evident that Mahayana is observed with more vigour. Incense smoke clouds the air, sticks are shaken out of canisters to tell fortunes, paper money is burned for use by deceased ancestors, bells are rung and the din of piety permeates every corner.

PRECEDING PAGE: nearly every Thai male spends time as a monk, at any age. **LEFT:** lighted candles and lotus buds at Bangkok's Wat Benchamabophit. **RIGHT:** the golden glow of a temple's Buddha image.

Temple life

Thailand's 300,000 monks typically live in a *wat,* practising and teaching the rules of human conduct laid down by the Buddha more than 2,500 years ago. There are literally hundreds of Buddhist wats in the cities and suburbs, usually sited in serene pockets of densely packed neighbourhoods and serving as hubs for spiritual and social life.

The term wat defines a large walled compound made up of several buildings, including a *bot* or hall where new monks are ordained, and one or more *viharn* where sermons are delivered. It may also contain a belltower, a *ho trai* (library), and *kuti,* or monk meditation cells, as well as stupas, called *chedi* in Thailand. Chedi contain the ashes or relics of wealthy donors, or important persons, emulating the Buddha whose ashes and relics were placed, by his instruction, in a mound of earth.

There may even be a school on the premises to educate the local children. And if there is any open space in the temple grounds, it is a sure bet that it will be filled with happy kids playing soccer or *takraw*.

The total number of monks in residence at Thailand's nearly 30,000 wats varies from season to season, swelling during the rainy season,

the normal time for a young man to enter the priesthood. Thai tradition requires that every Buddhist male enter the monkhood, for a period ranging from seven days to six months, or even a lifetime. Regulations require that government offices and the military give a man time off to enter the monkhood; companies customarily grant leave time with pay for male employees entering the monkhood.

The entry of a young man into monkhood is seen as repayment to parents for his upbringing, and as bestowing special merit on them, particularly his mother. Since women cannot be ordained, it is the son, as monk, who also makes merit for his mother and other female relatives. That merit advances her along the road to *nirvana*, which is attained for her, as for all Buddhists, when she acquires so much merit that she vanishes from the painful cycle of earthly death and rebirth.

Prior to being ordained, the would-be monk is shorn of all his hair. He then answers a series of questions put to him by the abbot, assuring that he is in good mental and physical health. He then moves to a monks' dormitory, or to a small *kuti* or meditation house.

SIGNIFICANT NAMES

Wat compounds that were founded by Thai royalty, or perhaps hold a special sacred status because something revered is kept within, often have names that begin with *Maha-, Rat-,* or *Ratcha-*.

chant in a group separate from the men, and receive whatever food has not earlier been consumed by the monks. A Buddhist monk must not only abstain from stealing, lying and idle talk, taking life, indulgence in sex, intoxicants, luxuries and frivolous amusements, he must also obey no fewer than 227 rules that govern the minutiae of daily conduct and manners. These vows include having no possessions other than the yellow robes, alms bowl, razor and a few other personal necessities. Monks eat

While in the temple, he listens to sermons based on the Buddha's teachings, studies the *Tripitaka,* or *Three Baskets* (the teaching of Buddha in Pali), practises meditation, and learns the virtues of an ascetic life. He shares in the work of the monastery: washing dishes, keeping the quarters clean. He goes out at dawn to receive his daily food.

There are nuns who wear white robes, but they do not share the same rights as the monks, as there is no provision for the ordination of women. They live in side areas of the wats,

LEFT: monk's quarters at Wat Arun, Bangkok.
ABOVE: morning offerings, Wat Benjamabophit.

only twice a day, once at dawn and again just before noon, and may eat only food offered by lay worshippers. They are also forbidden to touch money, sing or dance.

Communal centre

For all its Spartan life, however, a Buddhist wat in Thailand is by no means isolated from the real world. Most wats have schools of some sort attached to them; in fact, for centuries, the only schools in most of Thailand were those run by monks. The wat has traditionally been the centre of social and communal life in the villages, with monks serving as herbal doctors, psychological counsellors, and arbitrators of disputes.

Monks also play an important part in daily life, such as the blessing of a new building, or a birthday or funeral.

Except during the period of Buddhist Lent, from July to October, monks are free to travel about from one temple to another at will. Moreover, wats are open to anyone who wishes to retire to them.

On *wan phra,* a day each week determined by the lunar calendar, Thais go to the wat to listen to monks chant scriptures and deliver sermons. In addition

> **FOOLISH BELIEFS?**
>
> King Mongkut (Rama IV), who welcomed Christian missionaries to Siam and learned the English language from them, said to them: "What you teach us to do is admirable, but what you teach us to believe is foolish."

constitution declares that the king is the "upholder" of all religions. Islam is the second largest religion in Thailand, and all over the country, but especially in the south, there are hundreds of mosques. The Thai government contributes to the repair and construction of these mosques, as well as to that of the Buddhist temples.

Christian missionaries have struggled for more than a century for converts in Thailand, without great success. Today, there are around 500,000 Christians in

to providing monks with food, the laity earns merit by making repairs on the temple or, even better, replacing an old and derelict building with a new one. At the end of the lenten season, groups of Thais board boats or buses and travel to distant villages to make donations, an occasion filled with as much riotous and festive celebration as solemn ceremony.

Religious tolerance

Nearly 95 percent of the Thai people are Buddhist, but religious tolerance is (and always has been) extended to other religions. Around 5 percent of Thais are Muslim, with the remainder Christian, Hindu and Sikh. Indeed, the national

Thailand. King Mongkut suggested that Christianity had succeeded only where the indigenous religion was weak. There are pockets of Christians – notably protestants in Chiang Mai and Catholics in Chanthaburi – but few steeples amidst the chedi spires.

Spirits and amulets

Nearly every Thai male, and a large number of women as well, carry some sort of amulet, usually on a chain around their necks. Some wear as many as half a dozen charms to protect them from automobile accidents, gunfire, snakebite and almost any other disaster. In the provinces, tattoos ward off evil. Astrologers are consulted regularly to learn auspicious times for weddings, important journeys, moving into a new house, and even the promulgation of a constitution or other governmental action.

Brahman influences

Many of the Thais' non-Buddhist beliefs are Brahman in origin, and even today Brahman priests officiate at major ceremonies. The Thai wedding ceremony is almost entirely Brahman, as are many funeral rites.

The rites of statecraft pertaining to the royal family are presided over by Brahman priests. One of the most popular and impressive of these, the Ploughing Ceremony, takes place each May in Bangkok to signal the beginning of the rice-planting season. A team of sacred oxen is offered a selection of grains. Astrologers watch carefully, as the grains that the oxen choose will determine the amount of rainfall, and the degree of success or failure of the year's crops. Afterwards, the oxen draw a gilded plough around the field and seeds are symbolically sown (and afterwards eagerly collected by farmers to bring them luck). The head priest, after complex calculations, makes predictions on the forthcoming rain and bounty of the next harvest.

Spirits outnumber people

The variety of *phi* (spirits) in Thailand is legion, outnumbering the human population many times over. A seductive female phi, believed to reside in a banana plant, torments young men who come near. Another bothersome one takes possession of her victims and forces them to remove their clothes in public.

A very common sight in any town in Thailand, including sophisticated Bangkok, is a small house, generally set atop a post on a site selected after complex astrological consideration. In ordinary residences, the house may resemble a Thai dwelling; in hotels and offices, it may be an elaborate mini-temple, made of cement and painted and gilded.

In either case, these spirit houses serve as the abodes of the locality spirits. It is within their power to favour or plague the human inhabitants, so the spirit house is regularly adorned

LEFT: an extravagant and large spirit house.
RIGHT: a *malai*, made of jasmine flowers; while beautiful at first, it reflects the impermanence of things and life as it withers and decays.

with placatory offerings of food, fresh flowers and incense sticks. If calamity or ill luck befalls the compound, it may be necessary to call in an expert to consult the unhappy spirit to determine what is wrong.

One of the most famous spirit houses in Bangkok is the Erawan Shrine *(see page 170)*, at the junction of Thanon Ratchadamri and Thanon Ploenchit, adjacent to the Grand Hyatt Erawan Hotel. This shrine, honouring the Hindu god Brahma, was erected by the owners during the construction of the original hotel in the 1950s, after several workers were injured in mysterious accidents. The shrine soon acquired

a widespread reputation for bringing good fortune to outsiders as well.

A less well-known shrine sits in the compound of the Nai Lert Park Hotel on Thanon Witthayu. Its offerings consist entirely of phalluses, ranging from small to gargantuan, sculpted from wood, wax, stone or cement with full fidelity to life. They are left by women hoping to conceive a child.

To the average Thai, there is nothing inconsistent about the intermingling of such practices and beliefs with Buddhism. In the end, although deeply founded on Buddhism, Thai beliefs are both pragmatically and spiritually harmonious with the needs of the Thai people. ❑

IMAGES OF THE BUDDHA

From the gigantic seated Buddha at Wat Si Chum to tiny Buddhas worn as amulets, Thai artists have produced religious icons that rank among the world's greatest expressions of Buddhist art.

Images of the Buddha are devotional objects and are not considered to be works of art by their makers. When artists make an image of the Buddha, they follow specific rules – the Buddha is defined by a set of peculiar characteristics, a particular monastic garb and a series of *mudra* (attitudes, postures or gestures). The 32 bodily marks, evident at the time of the Buddha's birth, include hands that reach the knees without bending, a lion-like jaw, and wheel marks on the base of the feet. Buddhist artists have interpreted these marks according to the era in which they were working and the school of interpretation they chose to follow.

SUKHOTHAI SCHOOL

Thai Buddhist imagery was at its artistic height during the Sukhothai period (late 13th to early 15th centuries), when the smoothness and sheen of cast metals perfectly matched the graceful, elongated simplicity of the basic form. During this era, the Buddha was usually represented sitting cross- legged or with one foot forward in the "striding" position. One hand is raised in *abhayamudra* (dispelling fear). Slightly androgynous in appearance, the images also feature a flame-like *ketumula* on the crown of the head, protruding heels, flat soles and toes all the same length.

◁ **SPIRITUAL DETAILS**
Thai artists simplify anatomical details in their images of the Buddha to emphasise the spiritual qualities of Buddhism and to convey enigma and serenity.

COLOSSAL CHEDI ▷
This standing Buddha in Phra Pathom Chedi, Nakhon Pathom, is said to be the world's tallest monument of its type. The relic chamber was raised to its present height of 125 metres (410 ft) in 1860.

▽ **FASTING FIGURE**
This statue of a fasting Buddha is in the grounds of Wat U Mong, in Chiang Mai. The wat was founded in 1371 by King Ku Na.

SYMBOLISM OF MUDRAS

The Buddha can be seen either sitting, standing, lying or, in Thailand, walking. Every image of the Buddha is represented in a particular *mudra* or attitude. Hand gestures in particular are key iconographical elements in representations of the Buddha:

• *Abhayamudra* is the mudra of dispelling fear or giving protection: the Buddha is usually in a standing position, the right hand raised and turned outwards to show the palm with straight fingers.

• *Bhumisparsamudra* or calling the earth as witness: this is made by a seated figure, with the right hand on the knee and the fingertips touching the ground.

• *Dharmacakramudra* means spinning the Wheel of Law: both hands are held in front of the body, with the fingertips of the left hand resting against the palm of the right hand.

• *Dhyanamudra* is the meditation mudra: the hands rest flat in the lap, one on top of the other.

• *Varamudra*, giving blessing or charity: made by the seated or standing Buddha with the right arm pointing downwards, the palm open and fingers more or less straight.

• *Vitarkamudra* is the preaching mudra: the end of the thumb and index finger of the right hand touch to form a circle, symbolising the Wheel of Law.

△ **SUKHOTHAI SCHOOL**
Buddha images at Wat Phra Sri Sanphet, Ayutthaya, are seen in the attitude of *Bhumisparsamudra* (calling the earth as witness). The images date from the 13th and 14th centuries.

▽ **WHEEL OF LAW**
This Chinese-style Buddha can be found in Chiang Rai, at Wat Phra Singh. The Buddha is represented in the *Vitarkamudra* (preaching mode). The gesture of the right hand symbolises the Wheel of Law.

△ **RECLINING GIANT**
Phra Phuttahatmongkol in Wat Hat Yai Nai is the world's third largest reclining Buddha (attaining *parinibbana* – nirvana – in death). It measures 35 metres (115 ft) from head to toe. Visitors can climb inside the Buddha's chest.

▽ **SEATED IMAGE**
The Temple of the Big Buddha, Ko Samui, contains a modern 12 metre (40 ft) Buddha in the attitude of *Bhumisparsamudra*.

PERFORMING ARTS

In Thailand, "dance" and "drama" are nearly one and the same.

Many performances are derived from the epic tale, Ramakien

The Thai people have combined a lively imagination, a superb aesthetic sense and a fine hand to produce some of the most detailed and arresting visual arts found in Asia. In the performing arts, Thai dance-dramas are among the world's most dazzling, with elaborate and colourful costumes, and graceful, enchanting movements.

When discussing Thai theatre, one cannot use the word "drama" without uttering the word "dance" immediately before it. The two are inseparable, the dancer's hands and body expressing the emotions that the silent lips do not. In effect, the actor is a mime, with the story line and lyrics provided by a singer and chorus to the side of the stage. An orchestra creates not only the atmosphere, but an emotive force.

It is thought that the movements of dance-drama originated in *nang yai* (shadow puppet) performances of the 16th and 17th centuries. Huge buffalo hides were cut into the shapes of characters from the *Ramakien (see page 101)*. Against a translucent screen, which was back-lit by torches, puppeteers manipulated these figures to tell complex tales of good and evil. As they moved the hide figures across the screen, the puppeteers danced the emotions they wanted the stiff figures to convey. It is thought that these movements evolved into an independent theatrical art.

The most popular form of dance-drama is the *khon*, performed by dancers wearing brilliantly crafted masks. An evening's entertainment comprises several episodes from the *Ramakien*. (The entire *Ramakien* would take 720 hours to perform, slightly longer than even the most feverish theatregoer is prepared to endure.)

The expressionless masks focus the viewer's attention on the dancers' movements, where one sees grace and control of surpassing beauty – a dismissive flick of the hand, a finger

pointed in accusation, a foot stamped in anger. The favourite character is Hanuman, in his white monkey mask, whose dance movements would tax even the strongest viewer. Only the characters of Rama, Sita and Phra Lak appear without masks, but their features are kept stiff, looking like masks.

The most graceful of the dramatic arts is the *lakhon*. There are two forms: the *lakhon nai* ("inside" lakhon), which was once performed only inside the palace walls, and then only by women, and the *lakhon nawk* ("outside" lakhon), performed beyond the palace walls by men. Of the two, lakhon nai is the more popular entertainment.

Garbed in costumes as elaborate as their movements, the performers glide slowly about the stage, even in the most emotional moments, their faces impassive and devoid of smiles or expression. The heavily stylised movements convey the plot and are quite enchanting, though for most foreign visitors, 30 minutes is

---

PRECEDING PAGE: young classical dancers at the royal court. **LEFT:** a painted screen depicting *nang yai*, or shadow puppets. **RIGHT:** young dancers in traditional dance costumes.

sufficient to absorb the essentials of the play. Lakhon's rich repertoire includes the *Ramakien*, and tales that have romantic storylines.

There have always been two cultures in Thailand: palace and village. The village arts are often parodies of the palace arts, but more like burlesques with pratfalls and heavy-handed humour. *Likay* is the village form of lakhon. Broad, bawdy humour is its mainstay, played out against gaudy backdrops to an audience that walks in and out of the performance at will, eating and talking and having a good time, regardless of what takes place on stage. You may come across *likay* at a *ngaan wat* (temple fair) or rural festival.

Another variation on Thai classical dance is *lakhon kae bon*, which consists of a 20-member ensemble of dancers and musicians hired to perform at shrines to give thanks for a wish granted. Bangkok's Lak Muang, the city pillar shrine, is a popular *kae bon* venue, as is the city's Erawan Shrine.

Bangkok's *ngiew* or Chinese opera theatres have closed their doors forever, victims of television with its unending *kungfu* programmes. Wandering in a market at night, however, one may come across a performance that has been arranged as part of the entertainment during a funeral. (Grief is experienced privately; what

INDIAN EPICS

One of the two great Indian epics informing Thai theatre and dance is the *Ramayana*. (The other is the *Mahabharata*, a major Indian work whose original Sanskrit text is quite possibly the word's largest book.) From the Sanskrit meaning "romance of Rama", the *Ramayana* is the basis for many regional epic tales, including the *Ramakien* in Thailand.

The *Ramayana* is a moral tale, full of instructions and examples for leading a good, ethical life. In its homeland, India, it has been told for 3,000 years. With the spread of Indian culture throughout Southeast Asia, the *Ramayana* has become part of the mythology of Burma, Laos, Cambodia, Indonesia and Thailand. (See page 101 for more on the *Ramakien*.)

one shares with friends is happiness.) They may also be seen at wat fairs during the winter.

Puppet theatre has also lost most of its Bangkok audiences to television, but a few troupes remain. *Hoon krabok* puppets, similar to Punch and Judy puppets, tell the story of Phra Aphaimani. Delicately crafted, they are charming to watch. Performances are often arranged by major hotels for their guests during the year-end holiday season.

Modern Thai drama has yet to come into its own in a major way. Leading hotels produce stage plays, but they are primarily for popular entertainment – soap operas, comedies, and translations from Western plays.

Rural performances

The counterparts to the grace and beauty of classical dance are the more traditional and less structured dances performed in rural villages by farm families. Each region has a special form unique to it.

Harvest, fingernail, candle and fishing dances are performed by groups of women in village costumes. In flirtation dances, they are joined by male dancers attempting to weave romantic spells on unsmiling but appreciative partners.

> **MOOD MUSIC**
>
> Try listening to Thai music as you would listen to jazz, picking out one of the instruments and following it for a while, before switching to another instrument as the mood takes you.

regard to how others are playing it. (Some say the same about Thai politics.)

Seldom does an instrument rise in uninterrupted solo; it is always being challenged, cajoled by the other instruments of the orchestra. In a sense, it is the aural counterpart to Thai classical painting, with every space filled and a number of separate strands woven together, seemingly at random but with a distinct pattern. A classical *phipat* music orchestra is made up of a single reed instrument, the oboe-like *pi nai*, and a vari-

Music

Classical Thai music eludes many finely tuned Western ears. To the uninitiated, it sounds like a mishmash of contrasting tones without any pattern. To aficionados, it has a very distinct rhythm and plan.

Thai music is set to a scale of seven full steps, but it is normally played as a pentatonic scale (the scale of *Auld Lang Syne*). The rhythm is lilting and steady, with speeds varying according to section. Each instrument plays the same melody but in its own way, seemingly without

ety of percussion instruments. The pitch favours the treble, with the result that the music sounds airy rather than stentorian. The pace is set by the *ching*, a tiny cymbal, aided by the drums beaten with the fingers. The melody is played by two types of *ranat*, a bamboo-bar xylophone and two sets of *khong wong*, tuned gongs arranged in a semicircle around the player. Another type of orchestra employs two violins, the *saw-oo* and the *saw-duang*. It is usually heard accompanying a Thai dance-drama.

The *ja-khe*, a stringed instrument similar to a Japanese *koto*, sits flush with the floor and is often played as a solo instrument in the lobbies of some of Bangkok's larger hotels and restau-

LEFT: dance-drama students learning the moves.
ABOVE: *phipat* ensemble, with oboe-like *pi nai*.

rants. A separate type of orchestra performs at a Thai boxing match to spur the combatants to action. It is composed of four instruments: the ching, two double-reed oboe-like flutes, and a drum. It plays a repertoire entirely its own.

Originating in the countryside, but having found a permanent home in the city as well, are the *klawng yao* or long drums. They are thumped along with gongs and cymbals as accompaniment to group singing. Never played solemnly, they lend an exuberant note to any occasion – and for a Thai, it doesn't take much of an excuse to have an occasion. It may be a procession on the way to ordain a new monk, a

bus trip upcountry, or a *kathin* ceremony in the late autumn, when groups of Buddhists board boats to travel upriver to give robes to monks at the end of the three-month lenten season.

Literature

Thais have always placed a heavy emphasis on oral tradition, and it's a good thing, too, because most of its printed classical literature was completely destroyed by the flames of Ayutthaya's destruction in 1767.

Moreover, as tropical insects have a particular relish for the palm-leaf paper on which manuscripts were traditionally written, books are manifest examples of the Buddhist tenet that

nothing is permanent. The classical works existing today came from late-night sessions during the reigns of Rama I and II, when scholars delved into their collective memories and, on breeze-cooled palace verandas, recreated an entire literature.

At the heart of Thai literature is the *Ramakien*, the Thai version of the Indian classical tale, *Ramayana*. This enduring story has found a home in the literature of every Southeast Asian nation. In Thailand, it forms the basis of a dance-drama tradition. Understanding it allows one to comprehend a wide variety of dramatic forms, its significance for Thailand's monarchs who have adopted the name Rama as their own, and its role as model for exemplary social behaviour.

The *Ramakien* is the vividly told tale of the god-king Rama and his beautiful wife, Sita, paragon of beauty and virtue, and model for all wives to follow.

Sita is abducted by the nasty 10-headed, 20-armed demon king Tosakan, who imprisons her in his palace on the island of Longka (Sri Lanka), importuning her at every turn to divorce Rama and marry him. With his brother Phra Lak, Rama sets off in pursuit, stymied by mammoth obstacles that test his mettle. Along the way, he is joined by the magical white monkey-god, Hanuman, a mischievous but talented general who is one of the Thais' favourite characters. Hanuman and his army of monkeys build a bridge to Longka. After a pitched battle, Tosakan is killed, Sita is rescued, and everyone lives happily ever after.

Another classical work, pure Thai in its flavour and treatment, is *Khun Chang, Khun Phaen*, a love triangle involving a beautiful young woman with two lovers – one a rich, bald widower, and the other, a poor but handsome young man. This ancient soap opera provides a useful insight into Thai customs, manners and morals of the Ayutthaya era.

Written by Sunthorn Phu, the poet laureate of the early 18th century, *Phra Aphaimani* is the story of a rebellious prince who refuses to study to be king, instead playing the flute, much to the disgust of his father. After numerous exciting adventures, this prodigal son returns home to don the crown and rule his father's realm. ❑

LEFT: traditional *nang yai* performance of *Ramakien*.
RIGHT: live characters from *Ramakien* performance.

The Ramakien

If Thai literature has a long tradition and a short history, there can be no better illustration than the *Ramakien*, the Thai version of the Indian legend of *Ramayana*, an epic tale that arrived in what later became Thailand some 1,000 to 2,000 years ago, with the first wave of Buddhist missionaries from Sri Lanka.

As was true for many early cultures around the world, in Southeast Asia there were few written languages, or limited literacy, and the history, myths and stories of the various peoples were passed down by skilled storytellers from generation to generation, orally. In retelling the *Ramayana*, the characters and tangled plot remained, but the tale changed, becoming identifiably Thai as character names were changed and various Buddhist ceremonial elements were added to what was, originally, a Hindu text. It was not until when the Thai capital was in Ayutthaya – named for the primary city in the *Ramayana* – that the work was finally transcribed. Sadly, only fragments of that version of the epic story remained following the sacking of the city in 1767 by the Burmese, who burned virtually all of the written literature. Today, it is a required part of the school curriculum, so it is an allegory of the triumph of good over evil that is familiar to virtually every Thai.

The story opens in India with a demon, who was given great physical strength by Shiva, the Hindu lord of the universe. Betraying the trust, the demon rolled up the surface of the Earth like a carpet, removing all signs of life so he could be the sole survivor. Shiva called on the powerful god Vishnu the Preserver for vengeance, who turned himself into a white boar, decapitating the demon with his tusks and restoring life to the planet.

Upon returning to his celestial home in the Cosmic Ocean, Vishnu meditated until a lotus appeared, unfolding to reveal a young man who was taken to Shiva as the future king. Shiva dispatched the god Indra to find a new city for the king, travelling on a white elephant named Erawan, leading a host of angels to Earth. A city called A-Yu-Da-Ya was founded, named for four hermits who resided there, praying for 4,000 years. It was a paradisiacal metropolis with a bejeweled palace, sumptuous gardens, and 56,000 maidens to cater to the king's every whim.

And this is merely the start of the story. Immodest or subtle the *Ramakien* is not, and in this lush and exuberant excess lay much of its popularity. Battles were of such cosmic proportion that a collaboration between Steven Spielberg and Walt Disney would be required to convey them properly. Fire streamed from a god's third eye to vaporise demons caught debauching celestial maidens. A magical snake arrow was sent to coil itself around an enemy and elevate him into a fearsome thunderstorm. The monkey god Hanuman was able to levitate and fly, aiding his beloved master, Phra Ram, the king of Ayutthaya (and a reincarnation of Vishnu), to defeat the dreaded King Thotsakan of Longka (Sri Lanka), the 10-headed villain who had kidnapped Phra Ram's wife. It is an imaginative and captivating tale that blends romance, high adventure, and fantasy,

three key elements that some say are essential to understanding life in Thailand today. In fact, in the earliest written Thai version, there were 60,000 verses, 25 percent more than were in the Sanskrit original transcribed in Sri Lanka. A performance of the 138 acts, or episodes, involving more than 300 characters, lasted longer than 700 hours. Today, popular episodes may be seen in briefer performances of Thai classical dance, *khon*.

Artistic representations of the plot and characters may also be seen in murals and bas-relief throughout the country, from stone carvings at Prasat Hin Phimai and other Angkor-period temples in northeastern Thailand to wall paintings at Bangkok's oldest temple, Wat Pho. ❑

ARTS AND CRAFTS

With numerous cultural and aesthetic influences from around Asia, it's no wonder that Thailand's creative arts and crafts have an almost universal appeal

As is true of its architecture, music, religion, and cuisine, the handicrafts of Thailand are the clever result of outside ingredients being stirred by skilled practitioners over centuries to form something clearly and uniquely Thai. Someone with some knowledge in the field may say, "That bit's Chinese...and

that bit's Indian...and that bit's European," yet it must also be concluded that the effect, the end-product, is entirely home-grown.

Thailand is renowned worldwide as a centre of flourishing arts and crafts – one of the reasons it's a shopper's delight – and the best-known arguably are the textiles, most notably the colourful, shimmering silk. Villagers in the northeast had woven and worn silk for centuries, but it wasn't until after World War II – when the leading silk industries in Japan, China, Italy, and France were destroyed – that Thailand emerged as a primary source. Credit is given to an American expatriate, Jim Thompson, who organised provincial weavers, introduced long-

lasting chemical dyes and improved looms, and took samples of the gleaming cloth to New York. There, the costumes were made from his silk for a new Broadway musical, *The King and I*. *Vogue* magazine followed along and within a short time, a world market had been created. In recent years, the distinctive northeastern tie-dyed fabric called *mud mee* has become popular world-wide, largely due to the recognition and promotion given to it by Her Majesty Queen Sirikit. Thailand also produces excellent cotton garments and, from the hill tribes in the north, skirts and other items with remarkable embroidery.

Jewellery and gemstones

Thailand is equally famous for its gold and silver jewellery and gemstones, now the country's sixth-largest export category. It commands a part of the global jewellery market rivalled only by Sri Lanka and India. In the Ayutthaya and early Bangkok eras, gold's use in a variety of royal household items, such as cosmetic jars and tableware, as well as on thrones and ceremonial objects, brought honour to the owners and to the artisans who were commissioned by royal and other wealthy families. Today, most of the gold jewellery sold is less imaginative, taking the form of heavy chains purchased as a hedge against a fluctuating currency and as a status item.

More affordable items in great variety are fashioned from silver. Not so long ago, the silver used came from melted-down Indian, Burmese and French coins from Indochina. Nowadays, most of it is imported and then pounded into delicate and ornately crafted trays, boxes, bowls, and other containers noted for their raised designs. The finest work is done in the north and usually sold in shops in Chiang Mai and Chiang Rai.

Most of the gems sold in Thailand today are imported from neighbouring Burma and Cambodia, the bulk arriving in Thailand by sometimes questionable means. A century ago, gems were set in gold and silver jewellery noted more for the artistic fittings than for the stones themselves. Precious stones also played a prominent role in the decoration of crowns and other royal implements. The Nine Gems of the Brahman faith – diamonds, rubies, emeralds, yellow sapphires, blue sapphires, garnets, moonstones, zircons, and the cat's eye – were thought to have special powers.

Contemporary jewellery, some of it adapted from traditional Thai motifs, still utilises a variety of stones, but more and more, they are being purchased without settings and resold by the buyers in the West. The Khmer gem market in Chan-

skilled and patient artists who laboriously apply layer after layer of a resin to containers most often made from wood or woven bamboo. Some of the finest work may require several weeks or months. This art form also is used to decorate temple and palace doors, which are further illuminated by paintings depicting Buddhist legends and tales from the epic *Ramakien*.

Still another craft from China, related to lacquering, is mother-of-pearl decoration. Most of the iridescent shell comes from the Gulf of Thailand and adorns lac-

CRYSTAL POWER

During the Ayutthaya period, generals would ride into battle on elephants, wearing sashes encrusted with jewels that they believed would give them protection and strength.

thaburi, near the Cambodian border, and Burmese markets in Mae Hong Son offer an exciting alternative to the high-pressure Bangkok "factories", where quality is often poor and the prices are ridiculous. Unless you know gems, beware. Never buy gems from a source recommended by someone you have just met.

Laquerware and pottery

Lacquerware is another Burmese-Chinese import, and much of that made today – again, mainly in the north – is fashioned by highly

quered boxes, furniture and statuary. One of the more stunning examples is on the soles of the feet of the huge reclining Buddha figure in Bangkok's Wat Po, but displays may also be seen in Chinese restaurant tables and chairs.

Clay pots found in the northeast have been carbon-tested to 3600 BC. Yet even with that long history, ceramic handicrafts generally don't get the attention they deserve. Best known, perhaps, is the pale-green celadon used for everything from ash trays to dinner settings to large vases, and the enamelled terracotta ware with floral and Buddhist decorations, called *bencharong*, another imported Chinese art improved upon. Realistic reproductions of those

LEFT: finely woven silk is sold in countless hues and colours. **ABOVE:** lacquer hats on Royal Barge oarsmen.

early clay pots from the Bronze Age may also be found in antique stores and at a museum shop at Ban Chiang, and replicas of old stone sculpture are offered in Ayutthaya.

Antiques and woodcarvings

A word about antique stores. Real antiques cannot be taken out of Thailand without a permit from the Department of Fine Arts. In recent years, the government has been going after museums and private collectors around the world, demanding – and getting – many old religious artefacts back. Buddha images are sold widely, but they are for local use, and unless you

can wear it around your neck, its export is strictly forbidden, even if it was manufactured last week. Also, Thai craftsmen are ingenious when it comes to copying something, from a Versace shirt to a Rolex watch. Many of the "antiques" offered are no such thing.

Another handicraft, distinctly Thai, is ornamental woodcarving. In this, the Thais have no peers, developing, over time, traditional motifs such as the lotus and other flowers, mythological creatures from India, serpents and dragons from China. Usually this decorative work is found on furniture and in the adornment of religious and royal buildings, royal barges and carriages, and in a modest style even in the

humblest homes. When visiting a *wat*, look up towards the eaves and don't just pass through an open door, stop to examine it; some of what you see will surprise. When Thailand was covered by forest, such carving was at its peak and much of this painstaking carving has survived the wicked Thai climate. However proficient the product, it is unfortunate that most of the woodwork sold today is made from rattan and bamboo. Teak is now an endangered plant.

Other bric-a-brac

A category of handicrafts that never really went away and now is attracting attention are the objects of everyday rural life. Baskets whose origins were strictly utilitarian – to winnow, store, cook and carry rice to the table, to transport crops from the fields, even to tote small children – are now regarded by many as "folk art." Some of the woven containers, using thinly cut bamboo and other plants, are lightly lacquered for strength. Others are given modern handles and serve Western women as purses.

Brightly painted wooden "bells," or clappers that are hung around the necks of water buffaloes, baskets used to catch fish in the flooded rice paddies, kitchen implements made from coconut shells and carved wood, machetes used in the fields, coconut graters, large earthen water jars, even the worn wood and bamboo yokes used by villagers and street vendors to carry their heavy baskets of food to market – everything "authentic" is now in great demand. Poor northern hill-tribe villages, induced by the government and international organisations to stop growing opium, are now supplementing their meagre subsistence economy with the production of embroidered shoulder bags and native silver jewellery.

Because so much is being produced quickly to satisfy the new demand, much of the quality is slipshod. A visit to the National Museum *(see page 147)* or the Jim Thompson House *(see page 172)* in Bangkok – Thompson was an avid collector blessed with impeccable taste – will reveal appropriate guidelines. The present Queen of Thailand, under her self-help organisation called SUPPORT, also sponsors a number of provincial workshops, with the product so identified and sold in many stores. ❑

LEFT: common cooking items have an elegance.
RIGHT: silver-working near Chiang Mai.

ARCHITECTURE

The temples of Thailand are top on all visitors' agendas. Beyond the temple, the traditional Thai house reflects a nearly perfect adaptation to the environment

If culture is an expression of the best of a society, architecture must occupy society's zenith, for it is defined by the designs and spaces created for home life, worship, and work. As is true in much of Thailand's artistic expression, many of the finest temples, palaces and other buildings in the kingdom show the influences of several cultures, yet all are identifiably Thai. Indian, Khmer, Burmese, and Chinese architectural styles have had substantial effect through the centuries, but there is no mistaking the swooping multi-tiered roof lines, the distinctly ornamental decorations and blinding colours, the stunning interior murals and lovingly crafted and gold-adorned Buddha images, and the miles of interlocking waterways.

Sadly, many of those canals, called *khlongs*, have been replaced with traffic-jammed roadways, but thousands of the classical Thai structures may still be seen. There are approximately 30,000 temples in Thailand, and hundreds of these compounds established for the veneration of Buddha are worth visiting. So, too, the several royal residences, some blending Western neoclassical features, the result of visits to Europe by early Thai kings and the European expatriate's presence in Thailand.

Any study of Thai architecture begins with the temple, or *wat*, whose traditional role was as a school, community centre, hospital, and entertainment venue, as well as the place where the lessons of Buddha were taught. Every part of a Thai wat has symbolic significance. The capitals of columns are shaped either like water lilies or lotus buds, the lotus symbolising the purity of Buddha's thoughts – it pushes through the muck to burst forth in extraordinary beauty.

These compounds – some, like Wat Pho in Bangkok, are vast, while others in rural villages are quite modest – generally include an assembly hall, or *bot*, where monks perform ceremonies, meditate, and sermonise. A second

assembly hall, or *viharn*, is where lay people make offerings before a large Buddha figure. Dome-shaped *chedi* are where relics of the Buddha may be housed. There may also be towering, phallic spires, called *prang*, epitomised by the Wat Arun on the banks of the Chao Phraya in Bangkok, opposite the Grand Palace.

As different as the wats may be, there are similarities, or themes. Symbolism abounds in the ornate decoration. Bots are bounded by eight stones, believed to keep away evil spirits, an example of how animist beliefs coexist with Buddhism. Roof peaks are adorned with *chofa*, the curling, pointed extensions at each end that represent the *garuda*, the vehicle of Vishnu. In its claws it holds two *naga*, mythical serpents that undulate down the eaves. The garuda is a royal symbol, imported from India. Companies bearing it on their building facades operate "by royal appointment". At the top of a chedi may be a stylised thunderbolt sign of Vishnu, ancient Hindu lord of the universe. Palace architecture

PRECEDING PAGE: traditional house, Nonthaburi, north of Bangkok. **LEFT:** from a mural at Wat Bowon Niwet, Bangkok. **RIGHT:** Sri Lankan-influenced temple stupa.

conveys a lightness similar to that of the wat, employing many of the same motifs and construction materials.

The various outside influences are evident in other ways. Most of the ancient remains in northeastern Thailand reveal a heritage shared by the more famous Angkor Wat in neighbouring Cambodia, as this region was once a part of the sprawling Khmer empire. In the north, many of the older chedi are Burmese in style, constructed during that country's occupation of what was then the kingdom of Lanna.

Window panels and murals in Bangkok dating to the early 18th century cross many cultural

Traditional dwellings

Homes for ordinary people share the same sensitive treatment as those for the exalted. Thai-style teak houses, with their inward-sloping walls and steep roofs, seldom fail to charm with their airiness and their marvellous adaptation to tropical climates.

Like the wat, the Thai house has gone through a centuries-old evolution. Some trace the style to southern China, origin of today's Thai population and where many ethnic Thais still live. Steep roofs, sometimes multi-layered like the wats that dominated village life, with only a few rooms or one large, divided room elevated on

DOMESTIC DESIGNS

The design of the traditional Thai dwelling is well suited for Thailand's tropical weather: they are often built on stilts to rise above flood water; they have steep roof lines for shedding rain, materials that retain coolness, and ventilation that takes advantage of any breezes.

The architectural styles of traditional homes vary depending upon region, although the characteristics noted above are common throughout. In the flat central plains north of Bangkok, an open verandah is often the focus of home life, an outside living space. To the north of the country, where the temperatures are cooler, design of ventilation and living spaces often retains warmth. In most traditional dwelling, the central, innermost room is both a sleeping area and the home for any ancestral spirits.

Outside most Thai homes and commercial buildings stands the spirit house, a miniature dwelling intended for the natural spirits that are found on the land. These spirit houses vary between plain and modest, or gaudy and quite large.

and international boundaries, and are decorated with mythological figures from the Indian *Ramayana*, Chinese dragons, Indian *nagas* (or serpents) and foreign merchants wearing distinctly European garb.

"They are gorgeous," summarised Somerset Maugham, the British novelist and traveller who frequently visited Southeast Asia during the 20th century and wrote extensively about both Thailand and Southeast Asia. "They glitter with gold and whitewash, yet are not garish; against that vivid sky, in that dazzling sunlight, they hold their own, defying the brilliancy of nature and supplementing it with the ingenuity and playful boldness of man."

pilings distinguished the earliest homes. The structures were positioned to take advantage of prevailing winds, and many of the components were prefabricated, then fitted together with wooden pegs.

In time, the elevation of the houses increased, to protect the home from flooding and unwanted animal visitors, while producing a space beneath the house for keeping livestock or to be used for daily work such as weaving. Such homes are common in villages throughout Thailand today, although in urban areas, nearly all houses are now more Western in design and steadfastly anchored to the ground. Most of the early homes were made of native woods such as teak and bamboo, materials that are still used today, although teak is now on the nation's endangered list. The Jim Thompson House is a good example. Numerous other examples line the banks of the silvery network of canals that crisscross the Thonburi suburbs.

In Thailand's southern provinces, a different design evolved, reflecting the warmer, wetter climate. Here, the pillars were shorter, there was no exterior verandah, and windows had hinged shutters that closed from the top during torrential monsoon rains. With the arrival of Western traders and missionaries in the 18th century and early trips to Europe by Thai monarchy in the 19th century, Western-style buildings joined the traditional Thai structures along both sides of the Chao Phraya River, the centre of Bangkok's government and commerce.

Much of this early architecture remains today, including a part of the Oriental Hotel and the original French embassy next door, both designed by European architects. Shophouse architecture in the Sino-Portuguese style uses stout walls and often ornate window and roof treatments that were the hallmark of a type of housing once preferred by Chinese shopkeepers. As in yesteryear, the downstairs serves as a place to market one's goods; the upstairs is the family home. Shophouses at Tha Chang boat landing on the Chao Phraya, to the northwest of the Grand Palace, are good examples.

The Vimarnmek, in Bangkok's Dusit district and built entirely of teak but appearing decidedly more Western than Thai, and the Italianate palace built by King Chulalongkorn at Bang Pa-In near Ayutthaya, offer ample evidence of Thailand's passionate embrace of Western styles that continues to this day. (The present king and queen live in a modern palace with satellite dishes on the roof.)

Most contemporary architectural efforts show little regard for the past, as hundreds of new high-rises go up each year in the cities, while tract homes and lookalike rows of townhouses are erected for the country's growing middle class in the suburbs and small towns. During the building boom of the 1980s, many architects seemed to be trying to outdo each other. See the "robot building" on Bangkok's Thanon Sathorn, its sides decorated with outsized nuts and bolts,

and the headquarters for *The Nation* newspaper in Bangkok's Bang Na district, looking like two stylised grand pianos turned on their sides. At the same time, Corinthian columns and curvilinear banisters appeared on the balconies of virtually every new townhouse, appearing not only incongruous but in many cases ridiculous.

Seeing the past

Nothing beats seeing the surviving traditional structures in their natural settings, of course, but for the traveller with limited time, a visit to the Ancient City, half an hour south of Bangkok, is a must. Here, arranged over 80 hectares (200

acres) set out in roughly the shape of Thailand itself, are more than 100 full-sized and reduced-scale replicas of the country's most important monuments, temples, and palaces, as well as a typical early 20th-century commercial street, a floating market, and khlong-side village. Visitors in Bangkok should also consider hiring a long-tailed boat for a tour of the Thonburi khlongs and visits to the Jim Thompson home, which was constructed from three traditional homes moved from Ayutthaya, and the Kamthieng House on the grounds of the Siam Society, a simple but elegant home transported from Chiang Mai. A visit to the Grand Palace and the adjacent Wat Pho is assumed. ❑

LEFT: ornate ceiling of a wat, or temple. **RIGHT:** traditional architecture depicted in a temple mural.

TEMPLE ART AND ARCHITECTURE

The wat *plays a vital role in every community, large and small. They are also home to the country's 300,000 monks. For many visitors, they are one of the most memorable sights of Thailand.*

A typical Thai *wat* (loosely translated as monastery or temple) has two enclosing walls that divide it from the secular world. The monks' quarters or dormitories are situated between the outer and inner walls. This area may also contain a bell tower (*hor rakang*). In larger temples the inner walls may be lined with Buddha images and serve as cloisters or galleries for meditation. This part of the temple is called *buddhavasa* or *phutthawat* (for the Buddha).

Inside the inner walls is the *bot* or *ubosoth* (ordination hall) surrounded by eight stone tablets and set on consecrated ground. This is the most sacred part of the temple and only monks can enter it. The bot contains a Buddha image, but it is the *viharn* (assembly hall) that contains the principal Buddha images. Also in the inner courtyard are the bell-shaped *chedi* (relic chambers), which contain the relics of pious or distinguished people. *Salas* (rest pavilions) can be found all around the temple; the largest of these areas is the *sala kan parian* (study hall), used for saying afternoon prayers.

POPULAR TEMPLE ICONS

During the 10th century, the Thai Buddhist and Khmer-Hindu cultures merged, and Hindu elements were introduced into Thai iconography. Popular figures include the four-armed figure of Vishnu; the *garuda* (half man, half bird); the eight-armed Shiva; elephant-headed Ganesh; the *naga*, which appears as a snake, dragon or cobra; and the ghost-banishing giant Yak.

SINGHA HEAD ▷
Fierce-looking bronze *singha* (mythical lions) stand guard outside the ordination hall of Wat Phra Kaew in Bangkok.

△ **WAT PHRA KAEW**
The Temple of the Emerald Buddha is one of the most impressive examples of Thai temple art, and one of the world's great religious buildings.

△ SYMBOLIC ROOF DECOR
The *bot* (ordination hall) roof of Wat Pho in Bangkok is adorned with a carving of a mythical *garuda* (bird-man) grasping two *naga* (serpents) in its talons.

CHEDI ▷
Wat Pho has 95 *chedi*. They contain the ashes of royalty, monks and lay people. The four large chedi are memorials to Thai kings.

◁ THE CLOISTERS
The cloisters of Wat Pho are lined by 394 seated bronze Buddhas dating from the reign of Rama I.

THE LIBRARY ▷
Phra Mondop (the library), Wat Phra Kaew. Libraries or scripture repositories *(hor trai)* are built high up above the ground in order to protect the religious scriptures from flood damage.

THE ART OF MURAL PAINTING

Thai murals are found on the interior walls of *bot* (ordination halls) and *viharn* (assembly halls). Usually painted in solid colour without the use of perspective or shading, the murals are used by monks as meditation and teaching aids. Not many murals over 150 years old remain intact in Thailand, as they were painted straight onto dry walls and therefore could not survive the ravages of the Thai climate.

The mural above comes from Wat Phumin in Nan, northern Thailand. It was painted in the mid-19th century as part of restoration carried out by Thai Lu artists. The murals depict *jataka* (Buddha's birth) tales and also illustrate aspects of northern Thai life.

Murals dating from this period commonly contain scenes from everyday life, local myths, birds, animals and plants, as well as religious themes.

Mural painting was at its height during the reign of Rama III of Thailand (1824–51), who encouraged a huge program of construction and restoration of Buddhist temples. Of special note from this period are the fine murals in Wat Thong Thammachat in Thonburi, painted in 1850.

CUISINE

You bet it can be hot. It can also be cool. There is nothing bland about Thai cuisine, which most likely explains its universal appeal

Good food in Thailand is found in fascinating places, from seafood markets to floating restaurants to hawker stalls. Wherever one travels in the country, aromas and attractive food presentations are very appealing.

Thais take time over their meals, talking and making an entire evening of the affair. Since dishes are placed in the middle of the table and shared by all, it makes sense to take several friends so that one can order more dishes and sample more tastes.

While it's true that there are very spicy regional dishes – certain southern Thai curries and northeastern dishes – not all Thai food is hot and spicy. Generally, an authentic Thai meal will include at least one very spicy dish, a few that are less hot, and some that are flavoured with only garlic or herbs.

Usually, purely Siamese creations will take their place alongside adapted Chinese and Indian dishes, influences easy to spot.

Rice has always been the most important dish in any Thai meal, so much so that the Thai form of asking if one has eaten translates as "Have you eaten rice?". In times past, Thais would eat rice with just a few condiments, or in times of hardship with nothing more than fish sauce.

Curries and sauces have become more sophisticated as Thailand has become more affluent, and now it is commonplace for the central rice bowl to be accompanied by a selection of other dishes, often including chicken, pork and fish.

At the start of the meal, heap some rice onto a plate and then take a spoonful or two of curry. It is considered polite to take only one curry at a time, consuming it before ladling another curry onto the rice. Thais eat with the spoon in their right hand and fork in their left, the fork being used to push the food onto the spoon for transport to the mouth. Chopsticks are used only for Chinese noodle dishes.

PRECEDING PAGE: the cuisine of Thailand is known for both taste and aesthetics. **LEFT:** only the freshest of produce is used. **RIGHT:** grinding fresh chillies the traditional way with a mortar.

There seems to be some confusion among those who have sampled their first Thai meals abroad regarding the proper condiments to add to the food. Contrary to popular belief, peanut sauce, an "indispensable" addition to nearly every dish in Thai restaurants found in Western countries, is really of Malayan and Indonesian

origin and is used in Thailand only for *satay*. Similarly, instead of salt, Thais rely on *nam plaa,* or fish sauce, for their salt intake, often serving it with chopped chilli peppers to make a spicy dip.

Spicy and hot dishes

Kaeng means curry. The group includes the spiciest of Thai dishes and forms the core of Thai cooking.

Among the green curries is *kaeng khiaw wan kai,* a gravy filled with chunks of chicken and tiny pea-sized aubergines. A relative, *kaeng khiaw wan nua,* has slices of beef in it. *Kaeng leuang,* a category of yellow curries, includes *kaeng karee*, an Indian-style curry that is made with chicken or beef. *Kaeng phet* is a red curry with beef or pork. A close relative is *phanaeng nua*, a southern-style "dry" curry with a characteristic coconut flavour. *Kaeng som* is cooked in a hot-sour soup generally filled with pieces of either fish or shrimp.

Among the fiery favourites is *tom yang kung*, a lemony broth teeming with shrimp. It is served in a metal tureen that is wrapped around a mini-furnace heated by charcoal, so that it remains piping hot throughout the meal. *Po taek* (The Fisherman's Net Bursts) is a cousin of tom yang kung, containing squid, mussels, crab and fish.

Yam is a very hot and spicy salad combining meat and vegetables.

Mild curries

Tom kha kai, a thick coconut-milk soup of chicken chunks with galangal, is milder than the average Thai dish and a great favourite with foreign visitors.

Plaameuk thawt krathiam phrik thai is squid fried with garlic and black pepper. When ordering, ask that the garlic *(krathiam)* be fried crispy *(krawp krawp)*. The dish is also prepared with fish. *Kaeng jeut* is a non-spicy curry, a clear broth filled with glass noodles, minced pork and mushrooms. *Nua phat nam man hoi* is beef fried

in oyster sauce garnished with chopped shallots and green vegetables.

Muu phat priaw wan – sweet and sour pork – is probably of Portuguese origin and may have arrived in Thailand via Chinese émigrés. It is also possible to order it in most restaurants with red snapper *(plaa krapong)*, beef *(nua)* and shrimp *(kung)*.

Ho mok thalay is a seafood casserole of fish and shellfish chunks in a coconut mousse, steamed in a banana-leaf cup.

Kaeng matsaman is a southern-style curry. It consists of pieces of beef or chicken, combined with potatoes, onions and peanuts in a mildly spiced curry sauce flavoured with coconut milk.

Of Chinese origin but having secured a place in Thai cuisine is *plaa jaramet nung kiem bueh*, a dish of steamed pomfret with Chinese plum and bits of ginger. *Pu phat pong karee* is pieces of unshelled, steamed crab smothered in a curry sauce laden with shallots.

Hoi maleng pu op moh din is a thick, savoury coconut milk gravy filled with mouth-watering mussels cooked in a clay pot.

Noodles and others

Most noon-time dishes are derived from Chinese cuisine, and noodle dishes, a Chinese invention, have been adopted by the Thais. Those served at street-side, open-front shops come in two varieties: wet and dry. When ordering either, specify the wetness by adding the word *nam* (wet) or *haeng* (dry) to the dish's name. Thus, a soupy *kuay tiaw* would be *kuay tiaw nam*.

Kuay tiaw is a lunchtime favourite, a soup of noodles with balls of fish or slices of beef. *Ba-mee* is egg noodles with pieces of meat and vegetable. Some rice-based lunchtime dishes are also Chinese and include *khao man kai*, boiled rice topped with slices of chicken and chopped ginger; *khao moo daeng*, a similar dish with red pork slices; and *khao kaa moo*, stewed leg of pork with greens on rice.

Then, there are the variants using noodles. *Kuay tiaw raat naa* is broad white noodles boiled and served in a dish with morning glory. *Pat tai* is noodles fried in a wok with tofu, chopped vegetables and dried shrimp. *Phat siew* is of white noodles cooked with thin slices of meat (beef, chicken or pork), fresh greens and soy sauce. Served late at night and early in the morning are two soup-like dishes filled with boiled rice. The rice in *khao tom* is watery and augmented with minced pork and shallots.

A close relative is *jok,* a viscous-like rice porridge mixed with ginger, coriander, slices of meat and generally a fresh egg.

Each of Thailand's four regions has its own cuisine. Northern and northeastern dishes are related to Lao cooking, which is eaten with glutinous rice. Southern food is flavoured with the tastes of Malaysian cooking. Central cuisine corresponds closely to the food in Thai restaurants abroad.

ing to explode on the tongues of the unwary.

Khao soy originated in Burma. This egg noodle dish is filled with chunks of beef or chicken and is lightly curried in a sauce of coconut cream, and then sprinkled with crispy noodles and served with chopped red onions and lime.

Nam phrik ong combines minced pork with chillis, tomatoes, garlic and shrimp paste. It is served with crisp cucumber slices, parboiled cabbage leaves, and pork rind.

Laap is a minced pork, chicken, beef or fish dish normally associated with northeast-

> ### SPOON SHOCK
>
> A surprise to some visitors is that most Thais use a spoon and fork, not the chopsticks found in Thai restaurants in Europe and North America.

Northern cuisine

Northern specialties are generally eaten with *khao niaw* or sticky rice, which is kneaded into a ball and dipped into various sauces and curries. *Sai oua* is an oily, spicy pork sausage that epitomises northern cooking. The sausage is roasted over a fire fuelled by coconut husks, which impart an aroma to the meat. While this food is generally prepared hygienically, it is best to buy it only at better restaurants. Beware the *phrik khee nuu* chillis, which lurk inside wait-

LEFT: cooking giant prawns in a street market.
ABOVE: like many Asian foods, Thai meals are a balance of spicy and cool, *yin* and *yang.*

ern cuisine. While northerners traditionally eat the meat raw, northeasterners cook it thoroughly. It is served with long beans, mint leaves and other vegetables that contrast with its pungent flavour.

Kaeng hang lay, another dish of Burmese origin, is a relatively mild northern dish that is popular with foreign visitors. Pork and tamarind flesh give this curry a sweet-and-sour flavour. The curry is especially suited to dipping with a ball of sticky rice.

Northeastern cuisine

Northeastern food is simple and spicy. Like northern food, it is eaten with sticky rice, which

Isaan (northeastern) diners claim weighs heavily on the brain and makes one sleepy.

Kai yang, or northeastern roasted chicken, has a flavour found in no other chicken. Basted with herbs and honey, it is roasted over an open fire and chopped into small pieces. Two dips, hot and sweet, are served with it.

Nua yang is beef dried in a similar way to jerk. One can chew for hours on a piece and still extract flavour from it. *Som tam* is the dish most associated with the northeast. It is a spicy salad made from raw shredded papaya, dried shrimp, lemon juice and chillis.

Southern cuisine

Khao yam is a popular southern Thai breakfast dish made by tossing cooked rice with toasted, shredded coconut, thinly sliced Kaffir lime leaves, lemongrass, dried shrimp, powdered chilli and a thick brown sauce made from shrimp paste and palm sugar. *Phat phet sataw* looks like a lima bean but has a slightly bitter yet pleasant flavour. This dish is cooked with shrimp or pork, together with a sprinkling of chillis.

Khao mok kai, essentially a Thai *biriani*, lays roasted chicken on a bed of saffron rice topped with crisp-fried shallots.

Khanom jeen is found throughout Thailand but is thought to be of Mon origin. Minced fish is stewed in a red sauce and then served atop rice noodles. It is generally sold in markets in the early morning.

Nam phrik kung siap, or dried prawn on a stick, is grilled and served with chillis, *kapi* (fermented shrimp paste) and lime.

Kaeng tai plaa was created by bachelor fishermen who wanted a dish that would last them for days. Fish kidneys, chillis and vegetables are blended in a curry sauce and stewed for up to seven days. *Ho mok khai plaa* is made from fish stirred into a mousse of coconut cream, curry paste and egg, wrapped in leaves and steamed.

Chinese

Most Thai Chinese are of Teochow descent, so the typical Thai Chinese restaurant serves Teochow dishes with a distinct Cantonese flavour. Teochow is famed for dishes such as thick shark's fin soup, goose doused in soy sauce, and roasted duck with fresh green vegetables. Fruits and teas are integral parts of every meal. Poultry, pork and seafood are essentials, as are a huge variety of fungi and mushrooms.

Other Chinese cuisines are well represented in Thailand. Shanghai food is typified by dishes that are fried in sesame or soy sauce for a long time, making them sweeter and oilier than the other cuisines.

Libations

The main local beers are Singha (lion) and Chang (elephant), and which has a kick like one. Locally brewed Western beers such as Carlsberg, Kloster and Heineken are widely available. The local rice whisky packs a wallop. A bit sweet, it is drunk neat, or more popularly, mixed with club soda and lime. The most popular brands are Sang Som and Mekong.

Thailand has its own special coffee, made with a thick black melange of coffee, tamarind seed and who knows what else, strong enough to set a dead person's heart beating. In the markets, Thais fill the bottom of the glass two fingers high with sweetened condensed milk and pour the coffee over it. Ask for it black (the iced version is called *oliang*) in order to gain the full flavour of this exotic mixture. Tea is usually served with a considerable amount of condensed milk, and thus is quite sweet.   ❏

LEFT: cheap and ready offerings. **RIGHT:** some of Thailand's hearty sweets are of Portuguese origin.

Sweets

In Bangkok, desserts and sweets *(khanom)* come in a bewildering variety – from light concoctions through to custards, ice creams and cakes, and an entire category of confections based upon egg yolks cooked in flower-scented syrups. Bananas and coconuts grow everywhere in Thailand, and if they were to be removed from the list of ingredients available to the khanom cook, the entire edifice of Thai dessert cookery would come crashing down.

The heavier Thai confections are rarely eaten after a big meal. Desserts, served in small bowls,

Many of these sweets are made amazingly inventive, putting familiar ingredients in surprising surroundings. You may finish off a rich pudding, for example, before realising that its tantalising flavour came from crisp-fried onions.

Excellent khanom of various types can also be bought by the bag-full from roadside vendors, who prepare them fresh on portable griddles. One such sweet is the **khanom beuang**, or "roof-tile cookie", which consists in one version of an extremely thin crispy shell folded over taco-style, and filled with coconut, strands of egg yolk cooked in syrup, spiced and sweetened dried shrimp, coriander and a sugary cream.

are generally light and elegant. **Kluay buat chee**, a popular after-dinner sweet, consists of banana chunks stewed in sweetened, slightly salted and scented coconut cream, and served warm. Another favourite, **thap thim krawb**, is made from small balls of tapioca flour, dyed red and shaped around tiny pieces of water chestnut. These are served in a mixture of sweetened coconut cream and ice.

Anyone walking through a big Bangkok market is bound to come across a sweets vendor selling anything from candied fruits to million-calorie custards made from coconut cream, eggs and palm sugar. They are generally sold in the form of three-inch squares wrapped in banana leaves. Such snacks are good for a quick boost of energy.

Sangkhya maphrao awn is a magnificent custard made from thick coconut cream, palm sugar and eggs, then steamed inside a young coconut. **Khao laam** is glutinous rice mixed with coconut cream, sugar and either black beans or other goodies, and cooked in bamboo segments, then slit open and the rice eaten. **Taeng thai nam kati** consists of a Thai melon cut into small cubes and mixed with ice and sweetened, flavoured coconut cream. **Khanom maw gaeng** is a custard-like sweet, again made with coconut cream and eggs, but this time with soybean flour to thicken it. **Kluay khaek** uses bananas sliced lengthwise, dipped in coconut cream and flour, and deep fried until crisp. **Kati** is a rich coconut ice cream. ❑

PLACES

*A detailed guide to the entire country, with principal sites
cross-referenced by number to the maps*

Diversity and contrast characterise both Thailand's people and
its geography. Within an area of around 514,000 sq km
(199,000 sq miles) – roughly the size of France – are tropical
rainforests, broad rice plains and forest-clad hills that lie between 5
degrees and 21 degrees north of the equator, in the centre of the geographical jigsaw puzzle of Southeast Asia.

There is an abundance of natural resources. Under the canopies of
its rainforests, a wide variety of flora and fauna abound: iridescent
kingfishers, parakeets, pheasants, hornbills, flying squirrels and
lizards, gibbons, hundreds of species of butterflies, and nearly a thousand varieties of orchids. A cornucopia of fruit grows as well, wild
in the jungles, or tended carefully on small family holdings and in
larger plantations. Nearly 30 varieties of fruit are here: banana and
plantain, coconut, durian, orange, lime, mango, papaya, breadfruit,
jackfruit, mangosteen, rambutan, lychee and lamyai abound.

Elevations of the terrain run from sea level along the 2,600-km
(1,600-mile) long coastline to a peak of 2,596 metres (8,517 ft) in
the north, a region of hills clad in teak forests and valleys carpeted
in rice, fruit trees and vegetables, and bordered by Burma and Laos.

The northeast is dominated by the arid Khorat Plateau, where farmers struggle to cultivate rice, tapioca, jute and other cash crops. With
strong cultural affinities with neighbouring Laos and Cambodia, the
region is rimmed and defined by the Mekong River.

In the central plains, monsoon rains transform the landscape into a
vast hydroponic basin, which nourishes a sea of rice, the country's
staple and an important export. Through this region flows the Mae
Nam Chao Phraya – *mae nam* means river – carrying produce and
people south to Bangkok, washing rich sediment down from the
northern hills, and during the monsoons, flooding the rice fields.

The south of Thailand runs down a long, narrow arm of land leading to Malaysia. An area strongly influenced by Malay culture and
Islam, this southern isthmus is peppered by rubber and palm-oil plantations that alternate with rice and fruit trees.   ❑

PRECEDING PAGES: monks on a northern road; Silom area, Bangkok; dusk near
Chiang Rai; limestone islands, Krabi. **LEFT:** Wat Prathat Chom Kitti, Chiang Saen.

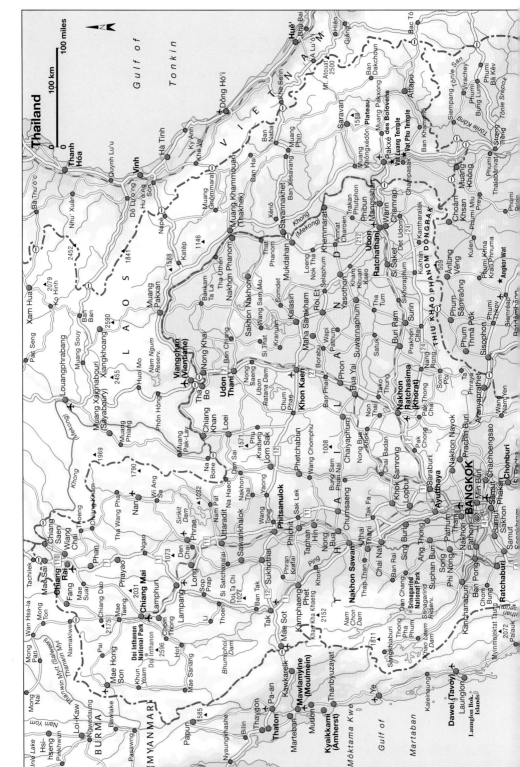

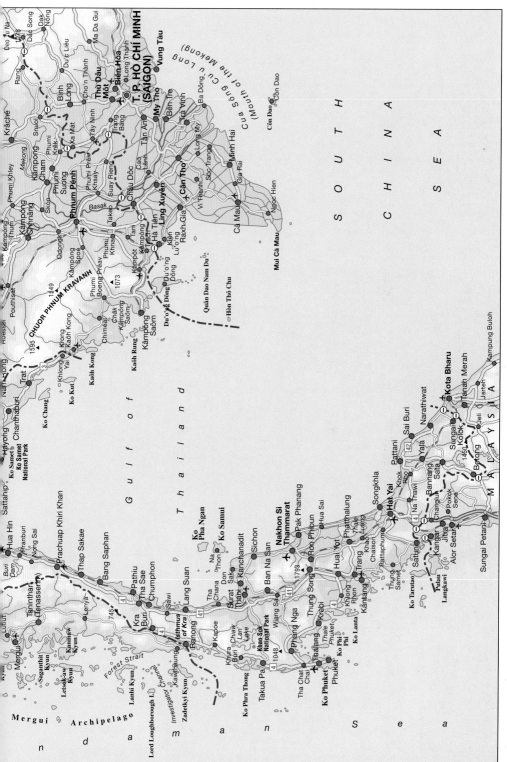

BANGKOK

A city of wild plums or angels it is not. Bangkok is rather a city of uncanny chaos anchored by the grandest of palaces

The Thai people call Bangkok, which means City of Wild Plums, Krung Thep, or City of Angels. To be perfectly correct, however, Bangkok's full name is Krungthepmahanakhon Amonrattanakosin Mahintharayutthaya Mahadilokphop Nopphosin Ratchathaniburirom Udomrathaniwetmahasa Amonphiman Awatansathit Sakkathatiya Witsanukamprasit, or in English, City of Angels, Great City of Immortals, Magnificent City of the Nine Gems, Seat of the King, City of Royal Palaces, Home of the Gods Incarnate, Erected by Visvakarman at Indra's Behest.

Bangkok began as a city of canals and elephant paths. When motor vehicles redefined urban transportation, the old thoroughfares were simply filled in or paved over for the new wheels.

The population of Bangkok has grown nearly tenfold since World War II. Today, one out of every six Thais lives in Bangkok and its environs. Growth in Bangkok seems out of control, a perception that is heightened by traffic snarls that are almost impossible to avoid.

At first (and often second) glance, the greater metropolitan area of more than 15 million people appears to be a bewildering melange of new and old, exotic and commonplace, all seemingly tossed together into a gigantic urban fuss. This, in fact, is what Bangkok is. If the city seems to lack order, it is because it never has had any, save for Rattanakosin, the royal core of the city where kings chose to build their palaces.

Chaos in construction began in earnest during the late 1950s, and a large part of what now assaults the senses began then – lofty office buildings and international hotels cheek-by-jowl with decades-old shophouses and religious shrines.

To cope with the massive traffic jams that has resulted from the Thais' love affair with the automobile – Thailand fancies itself as the Detroit of Asia – numerous expressways have been constructed. Realising that a better long-term solution to Bangkok's traffic woes is the provision of a metropolitan train system, on December 5, 1999 – on the auspicious occasion of His Majesty King Bhumibol's Sixth Cycle Birthday Anniversary – the Bangkok Mass Transit System, or BTS, opened for business.

Dubbed the Skytrain because of its elevated rail system, locals were at first slow to take to the service. Now everyone, both local and visitor, realises that it's the perfect way to deal with the city's seemingly endless traffic jams as one travels in cool air-conditioned comfort. Proposed extensions to outer Bangkok are in progress. A second mass transit system, the Metropolitan Rapid Transit Authority subway (MRTA, popularly known as "the Metro", or sometimes subway), opened in 2004, further improving life in this frenzied city. ❏

PRECEDING PAGE: Grand Palace and Wat Phra Kaew, Bangkok.
LEFT: the never-ending journey of life in Bangkok.

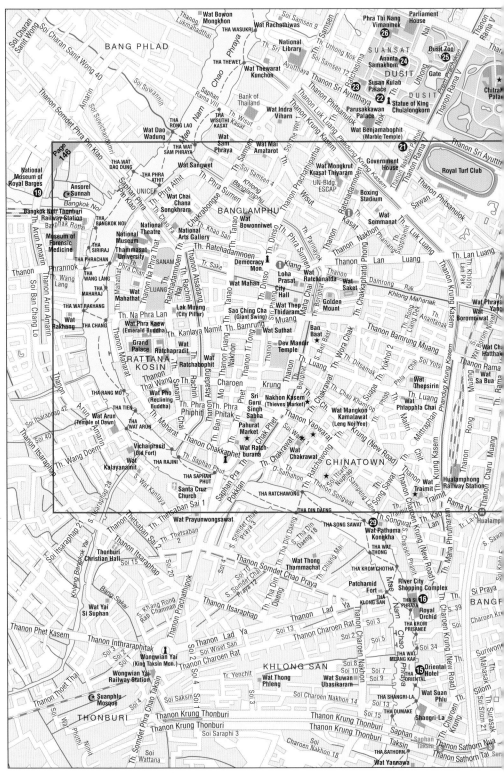

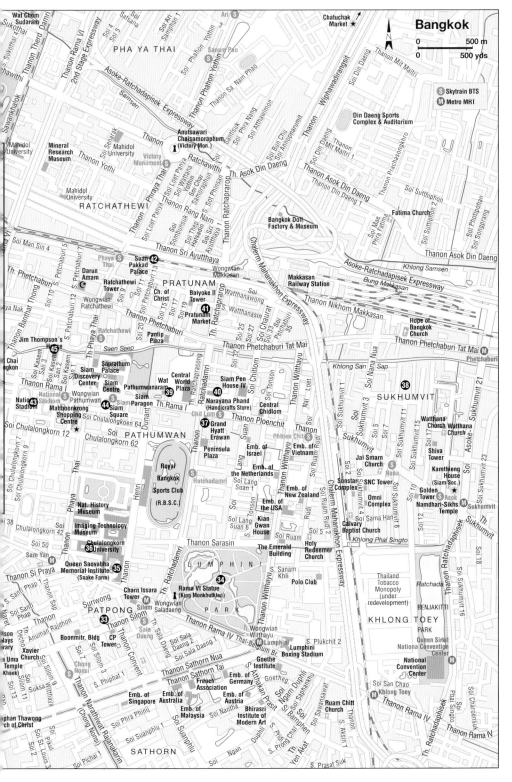

Bangkok

0 — 500 m
0 — 500 yds

Ⓢ Skytrain BTS
Ⓜ Metro MRT

Wat Chom Sudaram
Sukothai
Thanon Thierd Damri
2nd Stage Expressway
Thanon Rama VI
Asoke-Ratchadapisek Expressway
PHA YA THAI
Soi 4
Soi 5
Soi Satsana
Soi Ari
Sanphan 1
Ari Ⓢ
Soi Phahon Yothin
Sanam Pao
Soi Phra Nang
Soi Sa Nam Phao
Chatuchak Market ★
Thanon Phahon Yothin
Thanon Mit Maitri
Soi Din Daeng
Wiphavadirangsit
Samsen
hawithi
Sawankhalok
Mahidol University
Mineral Research Museum
Thanon Yothi
Mahidol University
Mahidol University
RATCHATHEWI
Thanon
Victory Monument
Anutsawari Chaisamoraphum (Victory Mon.)
Thanon Ratchawithi
Phraya Thai
Soi Senaak
Thanon Rang Nam
Soi Loet Panya
Soi Wattana Yothin
Soi Chai
Saimosaphan
Thanon Ratchaprarop
Soi Atthawimon
Soi Phra Ram
Soi Bun Chu
Soi Ampornpanich
Th. Asok Din Daeng
Thanon Asok Din Daeng
Thanon Din Daeng 1
Thanon Din Daeng
Thanon Mit Maitri 1
Thanon Prachasongkhro
Din Daeng Sports Complex & Auditorium
Soi Sutthiphon
Fatima Church
Soi Phattiphohan
Thanon Asok Din Daeng
Soi Man Sin 4
Soi Loet Panya
Soi Sombunsuk
Soi Si Ayutthaya
Thanon Sri Ayuthaya
Wongwian Makkasan
Bangkok Doll Factory & Museum
Chalerm Mahanakhon Expressway
Khlong Samsen
Soi Mae Phra Fatima
Soi Sutthiphon 2
Soi Songprang
Th. Phetchaburi
S. Petchaburi 7
S. Petchaburi 5
Darun Amam
Phaya Thai Ⓢ
Suan Pakkad Palace ㊷
Wongwian Makkasan
Asoke-Ratchadapisek Expressway
Makkasan Railway Station
Bung Makkasan
Soi 10
S. Petchaburi 12
Wongwian Ratchathewi
Ratchathewi Tower
Ratchathewi Ⓢ
Soi 11
Soi 15
Soi 17
Ch. of Christ
PRATUNAM
Thanon Watthanawong
S. Watthanasin
Thanon Nikhom Makkasan
aya Nak
Soi Kasem San 3
Soi Kasem San 2
Soi 20
Thanon Phetchaburi
Soi 25
Soi 27
Soi 33
Soi 35
Soi Chaurat
Baiyoke II Tower
Pratunam Market ⑪
Thanon Phetchaburi Tat Mai
Hope of Bangkok Church
Thanon Phetchaburi Tat Mai Ⓜ
Phetchaburi
Jim Thompson's House ㊺
Chai ngkon
Saen Saep
Pantip Plaza
Th. Phaya Thai
Ratchathewi Ⓢ
Khlong San Nap Sap
Soi Nana Nua
Soi Sukhumvit 21
Thanon Rama I
Saprathum Palace
Siam Discovery Center
Siam Centre
Pathumwan Ⓢ
Wongwian Pathumwan
Wat Pathumwanaram
Central World Plaza ㊴
Thanon Ratchadamri
Thanon Ratchaprasong
Siam Pen House IV ㊵
Narayana Phand (Handicrafts Store)
Thanon Witthayu
Soi Chitlom
Soi Tonson
Soi Sukhumvit 3
Soi Sukhumvit 5
Soi 7
Soi Sukhumvit 11
Soi Sukhumvit 15
Soi 17
SUKHUMVIT
Watthana Church Watthana Church
Asoke
㊳
Soi Sukhumvit 23
National Stadium Ⓢ
Nat'l Stadium
Mahboonkrong Shopping Centre
Siam Paragon
Siam Square
Soi Chulalongkoen 64
Chit Lom Ⓢ
Central Chidlom
Thanon Ploenchit
Phloen Chit Ⓢ
Thanon Sukhumvit
Nana Ⓢ
Shiva Tower
Kamthieng House (Siam Soc.)
Golden Tower
Asok Ⓢ
Namdhari-Sikhs Temple
Soi Chulalongkorn 12 ★
㊸
㊶ Siam
Soi Chulalongkorn 64
Dunant
㊲ Grand Hyatt Erawan
Peninsula Plaza
Emb. of Israel
Emb. of Vietnam
Jai Smarn Church
Sunstar Complex
SNC Tower
Omni Complex
Soi Sama Han
Th. Sukhumvit
Soi Chulalongkorn 9
Soi Chulalongkorn 11
Soi Chulalongkorn 62
PATHUMWAN
Royal Bangkok Sports Club (R.B.S.C.)
Thanon Ratchadamri
Soi Lang Suan 1
Emb. of the Netherlands
Emb. of New Zealand
Emb. of the USA
Soi Ruam Rudi
Soi Ruam Rudi 2
Chalerm Mahanakhon Expressway
Calvary Baptist Church
Soi Sukhumvit 12
Thanon Ratchadaphisek
i 38
Soi Chulalongkorn 42
Nat. History Museum
Imaging Technology Museum
Henri Dunant
Phaya Thai
Ratchadamri
Soi Lang Suan 6
Kian Gwan House
Soi Ruam 5
Holy Redeemer Church
Khlong Phai Singto
Soi Sukhumvit 16
Soi 50
Chulalongkorn University ㊱
Sam Yan Ⓜ
Queen Saovabha Memorial Institute (Snake Farm) ㉟
Thanon Sarasin
LUMPHINI PARK
The Emerald Building
Thanon Witthayu
S. Sanam Khli
Polo Club
Thailand Tobacco Monopoly (under redevelopment)
Ratchada
BENJAKITTI PARK
Thanon Si Praya
S. Santi Phap 1
S. Santi Sao
Charn Issara Tower
Silom Ⓜ
Wongwian Saladaeng
Rama VI Statue (King Monkbutklap) ㉞
Thanon Rama IV
Thai-Belgium Br.
S. Plukchit 2
Lumphini Ⓜ
Lumphini Boxing Stadium
Wongwian Witthayu
Queen Sirikit National Convention Center
National Convention Center Ⓜ
SURIWONG
PATPONG
Thanon Silom ㉝
Suriwong
Sala Daeng Ⓢ
Sala Daeng
Soi Sala Daeng 2
Soi Sala Daeng 1
Thanon Rama IV
Goethe Institute
Emb. of Germany
Ruam Chitt Church
Soi San Chao
Khlong Toey Ⓜ
Khlong Toey
Thanon Rama IV
ison days rary
Xavier Church
Uma Temple (Khaek)
Soi Silom 13
Boonmitr. Bldg
CP Tower
Chong Nonsi Ⓢ
Soi Silom 3
S. Phiphat 1
Thanon Convent
Thanon Sathorn Nua
Thanon Sathorn Tai
French Association
Emb. of Singapore
Emb. of Australia
Emb. of Austria
Emb. of Malaysia
Bhirasi Institute of Modern Art
SATHORN
phan Thawong ch of Christ
Soi Pipat
Soi Pipat
Soi St Louis 3
Soi Suksa
Soi Witthaya
Thanon Narathiwat Rajanakarin (Chong Nonsi)
Soi Phra Phinij
Soi Suanphlu
Soi Suanphlu
Soi Nantha
S. Pridi Chai
S. Pront Chai
Soi Ngam Duphli
Thi.
S. Bamphen
Soi Saphankhu
Soi Sawasdi
Yen Akat
Soi Aksin 1
Thanon Rama IV
Thanon Ratchadaphisek
Soi Phai Singto
Soi Charoensuk
Soi Pichai
S. Ngan
Duphli
S. Prasat Suk

THE OLD ROYAL CITY

*At the centre of Rattanakosin, the old royal city, is the Grand Palace
and the mystical Emerald Buddha of Wat Phra Kaew. Just outside
the palace grounds are the sacred Wat Pho and Lak Muang*

Although it's difficult to perceive from ground level, a bird's-eye view
would reveal that the old royal city occupied an oval island, part natural,
part artificial. The western bank of this island is formed by Bangkok's
defining river, **Mae Nam Chao Phraya**, and the eastern side by an artificial
canal or moat, Khlong Lot. After a brief sojourn across the river in Thonburi, in
the early 1780s Rama I set out to construct a protected city on the Ayutthayan
model by using the artificial canal to create an island at a bend in the river, what
is called **Rattanakosin**. Until the 1932 revolution, this district housed all the
royal quarters, administrative offices and the most royal temples.

A bird's-eye view would also reveal that this inner island, Rattanakosin, is
only the western half of a larger oval island. Outer Rattanakosin is bordered on
the east by yet another canal, Khlong Ong Ang, which is renamed Khlong
Banglamphu north of the Rathadamnoen intersection. Long settled by merchants
and artisans, this outer part of Rattanakosin still holds reminders of old Bangkok.

Wat Phra Kaew and Grand Palace Complex

The southern side of Thanon Na Phra Lan is lined by the white walls of the **Wat
Phra Kaew and Grand Palace ❶** complex (open daily 8.30am–3.30pm; tel: 0
2222 0094; admission fee covers sites A–G described
below, as well as entry to Vimanmek and the Abhisek
Dusit Throne Hall). The only entrance and exit to the
complex is in the middle. On the right are the Royal
Household offices; on the left is the ticket booth.

Wat Phra Kaew (Temple of the Emerald Buddha)
serves as the royal chapel of the Grand Palace. The
magnificent temple compound is modelled after palace
chapels in the former capitals of Sukhothai and Ayutthaya, and contains many typical monastic structures,
except living quarters for monks, a feature found in
most other Thai temples.

At the main entrance to the temple compound is the
statue of Shivaka Kumar Baccha, who was reputed to be
the Buddha's private physician. Just behind it is the Temple of the Emerald Buddha. To get to it you need to begin
walking in a clockwise direction. First to capture the eye,
on the upper terrace on the left, are the gleaming gold
mosaic tiles encrusting the Sri Lankan-style circular **Phra
Si Rattana Chedi ❹**. Erected by King Mongkut (Rama
V), it is said to enshrine a piece of the Buddha's breastbone.

In the centre is **Phra Mondop ❸** (Library of Buddhist Scriptures), surrounded by statues of sacred white
elephants. The building is studded with blue and green
glass mosaic, and topped by a multi-tiered roof fashioned like the crown of a Thai king. Adjacent to it is the
Prasat Phra Thep Bidom ❻ (Royal Pantheon). This
contains life-sized statues of the Chakri kings and is open

LEFT: Wat Phra
Kaew and the
Emerald Buddha.
BELOW: the Emerald
Buddha.

to the public only on Chakri Day, 6 April. From this terrace are good views of the royal mausoleum, bell towers and eight *prang*, or Khmer-style towers. The walls of the cloister surrounding the temple courtyard are painted with vivid and detailed scenes from the *Ramakien*. Originally completed during the reign of King Rama III (1824–50), they have been meticulously restored.

Finally you come to the **Bot of the Emerald Buddha** ⒟. Outside this main hall, at the open-air shrine, the air is always alive with supplicants' murmured prayers and heavy with the scent of floral offerings and joss sticks. The small, clothed, 75-cm (30-inch) tall jadeite Emerald Buddha is perched high on an altar near the far wall, shielded by a nine-tiered umbrella and enclosed in a glass case. Non-Buddhists may be disappointed by the small size of the Emerald Buddha, but its power and importance stems from the image's mystique, which should be instantly apparent from the demeanour of the pilgrims inside the bot.

Supposedly made in Sri Lanka, the image apparently was discovered in Chiang Rai in the early 1400s. Credited with miraculous powers, it was shifted to many locations as a prize of war over the centuries. While still a general, the future Rama I spirited the image away after sacking Vientiane in 1779 and placed it here in 1784. The removal is still fresh in the minds of Laotians.

Wat Phra Kaew's exit in the southwest wall leads to the Grand Palace's temporal sector. Although the royal family decamped to the more modern Chitralada Palace to the north in the Dusit district in 1946, most of the Grand Palace's labyrinth of structures and gardens remains closed to the public. Some official ceremonies are still held here. What visitors can glimpse is a bit of the complex's northern fringe.

Directly in front is the unassuming **Amarin Vinitchai Throne Hall** ⒠, the northernmost of a three-building group. The three-roomed throne hall served as

The Emerald Buddha is graced with three costumes, which change with the seasons: a crown and jewellery in summer; a gilded robe during the rainy season; and a golden cloak in winter. The change is done in a ritual ceremony by the king.

BELOW: throne in Chakri Maha Prasat, and Dusit Maha Prasat.

Map, page 143

the bedchamber for Rama I and a residence for Rama II and Rama III. In the early days of Bangkok, it also did duty as a court of justice, where cases were judged by the king or his ministers. Each new king has spent his first crowned night here. The gold-topped red poles standing at the entrance once tethered the elephants of visiting dignitaries. Inside, a throne sits atop a boat-shaped base. In the old days, this throne and base were hidden by a screen of curtains. At the appointed time, conch shells blew and the curtain was drawn back to reveal the seated king.

To the right (or west) is the grander, perhaps incongruous, **Chakri Maha Prasat ᖴ**. An audience and reception hall, it was designed by an English architect on neoclassical lines on the request of King Chulalongkorn. Court elders were disturbed by this strong dose of Westernisation and persuaded the king to add the three Siamese towers to the roof. The top floor contains ashes of Bangkok kings.

On the left-hand side of this building is a door, always closed to the public, that leads to the Inner Palace. This was once the domain of the king's scores of concubines, and no adult male, save the king, could enter it. Nowadays, the modern king sometimes hosts receptions here for high-ranking diplomats. A cooking school for upper-class Thais also operates here.

To the far right, on the western side of the courtyard, the building with the four-tiered roof and nine-tiered spire is the **Dusit Maha Prasat ᖴ**. Dating from 1789, it is a splendid example of classical Thai architecture. The balcony on the north wing contains a throne once used for outdoor receptions. Traditionally, deceased kings and queens lie here in state until their cremation on Sanam Luang. The exquisite pavilion in front of Dusit Maha Prasat was built to the height of the king's palanquin, so that he could alight from his elephant and don his ceremonial hat before proceeding to the audience hall.

Dusit Maha Prasat holds Rama I's teakwood throne, adorned with inlaid mother-of-pearl.

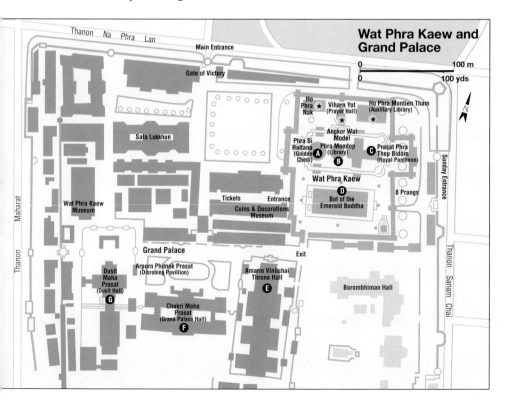

Wat Phra Kaew and Grand Palace

0 — 100 m
0 — 100 yds

Thanon Na Phra Lan

Main Entrance

Gate of Victory

Sala Lukkhun

Ho Phra Nak ★ Viharn Yot (Prayer Hall) Ho Phra Montien Tham (Auxillary Library)

Angkor Wat Model

Phra Si Rattana (Golden Chedi) **A** Phra Mondop (Library) **B** **C** Prasat Phra Thep Bidom (Royal Pantheon)

Wat Phra Kaew

D

Bot of the Emerald Buddha

8 Prangs

Wat Phra Kaew Museum

Tickets Entrance
Coins & Decorations Museum

Grand Palace Exit

Dusit Maha Prasat (Dusit Hall) **G**

Arporn Phimok Prasat (Disrobing Pavillion)

Amarin Vinitchai Throne Hall **E**

Borombhiman Hall

Chakri Maha Prasat (Grand Palace Hall) **F**

Thanon Maharat

Thanon

Sunday Entrance

Thanon Sanam Chai

Detail from Wat Pho.

Wat Pho

Exiting from the Grand Palace, turn left on Thanon Maharat and walk south past Thanon Thai Wang (which runs into the Tha Tien river-taxi dock, after passing a fresh market surrounded by early 20th-century shophouses). Turn left (that is, east) onto Soi Chetuphon and head to the entrance gate of **Wat Pho ❷** (open daily 8am–5pm; admission fee), Bangkok's largest and oldest temple, predating the Chakri dynasty. Its first buildings were constructed in the 16th century. If the Grand Palace seemed a preserved museum piece, these sprawling grounds are a living, breathing organism, still the home of 300 monks.

Most tours only tarry at the temple housing the **Reclining Buddha** in the western courtyard. Virtually filling a chapel, the brick-and-gold-plated statue is 46 metres (150 ft) long and 15 metres (50 ft) high. It depicts the dying Buddha on his side, awaiting his escape to *nirvana*. Observe the soles of his feet, which are inlaid with intricately wrought mother-of-pearl. The 108 designs are the ancient symbols by which an enlightened one can be identified.

In the eastern courtyard, screened by cloisters, is the large beautiful bot, Wat Pho's principal praying and ordination hall. Girdling its base are sandstone panels with 152 superbly carved scenes from the *Ramakien*. Nearby vendors sell rubbings of them. Yet more *Ramakien* tales are depicted in mother-of-pearl on the teak doors.

The courtyard is strewn with chedi and stone statues in strange positions. They are *rishi*, or Hindu hermits, and they were once used to instruct illiterate people on the nature of illnesses and the massage methods for treatment. Wat Pho still runs a herbal medicine school. Continue to the far eastern wall to find the massage hall, where an expert, vigorous one-hour massage costs foreigners a couple

BELOW: feet of the Reclining Buddha, Wat Pho.

of hundred baht. Those who wish to study can take 30-hour courses, which are regularly offered in English.

Rejoining Thanon Maharat and walking south past the Ministry of Commerce and police station, you'll shortly find yourself at the very southern tip of the inner Rattanakosin oval. The landmark here is the Charoen Rat Thirty-One Bridge, built in 1910. While the reinforced concrete structure itself is nothing special, note the monkeys holding up the plaster balustrade. This was the first, but certainly not the last, bridge with *Charoen* in its name. A favourite Thai word, it means "growth" or "development". The new King Vajiravudh (Rama VI) was 31 years old the year it was built. Follow the road as it turns north and becomes Thanon Rachini. On the other side of Khlong Lot, Thanon Atsadang runs parallel. Shophouse fans may want to cross the canal at Thanon Phra Phitak to peer at the canal-side Atsadang structures, which were probably built late in the 19th century. Note the European style of pediments and doorway decorations. Early in the 20th century, this was a fashionable precinct of car showrooms and boat-engine shops. As is apparent, it is still a thriving market area, but the run-down shophouses now house truck-transport companies and warehouses.

Lak Muang

If one heads on Thanon Na Phra Lan in the opposite, easterly, direction, at the far edge of Sanam Luang appears a gilded tree trunk that is the official centre of Bangkok. Erected by Rama I in the late 1700s, this is the **Lak Muang ❸**. Similar to the Shiva *lingam* that represents potency, the Lak Muang is the capital's foundation stone, where the guardian deity lives and from where the city's power emanates. Many Thai cities have such a spiritual anchor.

Map, page 146

Lak Muang, the foundation pillar.

BELOW: vendors at Wat Pho, and exterior of Lak Muang.

Sheltered by a graceful, recently renovated shrine, Lak Muang and its attendant spirits are believed to have the power to grant fertility and other wishes. Floral offerings are piled high around the pillar, and the surrounding air is laden with incense. Devotees bow reverently before pressing a square of gold leaf to the monument. In an adjoining *sala*, classical dance and music are usually underway by a resident troupe hired by supplicants whose wishes have been granted.

Retracing your steps back to the inner island, turn northwards and walk to the Ministry of Foreign Affairs, formerly the **Saranrom Palace**. This entire area was once the site of the "palaces" of members of the much-extended royal family. Most were torn down during the Chulalongkorn era to make way for useful office buildings. Built in 1868, Saranrom is one of the few to survive.

Once a royal mini-zoo and crocodile garden, the front the palace today is a soothing, monument-studded public garden. The memorial at the centre honours one of Chulalongkorn's 92 concubines. On a boat journey to the summer palace in Bang Pa-in, she fell into the river and drowned before scores of peasants. They were unable to save her because commoners couldn't touch royalty.

In early May, Sanam Luang is the site of the Royal Ploughing Ceremony, which is the official start of Thailand's rice-growing season. Sanam Luang's use as a kite-flying field began when King Chulalongkorn, an avid kite flyer, okayed using the royal field for kites.

Sanam Luang

Directly north of the Grand Palace is a clipped, circular-shaped lawn, **Sanam Luang ❹** (Royal Field). Another by-product of the destruction of the "second king's" palace, it was established as a cremation ground for royalty. In a city so short of green spaces, it now provides desperately needed space for impromptu soccer games, jogging, kite flying and children's games. It is also the natural venue for public protests. Massacres during pro-democracy demonstrators in 1973, 1976 and 1992 took place in and around Sanam Luang.

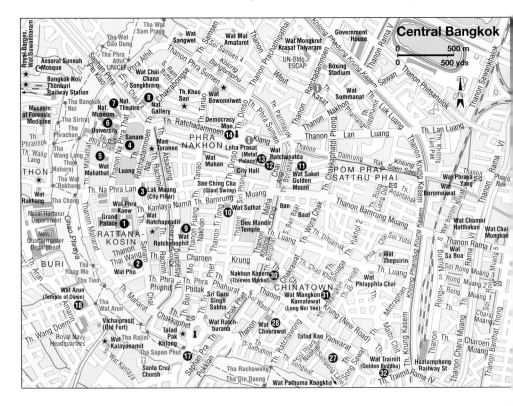

Turn right onto narrow Thanon Phra Chan (which runs into the Tha Prachan/Wat Mahathat river-taxi dock). The sidewalk becomes progressively denser with vendors of new and antique amulets, featuring Buddha, famous monks and occult objects. The amulets are guaranteed to fend off bullets, create fortunes, or induce potency or fertility. The vendors' trail eventually leads to the entry to **Wat Mahathat ❺** (open daily 8am–5pm). The buildings here are undistinguished, but one of two universities for monks is in the wat. It is also an important meditation centre. On Buddhist holidays, it blooms with herbal medicine vendors and stalls.

Just south are former royal office buildings that belong to the government Fine Arts Department and **Silpakorn University**, Thailand's first fine-arts school. Silpakorn sometimes sponsors art exhibits of both Thai and foreign artists. But if you want to be certain of seeing some contemporary art, turn right when Thanon Na Phrathat ceases, at Thanon Na Phra Lan. The Na Phra Lan Café has art on the walls, pretty food and a handsome, artsy clientele.

Continue along Thanon Na Phra Lan to discover two groups of 19th-century shophouses. The L-shaped Tha Chang group, near the end of the road at the Tha Chang cross-river ferry jetty, is the better-preserved. A century ago, there were about 10,000 shophouses on Rattanakosin; today there are probably fewer than 1,000. Thai builders were inspired by the Sino-Portuguese models of colonial Singapore and Malaya. Bangkokians were smitten with the stucco and cement materials as much as the idea of harmonious facades. Tha Chang's 33, two-storeyed units have sloped roofs with pediments, pilasters and balconies at the end units. Walls and windows are adorned with Chinese baroque touches. Like shophouses elsewhere on the island, these do not have the ground-floor open colonnades characteristic of Singapore and Malaysia.

Not coincidentally, **Thammasat University ❻** monopolises much of the western stretch of Sanam Luang. It was founded as a law university in 1932 by Pridi Phanaomyong, an architect of the revolution and star-crossed figure of modern Thai history. Thammasat retains a radical reputation, and its students are always at the forefront of popular protests. Foreign visitors are welcome to stroll the grounds, although they may be shocked by the dilapidated buildings and ill-supplied libraries. After Chulalongkorn University, this is the second-oldest and most prestigious university in the country.

A treasure house of both Thai and Southeast Asian riches is the **National Museum ❼** (open Wed–Sun 9am–4pm; admission fee; tel: 0 2224 1333 for details of guided tours), comprising a half-dozen old and new buildings. One of oldest is at the rear of the compound, the **Wang Na**, dating from 1782. The name refers to the palace of the "second king." His vast palace once extended across to Khlong Lot and up to the Grand Palace. It was occupied by the second-in-line to the throne. When his heir-apparent attempted a violent overthrow, however, King Chulalongkorn abolished the office in 1887 and tore down most of the buildings. The Wang Na today is one of the remnants; it houses artefacts like *khon* masks, gold and ceramic pieces, weapons, musical instruments and an elephant riding-seat of ivory.

Map, page 146

BELOW: Buddha image from the National Museum.

TIP

While Bangkok's National Museum is the finest of them all, there are nearly three dozen branches of the National Museum throughout Thailand, in most of the urban and cultural centres.

In front of the Wang Na's entrance is the similarly aged **Buddhaisawan Chapel**, once the second king's private place of worship. Today it shelters the bronze, Sukhothai-style Phra Buddha Sihing. Like the Emerald Buddha, it has a tangled history as one of the spoils of war and is reputed to have miraculous powers. On the day before the Songkran festival every year, it is paraded through the streets. Note the chapel's beautiful, well-preserved murals of Buddha's life. The two modern buildings in the rear of the complex cover an awesome chronological spectrum of Thai and Asian art. The southern building has the oldest pieces, representing the Dvaravati and Srivijaya periods, as well as examples of Khmer, Lopburi and Chaiya sculpture. Later periods are represented in the northern building. Besides ceramics and sculpture from Sukhothai and Ayutthaya, there are articles from the Lanna and Chiang Saen kingdoms.

One of the museum's most valuable possessions, familiar to every student of Thai history, is located elsewhere: a black, stone stele that is controversially accredited to King Ramkamhaeng and which is believed to bear the oldest sample of Thai script. If this theory is true, it dates from 13th-century Sukhothai. The stele's message describes or prescribes a kingdom of peace and prosperity. It is located in the same building as the ticket office, formerly an open-sided audience hall. Here you can also find bronze tools from Ban Chiang, an archaeological site in the northeast that indicates humans settled there 5,000 years ago. The museum provides guided tours several mornings a week in English and one day a week in French, German and Spanish. Check with the tourist authority or the museum for times.

The **National Gallery** ❽ (open Wed–Sun 9am–4pm except public holidays; tel: 0 2281 2224; admission fee), on the northern tip of Sanam Luang on Thanon

BELOW: Buddhaisawan Chapel.

Chao Fa, was once the national mint. Today, the National Gallery shelters a few gems of 20th-century Thai art and the Thai film archive. It occasionally hosts shows of foreign and Thai artists. If time is limited, however, it's more rewarding to visit the National Museum immediately south.

Map, page 146

East of the Grand Palace

To the east of the Grand Palace is the first of Rattanakosin's canals. Before crossing over the canal, notice immediately to the north what, yes, appears to be a golden pig lording over a construction site. The Pig Memorial was built in 1913 as a birthday present from friends to Queen Saovabha, Chulalongkorn's favourite wife. (She was born in the Year of the Pig.) The construction site is part of an ongoing archaeological search for city walls built by Rama I.

Wat Ratchabophit ❾ (open daily 8am–6pm) is easily recognisable by its distinctive doors, carved in relief with jaunty soldiers wearing European uniforms. Built in 1870, the design was intended to meld Western and Thai art forms. Note the unusual layout, with a tall, gilded chedi at the centre of the courtyard and enclosed by a circular cloister. Built into the northern side of the yellow-tiled cloister is the bot, itself covered in brightly patterned, multi-hued tiles.

Exterior detail of Wat Ratchabophit.

The bot's windows and entrance doors are works of art. Tiny pieces of mother-of-pearl have been inlaid in lacquer, in an intricate rendition of the insignias of the five royal ranks. In a recess beside one of the doors is a bas-relief of a god named Khio Kang – or Chew Hard, meaning "the one with long teeth" – who guards this sanctuary. Four chapels, connected to the central gallery by small porticoes, further enlarge this colourful temple. The doors open into a startling temple interior. Instead of murals and the customary shadowy interior of Thai temples, this has been rendered like a Gothic chapel, with all the light and delicacy of a medieval cathedral if it were infused with a Versailles salon.

BELOW: gilded stucco decor, Wat Ratchabophit.

Since the temple was begun before King Chulalongkorn's visits to Europe, he may have been inspired by his visit to the British colonial city of Singapore. The outside garden is studded with memorials, many modelled after pint-sized Christian churches. These enclose the ashes of Chulalongkorn's numerous concubines and children. The wat occupies the corner of Thanon Ratchabophit and Thanon Fuang Nakhon.

Continue north up Thanon Fuang Nakhon, and turn right at the second corner onto Soi Sukhat. Two short blocks east is **Wat Suthat** ❿ (open daily 8.30am–9pm), built at the turn of the 18th century. The outdoor compound is populated by pagodas and statues, mostly brought from China as ship ballast in the early 19th century. The statues include bronze horses, Chinese scholars and homely *farang* (European) sailors wearing goofy hats. Wat Suthat's fame stems from the enormous dimensions of its *ubosot* and *viharn*, respectively the ceremony and main halls. Both have galleries of gilded Buddha images. Dominating the viharn is an 8-metre (26-ft) tall meditating Buddha cast in 14th-century Sukhothai. Brought to Bangkok down the Chao Phraya on Rama I's orders, the statue is now surrounded by well-preserved 19th-century murals tracing the last 24 lives of Buddha. Note the depictions of fabulous sea monsters and foreign ships on the columns of the viharn. The doors are one of the wonders of Thai art. Carved to a depth of 5 cm (2 inches), they follow the Ayut-thayan tradition of floral motifs, with tangled jungle vegetation hiding small animals. Accounts vary as to whether Rama II designed or carved the doors him-self. When they were completed, he ordered the chisels thrown into the river so that the fine carving could not be duplicated.

Immediately north of Wat Suthat is a giant red wooden gateway. This is the 200-year-old **Sao Ching Cha** (Giant Swing), once the centrepiece of an annual cere-mony honouring the Hindu god Shiva. A bench bearing teams of two to four standing young men was suspended from the crosspiece. When the swing was swung, the men would attempt to catch with their teeth a bag of gold suspended from on high. Accidents were so common that the ceremony was abandoned in 1933, although lately city officials have considered reviving it as a tourist attraction.

Just northwest of Giant Swing is the city's only Brahman temple. The three holy halls are about the same age as the swing and are still used. Although Thai-land is a devoutly Buddhist state, Hindu Brahman rituals accompany many ancient royal ceremonies, with Brahman priests always at hand.

The stretch of road running eastward from this very busy intersection is called Bamrung Muang. It was one of the first paved roads in Bangkok. Today it is noisy, polluted, traffic-choked and frequently bereft of pavements. It can be hell to negotiate if not nimble-footed and quick of reflexes; the cautious may think it wise to take this route only on Sunday or holidays. Still, those who toss caution to the winds and venture a few blocks east to a cluster of alleys on the right called **Ban Baht** will note that many shops here make or sell monks' alms bowls and other religious articles for monks and laity.

Self-explanatory rule at all temples.

BELOW: Wat Suthat and Giant Swing.

Golden Mount

Until the 1960s, the **Golden Mount** ⓫ (open daily 8am–6pm) was the highest spot in the city. Although Rama III was never able to achieve the desired height because the soft earth underneath kept sinking, King Mongkut (Rama IV), his successor, firmed it up in the mid-19th century by placing a thousand teak logs in the boggy soil. His son, Chulalongkorn, finally completed the task.

The Golden Mount is still an excellent viewing and photographic perch. Standing 78 metres (256 ft) high, the top level is reached by a stairway that ascends around the base of the hill. The gilded chedi on top is believed to contain Buddha relics. During World War II, sirens here warned of Allied air raids.

From the Golden Mount, it is easy to spy **Wat Saket** (open daily 8am–6pm) to the east on the same grounds. Long before the arrival of the Bangkok kings, a temple stood here during the Ayutthaya period. Rama I built Wat Saket just outside the city walls to serve as a commoners' crematorium. In the late 19th century, it became a dumping ground for the corpses of the poor felled by cholera epidemics. Dogs and vultures waited to feast on them.

Back towards the east

At the northwestern corner of the Golden Mount's grounds is the intersection of two canals holding three names: Khlong Banglamphu, which turns into Khlong Ong Ang, and Khlong Mahanak. During daylight hours, one can catch a boat traversing the Mahanak canal in an easterly direction, and get off at Jim Thompson House, the Central World Plaza, Soi Asoke or beyond. The much smaller motorised long-tails on Khlong Mahanak originating from Banglamphu canal veer southward to the Hualamphong Railway Station in less than 15 minutes.

Map, page 146

The spire atop the Golden Mount, like atop many of Thailand's sacred Buddhist structures, symbolises Mount Meru, a mythical mountain.

BELOW: the swing ceremony, and making a monk's alms bowl.

**Map,
page 146**

*Murals at Wat Bowon
Niwet were painted
by Krua In-khon,
who had never been
outside of Thailand.
Look for southern
America antebellum
mansions, race
tracks and people
dressed in the fash-
ions of 19th-century
America.*

BELOW: Golden
Mount at sunset.
RIGHT: Golden
Mount, late 1800s.

Just north of the Golden Mount is an intersection where six roads converge. Thanon Ratchadamnoen Klang, the broad western avenue leading to Democracy Monument, was inspired by Paris's Champs d'Elysees, and until 1941 it was lined with mahogany trees. To reach it, take the Mahathai Athit Bridge across the Mahanak canal – Thais call it the Weeping Bridge because of its bas reliefs of sobbing figures. Or else take a little detour back across Ong Ang canal via the larger Phanfalilat Bridge. This leads to **Mahakan Fort**, originally built at the turn of the 18th century, but much restored since. It is one of only two remaining watchtowers of the old city wall.

If strolling south along the busy, canal-side Thanon Mahachai, some of the other remnants of the city wall that encircled Rattanakosin in the 19th century are visible. Go through the very first archway to reach "dove's village", a calm refuge specialising in antiques, bird cages, bird accessories and birds themselves. This is where connoisseurs purchase doves for competition in singing contests. A silver-tongued dove may be worth more than US$10,000.

Directly behind, to the west, is **Wat Ratchanatda** ⑫ (open daily 8am–6pm), a thriving centre for amulet vendors. The best-selling amulet depicts a monkey holding a phallus in its hands. Sunthorn Phu, the greatest Thai poet, once resided in the monks' cloisters. Don't miss the large, multilayered metal pagoda: **Loha Prasat** ⑬, (open daily) recently opened after 150 years of sporadic construction. Visitors can roam ground-floor corridors lined with Buddhas.

Backtrack or pick any lane northward to arrive at **Democracy Monument** ⑭ – or at least a view of the 24-metre (78-ft) tall wings in the middle of a hectic traffic circle. A major city landmark, the monument was built in 1939 to commemorate the overthrow of the absolute monarchy in June 1932. The 75 cannons about the base are symbolic of the Buddhist year 2575, equivalent to AD 1932. Plaster reliefs at the base represent the revolutionaries.

The resemblance to fascist architecture is not coincidental. The monument was designed by the Italian-born Corrado Feroci, who took the Thai name Silpa Bhirasi and is much honoured today as the founder of Silpakorn University, and as the father of the modern Thai art movement. As evident in some of his other works, Silpa was much taken by Italian fascist ideas concerning art, if not the political philosophy. Regardless, the monument is a potent symbol of democracy. The avenue between here and Sanam Luang to the west is a natural site for public demonstration. It was in this vicinity that the massacres of 1973, 1976 and 1992 took place. The monument also serves as a memorial place for making offerings to those that died in those violent years.

To the northwest is **Wat Bowonniwet** (open daily) on the southern corner of Thanon Bowon. It was built between 1824 and 1832 by Rama III. His son, the future king Mongkut, spent many of his 27 years as a monk here, attempting to purge Thai Buddhism of superstitions and aberrant practices. Subsequent kings have served their brief monkhoods here.

The buildings are undistinguished, except for the murals inside the bot. They display a knowledge of Western perspective that is startling compared to the traditional, two-dimensional Thai mural scenes. ❑

Map, page 138

MAE NAM CHAO PHRAYA

It was the river of kings, and is now the river of commerce. Dividing old Bangkok and Thonburi, the Chao Phraya is the most splendid part of Bangkok, lined with hotels, temples and eclectic architecture

The Mae Nam Chao Phraya, Thailand's celebrated River of Kings, snakes 365 km (225 miles) south from Nakhorn Sawan in the central plains, past the ancient city of Ayutthaya, down to Bangkok and finally out at Samut Prakarn into the Gulf of Thailand. Nowadays, this historic river appears at first glance as a rather unprepossessingly murky flow of water, buzzing with industrial-looking tugs, express-boat taxis, and noisy *rua hang yao*, or long-tailed boats. Nonetheless, exploring this famous river and its intricate network of *khlong*, or canals, is one of Bangkok's more appealing highlights. Besides the towering modern apartments and the luxurious riverside hotels, there are ancient temples and the fairytale spires of the Grand Palace. And along the smaller connecting canals are rustic wooden houses, floating markets and smiling children diving unselfconsciously naked into the muddy waters – an appealing glimpse of the old ways of life away from the city's pollution and congestion.

For centuries, the Chao Phraya has been the lifeblood of Thailand. It was along this river that the Thais fled from their ancient stronghold of Ayutthaya (an excellent river-cruise excursion from Bangkok) after defeat by Burmese invaders in 1767 to establish their new kingdom briefly in Thonburi, before moving to the more protected Bangkok on the opposite bank. To this day, Mae Nam Chao

BELOW: old house and spirit house on the river, and speeding along a back canal.

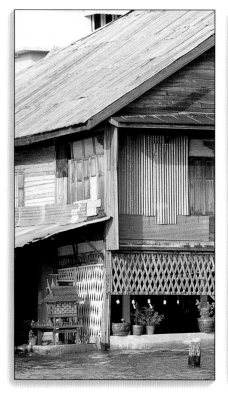

Phraya remains a working river as the means by which rice and a whole host of other supplies from the fertile central plains are transported to the capital.

For travel writers and other visitors, the Chao Phraya is central to the romance of Bangkok. In 1888, a little known 30-year-old Polish seaman, Teodor Konrad Korzeniowski, wrote: "There it was, spread largely on both banks, the Oriental capital which had yet suffered no white conqueror. Here and there in the distance, above the crowded mob of low, brown roof ridges, towered great piles of masonry, king's palace, temples, gorgeous and dilapidated, crumbling under the vertical sunlight, tremendous, overpowering, almost palpable, which seemed to enter one's breast with the breath of one's nostrils and soak into one's limbs through every pore of the skin."

Bangkok's venerable **Oriental Hotel ⓯**, established in 1876, named a suite in its author's wing after this scribe, who later changed his name to Joseph Conrad. Today, the grand hotel that overlooks the banks of the Chao Phraya and operates its own luxury river cruises upstream to Ayutthaya is also where most visitors embark for their first taste of the Chao Phraya. Two minutes' walk from the hotel is the **Tha Orienten** (pier), where one can take a cheap ride on an express river taxi and get off at any of the stops along the route, as far north as Nonthaburi. Alternatively, charter a long-tail boat for a faster, private, but considerably more expensive glimpse of river life. Remember to bargain fiercely for the boat hire; expect to pay at least 500 baht for an hour or two.

There are several pier stops south of Tha Orienten, but most of the highlights of the river are to the north, and also to the west along Khlong Mon. As the express boat noisily chugs off, filled by a mix of local commuters, tourists and saffron clad monks, take a glimpse of the old colonial buildings on the Bangkok

Oriental Hotel swimming pool and Chao Phraya.

BELOW: Wat Arun and a cross-river ferry during flooding of the Chao Phraya River.

**Maps
on pages
138 & 146**

*In the mid 1800s,
perhaps 90 percent of
the city's half-million
population lived
along the city's
khlong, or canals.*

BELOW: river pier at
the Oriental Hotel.
RIGHT: driver of a
rua hang yao, or
long-tail boat.

side of the river: the **French Embassy**, the crumbling **Old Customs House** and the **General Post Office**. On the Thonburi side are Peninsula Hotel and Sofitel Hotel. On the right side of the river is the **River City Shopping Complex** ⑯, as well as a patch of rather tatty warehouses and shacks fronting the Chinatown area by the Tha Ratchawong pier. Just beyond a singularly tacky modern high-rise with a mock St Paul's Cathedral dome are two bridges: **Phra Pok Klao Bridge** and the **Memorial Bridge** ⑰, the first to span the Chao Phraya and opened by King Rama VII (Prajadhipok) in 1932 to commemorate the 150th anniversary of the Chakri dynasty. The bridges mark the beginning of the royal district of Rattanakosin.

On the left and directly opposite the Grand Palace is **Wat Arun** ⑱ (open daily 8.30am–5pm), unmistakable and one of the river's oldest and most distinctive landmarks, dating back to the Ayutthayan period before King Taksin moved the Thai capital south to Thonburi and later to Bangkok. The temple's 82-metre (270-ft) high *prang*, which is featured on the 10-baht coin, is bedecked with millions of tiny pieces of Chinese porcelain donated by ordinary Thai citizens during the reign of King Mongkut (Rama IV).

Named after Aruna, the Hindi god of dawn, the recently renovated Wat Arun is a spectacular sight from the river. The central prang, which symbolises Mount Meru, the mythical Buddhist peak, is surrounded by four minor prangs at the corners of the wat. In between the minor prangs are four *mondop*.

Just beyond Wat Arun, also on the Thonburi side of the river, is **Wat Rakang**, the bell wat, which has a lovely collection of bells that are rung each morning. In the library, superb murals, dating from 1788, depict scenes from the *Ramakien*. Further on is **Khlong Bangkok Noi** and the **National Museum of Royal Barges** ⑲ (open daily 9am–5pm; tel: 0 2424 0004; admission fee). The Royal Barges are a fascinating collection of superbly crafted and regal river vessels, which are kept housed in a rather nondescript warehouse. The most famous of the Royal Barges is the 46-metre (150-ft) *Subanahongsa*, constructed in 1911, which normally conveys the king during a Royal Barge procession. The craft requires a crew of 54 oarsmen, two steersmen, two officers, one flagman, one rhythm keeper and one singer, who chants to the cadence of the oars. Two seven-tiered umbrellas are placed in front of and behind the golden pavilion that shelters the king. On the prow of the barge is a gilded *hong*, or sacred swan.

Should you have the opportunity to witness this rare event, which only happens once every few years, do not miss it. Oarsmen in traditional costumes propel the mighty vessels in a lengthy procession, chanting ancient barge songs, called *bot heh reua*. Instruments play and thousands cheer. It is a sight that evokes the pomp and splendour of the early kingdom that gave the Chao Phraya its old name, River of Kings.

Further upstream on Khlong Bangkok Noi is **Wat Suwannaram**, built by Rama I on the site of an earlier temple and extensively renovated since. Within the *viharn* are well-preserved murals from the early 1800s depicting, among other events and scenes, the ten lives of Buddha. Commissioned by Rama III, they are thought by many to be Bangkok's best temple murals. ❑

Waterways

For centuries, the river and *khlong*, or canal, served as the transportation arteries of Thailand. In a land that flooded whenever the monsoon-swollen rivers overflowed their banks, it made little sense to build roads that would be washed away. Rivers and canals also provided natural defences as moats against invaders.

In the central plains, and especially at Ayutthaya, master engineers diverted a river to turn Ayutthaya into a fortified island. Later, in Bangkok, engineers dug a canal across a neck of land between the present site of Thammasat University and Wat Arun, thereby eliminating a long roundabout route to the mouth of the Chao Phraya. Erosion eventually widened the canal, which has now become the river's main course. The original river loop became the khlong of Bangkok Noi and Bangkok Yai. When King Rama I established Bangkok, he had three concentric canals constructed, turning the royal city into an island. Other canals were dug to connect them. In the 19th century, it was estimated that more than 100,000 boats plied Bangkok's canals.

The most extensive rural canal expansion came during the reign of King Chulalongkorn. His engineers mapped the central plains, and the monarch gave farm land to whoever would dig the section of canal passing through his property. In a few years, thousands of kilometres of canals crisscrossed central Thailand. The magnitude of this enormous project can only be appreciated from the air.

In the mid 20th century, Bangkok shifted from boats to cars. Canals were filled in to create roads, and houses were built on solid ground. The result is evident: congested and noisy streets in the hot season, flooded streets in the monsoon season.

Zipping along at water level in a *rua hang yao,* or long-tailed boat, is one of the coolest ways to tour the city. The rua hang yao is a particularly Thai invention, born of necessity. In engineering terms, it is simplicity itself: A car or truck engine is mounted on a pivot at the stern of a long, low and narrow boat. A long shaft, or "tail", extends from the back of the boat, the small propeller spinning furiously in the water, spitting a rooster tail and propelling the boat at rapid speeds. In the narrow canals, the pivot allows the boatman to turn the craft in a very tight radius.

A lovely 90-minute route zips upriver to Khlong Bangkok Noi. A short way beyond the Bangkok Noi Railway Station is the Royal Barge Museum. If asked, the driver will stop for a few minutes for a tour of the museum. Continue up the canal, turning left into Khlong Chak Phra, which soon changes its name to Bang Kounsri and eventually to Bangkok Yai.

One of the most scenic khlong in the eastern section of Bangkok is Khlong Saen Sap, dug to carry troops to Chachoengsao to fight invaders from the east, and to join the Bangpakong River for a journey into the sea. The canal begins at Pratunam, but the water is filthy and fetid there.

Better to start at the Ekamai Bridge or at Phrakanong Khlong Tan Bridge. The canal is straight and unshaded, so it's less attractive than the twisting and convoluted Thonburi canals, but nevertheless it passes through lovely rice country. In any case and on any khlong, take a look. ❑

BEYOND THE ROYAL CITY

Map, page 138

To the north of the royal city is Dusit, with the modern palace and Thailand's parliament. South is Chinatown and the old foreigners' district. East is the clutter and high-rises of a modern city

The royal district of old Bangkok – with its brightly coloured exotic temples, saffron-clad monks and the stately allure of the magnificent Grand Palace – rightly draws the first attentions of most visitors to Thailand. But it is the less picturesque, more chaotic contemporary Bangkok that gets its tenacious grip on travellers, overloading the senses with an intoxicating mixture of sun-baked petrol fumes, the hot steam of stir-fried noodles, the screech of *tuk-tuks* and the sing-song haggling of night-market hawkers and go-go bar touts. It's a city that doesn't so much appeal to the senses as bludgeon them with striking, vivid, noisy and contrasting images. One night in Bangkok, or even one day of wandering through the sweltering heat, is not for the fainthearted, but it is certainly a memorable experience.

Dusit, north of the royal city

To the north of Rattanakosin, the old royal city, is the much more serene and dignified Dusit area. Just past the railway line on the north side of Thanon Sri Ayutthaya is a huge leafy set of grounds surrounded by a moat and high railings. Within these grounds are grazing cattle, milk churns and fishponds. It would be easy to think this was a farm, but in fact it is the **Chitralada Palace ⓴**, (closed to the public) where the king and queen live. The current king, Bhumibol Aduljadej, has lived here throughout his reign. Chitralada Palace was built in 1913 by King Rama VI (Vajiravudh), who at the time still lived in the Grand Palace but wanted a quiet retreat from the pomp and grandeur of the court. The villa itself is a low-rise structure obscured by the greenery, but the grounds are put to good use for experimental farming projects.

Just past the Chitralada compound, on the other side of Thanon Sri Ayutthaya, is **Wat Benjamabophit ㉑** (open daily 8am–6pm), or the Marble Temple. The last major temple built in Bangkok, it was started by Rama V (Chulalongkorn), in 1900 and was finished 10 years later. Designed in cruciform shape, the exterior of the main prayer hall is clad in Italian marble. Through the rear entrance of the courtyard is a huge *bodhi* tree approaching a century in age, and said to be derived from a tree that came from Buddha's birthplace in India.

Just past Wat Benjamabophit is Thanon Ratchadamnoen, a pleasant, tree-lined boulevard that leads past a huge square dominated by a **Statue of King Chulalongkorn ㉒** on horseback, who was responsible for much of this part of Bangkok. On the anniversary of his death on 23 October, the square is crowded with students and government officials honouring him by laying wreaths at the base of his statue.

To the left of the square is **Suan Amporn ㉓**, a spacious park with fountains and trees. It is the setting for

PRECEDING PAGES: skyline from downtown looking west. **LEFT:** looking west from Chao Phraya. **BELOW:** Bangkok's traffic.

many royal social functions and fairs. Directly behind and north of the square and statue stands **Ananta Samakom** ㉔ (Royal Throne Hall; closed to the public), an Italianate hall of grey marble crowned by a huge dome. It was built in 1907 by King Chulalongkorn as his throne hall, later housing the Parliament until 1974. Special permission is required to go inside the building, decorated with huge murals depicting famous events in Thai history.

East is **Dusit Zoo** ㉕ (open daily 9am–5pm; tel: 0 2281 2000; admission fee), the city's main animal park and one of the most popular places in Bangkok for family outings. A lake with boats for rent is surrounded by an aviary and enclosures containing the exotic wildlife of Asia: gibbons, Sumatran orangutans, snakes and elephants.

Vimanmek.

Behind the old National Assembly building is **Vimanmek** ㉖ (open daily 9am–4pm; tel: 0 2281 1569; admission fee), billed as the world's largest golden teak-wood mansion. As much a work of art as the treasures it holds within, Vimanmek, or Cloud Mansion, was built by King Chulalongkorn as a residence for his family in what were, in 1900, the suburbs of Bangkok. The airy, 100-room home is filled with crystal, Faberge jewellery and other objets d' art brought from Europe. It demonstrates the extent to which the royal family were influenced by European culture in the late 19th and early 20th centuries.

Chinatown

South of the Dusit area, east of the old royal city, and on the north side of the winding Chao Phraya is Bangkok's Chinatown.

BELOW: studio in Vimanmek.

Chinese merchants originally settled the area that now comprises the old royal city but were asked to move to the present **Sampeng Lane** ㉗ (Soi Wanit 1)

when construction began on the Grand Palace in the 1780s. In 1863, King Mongkut built Charoen Krung (New Road), the first paved street in Bangkok, and Chinatown soon began to expand northwards towards it. Charoen Krung runs over 6 km (4 miles) from the Grand Palace southwards to where it terminates at the river, just south of the Krung Thep Bridge. Chinatown was followed at Khlong Krung Kasem by a Muslim district that, in turn, was followed by an area occupied by *farang* (where the Oriental Hotel now stands). Later, a third road, Thanon Yaowarat, was built between Charoen Krung and Sampeng, becoming the principal road of Chinatown and the name by which this area is frequently known, **Yaowarat**.

The area has had a somewhat rowdy history. What began with mercantile pursuits soon degenerated into a lusty, earthy entertainment area. By 1900, alleys led to opium dens and houses whose entrances were marked by green lanterns *(khom khiew)*. A green-light district was like a Western red-light district, and while the lanterns have disappeared, the term *khom khiew* still signifies a brothel. Eventually, Sampeng was tamed into a sleepy lane of small shops selling goods imported from China. Sampeng Lane begins on Thanon Maha Chai and is bound at either end by Indian and Muslim shops. The western end, Pahurat, has a warren of tiny lanes filled with Indians selling cloth. Across the canal is Sampeng proper, with shops selling inexpensive jewellery, tools, cloth, clothes, toys, shoes and novelties.

After leaving the old royal city and crossing Thanon Chakrawat, turn right a short distance to the entrance of **Wat Chakrawat** ㉘ (open daily 8am–6pm), an odd amalgam of buildings. Dating from the Ayutthaya period and thus predating Chinatown, it has a small grotto with a statue of a laughing monk. Myth

Maps on pages 138 & 146

Thailand's first Chinese immigrants were merchants in the 1500s. In the centuries since, the kingdom's Chinese population has become strongly integrated in Thai society.

BELOW: shy girl in Chinatown.

Street sign for a palm-reading expert, Chinatown.

BELOW: paper images are burnt for the ancestors.

says that it is the likeness of a monk who was once so slim and handsome that he was constantly pestered by women. His devotion to Buddhism led him to the unusual remedy of eating until he grew so gross that the women lost interest. Near the end of Sampeng, the shops bear Muslim names. The merchants here trade gems. Marking the eastern end of Sampeng is another temple from the Ayutthaya period, **Wat Pathuma Kongkha** ㉙ (open daily 8am–6pm). It was here that criminals of royal birth were executed for crimes against the state.

At places, Thanon Yaowarat looks like a somewhat dowdier version of a Hong Kong street with its forest of signs. It is best known for its gold shops, all of which seem to have been designed by a pastry cutter, so alike they look. Daily prices are scrawled on the windows of shops painted red for good luck. Mirrors and neon lights complete the decor.

Yaowarat is also an old entertainment area. Halfway down on the north side of the street is the famous "Seven Storey Mansion" that flourished well into the middle part of the 20th century. It was designed so that those interested only in dining could do so on the ground floor. As the evening progressed and one relaxed, one would ascend the stairs, floor by floor, to more sybaritic delights. Unrepentant hedonists headed straight for the top floor. Between Yaowarat and Charoen Krung, near the western end of Chinatown, is **Nakhon Kasem** ㉚ (Thieves Market). A few decades ago, it was the area a householder searched after being robbed, a likely place where one might recover stolen goods for a very reasonable price. It later became an antique dealer's area, but now handles mainly more prosaic household items.

Near the eastern end of New Road is Chinatown's biggest Buddhist temple, **Wat Mangkon** ㉛ (open daily 8am–6pm). From early in the morning it is aswirl

with activity and incense smoke reminiscent of old China. The most interesting lane is Isara Nuphap, which runs south from Thanon Phlab Phla Chai. Around the entrance to Isara Nuphap are shops selling paper effigies of houses, Mercedes-Benzes, household furniture and other items. These are burnt in the Chinese *kong tek* ceremony, a ritual, the participants believe, which sends the effigies to the afterlife for use by deceased relatives.

Just east of the point where Thanon Yaowarat meets Thanon Charoen Krung (not far from Hualamphong Railway Station, which connects Bangkok to the rest of the country by rail) is **Wat Traimit** ㉜ (open daily 8am–6pm; admission fee) and the famous Golden Buddha. Found by accident in the 1950s at a riverside temple, when a construction company was extending its dock, the huge stucco figure of the Buddha was too heavy for the sling. It snapped and, to the horror of all, smashed to the ground, breaking one corner. A close examination showed a glint of yellow through the crack. Further investigation revealed that the stucco was only a thin coat and that inside was an image of solid gold weighing over five tons. Like many similar statues, it was probably made elsewhere in Thailand during the Ayutthaya period. To preserve it from Burmese invaders, it was covered to conceal its true composition and rested undetected for centuries.

Bangkrak and Silom

Further south and just east of the Chao Phraya is **Bangkrak**, a vibrant modern district that has risen in just the past few decades. This area has long been a neighbourhood of *farang*, the expat foreigners. Anchoring the western end is the grand **Oriental Hotel**, right on the bank of the Chao Phraya. From the Oriental, stroll past the gaggle of *tuk-tuk* drivers, long-tail boat touts and

Maps on pages 138 & 146

Wat Traimit's Golden Buddha may be the world's largest solid-gold Buddha at 4 metres (13 ft) in height. Of Sukhothai style, it may date from the 13th century.

BELOW: wholesale market, Chinatown.

Fate or Choice?

Thailand has a prostitution problem. It is of neither recent nor imported vintage. Contrary to the impression of many foreigners, prostitution has been illegal for over 30 years. Social scientists and non-governmental organisations estimate that there are between 300,000 and 2 million Thai prostitutes in Thailand and overseas in places like Japan. In Thailand, no truck stop or town with a population of 20,000 would be complete without a few ramshackle brothels.

According to a Thai newspaper editor, except for the area surrounding the Grand Palace, there is not a single neighbourhood in Bangkok where sex is not for sale, mostly to Thai men. The venues include brothels, hotels, nightclubs, massage parlours, bars, barber shops, parks, karaoke lounges and even golf courses. At the top are private-member clubs, advertised in the glossiest magazines. At the bottom are locked brothels, where the women – and young girls – are

virtually enslaved. As measured by compensation and working conditions, the tawdry bars serving foreign men in Patpong are somewhere in between.

There is no single reason why Thailand has more prostitutes than many poorer countries. The traditional explanation of poverty, however, carries less and less weight. While most patrons of Thai prostitutes are Thai men, foreigners also contribute to the demand. Besides the infamous sex tours from Japan, Germany, Australia and elsewhere, there is also a sizeable community of Western men, notably in Pattaya and Phuket, who live in Thailand solely because of the cheap sex, child sex or teenage wives.

Agents kidnap young girls from remote provinces or trick them with offers of factory jobs in the city. These girls may end up in locked brothels, from which they may eventually be smuggled to other Asian countries.

It's hard for poor families to resist the blandishments. Particularly at April "harvest time", when 12- and 13-year-old girls finish the customary 6 years of schooling, agents flock to villages, where they offer parents hundreds of dollars or electric appliances in exchange for pretty daughters. A girl typically has to work off a debt that is twice her sale price, although she may have to start over if she is resold before reaching her goal.

When asked why she became or remains a prostitute, a young woman will usually talk about luck or fate. Yet true Buddhists believe in neither, and don't subscribe to predestination. Buddhism, of course, doesn't sanction prostitution at all.

Feminist NGO's don't focus their primary efforts on extricating girls and women from prostitution. They have found that regardless of how women were originally lured into prostitution, few are strongly motivated to get out. The work is easy, the money is too good, and the family pressure overwhelming. Instead, the advocates concentrate on prevention, teaching marketable skills.

Prostitution is probably the principal reason why the Aids epidemic is so extensive in Thailand. Random blood testing indicates that just under 1 million men, women and children are now infected with Aids in Thailand. It is neither a Thai nor a *farang* (European) problem. It is a human problem. ❑

"copy-watch" sellers to the end of the *soi*, turn right and you'll soon be at the less exciting end of one of Bangkok's most exciting streets, Thanon Silom. Cross over and start walking down Silom and you will quickly pick up the flavour of the city – the end to end gridlock of cars, the small clusters of motorcyclists with gaudy numbered vests who act as a taxi service (if you're in an adventurous mood, take one to the end of the street and feel them weaving skilfully among the cars, buses and tuk tuks). On either side of the street are jewellery and handicraft stores, banks and restaurants, offices and shopping malls. There are some big brash eateries popular with tourists such as Silom Village, but much more appealing are the elegant restaurants for the locals tucked discreetly away in the lanes off Silom, especially Thanon Pramuan, near a Hindu temple, **Maha Uma Devi**, founded in the 1860s. In the neighbourhood is Thanying, a Thai restaurant in the style of an aristocratic Thai home, set in leafy gardens and run by a Bangkok socialite who is also closely related to the Thai royal family.

Silom really comes to life at night. The Silom night-market begins about half way down on the left hand side of the street, crowding the narrow pavement with a colourful array of stalls on both sides. Here you must bargain fiercely for the fake watches, jeans, t-shirts, shirts and luggage on offer. Most bargaining is done with the aid of calculators, though if you can get the hang of Thai numbers, it'll probably help bring down the price. About half way along the night-market, the stalls curve off to the left along a noisy neon-lit street. Love it or hate it, and few have any other opinion, the notorious **Patpong** ❸❸ (which is actually two streets – Patpong I and Patpong II) has an electric, sinful atmosphere that any visitor ought to experience at least once. It's hard to imagine a starker contrast to the serene temples and palaces and the gracious smiles and

Map, page 138

TIP

In November, Maha Uma Devi is the centre of the Hindi festival of lights, Deepavali.

LEFT: Patpong dancer.
BELOW: transvestites in Patpong.

BELOW: morning *tai
chi*, Lumphini Park.

wai of hotel staff than the raucous touting and outrageous sex shows of Patpong.
Nowadays, there seem to be far more curious middle-aged couples than die-
hard sex tourists in and around the bars of Patpong, and the atmosphere is sometimes more racy fun than unrelenting sleaze. Indeed, the cramped hawker stores
choking Patpong I at night often appear to do better business than the bars. There
are more bars on Thanon Suriwong, which runs parallel to Silom, and on Silom
Soi 4, which runs parallel to Patpong and Patpong II. The bars in Soi 4 attract a
very different kind of crowd, generally younger. Some are gay bars while others
are trendy bar-cafes popular with resident expatriates.

At the end of Silom is a huge and busy intersection that can take a good fifteen
minutes to cross. But to the northeast across the intersection lies respite from
the relentless dust and petrol fumes of the city. **Suan Lumphini** ❸❹ (Lumphini
Park; open daily 4.30am–8pm; no fee), which Bangkokians call the lung of the
city, is a tranquil and tropical oasis of greenery with boating lakes, open-air exercise areas and outdoor cafes. In the morning, people jog, practise *tai chi* exercises, lift weights, even dance under the trees. Along the park's lakes, kiosks
rent rowboats or paddleboats. In the afternoons, boys play *takraw* and soccer,
or during the hot season, fly kites. Everything stops, momentarily, at 6pm, when
the Thai national anthem is played in the park and people stand rigidly to attention in a moving and sincerely felt display of patriotism.

Directly west along Thanon Rama IV is the **Queen Saovabha Memorial
Institute** ❸❺ (open 8.30am–4.30pm on weekdays and 8.30am–noon on holidays; tel: 0 2252 0161-4; admission fee), or as it is better known in English, the
Snake Farm. Operated by the Thai Red Cross, its primary function is not to
entertain tourists but the more serious business of producing anti-venom serum

to be used on snakebite victims, of which there are many every year throughout the country. The Snake Farm, the second oldest of its kind in the world, produces serum from seven types of snake: the king cobra, Siamese cobra, banded
krait, Russell's viper, Malayan pit viper and the green and Pope's pit viper. This
snake farm is professionally run, informative and well worth a visit. Adjacent
is a respected clinic for sexually transmitted diseases.

Map,
page 138

Into central Bangkok

Coming out of Lumphini Park at the northwestern end onto Thanon
Ratchadamri, head north along Ratchadamri, which eventually reaches
Bangkok's prime shopping district. Along the way on the left is another section
of greenery, the **Royal Bangkok Sports Club**, a private club with sports facilities, golf course, swimming pool, tennis courts and horseracing on Sundays
during all but the rainiest months. The club is closed to non-members, but the
racecourse is open to the public. There is no off-track betting, so you'll have to
wait till other people put their baht on the line to get any idea of the winning
odds. These are then displayed on a huge computerised board and the prices
change dramatically as everyone places their bets at the last minute.

Access to the racetrack is from the other side along the parallel Thanon Henri
Dunant. (Thais still use its old name of Sanam Ma, or Thanon Racecourse.) Across
this road stands the temple-like buildings of **Chulalongkorn University ㊱**, the
country's oldest and most prestigious institution of higher learning. Built in a mixture of Thai and Western styles, the university was founded by King Vajiravudh,
who reigned from 1911–1925 and named the university after his father.

Heading north along Thanon Ratchadamri towards the intersection with

BELOW: Lumphini
Park, and down-
town twilight.

Thanon Rama I, one passes two of the city's most opulent hotels, the Regent and the Grand Hyatt Erawan. At the intersection, the **Erawan Shrine** ❸❼ (open daily) draws visitors and locals. To improve their fortunes or to pass exams, believers make offerings at a statue of a four-faced deity. Floral garlands or wooden elephants are placed at the god's feet in thanks for wishes granted. Most days dancers in traditional costume add to the colourful scene. Outside are little stalls where people sit all day making garlands that worshippers purchase as offerings. This attractive corner is, however, now somewhat marred by the elevated transit rails overhead, which dwarf the intersection.

This intersection also marks the centre of Bangkok's prime shopping land. In the future there are plans for a series of air-conditioned walkways that will link the main shopping malls within a 1-km (½-mile) radius. East of the intersection is Thanon Ploenchit, either side of which are ritzy malls, including the international-designer showcase Gaysorn Plaza, and adjoining Thanon Chitlom has the largest branch of Thailand's Central Department Store. This was burnt down in 1995 but has now been rebuilt.

Thanon Rama I turns into Thanon Ploenchit heading east. Beyond the British Embassy, the boulevard eventually turns into Thanon Sukhumvit – an area known simply as **Sukhumvit** ❸❽ – and stretches virtually as far as the resort town of Pattaya. Sukhumvit is a very busy commercial and residential district, with many restaurants and bars that cater to locals and expats, though relatively few tourists; the area is not rich in cultural attractions. There is, however, the enormous **seafood market** on Soi 24, and the **Kamthieng House**, a lovely 130-year-old Thai-style house in the Siam Society compound on Sukhumvit Soi 21.

To the northwest of the Erawan Shrine – diagonally opposite across the inter-

BELOW: Erawan Shrine.

section – is the **Central World Plaza**, yet another huge shopping mall. If feeling trapped by malls and commerce, duck into **Wat Pathumwanaram** ❸❾ (open daily 8.30am–6pm), a quiet temple tucked in behind the Central World Plaza. The temple was built by King Mongkut in a large park that also held a palace and a lotus pond (after which the temple was named), so that he could escape the summer heat of Rattanakosin. The palace is gone, the trees have been cut and the ponds filled in to build the Central World Plaza complex. Wat Pathum Wanaram is the most popular temple in Bangkok among taxi drivers, who drive here to have their vehicles blessed against accidents. It also holds regular meditation classes.

Opposite the Central World Plaza is the government's handicrafts store **Narayana Phand** ❹❶ (open daily 10am–9pm), which has an excellent selection of Thai-made goods on several floors and is worth exploring, if for no other reason than to learn about the wide variety of Thai crafts. Along the way up Ratchadamri to Ratchadamri Arcade and Bangkok Bazaar are numerous small shops crammed into a small space and vendors spilling off the pavements. One can often find some good handicraft bargains at small shops in Ratchadamri Arcade. The pair serve as a link between the chic shops of Ratchaprasong and the bazaar atmosphere of the vast, sprawling **Pratunam** ❹❶, a little further to the north and a favourite shopping place for many Thais and budget travellers. Pratunam means "water gate" and refers to the lock at the bridge to prevent Khlong San Sap, to the east, from being flooded by the one to the west, which leads to the Chao Phraya.

North is **Wang Suan Pakkad** ❹❷ (open daily 9am–4pm, tel: 0 2245 4934; admission fee), also known as the Cabbage Patch Palace (*suan* means garden, *pakkad* means cabbage), at 352 Thanon Sri Ayutthaya. The splendid residence

Map, page 138

Two high-rise towers loom near Pratunam: a tall one and a short one. For nearly a decade, the short one was Thailand's tallest building. The taller skyscraper, 90-storey Baiyoke Tower, has been under construction for what seems like an eternity.

BELOW: tourist police ready to help.

Map, page 138

Store offerings of silk.

BELOW: looking for a bus.
RIGHT: garden outside Jim Thompson's house.

belonged to the late Princess Chumbhot, one of Thailand's leading gardeners and art collectors. The beautifully landscaped grounds contain numerous plants the princess brought from all over the world, as well as varieties found in the Thai jungle. One probably would not wish to wander much further north than here, except perhaps by Skytrain to **Chatuchak Weekend Market** (open weekends only 6am–6pm), one of the biggest outdoor markets you are ever likely to see and a real highlight for shoppers.

Continue west along Thanon Rama I to yet more shopping. The intersection of Thanon Rama I and Thanon Phaya Thai is one of the best areas to shop, especially for those who like a little local colour and confusion. On the southwest corner next to the **National Stadium** ㊸ is the air-conditioned **Mahboonkrong** or MBK Centre, one of Bangkok's biggest complexes. It's more like an indoor market than a mall, with five crowded floors of cheap local clothes, stalls, supermarkets, boutiques and fast-food joints.

To the east across Phaya Thai is the **Siam Discovery Centre**, a plush airconditioned mall comprising mainly international brand names at extravagant international prices. Of more interest to visitors is the adjacent **Siam Centre**, a mecca for young Thai trendies looking for locally made international labels. Next to Siam Centre, the **Siam Paragon** mall is being constructed and slated for completion at the end of 2005. This retail haven, which has a gourmet market, restaurants, and cineplex and entertainment facilities, will incorporate gardens and waterfalls as part of its architecture. Across the road is one of the oldest shopping areas in Bangkok, **Siam Square** ㊹. Inside are cinemas, bookstores and restaurants. There is also the British Council, with its excellent library, and the Hard Rock Cafe. But there are other attractions besides shopping and eating in this

area. On Khlong Maha Nag at the north end of Soi Kasemsan II, is the **Jim Thompson House** ㊺ (open daily 9am–5pm; tel: 0 2215 0122; admission fee). This Thai-style house is, in truth, a collection of seven Thai houses acquired from central Thailand, disassembled and brought to Bangkok, and joined together by the remarkable American. Thompson came to Thailand at the end of World War II as an intelligence agent and later revived the Thai silk industry. In 1967, while on a visit to the Cameron Highlands in Malaysia, Thompson mysteriously disappeared; despite an extensive search, no trace has ever been found of him. Some say he simply died of a heart attack, while others suggest CIA shenanigans. Nonetheless, his sumptuous traditional Thai style home remains and is open to the public. The silk business he founded continues to flourish and if you are looking for expensive and tasteful souvenirs to take home, Jim Thompson silks are good value.

Inside the houses and throughout the grounds are 14 centuries' worth of Southeast Asian antiques. If looking to invest in antiques, come here first to see the best. There is, for example, a limestone torso of a Buddha image, said to be one of the oldest existing Buddha figures in Southeast Asia. Throughout the house are carved images, in wood and stone, of Burmese spirits and Buddhas. Superb paintings from the 1800s fill the master bedroom, while blue-and-white Ming-dynasty porcelain is displayed elsewhere in the house. ❑

OUTSIDE OF BANGKOK

Escaping the fuss of Bangkok is easier than might be imagined. Crocodiles, roses, immense Buddhas, World War II relics, wild tigers and elephants, waterfalls, and markets await on day-trips

Map, page 179

L ocated near enough to Bangkok for a comfortably paced day trip, the eastern province of Nakhon Nayok offers waterfalls and a pretty park. The most scenic route to this province is Route 305, which branches off Route 1 just north of Rangsit, 30 km (20 miles) north of Bangkok. A wide road runs northeast along a lovely canal, passing rice fields and small rivers to **Nakhon Nayok ❶**, about 140 km (90 miles) northeast of the capital. From the town, Route 33 heads northwest and then, within a few kilometres, Route 3049 leads off to the right towards two waterfalls, including Sarika Falls. Near the car park are pleasant outdoor restaurants and stalls selling fruits and drinks. Sarika Falls itself is impressive around the end of the rainy season, from September to November. Wear good shoes; the stone paths are slippery.

Nearby is **Wang Takrai National Park**. Along the way is the temple of Chao Pau Khun Dan, named after one of King Naresuan's advisers whose spirit is believed to protect the area. Prince Chumbhot, who established Suan Pakkad in Bangkok, also established the 80-hectare (195-acre) Wang Takrai Park in the 1950s; a statue of him stands on the opposite bank of the small river flowing through the park. His wife, Princess Chumbhot, planted many varieties of flowers and trees, including some imported species. Cultivated gardens sit among tall trees, which line both banks of the river flowing through the park. Bungalows are available.

Khao Yai National Park ❷ (open daily 8am–6pm; tel: 0 3731 9002; admission fee), the nearest highland escape to Bangkok, lies 200 km (125 miles) northeast of the capital, and covers 2,170 sq km (840 sq miles). Established in 1962, it is the oldest national park in Thailand. With its proximity to Bangkok, it gets almost one million visitors annually. It takes about three to four hours to drive to Khao Yai from Bangkok.

Several years ago, extensive accommodation was available within the park, as well as a restaurant and an 18-hole golf course. These facilities, however, have been closed in an effort to reduce the environmental damage of development. Presently, there are a campsite and some simple dormitories within the park, and camping out on one of the observation towers may be a possibility as well. (Enquire at the TAT office or the forestry department in Bangkok, or at park headquarters.) Outside of the park and on the main road from Pak Chong to Khao Yai, resort hotels and guesthouses have proliferated in recent years.

Khao Yai's highest peaks lie on the east along a landform known as the Khorat Plateau. **Khao Khiaw** (Green Mountain) is 1,351 metres (4,433 ft) high and **Khao Laem** (Shadow Mountain), 1,328 metres (4,357 ft).

Khao Yai is comprised of broad-leaf evergreen forests and mixed deciduous trees, with grasslands and scrub

PRECEDING PAGES: white-handed gibbon, Khao Yai. **LEFT:** school lunch. **BELOW:** Khao Yai National Park.

as secondary growth. Even on a short walk through the park, unusual palms, lush ferns and tenacious vines abound and provide a welcome respite. In the cool season, many trees and shrubs come into flower, and numerous wild orchids may be seen, including *Bulbophyllum khaoyaiense*, native only to the park.

Pig-tailed macaques and white-handed and pileated gibbons are among the most commonly seen small mammals. Larger mammals including bears, wild pigs, guars, leopards and other large cats, and various species of deer are occasionally spotted. Khao Yai is also home to about 200 elephants and perhaps 40 tigers, but these are rarely seen. In addition, over 300 species of migrant and resident birds have been identified.

The visitor's centre, adjacent to park headquarters, has somewhat disjointed but interesting displays. It is a good place to begin a tour of Khao Yai. Guides are sometimes available at the headquarters, but you'll have a better chance of getting an English-speaking one if you organise a tour of the park through one of the guesthouses in the area. A dozen or so trails, from 2 to 8 km (1 to 5 miles) in length and of varying degrees of difficulty, snake through the park to waterfalls, and to grassy areas and salt licks. In several clearings there are observation towers to watch animals feed.

In the late afternoon, several guesthouses offer trips to a limestone cave at **Khao Rub Chang**, just north of the park and where, at dusk, a massive exodus of wrinkled-lipped bats darkens the sky for more than an hour.

After dark, night safaris can be arranged in which powerful halogen spotlights are used to illuminate night-feeding animals such as barking deer, sambar and civet. At night, winter temperatures may drop to below 15°C (60°F); warm clothes are handy.

TIP

At certain times of the year, the State Railways of Thailand may offer weekend day-trips to Khao Yai; however, the bus is more reliable and often faster.

BELOW: tiger cubs in Khao Yai, a rare sighting.

South of Bangkok

The **Crocodile Farm** ❸ (open daily 7am–6pm; tel: 0 2387 0020; www.paknam. com; admission fee) is located in Samut Prakarn Province, near the river-mouth town of Samut Prakam, half an hour's drive (30 km/20 miles) southeast of Bangkok on the old Sukhumvit Highway (Route 3). Started in the 1960s with an initial investment of about 10,000 baht (less than US$500 back then), the owner now has three farms worth 100 million baht. At present, this farm has about 60,000 fresh- and saltwater local crocodiles, as well as some South American caimans and Nile River crocodiles. They are hatched and raised in tanks, with netting to protect them from mosquitoes, which can blind them by biting their eyes.

The highlight of a visit to the farm are the shows in which handlers enter a pond teeming with crocodiles and toss them about rather roughly. While this sounds dangerous in print, the lethargic beasts are less likely to bite because of innate viciousness than because their noon nap has been interrupted. After the crocodiles are skinned, incidentally, their meat is sold to restaurants in Samut Prakarn and Bangkok. The farm also has a zoo and amusement park with rides. The irony of all this is that the owners have succeeded in preserving the animal; nearly all the wild Asian species have been hunted to extinction.

Also in Samut Prakarn, a few kilometres from the Crocodile Farm, is **Ancient City** ❹ (Muang Boran; open daily 8am–5pm; tel: 0 2323 9523; admission fee), which bills itself as the world's largest outdoor museum. The brainchild of a Bangkok millionaire with a passion for Thai art and history, it took around three years to construct. In what used to be 80 hectares (200 acres) of rice fields, designers sketched an area roughly the shape of Thailand and placed the individual attractions as close to their real sites as possible. There are replicas (some

Map, page 179

Crocodile Farm.

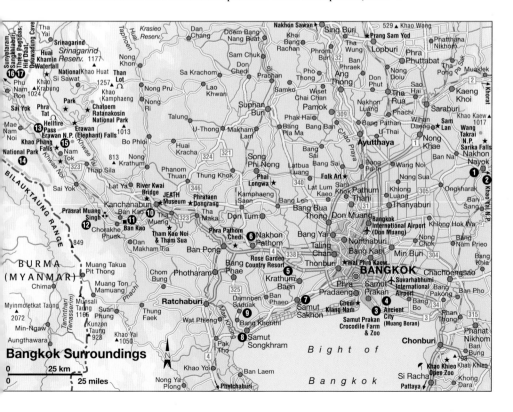

Bangkok Surroundings

0 — 25 km

0 — 25 miles

full-size, most others one-third the size of the originals) of famous monuments and temples from all parts of the kingdom. Some are reconstructions of buildings that no longer exist, like the Grand Palace of Ayutthaya, and some are copies of real places, like the Phimai sanctuary, northeast of Nakhon Ratchasima, and the huge temple of Khao Phra Viharn on the Thai-Cambodian border. Experts from the National Museum in Bangkok worked as consultants to ensure the historical accuracy of the reproductions. At present, there are more than 60 monuments, covering 1,500 years of Thai history. The monuments are spread out over a large area; it may be most convenient to drive between them. However, the grounds are beautifully landscaped with small waterfalls, creeks, ponds, rock gardens and lush greenery; deer graze freely among the many interesting sculptures representing figures from Thai literature and Hindu mythology. In addition to the monuments, Ancient City also has a model Thai village, in which artisans work on handicrafts, such as lacquerware, ceramics and paper umbrellas.

For those with time, Paknam is a bustling fishing town with an interesting market along its docks. Cross the river by ferry to the famous **Wat Phra Chedi Klang Nam**, which, contrary to its name ("the chedi in the middle of the river"), is now on solid land, the result of the river shifting its course. Thai kings used to stop at this temple on their way in and out of the country on state visits, praying for success in their journeys or offering thanks on their return.

West of Bangkok

Less than an hour's drive due west from Bangkok, **Suan Sam Phran** ❺ (Rose Garden; open daily 8am–6pm; tel: 0 3432 2588; admission fee) is the brainchild of a former lord mayor of the capital. The garden lies 30 km (20 miles) west of

BELOW: Ancient City.

the capital on Route 4, en route to Nakhon Pathom. Its large area of well-landscaped gardens contains roses and orchids, and includes accommodation, restaurants, a golf course reputed to be among the 25 best in the world, paddle boats on an artificial lake, and a children's playground. Its premier attraction is a daily Thai cultural show.

In a large arena, beautifully costumed Thai actors demonstrate folk dances, Thai boxing, a wedding ceremony, cock-fighting and other rural entertainment. Outside after this show, elephants put on their own show, moving huge teak logs as they would in the forests of the north. The elephants then carry tourists around the compound for a small fee.

Just 50 km (30 miles) west of Bangkok, beyond the Rose Garden on Route 4, is the town of **Nakhon Pathom ❻**, famous for **Phra Pathom Chedi**, which rises majestically over the surrounding countryside. At just over 125 metres (410 ft) in height, it is the tallest Buddhist monument in the world, a few feet taller even than the Shwedagon in Rangoon.

Nakhon Pathom is believed to be Thailand's oldest city. The name derives from the Pali for "first city." According to legend, it was the capital of Suvannabhumi, the "land of gold," and it was here that King Ashoka (268–232 BC) sent two missionaries from India to introduce Buddhism. The first archaeological records date from the 6th century when the area was populated by the Mons, Dvaravati-Buddhists who flourished in the Chao Phraya basin from the 6th to the 11th century. The original chedi is believed to have been constructed by the Mons in the late 10th century. In the early 11th century, Nakhon Pathom and the surrounding area fell to the Khmers, who built a Brahman (Hindu) *prang* some 40 metres (130 ft) tall, which enclosed the original Buddhist structure.

TIP

Southeast of the Phra Pathom Chedi is the Phra Pathom Chedi National Museum, with a nice collection of artefacts excavated from the area. Open Wednesday–Sunday. Admission fee.

BELOW: Nakhon Pathom's Phra Pathom Chedi.

In 1057, King Anawratha of Pagan besieged the city, leaving the chedi in ruins. Although the city regained brief importance in the 16th century as a defensive position against the invading Burmese, it wasn't until 1853 that repairs to the chedi were begun. King Mongkut, who had spent time in the area as a young monk before gaining the throne, was impressed with the history of the edifice, and believed it to contain a relic of the Buddha. The final structure was completed during the reign of King Chulalongkorn in the early 20th century. Set in a huge square park and covered with golden-orange tiles imported from China, the chedi rests upon a circular terrace, the perimeter of which is accented with sacred trees. Walking up the enormous main staircase brings you to the North Viharn and the Sukhothai-style standing Buddha, the stone head, hands and feet of which were discovered in Sawankhalok in 1900. King Vajiravudh commissioned a bronze body cast to match the stone pieces; the statue was enshrined in 1915 and is greatly revered by Thais. The king's ashes are buried at its base.

After investigating the chedi, wander around the grounds for a few moments. Have your palm read for a small fee (there's at least one fortune teller who speaks enough English to make it entertaining), enjoy a delicious iced coffee made fresh on the spot and served in a small plastic bag with a straw, and peruse the startling selection of porn magazines that are sold just at the base of the chedi.

In former times, a royal visit to Nakhon Pathom was more than a day's journey, so it is not surprising that a number of palaces and summer residences were built there. One of them, **Sanam Chand Palace**, 2 km (1 mile) west of Phra Pathom Chedi, has a fine *sala*, a meeting pavilion now used for government offices, and a building in a most unusual Thai interpretation of English Tudor architecture, used appropriately as a setting for Shakespearean drama. In front

BELOW: riverside laundry washing.

stands a statue of Yaleh, the pet dog of King Vajiravudh, who commissioned the palace. The fierce dog, unpopular with the court, was poisoned by the king's attendants. Even as a statue, Yaleh looks insufferable. Although most of the palace buildings are closed to the public, one of them serves as a small museum and contains memorabilia of Vajiravudh.

A good way to approach the coastal port of **Samut Sakhon ❼** (also known as Mahachai) is by a branch railway connecting it with Thonburi, on the other side of the Chao Phraya from central Bangkok. The line, called the Mae Khlong Railway, runs at a loss, but is subsidised for the benefit of those living in the provinces west of Bangkok. The 40-minute journey passes through the suburbs, then through vegetable gardens, groves of coconut palms, and rice fields.

A busy fishing port, Samut Sakhon lies at the meeting of the Tachin River, the Mahachai Canal and the Gulf of Thailand. The main landing on the riverbank has a clock tower and a restaurant serving excellent seafood. Nearby, fishermen at the fish market unload the treasures of the sea from their boats. At the fish-market pier, it's possible to hire a boat for a round-trip to Samut Sakhon's principal temple, Wat Chom Long, at the mouth of the Tachin River. Most of the buildings are modern, except for an old *viharn*, which dates back about a century, immediately to the right of the temple's river landing. The extensive grounds overlooking the water are charmingly laid out with shrubs and flowering trees. There is also a statue of Chulalongkorn. His homburg hat does not in the least detract from his immense dignity.

From Samut Sakhon, cross the river to the railway station on the opposite side. Here, board a second train for another 40-minute trip to **Samut Songkhram ❽**, on the banks of the Meklong River. The journey goes through

Map, page 179

BELOW: harbour at Samut Songkhram.

TIP

In late November and early December, Kanchanaburi has a week-long fair that features a nightly sound-and-light show celebrating the Allied attack on the bridge over the Kwai River. Make reservations well in advance – it's popular with locals.

broad salt flats, with picturesque windmills revolving slowly in the sea breezes. Samut Songkhram is another pretty fishing town; wandering its wharf is an olfactory and a visual experience. Return to Bangkok along the same rail route or hire a long-tailed boat for a trip up the Meklong River to Ratchaburi.

Eighty km (50 miles) southwest of Bangkok, near Samut Songkhram, lies the town of **Damnoen Saduak** 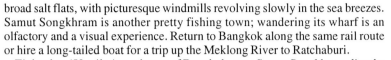, famous for its daily floating market. Beginning before dawn, women in traditional straw hats manoeuvre flat-bottomed boats laden with produce, fish and flowers into position along the canals. They hawk their wares in a colourful spectacle lasting most of the morning, but be there early (the majority of tourists arrive on buses around 9am) for the most authentic experience. Air-conditioned buses depart the Southern bus terminal for Damnoen Saduak every half hour beginning at 6am.

Kanchanaburi and the River Kwai

Established in the early 1800s, thus making it a young city by Thai standards, **Kanchanaburi** ⑩ is about 120 km (75 miles) northwest of Bangkok, past Nakhon Pathom, and not far from the Thai border with Burma. It prospers from gem mining and a teak trade with Burma. The world's smallest species of bat, about the size of a bumblebee, was discovered near an odd-looking railway bridge crossing the Meklong River, also known as the Kwai Yai, a few kilometres outside of Kanchanaburi. The bridge is contoured with a series of elliptical spans, with an awkwardly rectangular centre.

This bridge is often called the "Bridge on the River Kwai." In fact, it's not. The bridge that spanned the mightier Kwai River and inspired the novel and film was further north. Of course, the original bridge no longer exists.

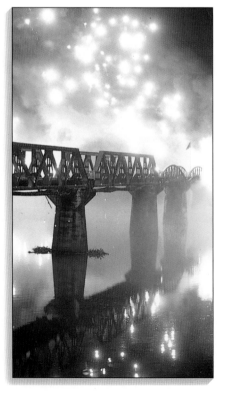

BELOW: sound-and-light show over the River Kwai Yai.

Seeking to shorten supply lines between Japan and Burma in preparation for an eventual attack on British India, the Japanese began work on a railway between Thailand and Burma in 1942. For a large part of its 415 km (260 miles), the railway followed the river valley. Although the logistics of doing so were often nightmarish, following the valley allowed construction of the railway simultaneously in different areas. At the end, there were nearly 15 km (9 miles) of bridges completed. The Japanese forced 250,000 Asian labourers and 61,000 Allied prisoners-of-war to construct 260 km (160 miles) of rail on the Thai side, to Three Pagodas Pass on the border. It is estimated that 100,000 Asian labourers and 16,000 Allied prisoners lost their lives from beatings, starvation, disease and exhaustion. In Kanchanaburi, graves mark 6,982 of those Allied soldiers. There are two cemeteries in Kanchanaburi. The larger is on the main road nearly opposite the railway station; the second, Chungkai, is across the river on the banks of the Kwai Noi. Both hold the remains of Dutch, Australian, British, Danish, New Zealander and other Allied prisoners-of-war; American dead were removed to Arlington Cemetery, outside Washington, DC.

An appreciation of the enormous obstacles the prisoners faced is provided by the JEATH **War Museum** (open daily 8.30am–6pm; admission fee), near the end of Thanon Lak Muang. (The name derives from the first initial of those nationalities involved in the construction: Japan, England, America/Australia, Thailand and Holland.) Established in 1977 by the monks of **Wat Chaichumpol** (Wat Chanasongkhram) next door, the museum was constructed like the bamboo huts in which the war prisoners lived. Utensils, paintings, writings and other objects donated by prisoners who survived share some of the horror of their hellish existence.

Exhibits at the newer **Thailand-Burma Railway Centre** (open daily 9am–5pm, tel: 0 3451 0067; admission fee), just south of the bridge, provide further detail on the history of the Death Railway and even include a full-scale replica of the original wooden bridge.

In spite of the fact that the memorial bridge is often mistaken for the one made famous in print and film, it is worthwhile visiting from a historical point of view. It can be reached by boat or *samlor* from Kanchanaburi. Visit at 10.50am or 4.30pm if you want to see the train passing by.

The memorial bridge has lost some of its artificial mystery with commercialisation, but walking across it is a sobering experience. (Niches between the spans provide an escape in case a train passes by.) A steam locomotive used shortly after the war is displayed beside the tiny station platform, along with an ingenious Japanese supply truck that could run on both roads and rails. Floating restaurants and hotels line the banks of the river, which is attractive and peaceful despite its grisly history.

Today, most of the old tracks have been removed, except for a section running peacefully from Kanchanaburi to the terminus at Nam Tok, a 50-km (30-mile) journey taking about 1½ hours and crossing one of the shakiest bridges in the world; the wooden pillars and sleepers creak and groan disconcertingly as the train moves slowly across them. ❏

Map, page 179

Detail from Wat Chaichumpol.

BELOW: hoping a train is elsewhere on the bridge over the River Kwai.

Map,
page 179

THAILAND

Bangkok

FAR TO THE WEST

Beyond the day-trip to Kanchanaburi are some of Thailand's wild lands. Keep going, and one reaches the border with Burma. Unfortunately, only Thais can continue onward beyond the frontier

To head out from Kanchanaburi towards the lush, mountainous west is to take a road to nowhere. Or so it seems. Remote Three Pagodas Pass has little to show beyond the modest markers that give it its name, a military checkpoint and a small thriving market. Nearby Sangkhlaburi is a somnolent, spacious outpost perched between lake and jungle. Beyond the peaks and clouds lies southern Burma, as inaccessible as it is close.

The highway out of Kanchanaburi winding northwest towards the Burmese frontier may be going nowhere much – no border crossings are permitted – but there is no shortage of natural and historical diversions along the way. An appropriate beginning, one which gives context to this jungled area's ancient origins, is the prehistoric burial site at the village of **Ban Kao ⑪**, on a side road about 30 km (18 miles) into the 250-km (150-mile) stretch from Kanchanaburi to the Burmese border. Neolithic remains discovered near the village may date as far back as 10,000 years, archaeologists believe. At a small museum near the site are pottery and human remains that date from 3,000 to 4,000 years ago.

Seven km (4 miles) and a few thousand millennia further on, the 13th-century remains of a Khmer city associated with the Angkor empire have been turned into an historical park. **Prasat Muang Singh ⑫** (open daily

BELOW: woman from near the Burmese border.

8.30am–4.30pm; tel: 0 3459 1122; admission fee), situated prettily on the Kwai Noi, covers 70 hectares (170 acres) and encompasses four groups of ruins. Sculptures of deities and the remains of an elaborate water system can be seen.

Jumping centuries ahead again, the tendency of jungle and time to erase the evidence of history has been energetically tackled at a World War II site 80 km (50 miles) beyond Kanchanaburi on Route 323. **Hellfire Pass** ⑬ is the largest of many mountain cuttings carved out of rock in atrocious conditions by Asians and Allied prisoners-of-war forced to build the so-called Death Railway, intended by the Japanese to link Singapore and India. The pass has been turned into a memorial for the thousands who died, mainly of malaria and dysentery. The prisoners worked with hammers, picks, shovels, steel tap drills and dynamite. Close examination of the sheer walls of Hellfire Pass reveals the marks of the old drills and blast holes. Most of the railway was abandoned or dug up soon after the war ended. A portion that remains takes visitors from Kanchanaburi to Nam Tok, a small touristy market town not far from the pass.

About 20 km (12 miles) further up Highway 323, and also reachable by boat from Nam Tok, **Sai Yok National Park** ⑭ (open daily 8.30am–4.30pm; tel: 0 3451 6163-4; admission fee) evokes a light-hearted atmosphere with picnickers and swimmers – in stark contrast to the gory Russian roulette scenes filmed here for the movie *The Deerhunter*. Sai Yok is quieter than the **Erawan National Park** ⑮ (open daily 8.30am–4.30pm; tel: 0 3457 4222; admission fee), which has one of Thailand's most popular waterfalls and lies about 80 km (50 miles) from Kanchanaburi along a different road. Beyond Erawan to the northeast are two limestone caves, Tham Phra That and Tham Wang Badan, as well as Huay Khamin Falls, with large, deep pools.

TIP

Within the 500 sq km (193 sq miles) of Sai Yok National Park, accommodations available include simple bungalows and houseboats.

BELOW: clouded leopard, and black-throated sunbird.

Map,
page 179

Parts of Burma
beyond Three
Pagodas Pass were
taken from ethnic
groups by Burma's
army in the 1990s.
Several refugee
camps on the Thai
side, most of them
well off main roads,
hold thousands of
Mon and Karen
refugees.

BELOW: on the lake
near Sangkhlaburi.
RIGHT: deciduous
forest north of
Sangkhlaburi.

Back on Highway 323, the **Hin Dat** hot springs make a restful stop. Just yards from the freezing and rushing river water, bathers soak quietly in calm, steaming, mineral-rich hot springs. Food stalls, shrines and pleasant walking areas add to the gently festive atmosphere. Just beyond, the Phatat waterfall is a short drive to the right from the main highway. Slightly further on, one of a number of elephant camps along this route is open to the public.

Thong Pha Thum, nestled under the mountains, is the last village before the winding, climbing ascent to Sangkhlaburi, where the combination of steep limestone mountains and a huge lake created by the Khao Laem hydroelectric dam make for dramatic views. At about the half-way mark along this stretch, the **Sunyataram Forest Monastery** is a meditation retreat associated with the charismatic Phra Yantra Bhikku – one of Thailand's most famous and revered monks until the mid 1990s, when he was involved in a series of scandals and had to flee the country. The monastery, quiet now for perhaps less happy reasons than its original meditative purpose, is an attractive, slightly ramshackle collection of wooden buildings spread out over a section of old forest. Small fish pools and winding trails add to the charm. Devotees here haven't given up on the disgraced monk: his posters still adorn walls and his sermons and books are for sale. Two other pleasant stops close by include the Dar Thongthong and Kroenkrawia waterfalls.

Sangkhlaburi ⑯, which may well be one of Thailand's prettiest towns, is still relatively undiscovered. Perched around the large Khao Laem, surrounded by high peaks and practically untouched by the kind of ugly concrete shophouse development that has spread throughout most of Thailand, it is a fascinating cultural meeting point. Thai, Burmese, Mon and Karen all live here, most involved in one way or another with border trade, legal and otherwise. Tourism is slowly but steadily increasing here, in low-key fashion. The town has no real hotels, but a growing number of guesthouses cater to hardy travellers. The attractions include unbroken tranquillity, river rafting and hiking.

A stroll across a part of the lake, over Thailand's longest wooden bridge, leads to an attractive Mon village. Villagers, who built the bridge themselves, are experts at negotiating on motorcycles the steep, bumpy lane that leads from the bridge to the main town. Just past the Mon village, the towering **Chedi Luang Phaw Utama**, which has fine vistas over the surrounding countryside, was built in the style of the Mahbodhi *stupa* in Bodhgay, India and is topped by about 6 kg (13 lbs) of gold. The striking **Wat Wang Wiwekaram** nearby is built in an amalgamation of Thai, Indian and Burmese styles. In front of the chedi, a market sells handicrafts, textiles and general goods.

Three Pagodas Pass ⑰ (normally open 8am–6pm daily, but can close at short notice depending on political conditions; tel: the Immigration Department of Sangkhla Buri 0 3459 5335), 16 km (10 miles) beyond Sangkhlaburi at an elevation of 1,400 metres (4,600 ft), has long been the main trade link between western Thailand and southern Burma, and was the entry point into Thailand for invading Burmese troops during the Ayutthaya period. The main draw for tourists is the busy market here. Over the border, the Burmese town of Paythonzu is open only to Thai day-trippers. ❏

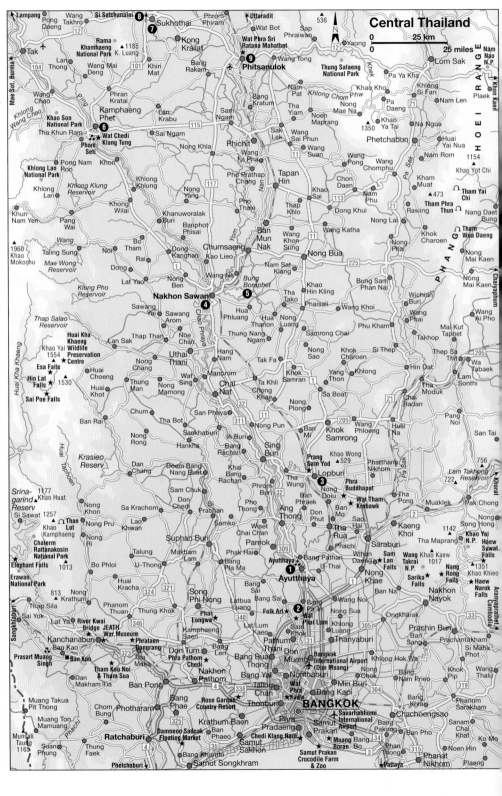

Central Thailand

CENTRAL THAILAND

Here in the plain defined by the Mae Nam Chao Phraya,
Thailand's rice culture blossomed, as did its great empires

The traditional source of Thailand's wealth is rice. Intricately irrigated rice fields have fed its people for more than 700 years. The central plains are the fertile heart of Thailand, towards which the early Thais steadily migrated from the mountains and valleys of the northern mountains.

Towards the end of the dry season, in May, the fields are alive with farmers turning the earth. A month or so later, when the rains have come, water covers the shallow paddies sprouting with young rice plants. In November, the rains fall off, and the grain turns golden: harvest time. Afterwards, there are the festivals that coincide with the burning of the harvested fields, as the earth is prepared for another cycle of cultivation.

Several major rivers water this fertile heartland – notably the Ping, Wang, Yom and Nan, which eventually combine to form the majestic Chao Phraya, emptying into the Gulf of Thailand below Bangkok. Thai history has followed these rivers with the establishment of great empires, all found in the central plains: the Angkor-style towers of Lopburi, where the Khmers once ruled to reap the bounty of the plains, and the sprawling ruins further south, near Bangkok, of once-great Ayutthaya. To the north, the flower of Sukhothai bloomed, perhaps the finest highlight of Thailand's past.

The wooden houses of the central plains, more than any other part of the country, reflect the classic style of Thai architecture. The panelled walls slant slightly inwards to achieve an oddly graceful effect, the steep roof seeming to strain towards the sky. The faces of the people here in the central lowlands are less likely to reveal the imprint of Chinese, Lao, Burmese or Malay ancestry, as these races have intermingled with the Thai in both the cities and in the border regions.

Like the heartland of many countries, the central plains are often ignored by travellers on their way elsewhere, to Chiang Mai and the north, for example. Yet for those who stop here, perhaps more than anywhere else in Thailand, the foundations of Thai culture and society are best uncovered, and most readily understood. ❏

PRECEDING PAGES: a water buffalo feeds in the cool of a central plain's dawn.

AYUTTHAYA AND LOPBURI

On its way south, Thailand's capital spent four centuries at Ayutthaya, north of Bangkok on the Mae Nam Chao Phraya, the great river through Thailand's central plains. It retains its history

Map, page 192

THAILAND

Bangkok

Were one ignorant of the importance and history of **Ayutthaya ❶**, one would nonetheless be impressed by the beauty and grandeur of this city built by 33 monarchs over 400 years. From the ruins, it is easy to appreciate the genius of the kings who built this great city. Located 85 km (55 miles) north of Bangkok, Ayutthaya was laid out at the junction of three rivers: Chao Phraya, Pa Sak, and Lopburi. Engineers had only to cut a canal across the loop of the Chao Phraya to create an island. Canals were also constructed as streets; palaces and temples were erected.

To approach the city as 17th-century visitors did, travel up Mae Nam Chao Phraya from Bangkok. Several deluxe boats make a pleasant voyage of the journey. Once in Ayutthaya, a river tour around the island in a long-tail boat can be arranged on the landing stage close to Chan Kasem Palace. Not only is this an excellent introduction to the ruined city, it is also the most convenient way to reach some of the more isolated sites on the mainland side of the river. Despite the claims of some Bangkok tour operators, there is modern accommodation here, as well as several clean, inexpensive Chinese hotels.

LEFT: chedi of Wat Phra Ram, Ayutthaya.
BELOW: canal-side homes in Ayutthaya.

Foundations of Ayutthaya

Ayutthaya was founded around 1350 by a prince of U-thong. Thirty years later, the kingdom of Sukhothai passed under Ayutthayan rule, which then spread as far as Angkor in the east, and Pegu, in Burma, to the west.

It was one of the richest cities in Asia by the 1600s – exporting rice, animal skins, ivory – and with a population of one million, greater than that of contemporary London. Merchants came from Europe, the Middle East and elsewhere in Asia to trade in its markets. Ayutthayan kings engaged Japanese soldiers, Indian men-at-arms and Persian ministers to serve in their retinues. Regular relations with Europe began in the early 1500s, with the Portuguese, and later with the Dutch, British, and especially the French. Europeans wrote awed accounts of the fabulous wealth of the courts and of the 2,000 temple spires clad in gilded gold.

As fast as it rose to greatness, it collapsed, suffering a destruction so complete that it was never rebuilt. Burmese armies had been battering at its gates for centuries – its strong fortifications, with ramparts 20 metres (65 ft) high and five metres (20 ft) thick, were generally effective – before occupying it for a period in the 16th century. Siamese kings then expelled the Burmese and reasserted their independence. In 1767, however, the Burmese triumphed again. In their victory, they burned and looted, destroying most of the city's monuments, and enslaving, killing, or scattering the population. Within a year, Ayutthaya had become a ghost town,

its population of over one million reduced to a few thousand. Today, the ruins stand by themselves on the western half of the island, with modern Ayutthaya a bustling commercial town concentrated in the eastern part of the island.

Start close to the junction of the Nam Pa Sak and Chao Phraya rivers, passing by the imposing **Wat Phanan Choeng** Ⓐ (open daily 8am–5pm; admission fee). Records suggest that the *wat* was established 26 years prior to Ayutthaya's foundation in 1350. The temple houses a huge seated Buddha, so tightly crowded against the roof that he appears to be holding it up. Wat Phanan Choeng was a favourite with Chinese traders, who prayed there before setting out on long voyages; it still has an unmistakably Chinese atmosphere.

Ayutthaya was at one time surrounded by stout walls, only portions of which remain. One of the best-preserved sections is at **Phom Phet**, across the river from Wat Phanan Choeng. Upstream west from Wat Phanan Choeng, the restored **Wat Phutthaisawan** Ⓑ (Buddhaisawan; open daily 8am–5pm) stands serenely on the riverbank. Seldom visited, the landing is an excellent place to enjoy the river's tranquillity in the evenings. Further upstream, the restored **Cathedral of St Joseph** is a Catholic reminder of the large European population that lived in the city at its prime.

Where the river bends to the north is one of Ayutthaya's most romantic ruins, **Wat Chai Wattanaram** Ⓒ (open daily 8am–5pm; admission fee), erected in 1630. Perched high on a pedestal in front of the ruins, a Buddha keeps solitary watch. The stately *prang* with its surrounding *chedi* and rows of headless Buddhas make a fine contrast to the restored **Queen Suriyothai Chedi** Ⓓ (open daily 9am–5pm; no fee) on the city side of the river. Dressed as a man, the Ayutthaya queen rode into battle, her elephant beside that of her husband. When she

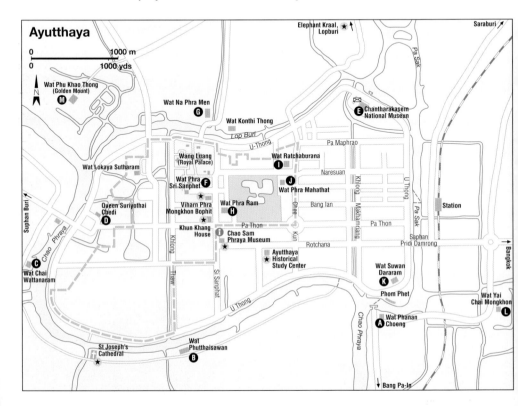

saw him being attacked by a Burmese prince, she moved between them with her elephant, receiving a lethal lance blow intended for her husband.

Chantharakasem National Museum ❸ (open Wed–Sun 9am–4pm; admission fee) was originally constructed outside the city walls, close to the junction of the rivers and the new canal. King Naresuan built it as a defensive bastion while he was engaged in wars against his northern rivals from Chiang Mai. In 1767, the Burmese destroyed the palace, but King Mongkut resurrected it in the 19th century as a royal summer retreat from Bangkok's heat. Now housing a small museum, the palace looks out on the busiest part of the modern town.

The old royal palace, **Wang Luang**, was of substantial size if the foundations for the stables of 100 elephants are any indication. It was razed by the Burmese and the bricks removed to Bangkok to build its defensive walls, so only remnants of the foundations survive to mark the site. Close by stand the three stately chedi of **Wat Phra Sri Sanphet ❻** (open daily 8am–5pm; admission fee), a royal temple built in 1491 that honours three 15th-century kings. The identical chedi have been restored and stand in regal contrast to the surrounding ruins.

For two centuries after Ayutthaya's fall, a huge bronze Buddha sat unsheltered near Wat Phra Sri Sanphet. Its flame of knowledge and one of his arms had been broken when the roof, set alight by the Burmese, collapsed. Based on the original, a new building, the **Viharn Phra Mongkol Bophit**, was built in 1956 around the restored statue. The resulting shrine works remarkably well, the giant, black-coloured Buddha exuding a genuinely numinous feeling of power.

Across the river from the old palace stands another restored temple, **Wat Na Phra Men ❼** (open daily 8am–5pm; admission fee). Here, a large stone Buddha is seated in the "European fashion" on a throne – a sharp contrast to the yoga

Map, page 196

An elephant-mounted Ayutthayan general prepares to lead his army against the Burmese.

BELOW: Ayutthayan jewellery, and Lopburi sculpture.

position of most seated Buddhas. Found in the ruins of Wat Mahathat, the statue is believed to be one of five that originally sat in a recently unearthed Dvaravati-period complex in Nakhon Pathom. The *bot* (central sanctuary) contains a seated Buddha on the altar. Across a bridge are the ruins of **Wat Konthi Thong**.

Back on the island and across the road from Phra Mongkol Bophit, **Wat Phra Ram** ⓗ (open daily 8am–5pm; admission fee) is one of Ayutthaya's oldest temples. Founded in 1369 by the son of Ayutthaya's founder, its 15th-century buildings have been restored twice. Elephant gates punctuate the old walls, and the central terrace is dominated by a crumbling prang to which clings a gallery of stucco *naga*, *garuda* and statues of the Buddha. The reflection of Wat Phra Ram's prang shimmers in the pool that surrounds the complex. Once a marshy swamp, the pool was dug to provide landfill for the temple's foundations.

In 1957, looters removed much of the gold from Wat Ratchaburana. Only part of it was finally recovered.

Two of Ayutthaya's finest temples stand side by side northeast across the lake from Wat Phra Ram. Built in 1424 by the seventh king of Ayutthaya as a memorial to his brothers, the well-known **Wat Ratchaburana** ⓘ (open daily 8am–5pm; admission fee) dominates its surroundings. Excavations during its restoration in 1958 revealed a crypt containing gold jewellery, Buddha images and other objects, among them a charming, intricately decorated elephant. These treasures are kept in the **Chao Sam Phraya National Museum** (open Wed–Sun 9am–4pm; admission fee) to the south. Some of Thailand's finest ancient paintings cover crypt walls.

BELOW: Wat Phra Ram, founded in 1369.

Across the road, **Wat Phra Mahathat** ⓙ (open daily 8am–5pm; admission fee) is one of the most beautiful temple complexes in Ayutthaya, and one of its oldest, dating from the 1380s. Its glory is its huge prang, which originally stood 46 metres (150 ft) high. The prang later collapsed, but it was rebuilt 4 metres (13 ft) higher than before. Stone Buddha faces, each a metre (over 3 ft) in height, stand

silently around the ruins. Together with the restored chedi that ring the prang, these combine to make this one of the most impressive sites in Ayutthaya. Next door, the government has built a model of how the royal city may have once looked.

Wat Suwan Dararam ⓚ (open daily 8am–5pm), to the southeast and constructed near the close of the Ayutthaya period, has been beautifully restored. The foundations of the *bot* dip in the centre, in emulation of the graceful deck line of a boat, meant to suggest a boat carrying pious Buddhists to salvation. Delicately carved columns support the roof, and the interior walls are decorated with brilliantly coloured frescoes. Still used as a temple, the wat has a magical atmosphere in the early evening when the monks chant their prayers. East is **Wat Yai Chai Mongkhon** ⓛ (open daily 8am–5pm; admission fee), originally established in the mid 1300s. In single-handed combat on elephant-back, King Naresuan slew the crown prince of Burma in 1592. The immense chedi, built to match the Phu Khao Thong Pagoda just north of Ayutthaya, was erected in celebration of the victory. Buddha statues line the courtyard.

Just north of Ayutthaya, the **Wat Phu Khao Thong** ⓜ (open daily 8am–5pm), better known as the **Golden Mount**, stands with its 80-metre (260-ft) high chedi alone amidst the rice fields, its upper terraces commanding a panoramic view of the countryside. While the wat dates from 1387, the chedi was built by the Burmese after their earlier and less destructive conquest in 1569. It was later remodelled by the Siamese in their own style. In 1957, to mark 2,500 years of Buddhism, a 2,500-gram (5.5 lb) gold ball was mounted on top of the chedi.

In the opposite direction from the Golden Mount, the road runs to the only elephant *kraal* left in Thailand. This 16th-century kraal is a reminder of the days when elephants were not only caught and trained to work in the jungles,

Map, page 196

BELOW: Wat Ratchaburana.

In 1688, as Narai lay mortally ill in his palace, an army officer seized the throne. The king called in a Buddhist abbot to ordain his loyal attendants as monks, to save them.

BELOW: elephant round-up at Ayutthaya's kraal, 1895.

but were also an essential requisite for a strong army. The last elephant roundup was in 1903. Standing at the edge of the restored stockade with its huge teak columns, one can imagine the thunder of the mighty beasts.

Bang Pa-In ❷ (open daily 8am–3.45pm; admission fee), a charming collection of palaces and pavilions once used as a royal summer retreat, lies a short distance downriver from the ruins of Ayutthaya. The rulers of Ayutthaya used it as long ago as the 17th century, but the buildings one sees today date from the late 19th- and early 20th-century reigns of Rama V and Rama VI.

Lopburi

The former summer capital of Siam, **Lopburi ❸**, lies 10 km (6 miles) north of Ayutthaya. Here, the hills of the Khorat Plateau appear on the horizon, the first break in the flatness of the central plains.

Artefacts from the neolithic and bronze ages have been found in large quantities in Lopburi, testifying to the great antiquity of the city. In the Dvaravati period, from the sixth to 11th century, it was a major religious centre thought to have attracted savants from around the region. At the height of the Angkor empire in the 11th and 12th centuries, it was a provincial capital. Then came the Thais, who put their imprint on most of the old buildings that now survive. It was not until the mid 1600s that Ayutthaya became a bustling international city with upwards of three dozen nationalities represented. Some French architects even ventured to Lopburi, where Narai retreated in summer to escape the heat.

The grounds of the **Lopburi Palace** (also called King Narai's Palace, or Narai Ratchaniwet, open daily 7am–5.30pm), built between 1665 and 1677, are enclosed by massive walls, which still dominate the centre of the modern town.

The grounds have three sections enclosing governmental, ceremonial and residential buildings. The middle section once enclosed the Dusit Maha Prasat Hall, Chantra Paisan Pavilion, and Phiman Mongkut Pavilion. The inner courtyard was that of the king, where his residence, **Suttha Sawan Pavilion**, was nestled amidst gardens and ponds.

Map, page 192

Of King Narai's buildings, the only one that has substantially survived is the **Dusit Maha Prasat**. This was built for the audience granted by the king in 1685 to the ambassador of Louis XIV. Near the Dusit Maha Prasat is the **Phiman Mongkut Pavilion**, a three-storey mansion in the colonial style and built in the mid-19th century by King Mongkut. The immensely thick walls and high ceilings show how the summer heat was averted most effectively before air-conditioning arrived. The mansion, small but full of character, displays a mixture of bronze statues, Chinese and Sukhothai porcelain, coins, Buddhist fans, and shadow-play puppets. Some of the pieces, particularly the Ayutthaya bronze heads and Bencharong porcelain, are superb.

The remains of a grand palace in Lopburi rival those of the royal palace. Located just north of Narai's residence, the buildings show strong European influence, with straight-sided walls and pedimental decorations over Western-style windows.

Also of note in Lopburi are three temple ruins built by the Khmers in the 11th and 12th centuries. **Prang Sam Yot** comprises three *prang*, originally intended to symbolise the Hindu deities Shiva, Vishnu, and Brahma. Of particular interest are the carved Khmer lintels over the *prang* entries. **Prang Khaek**, once dedicated to Shiva alone, is similar. **Wat Phra Si Rattana Mahathat** (open Wed–Sun 7am–5pm; admission fee), once the city's largest monastery, boasts a tall laterite tower with intact lintels and stucco ornamentation. ❑

BELOW: Phaulkon's palace, Lopburi.

Map, page 192

THAILAND

Bangkok

BELOW: central-plain smile, and a face at a local fair.

THE CENTRAL PLAINS

For most foreign travellers, Thailand's central plains are a fly-over or drive-through zone on the way to the north. Yet, culturally and agriculturally, this is one of Thailand's most important regions

Nakhon Sawan ❹, 250 km (150 miles) north of Bangkok, has long been an important commercial centre because of its location as the hub of roads and rivers connecting north and central Thailand. The Ping and Nan rivers, already swollen by their tributaries, meet the Wang and the Yom at Nakhon Sawan, forming the Chao Phraya. Route 1 divides here, sending a branch, Route 117, due north to Sukhothai and Phitsanulok, while itself continuing northwest towards Tak. Reaching one's destination in the central plains, as in most other parts of Thailand, is generally quick and comfortable. The main cities in the centre are linked to Bangkok by road, rail and air. Of these three modes, the most common is by coach.

Under its old name of Paknampoh, Nakhon Sawan played a vital role in the teak trade. It was here that the great teak rafts, which had sometimes been travelling for two or three years from the northern forests, were broken up into smaller rafts for floating down to Bangkok on the Chao Phraya River. Teak rafts may still occasionally be seen on the river below Nakhon Sawan, but since the government's banning of logging in Thailand, they are not nearly as numerous as they were in the heyday of Thailand's teak trade. Today, there are few traces of Nakhon Sawan's historic past in the modern commercial town.

The most notable shrine is outside the town, across the bridge over the Chao Phraya. Here, on a small hill stands **Wat Chom Kiri Nak Phrot**. On a clear day the views from the top of the hill are stunning. The main structure dates from the 14th-century Sukhothai period, but the Buddha image, seated on a throne supported by demons, is of the Ayutthaya period. Behind the main shrine is a massive, finely adorned bronze bell, about a century old, supported aloft on brick pillars.

A favourite outing for those living in and around Nakhon Sawan is a trip to **Bung Boraphet ❺**, a large lake a few kilometres to the east. Until they were hunted to extinction, crocodiles used to bask on its shores. This low-lying area acts as a catchment during the rainy season. At the height of the monsoon in September and October, the swollen lake covers an area of some 120 sq km (50 sq miles). A good time to visit is on a moonlit night, in the cool season, for a picnic on the island.

Found in the northern part of the Central Plains, this 10th–11th-century terracotta piece depicts a dvarapala or door guardian.

The "new" city of **Kamphaeng Phet ❻** lies 3 km (2 miles) off Route 1, about 120 km (75 miles) northwest of Nakhon Sawan and on the east bank of the Ping River. This city was built by King Li Thai (1347–1368), of the Sukhothai dynasty, to replace the older town of Chakangrao on the opposite bank. Both served as garrison towns for the Kingdom of Sukhothai.

Along the road to Kamphaeng Phet are the remains of a fort, **Phom Seti**, built to defend the former city of Chakangrao. Further along the road is the well-restored *chedi* of **Wat Chedi Klang Tung**, – the "Chedi in the Middle of the Fields" – another relic of the earlier city.

With its numerous rice and noodle houses, the modern part of town is on the other side of a bridge, over the Ping River. The well-designed **Kamphaeng Phet National Museum** (open Wed–Sun 9am–4pm; admission fee) contains

BELOW: ruins of Kamphaeng Phet.

**Map,
page 192**

one of Thailand's finest bronze statues of the Hindu god Siva. This life-sized image was cast on the orders of the governor of Kamphaeng Phet in the first quarter of the 16th century.

Early during the reign of King Chulalongkorn, a German visitor removed the image's head and two hands. Too afraid to arrest a *farang* (Westerner), the governor quickly sent word to Bangkok that the priceless fragments were on their way by boat. Officials in Bangkok detained the German, who declared that he was going to give them to the Berlin Museum.

King Chulalongkorn, a skilful diplomat, found a way to placate the German as well as keep the cultural treasures for his country. He promised to send an exact copy of the whole Siva image to Germany, so that the authentic fragments could remain in Thailand. And so it was done. The copy of the bronze is still in Berlin. Other exhibits in the museum include pre-Sukhothai bronzes, stucco Buddha heads from local monuments, and some ceramics.

A car or coach is necessary for a tour of the fortifications and temples, as they are some distance from the modern town. A visit to King Li Thai's fortifications reveals why the town was called Kamphaeng Phet, or Diamond Walls: the massive ramparts of earth are topped by laterite rising 6 metres (20 ft) above the outer moat, once overgrown with water hyacinths but now extensively restored.

The chief monuments of Kamphaeng Phet lie northwest of the walled city. The monks who built them were of a forest-dwelling sect, strongly influenced by teachers from Sri Lanka. Their temples, constructed of laterite, are thought to show Ceylonese influence. Most of them, however, underwent major changes during restoration in the Ayutthaya period.

The familiar themes of Buddhist architecture, *viharn* and chedi, are repeated in the ordination halls of two temples. These two temples are of special interest and should be seen even on a rapid tour.

BELOW: Wat Phra Si Iriyabot.
RIGHT: planting rice seedlings.

The first, **Wat Phra Si Iriyabot**, derives its name from Buddha images that are depicted in four postures (*si* meaning four, and *iriyabot*, postures) on the central square *mondop* (sanctuary): walking, standing, sitting and reclining. The standing image is largely intact, with the original stucco coating on its head and lower part of the body. This is an impressive and unaltered example of Sukhothai sculpture. Unfortunately, the other images are in very poor condition. The whole temple stands on a platform that is encircled by the original laterite railing and walls. The other temple, **Wat Chang Rawp**, or Shrine Surrounded by Elephants, consists of the base of a laterite chedi surrounded by elephant buttresses, a theme borrowed from Sri Lanka that claims the universe rests on the backs of these beasts.

The row of elephants on the south side is almost complete, but several are missing on the other flanks of the stupa. Unfortunately, the spire of the great monument has vanished, but the ruins of a crypt on the upper level of the stupa can still be inspected. The pillars of the former viharn also remain.

Repair work was completed in the late 1990s, restoring much of the original form without – luckily – robbing the elephants of their appeal. ❏

Culture of Rice

The Thai expression *kin khao* is translated as "to eat," but it actually means "to eat rice." Indeed, here where rice has been a staple for centuries, the two are synonymous.

The rice-planting season begins in May, when the king presides over the ancient ploughing ceremony at Sanam Luang, in Bangkok. This Brahmanic rite symbolises the attention that the spirits give to the prospects for the forthcoming rice harvest.

Cultivating rice is by necessity a cooperative effort, tightening the bonds of family and community. According to tradition, a farmer can ask fellow villagers to help with the work, and without having to pay for their labour. All that is expected from the host is a meal during the day, and perhaps some rice liquor in the evening. In the countryside, nearly everyone is a farmer as they put aside normal jobs to help with the preparation of paddy fields and the sowing of seed. Children are on holiday from school, as they will be when harvesting begins later in the year.

The social importance of this cooperation can hardly be exaggerated. It has a direct influence on individual behaviour, because if there are problems between individuals, families and communities, the work will not get done. Moreover, it is believed that quarrelling will upset the rice spirit and the crop may fail. Soon after the rice seedlings are transplanted into the paddy fields, villagers leave token packets of rice and other food in the fields, as offerings to the rice spirit.

A ceremony important to the crop is the Boon Bang Fai, or skyrocket festival, which assures abundant rains. The festival that takes place as the monsoon rains begin has Buddhist origins, although it also contains elements of Brahmanism and animism. Buddhists say it began at the death of the Lord Buddha, when one of his grieving disciples, unable to reach his torch to the top of the funeral pyre, hurled it up to the top in a manner similar to the appearance of skyrockets being shot off. Villagers make their own rockets with gunpowder, launching them from a ladder-like structure, or from a very tall tree. Monks are involved, and if the rockets do not go off properly, the monks will lose prestige.

The cooperative effort given to the rice crop continues through the growing months. One of the most onerous tasks is keeping birds away from the ripening grain. By early December, rice is ripe enough for harvesting in Thailand's rice bowl, the central plains, and in the north, but the harvest comes later in the south. Harvesting schedules are fixed by common consent within each village.

Finally, when the rice is in the barns, the farmers at last relax and enjoy themselves. And it is then that they celebrate Songkran – the most joyous festival of the year, which marks the beginning of the traditional Thai new year, in April.

Big commercial farmers and agribusiness companies produce rice on a mammoth scale. Chemicals have now supplanted the powers of the rice spirit. Former farmers have left their fields altogether, and instead work on roads, drive trucks, and maintain tractors. Rice is no longer the top Thai export, but it is still a vital one – Thailand continues to remain the world's top rice exporter, earning about US$ 2 billion annually. ❑

SUKHOTHAI

Map, page 192

Sukhothai, the first independent Thai kingdom, is considered to be from the golden era of Thailand's history. Fortunately, much of ancient Sukhothai remains today, at the northern extent of the central plains

The route towards the ancient city of **Sukhothai ❼** (Dawn of Happiness) passes through "new" Sukhothai, a bustling modern town of concrete shop-houses. About 10 km (7 miles) further on, the road enters the limits of old Sukhothai through the **Kamphaenghak** (Broken Wall) **Gate**.

The Sukhothai Kingdom began around 1240, when King Intradit asserted his independence from the Khmers. Sukhothai, which grew to include most of modern-day Thailand and parts of the Malay Peninsula and Burma, is synonymous with some of the finest artistic endeavours in Thai history, including perhaps the most exquisite Buddha images. Unfortunately, the golden age was relatively short-lived, just two centuries and nine kings long. The upstart Kingdom of Ayutthaya absorbed Sukhothai in 1438. The most notable Sukhothai king was Ramkamhaeng, who, among other accomplishments, reformed the Thai script, promoted Theravada Buddhism and established links with China.

The remains of ancient Sukhothai's massive walls reveal that the inner city was protected by no fewer than three rows of earthen ramparts and two moats. The city was begun by the Khmers, who left behind three buildings and the beginnings of a water system, similar to that of Angkor Wat. After the Angkorian empire began to contract, the Khmers abandoned ancient Sukhothai and the Thais moved in, building their own structures. They eschewed the intricate Khmer irrigation system, installing a much less complex one of their own. It is suggested that water, or the lack of it, in part contributed to the city's demise. It is possible that the city was originally served by the Yom River, which later shifted course and deprived Sukhothai of a dependable source of water.

Exploring the ancient city

A short distance from Kamphaenghak Gate is the **Ramkamhaeng National Museum** (open Wed–Sun 9am–4pm; admission fee), a good starting point for a tour of the enclave. The museum contains a fine collection of Sukhothai sculpture, ceramics and other artefacts, as well as exhibits from other periods. The entrance hall is dominated by an impressive bronze image of the walking Buddha. This style of image is regarded as the finest sculptural innovation of the Sukhothai period (1230–1440). There had been earlier essays in high and low relief, but the Sukhothai sculptors were the first to create statues of the walking Buddha. It also displays the elements that typify the Sukhothai style, including fluid lines, a somewhat androgynous figure, and strict interpretation of the 32 *raksana,* or characteristics by which a Buddha would be recognised: wedge-shaped heels, arms hanging to the knees, fingers and toes of equal length, among other distinguishing features.

Walking in Sukhothai.

In this period, the Thais definitively embraced Theravada Buddhism and invited monks from Sri Lanka to clarify points of scripture. While Buddhism was blossoming, Hindu influence remained strong, indicated by the two bronze images of Hindu gods flanking the walking Buddha in the museum. The one on the right, with the combined attributes of Vishnu and Siva, is especially fine. Also worth noting is a stone torso of an *apsara,* or celestial maiden, in the Khmer style. An important object proudly displayed on the mezzanine floor is a copy of the famous stone inscription of King Ramkamhaeng; the original is the most

LEFT: Wat Mahathat during Loy Krathong.

prized exhibit of the National Museum in Bangkok. It was at the **Non Prasat** (Palace Mound), now merely a slightly raised terrace of earth and brick, that the inscription was found. In 1833, the future King Mongkut, then a monk, discovered the stone, which had been inscribed in 1292. On it, King Ramkamhaeng had recorded his conquests in surrounding kingdoms, and the fact that in 1283 he improved the Siamese alphabet. However, some experts now doubt its authenticity and believe the inscription to be a much later forgery.

Once situated on the Non Prasat was the stone throne of Ramkamhaeng, and although there is little to be seen now, apart from the walled terrace, this was the numinous centre of old Siam. Alexander Griswold notes: "The political significance of the throne can scarcely be exaggerated, for the king sat on it when he discussed affairs of state… and when he received his vassals who came to do homage". The stone throne, called the *Manangasila*, is now in the Temple of the Emerald Buddha in Bangkok.

Over the centuries, until the 16th century, kings added to Wat Mahathat until there were 200 or so chedi.

Within the walls of Sukhothai are the ruins of some 20 temples and monuments. The greatest of them is **Wat Mahathat**, west of the museum. It is not known with certainty who founded this temple, which Griswold called "the magical and spiritual centre of the kingdom", but it is presumed to have been the first king of Sukhothai. Wat Mahathat owes its present form to a remodelling completed by King Lo Thai, around 1345.

The original design, discovered a few years ago during repairs, was a quincunx of laterite towers based on a laterite platform. The four axial towers, which can still be seen, are of the Khmer style but with stucco decorations added by Lo Thai. The central tower is now hidden in the basement of Lo Thai's "lotus bud" tower. The axial towers were linked to the central tower by laterite but-

BELOW: Wat Mahathat at sunset.

tresses, which are still visible. The principal Buddha image, cast in bronze by King Lu Thai (1347–1368), is now in Bangkok, at Wat Suthat. The stucco frieze of walking monks around the base of the main tower is unusual.

Among the 20 other shrines within the walls, and some 70 more in the neighbourhood, many repeat familiar architectural themes. The following short list reflects the monuments of special interest.

Wat Si Sawai, southwest of Wat Mahathat, was originally a Hindu shrine that contained an image of Siva. Triple towers remain, built in a modified Khmer style; the stucco decoration, added to the towers in the 15th century and showing mythical birds and divinities, is particularly fine.

Wat Chana Songkhram and **Wat Trakuan**, just north of Wat Mahathat, have especially nice Sri Lankan-style chedi, of which only the lower parts still stand. Wat Trakuan has revealed many bronze images of the Chiang Saen period.

Wat Sa Si, north on the other side of the highway and on the way to the southern gate, has a chedi of the Sri Lankan type. The ordination hall *(bot)* lies on an island to the east of the spire. The ruins of the main shrine consist of six rows of columns, which lead to a well-restored, seated Buddha image. As Achille Clarac, author of *Discovering Thailand*, put it: "The detail, balance and harmony of the proportions and decoration of Wat Sra Sri, and the beauty of the area where it stands, bear witness to the unusual and refined aesthetic sense of the architects of the Sukhothai period."

Leaving the walled city by the northern San Luang, or the Royal Shrine gate, and travelling about a kilometre, one arrives at the important shrine of **Wat Phra Phai Luang**. It originally consisted of three laterite towers covered with stucco, probably built in the late 12th century, when Sukhothai was still part of the

Map, page 192

BELOW: bullock cart decorated for Loy Krathong.

TIP

Perhaps the most
exquisite time of the
year to see Sukhothai
is during Loy Krathong,
during the November
full moon. This festival
celebrates the end of
the rainy season.

Khmer empire. This shrine might have been the original centre of Sukhothai, since Wat Mahathat is of a later period. A fragmentary seated stone Buddha image, accurately dated to 1191 and the reign of the Khmer King Jayavarman VII, was found here and is now in the grounds of the town's Ramkamhaeng Museum. During restoration in the mid 1960s, a large stucco image of the Buddha in the central tower collapsed, disclosing numerous smaller images inside. Some date these images to the second half of the 13th century.

To the east of the main shrine lies a pyramidal brick chedi that originally contained seated stucco Buddha images, dating from the late 13th century. Later, the niches were walled up with bricks, which were removed during a restoration started in 1953.

When heads of the stucco images began appearing on the antique market in Bangkok, authorities realised that the stupa was being pillaged. A team from the government was dispatched to the site, but most of the damage had already been done. Those heads – in the Chiang Saen style – that have not left the country are in private collections elsewhere in Thailand, or else in the custody of the National Museum in Bangkok.

Beyond Wat Phra Phai Luang to the west is **Wat Si Chum**, with one of the largest seated Buddha images in Thailand. The *mondop*, or enclosing shrine, was built in the second half of the 14th century, but the image itself, called *Phra Achana,* or The Venerable, is believed to be the one mentioned in King Ramkamhaeng's inscription. There is a stairway within the walls of the mondop that leads to the roof. The ceiling of the stairway is made up of more than 50 carved slate slabs with scenes from Buddhist folklore. Their function is to turn the ritual climbing of the stairs into a symbolic ascent to Buddhahood. Partly

BELOW: ruins of
Wat Chetupon.

because of the precarious nature of the stairway, and partially to avoid people standing above the Buddha's head, it is no longer permitted to climb the stairs.

Map, page 192

There is a story that troops gathered here before an ancient battle were inspired by an ethereal voice that seemed to come from the Buddha itself. Some suggest a cunning ploy by a general who hid one of his men on the stairway and instructed him to speak through one of the windows concealed by the body of the image; the effect was inspiring, however, and the soldiers routed the enemy.

South of the walled city is another group of shrines and monasteries. One of the most interesting is **Wat Chetupon**, where the protecting wall of the viharn is made of slate slabs shaped in imitation of wood. The gates are also formed of huge plates of slate mined in the nearby hills. They somewhat resemble the megaliths of England's Stonehenge, but on a smaller scale. The bridges across the moat that surround the temple are also made of stone slabs. On the central tower of Wat Chetupon are Buddha images in the standing, reclining, walking and sitting postures. The walking Buddha here is regarded as one of the finest of its kind.

"To the west of the city of Sukhothai", says King Ramkamhaeng's inscription, "is a forested area where the king has made offerings. In the forest is a large, tall and beautiful viharn which contains an 18-cubit image of the standing Buddha". This is now identified as **Wat Saphan Hin**, Monastery of the Stone Bridge. It is so-called because it is approached by a stairway of large stone slabs. The image is situated on the crest of a low hill and can be seen at a considerable distance. It is 12 metres (40 ft) high, with its hand raised in the attitude of giving protection, and is almost certainly the image described by King Ramkamhaeng.

Many other monuments are to be found in this western area. They were probably built by monks from Sri Lanka, who preferred to locate their monasteries in the forest. Another monument worth visiting, near the road and not far from the western gate of Sukhothai, is **Wat Pa Mamuang**, Shrine of the Mango Grove, where King Lu Thai installed a famous monk of the Theravada sect in 1361. Still standing are the shrine foundations and the ruins of the main chedi.

Outside Sukhothai

About 50 km (31 miles) north of the modern town of Sukhothai, along a concrete highway, lies the venerable city of **Si Satchanalai** ❽, on the banks of the Yom River. Founded in the middle of the 13th century, as was Sukhothai, it served as the seat of the viceroys of Sukhothai and was always mentioned as the twin city of the capital. Whereas restoration, removal of trees, and the installation of lawns have removed some of the grandeur of Sukhothai, Si Satchanalai's setting gives it an aura few other ancient sites have. It is a pleasure to wander through the wooded complex, rounding a corner and being surprised by a new wat or monument.

The first and most important monument to visit in Si Satchanalai is **Wat Chang Lom**. There can be little doubt that this is the "elephant-girdled shrine" described in King Ramkamhaeng's stone inscription. The great king records that he started to build it in 1285 to house some exceptionally holy relics of the Lord Buddha, and

BELOW: standing Buddha at Wat Saphan Hin.

Map, page 192

East a kilometre or so of Si Satchanalai is Chalieng, an earlier Khmer site from the late 1100s and early 1200s. It is thought to have been an outpost for travellers.

BELOW: Phra Buddha Chinaraj is venerated throughout Thailand.
RIGHT: Wat Chedi Chet Thaew.

that it was finished six years later. It is the only surviving stupa that can be attributed with virtual certainty to King Ramkamhaeng. Built of laterite and stucco, it is a large bell-shaped spire in the Sri Lankan style standing on a two-storey, square basement. The upper tier contains niches for Buddha images, now mostly empty, while the lower level contains 39 elephant-shaped buttresses, built of laterite blocks.

South of the Elephant Shrine are the ruins of **Wat Chedi Chet Thaew**, which include seven rows of chedi, believed to contain the ashes of the viceroys of Si Satchanalai. One of the stupas has a stucco image of the Buddha sheltered by the *naga* (divine serpent), which is in unusually good repair.

Further south still, and close to the massive walls of the city, are the remains of **Wat Nang Phya**, Temple of the Queen. This has fine stucco decoration on one of the external walls. Dating probably from the 16th century, this stucco work has some affinities with European baroque.

Other temples worth visiting include **Wat Khao Phanom Pleung** and **Wat Khao Suwan Kiri**, set on two scenic hills linked by a walkway. **Wat Phra Si Rattana Mahathat** in Chalieng, one of the most beautiful temples, lies a couple of kilometres southeast of the old city in a setting overlooking the Yom River.

Si Satchanalai is also associated with the famed Sawankhalok ceramics, which were among Thailand's first export products. The brown bowls and their distinctive double-fish design were sent to China aboard junks; remains of them have been found in the Gulf of Thailand. It is still possible to buy genuine antique Sawankhalok ceramics in the area; most, however, are copies.

Fifty km (31 miles) east of Sukhothai, **Phitsanulok** ❾ now has only a few mementos of the past; a fire over three decades ago razed most of the old town.

The new city is a rather dull collection of concrete shophouses. However, nothing can detract from its superb location along the Nan River, with its quays shaded by flowering trees and its houseboats and floating restaurants moored beside the steep banks. The great fire fortunately spared **Wat Phra Si Rattana Mahathat**, the principal shrine in Phitsanulok.

The **Phra Buddha Chinaraj**, the image in the main bot, is venerated throughout Thailand. This has given rise to a busy traffic in religious objects and souvenirs. The seated image was cast in the Sukhothai style.

The bot that enshrines the Phra Buddha Chinaraj comprises a three-tiered roof that drops steeply to head-high side walls, focusing attention on the gleaming image at the end of the nave. Flanking the image are two wooden pulpits of superb late-Ayutthaya workmanship. The large one on the left is for monks, who chant the ancient, Pali-language Buddhist texts; the smaller pulpit on the other side accommodates a single monk who translates the chants into Thai (since few of the congregation would understand Pali). Note the main doors inlaid with mother-of-pearl, dating from the late 18th century. The *prang* (spire) in the centre of the temple complex was rebuilt in the Khmer style by King Boromatrailokanat. The cloisters surrounding the prang contain Buddha images from several periods, some of them of great artistic value. A repository of art objects includes Thai and Chinese ceramics. ❏

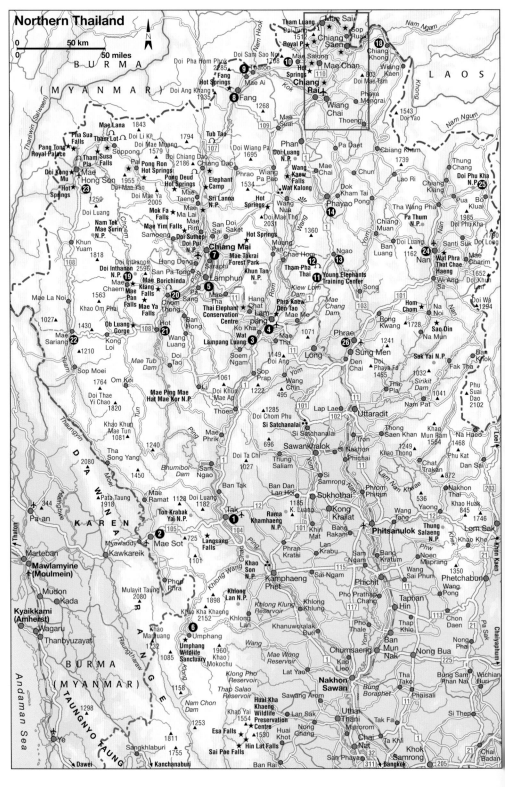

Northern Thailand

THE NORTH

Travellers not heading for the southern beaches head for the northern mountains, hill tribes and outdoor adventure

The north of Thailand has been the setting for epic battles involving Burmese and Chinese invaders, and it has witnessed the magnificent rise – and collapse – of ancient kingdoms. Until the early part of the 20th century, it was accessible from Bangkok only by a complicated river trip, or by a journey of several weeks on elephant back.

It is not surprising, then, that the region has retained a distinct flavour all its own, one still so strong that tourists from other parts of Thailand come here almost as if to visit another country. They marvel at the profusion and beauty of the temples, with their splendid teak carvings and intricate Burmese-inspired decorations; the splendour of the wild orchids that grow so profusely in the hills; the gentle and good manners of the people (among whose hospitable habits it is to place a basin of cool water outside their gates to quench the thirst of passing strangers); and the novelty of having to bundle up in a sweater in the cool season.

The north is a region of great natural wealth and scenic beauty. Although decades of logging have reduced the hardwood forests, a logging ban has ensured the remainder will survive, whilst reforestation is already far advanced. In these jungled mountains live unusual people, now a tourist industry in their own right: Hmong people whose women wear vast, bulky turbans and clanking silver jewellery; Mien tribespeople dressed in finely worked embroidery; several small nomadic groups – like the Phi Thong Luang, or Spirits of the Yellow Leaves – who some thought existed only in myth. The hill tribes are still an exotic thread on the fringe of Thai life, but gradually they are being woven into the national fabric and are venturing to the larger cities of the north. Some – notably the Mien – prosper, running trendy stalls in the Chiang Mai night bazaar. Others, particularly the Akha, do less well, sitting and selling their wares on the pavement amid the din and fumes of urban traffic.

It is hard for the authorities adequately to patrol this wild terrain, but easy for smugglers to slip back and forth across the borders with Burma and Laos in the notorious Golden Triangle. The government, however, with the active support of the king, has been quite successful in introducing alternatives to opium as a cash crop.

Long closed at most frontiers, Thailand's borders with its neighbours of Cambodia, Laos and Burma are slowly opening to international travellers. Already Laos and Cambodia are increasingly accessible overland from Thailand, and Burma may one day be, too.   ❏

PRECEDING PAGES: a Lisu village brings in the traditional new year.

TOWARDS CHIANG MAI

North of Thailand's central plains, the land begins rising into highlands of the north. The approach to the northern extents is classically transitional, whether regarding smuggling or history

Map, page 216

On the banks of the Mae Nam Ping, the quiet town of **Tak ❶** is the gateway to the north, Thailand's most scenic region. Northwest of Kamphaeng Phet and west of Sukhothai, Tak is but a ghost of its former brawling self. Once called Raheng, it was a logger's town, and just north of Tak was the confluence of the Wang and Ping, two of the four main tributaries of the Mae Nam Chao Phraya. Logs freed from the wild rapids on the upper Ping and the Wang were floated downriver to Nakhon Sawan. The rapids have since been submerged under the reservoir of Bhumibol Dam, but the town's wild-west reputation has been sustained, to a degree, by the smuggling of gems, drugs and teak from nearby Burma.

During the 19th century, Tak was a provisions centre for journeys west into Burma and north to Chiang Mai. Until the railway was completed in the 1920s, the only way north was by boat, propelled by poles against the swift current. As the rapids were the most formidable obstacle on the river, Tak was an essential stop for rest and replenishment.

Today, Tak is a prosperous town just off Route 1. It is entered either by a direct route, or by the old road that threads through tiny manicured gardens and around a pond near the provincial offices. Other than the river at sunset and the orange suspension bridge that resembles a miniature version of San Francisco's Golden Gate, Tak offers few exceptional sights. A broad esplanade separates the market from the Ping River; a dyke holds back the river's waters, which once flooded during the rainy season.

LEFT: officials with offerings en route to the monastery, Lampang.
BELOW: northern rice fields.

Towards Burma

Route 105 leads west through rugged hills towards the Burmese border town of Mae Sot. About 18 km (11 miles) outside of Tak lies **Lan Sang National Park**, with waterfalls that are hidden behind a screen of bamboo groves. Increasingly scarce bears, deer and even leopards make the area home. If time allows, stop at the *nikhorn*, or "settlement", on Doi Musoe to view Lisu, Lahu and Hmong hill-tribe life.

Freshly brewed, locally grown coffee is on sale here to restore the passing motorist, as well as wild orchids and forest flowers. The road rises to Phawo Mountain, where truck drivers make offerings at an elaborate, *naga*-headed shrine for safe passage. Beyond the pass, the road drops through forest into a peaceful valley dotted with small farmhouses, white *chedi*, and ornate Burmese-style temples.

The streets of **Mae Sot ❷**, a somewhat boisterous frontier town, is home to a diversity of ethnic groups. Along with a vigorous smuggling trade, especially in Burmese teak since 1989 a Thai logging ban, refugee camps on the outskirts of town have changed much of

Mae Sot's character. Shops advertise in Thai, Chinese, Burmese, and English. With its confusion of narrow streets, sidewalk stalls, bicycles, and pedestrian shoppers, it has the air of a frontier boom town.

From Mae Sot, it is a 5-km (3-mile) drive to the Burmese border. Worth a visit is an ornate Burmese temple with tiers of red-tiled rectangular roofs fringed with silverwork that are piled heavenward into a tower. Within the sanctuary are four Buddha images, one of which has gold jewellery distending its earlobes. Continue to the **Mae Nam Moei**, which forms the border with Burma. A new road bridge across the Moei to the Burmese town of Myawaddy has been completed, but is frequently closed because of political disagreements.

North of Tak to Chiang Mai

Bhumibol Dam.

Return to Tak and continue north on Route 1 and then on to Route 106, which describes an "S" and twines itself about Route 1. On the left, about 20 km (15 miles) past Tak, **Ban Tak** village lies on the banks of the Ping River. In the days when the river offered the only passage north, Ban Tak was a village of boat builders. Today, it is quiet but picturesque, with houses on stilts that teeter on the riverbank and a rickety bamboo footbridge overlooking children swimming. Opened in 1964 and named after Thailand's current king, **Bhumibol Dam** ❸ (also called Yanhee Dam), sits 30 km (20 miles) north of Ban Tak, on the left of Route 1. The dam, Thailand's largest, generates enough power to light Bangkok and a large number of Thailand's rural provinces. With permission, it's possible to drive across the 154-metre (505-ft) high cement retaining wall to view the reservoir stretching 120 km (75 miles) northwest.

BELOW: moving cattle on the open highway.

About 60 km (40 miles) north of the Bhumibol Dam turn-off, Route 1 arrives

at **Thoen**. Although Thoen can be passed through rapidly, it does enjoy a small claim to fame as the home of lucky *pohng kham* stones. Each pohng kham contains a variety of colours and encapsulated "scenes". Some of the clear pieces hold strange, crystalline formations resembling wisps of blue hair, jungle moss, or even a city skyline.

Map, page 216

From Thoen to Lampang, Route 1 undulates over teak-covered hills and a mountain pass sprinkled with spirit houses before dipping into the broad, cattle country of the Yom River Valley, dominated by the former kingdom of Lampang. Approximately 18 km (12 miles) south of Lampang is the junction with the road to **Ko Kha**.

Turn left past the town and cross the Wang River, bearing left for 1 km (½ mile), to reach one of the greatest treasures of the north: a revered temple, **Wat Phra That Lampang Luang ❹**. Cherished by scholars for its antiquity and delicate artwork, the temple compound is all that remains of a fortress city that flourished more than a millennium ago. It is said to have been founded by a 7th-century princess, Chama Dewi, who bore two sons; one became king of Lampang, the other, king of Lamphun. The wat, entirely rebuilt in the 16th century, played a key role in the golden period of the northern kingdoms. Nearly 200 years ago, Burmese invaders occupied the temple. According to legend, Lanna patriots sneaked into the temple through a drain, surprising and routing their enemy. Monks will point to a hole in the balustrade; it's said that the hole was caused by the cannon ball that killed a Burmese general.

The temple's museum features lacquered bookcases, jewelled Buddhas, and wooden *tong* banners that hang from poles like stiff flags. Most revered is a small Emerald Buddha believed to have been carved from the same stone as its

The main chedi at Wat Lampang Luang has taken on a bluish-green hue because of its copper covering oxidising from centuries of rain. Inside the chedi is said to be a relic of the Buddha, a strand of hair.

BELOW: teak viharn of Wat Phra That Lampang Luang.

**Map,
page 216**

Phra Kaew Don Tao.

BELOW: Wat Phra
That Hariphunchai.
RIGHT: Buddha, Wat
Kukut.

famous counterpart in Bangkok. It is displayed each November during the annual temple fair. The most important structures are the copper-plated chedi and the huge viharn with its low roofs.

About 20 km (12 miles) north past Ko Kha, Route 1 enters the provincial capital of **Lampang ❺**. Half the size of Chiang Mai, it has been developed almost to the level of its northern cousin. While much of its bucolic tranquillity has disappeared, it retains one relic of the past found in no other Thai city: horse-drawn carriages. These can be hired by the journey or by the hour. There are few more romantic pursuits to be found in Asia than clip-clopping down a moonlit back street.

Two Burmese-style temples in the town are worth visiting. Seven chapels, one for each day of the week, stand at the base of the chedi in **Wat Pha Sang**, located on the left bank of the Wang River. On the right bank, **Wat Phra Kaew Don Tao** is a lovely fusion of Burmese and northern Lanna architecture. In the pavilion, columns soar to ceilings covered in a kaleidoscope of inlaid enamel, mother-of-pearl and cut glass depicting mythical animals. North of town stand the 20 chalk-white spires of **Wat Chedi Sao**, set in the rice fields.

Straddling the Ping River and once an influential centre of the Mon culture – until King Mangrai overran the city in 1281 – **Lamphun ❻** is just 25 km (15 miles) south of Chiang Mai, via an attractive, tree-lined highway.

Lamphun is said to date from the mid-6th century and is famed for two elegant temples, attractive and confident women, and succulent *lamyai* fruit. Located on the banks of the Mae Kuang River, the provincial town was once on the main road from Lampang to Chiang Mai. A highway now bypasses Lamphun, making for a quiet and peaceful atmosphere. The town has managed to preserve a mellow upcountry quality, appropriate to its historical dignity.

To gain the best perspective on **Wat Phra That Hariphunchai**, enter it through its riverside gate, where large statues of mythical lions guard its portals. Inside the large compound, monks study in a Buddhist school set amidst monuments and buildings, which date as far back as the late 9th century, thus making the wat one of the oldest in northern Thailand. The base of the 50-metre (165-ft) high, gold-topped chedi in the centre of the courtyard is the oldest structure in the temple.

Ten centuries younger, but still respectably old, the gilt-roofed library stands to the left of a *sala* that shelters one of the world's largest bronze gongs. The somewhat disorganised temple museum contains a representative sampling of several styles of old Buddhist art.

A kilometre (½ mile) west of Lamphun's old moat stands **Wat Kukut**, dating from the 8th century (it is also known as Wat Chama Devi). The temple has a superb pair of unusual chedi. Erected in the early 1200s, the larger chedi consists of five tiers, each of which contains three niches. Each niche houses a statue of the Buddha, making an impressive display of 15 Buddha images on each side.

South of Lamphun, beyond the cotton-weaving town of **Pasang** – commonly believed by Thais to have the loveliest females in the country – is the hilltop pilgrimage centre of **Wat Phrabat Tak Pha**. A Buddha footprint on the hill is reached up a flight of 469 steps. ❑

CHIANG MAI

Map, page 216

Hill tribes lure travellers to the Chiang Mai area, although many hill villages and treks evoke commercialisation. Still, Chiang Mai's hospitality and the area's diverse offerings are reason enough to go

I t has become commonplace in many guidebooks to bemoan the supposed demise of **Chiang Mai ❼**, Thailand's once fabulous "Rose of the North". Noisy tuk-tuks are said to have replaced silent *samlor* pedicabs, concrete commercial buildings to have ousted traditional wooden housing, and high-rise condominiums to have marred the serene northern skyline. Happily, this is far from being the case. Chiang Mai has grown, it is true, and the volume of traffic has certainly increased along with urbanisation.

But high-rise buildings are a thing of the past, at least in the beautiful and historically important old city, where all new construction is strictly limited to three-storey buildings. In recent years, the city streets have been attractively cobbled in red brick, concrete lamp standards replaced by ornate Parisian-style lanterns, and the city walls and moats excavated and restored.

Despite its increasingly rapid urbanisation, 700-year-old Chiang Mai remains prized as a pleasant, cool-season escape from the sticky humidity of Bangkok. Situated 300 metres (1,000 ft) above sea level in a broad valley divided by the picturesque 560-km (350-mile) long **Mae Nam Ping**, the city reigned for seven centuries as the capital of the Lanna (Million Rice Fields) Kingdom. The city's northern remoteness kept the region beyond the close control of Bangkok – 700 km (400 miles) south – well into the 20th century. In its splendid isolation, Chiang Mai developed a culture quite removed from that of the central plains, with wooden temples of exquisite beauty and a host of unique crafts, including lacquerware, silverwork, wood carvings, ceramics and umbrella-making. Although hospitality of both the hill tribes and the northern Thais is sometimes strained by the sheer numbers of visitors, they remain more gracious than in many other cities.

LEFT: northern farming.
BELOW: modern Chiang Mai.

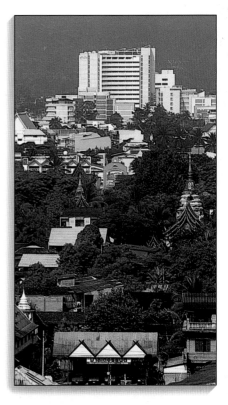

Origins

Chiang Mai's story begins further north, in the town of Chiang Rai. Its founder and king, Mangrai, ruled a sizeable empire that ran as far north as Chiang Saen, on the Mekong River. He founded Chiang Rai in 1281. But when the Mongol ruler, Kublai Khan, sacked the Burmese kingdom of Pagan in 1287, Mangrai feared that his realm might be threatened and so formed an alliance with the rulers of Sukhothai, then Siam's capital. With his southern boundaries secure, Mangrai captured the old Mon kingdom at Lamphun. To centralise his rule, he established a new base in the Ping River Valley in 1296. This new capital he named Chiang Mai, or "new city". The location was chosen by the auspicious sighting of white deer, and of a white mouse with a family of five, all at the same time, or so the story has it. Rather than building on the banks of the Ping, which often floods, he built his city – with the help of 90,000

TIP

Be careful on the
streets on April 13,
and for several days
thereafter. Songkran,
the traditional Thai
new year, is when one
sprinkles water on
friends to bless them.
In Chiang Mai,
especially, it rapidly
degenerates into a
deluge of cascading
proportions.

BELOW: grounds of
Wat Chiang Man.

labourers – half a kilometre to the west and surrounded it with stout brick walls.

Less than a century after Chiang Mai's founding, however, Ayutthaya replaced Sukhothai as the capital of Siam. This new kingdom had its own expansionist dreams and ambitions, including designs on its neighbour to the north. For the next 400 years, there was fierce competition and sometimes open warfare. In the 16th century, Ayutthaya crushed an invasion by Chiang Mai, and Chiang Mai's power waned. To compound its troubles, the region was invaded in the early 1700s by the same Burmese enemy who were laying siege to Ayutthaya.

Although the Burmese were finally defeated, the people of Chiang Mai were so exhausted and discouraged by the constant conflict that they abandoned the city. It remained deserted until 1796, when the Burmese army was finally defeated; new nobles began restoring the city to its former prominence. It continued to enjoy autonomy from Bangkok, at least until the railway brought meddling central government administrators. In 1932, following the death of the last king of Chiang Mai, the north was finally fully incorporated into the Thai nation.

Old Chiang Mai

The commercial centres of downtown are along Thanon Thaphae, with numerous hotels, shops and guesthouses. Hotels have sprung up along Thanon Huay Kaew, which leads out to Doi Suthep. Red *songthaew* pick-ups may be hailed all over town; fares are a fixed 10 baht for most journeys. More expensive, but still quite cheap, *tuk-tuk* noisily carry passengers to any point around town. A few pedal *samlor* still offer a more leisurely way of travel.

The city's history began with **Wat Chiang Man** Ⓐ (open daily 9am–5pm), which translates as "power of the city". It was the first temple to be built by

Mangrai, who lived there during the construction of the city in 1296. Located in the northeast part of the old walled city, it is the oldest of Chiang Mai's 300-plus temples. Two ancient, venerated Buddha images are kept in the abbot's quarters and can be seen on request. The first image, Phra Satang Man, is a small 10-cm (4-inch) high crystal Buddha image taken by Mangrai to Chiang Mai from Lamphun, where it had reputedly resided for 600 years. Apart from a short sojourn in Ayutthaya, the image has remained in Chiang Mai ever since. On Songkran in April, it is paraded through the streets.

The second image, a stone Phra Sila Buddha in bas-relief, is believed to have originated in India around the 8th century. Both statues are said to possess the power to bring rain and to protect the city from fire. The only other important structure in Wat Chiang Man is Chang Lom, a 15th-century square *chedi*, buttressed by rows of stucco elephants.

Imperiously positioned at the head of the old city's principal east-west thoroughfare is **Wat Phra Singh ❸** (open daily 8am–6pm), Chiang Mai's most important temple and also its largest. Founded in 1345, it dominates the quiet heart of the old, walled city, near the western gate of Suan Dok. Wat Phra Singh is noted for three monuments: a library, chedi and the Viharn Lai Kham. The magnificent Lanna-style wooden library, on the right side of the compound, is raised on a high base decorated with lovely stucco angels. Behind the main viharn, built in 1925, is a beautiful wooden *bot,* and behind this, a chedi built by King Pha Yu in 1345 to hold the ashes of his father. Wat Phra Singh's most beautiful building is the small Phra Viharn Lai Kham, to the left of the bot. Of all of Chiang Mai's temple buildings, it is perhaps the most outstanding. Built rather late in the Lanna period, in 1811, the wooden building's front wall is decorated

Map,
page 227

Carved and gilded door, Wat Phra Singh.

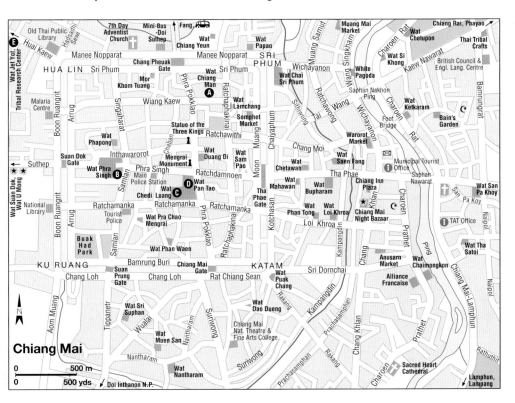

in goldleaf flowers on a red lacquer background. Intricately carved wooden window frames accent the doors. The interior walls of the Viharn Lai Kham are decorated with murals commissioned by Chao Thammalangka, who ruled over Chiang Mai between 1813 and 1821. Although focusing on the Buddhist stories of Prince Sang Thong (north wall) and the *Tale of the Heavenly Phoenix* (south wall), they also record in fascinating detail aspects of early 19th-century Lanna society and exhibit clear indications of persistent Burmese cultural influence.

Calamity is associated with **Wat Chedi Luang ⓒ** (open daily 8am–6pm), built in 1401 to the east of Wat Phra Singh. A century and a half later, a violent earthquake shook its then 90-metre (295-ft) high pagoda, reducing its height to 42 metres (140 ft). Its superstructure was never rebuilt, but the base and reliquary have been impressively restored. Even in its damaged state, the colossal monument is majestic. For 84 years the Emerald Buddha, now in Bangkok, was housed in this wat before being moved to Vientiane. King Mangrai was reportedly killed nearby by an untimely bolt of lightning. Close to the wat's entrance stands an ancient, tall gum tree. When it falls, says a legend, so will the city. As if serving as counterbalance, the *lak muang,* or city boundary stone, in which the spirit of the city is said to reside, stands near its base. The viharn of **Wat Pan Tao ⓓ** (open daily 8am–6pm), adjacent to Wat Chedi Luang, formerly a palace, is a masterpiece of wooden construction. Its doorway is crowned by a beautiful Lanna peacock framed by *naga,* or mythical serpents.

BELOW: chedi of Wat Suan Dok hold ashes of Chiang Mai's royal family.

Located 1 km (½ mile) northwest of the city walls, **Wat Jet Yot ⓔ** (open daily 8am–6pm; no fee) was completed by King Trailokaraja in 1455. As its name "Seven Spires" suggests, it is a replica of the Mahabodhi Temple in India's Bodhgaya, where Buddha gained enlightenment while spending seven weeks in its

gardens. The beautiful stucco angels that decorate its walls are said to bear faces of Trailokaraja's own family. Its similarity to a temple in Burma's then-capital of Pagan did not stop the invading Burmese from severely damaging it in 1566.

One of the most impressive city temple complexes is **Wat Suan Dok G** (open daily 8am–6pm), 1 km (½ mile) west of the western wall gate. At its northwest corner are whitewashed chedi containing the ashes of Chiang Mai's royal family; the huge central chedi is said to hold eight relics of Buddha. A short way out of town to the west, towards Doi Suthep, is 15th-century **Wat U Mong**, with its honeycomb of underground cells used for meditation. Lying amidst beautiful teak trees, the restored site is one of many quiet spots still left in Chiang Mai.

Beyond the old city

A steep series of hairpin curves rise up the flanks of **Doi Suthep G** – 15 km (9 miles) northwest of the city – to Chiang Mai's best-loved temple, **Wat Phra That Doi Suthep** (open daily 8am–6pm). The site was selected in the mid 1300s by an elephant that was turned loose with a Buddha relic strapped to its back. It climbed half-way up the mountain, then stopped and would climb no more. Doi Suthep was built at the spot where it halted.

The ascending road passes the entrance to the Huay Kaew Falls, where a minibus goes to the top. The scenery en route is spectacular, with the road winding its way to a large car park beneath Wat Phra That Doi Suthep. Seven-headed naga undulate down the balustrade of a 290-step stairway that leads from the car park to the temple. For the weary, a funicular makes the same ascent for a few baht. From Wat Phra That Doi Suthep, Chiang Mai is spread out below at one's feet.

From the upper terrace, a few more steps lead through the courtyard of the temple itself. In the late afternoon light, there are few sights more stunning than that which greet one at the final step. Emerging from cloisters decorated with murals depicting scenes from the Buddha's life, one's eyes rise to the summit of a 24-metre (80-ft) high gilded chedi, partially shaded by gilded bronze parasols. The chedi is surrounded by an iron fence with pickets culminating in praying *thewada,* or angels. Appearing in the east and west ends of the compound are two viharn. At dawn, the eastern one shelters chanting nuns in white robes. At sunset, the one on the west houses robed monks chanting their prayers.

From the parking area of Wat Doi Suthep, a road ascends 5 km (3 miles) to **Phuphing Palace H** (gardens only open Fri–Sun and holidays 8.30am–4pm when the royal family is absent; tel: 0 5321 9932; admission fee). Constructed in 1972 as the winter residence of the royal family, the palace, at 1,300 metres (4,265 ft) elevation, has audience halls, guest houses, dining rooms, kitchens and official suites. A highlight is its beautiful and well-tended gardens. The palace also serves as headquarters for the royal family's agricultural and medical projects for the benefit of the hill tribes and nearby villages.

Commercialised hill tribes

From the palace entrance, the road continues through pine forests to the commercialised Hmong hill-tribe village of **Doi Pui**. The village has been on the tourist track

Maps on pages 227 & 231

The architecture of Wat Phra That Doi Suthep is considered to be very representative of Lanna culture.

BELOW: covered children.

TIP

The area around
Chiang Mai is perhaps
best visited during
winter, late November
through early
February, when it is
abloom with an
astounding variety
of beautiful flowers.
Each February the
annual Flower Festival
fills the streets with
floral parades.

BELOW: umbrellas
made in the north
are famous.

for some time, but recent improvements have brought material benefits to its inhabitants, including a paved street lined with souvenir stands. Once subsistence farmers, the tribespeople have learned that visitors come bearing gifts, and a camera automatically triggers a hand extended for a donation. Hmong are itinerant farmers here, and in Burma and Laos. They once depended upon opium cultivation for their livelihoods; despite government efforts to steer them towards more socially acceptable crops, many still cultivate patches deep in the hills.

An interesting insight into opium farming is provided by Doi Pui's Opium Museum, which describes in detail the process of cultivation and harvest. For those who lack the time to go deeper into the northern hills, this Hmong village offers an example of hill-tribe life, though one doubts it retains much of its original personality.

Once an agricultural region, the **Mae Sa Valley** ❶ cultivates a new money-earner: tourism. Waterfalls, working elephant camps, butterfly farms, orchid nurseries and a charming private museum called Mae Sa House Collection (with prehistoric artefacts and Sukhothai ceramics, among many things) vie for the visitor's attention. The valley also has quiet resorts along its river.

North of Chiang Mai

To reach the northern town of Fang, take Route 107 north from Chiang Mai (beginning at Chang Phuak Gate) towards Chiang Dao. The road passes through rice fields and small villages, then begins to climb past Mae Taeng into the Mae Ping Gorge, which forms the southern end of the Chiang Dao Valley. Ahead, on the left as one follows the river's right bank through scenic countryside, is the massive outline of Chiang Dao mountain.

Map,
page 231

At the 56-km marker is the **Taeng-Dao Elephant Training Centre** (open daily 8am–5pm; tel: 0 5329 8553; admission fee), on the bank of the Ping River. Twice daily, a line of elephants walk into the Ping River to be bathed by *mahout* for the amusement of tourists, who reward the baby elephants with bananas. The elephants then move to a dusty arena to demonstrate how to make huge logs seem like toothpicks, picking them up or dragging them with great ease across the teak-shaded open space. After the show, one can take a short elephant ride, and then hire a small bamboo raft for a 45-minute trip down the Ping River.

About 60 km (40 miles) from Chiang Mai on Route 107, a dirt road branches left and goes to **Doi Chiang Dao** , which at 2,186 metres (7,175 ft) is Thailand's third-highest peak. A jeep or a trail bike is needed to negotiate this 9-km (6-mile) long track, which leads to the Hmong village of Pakkia up the mountain. Entry to the sanctuary is restricted and permission must be obtained from the wildlife head-quarters near Tham Pha Plong Monastic Centre at the foot of the mountain.

Elephant training.

The government's agricultural aid on Doi Chiang Dao is aimed at eradicating opium cultivation. From the government station here, officials trek out to assist hill tribes living on the slopes of Doi Chiang Dao and on the neighbouring mountains. At the nearby nursery, horticulturists experiment with new strains of tea that are gradually being introduced throughout the region.

Further north, Route 107 enters the town of **Chiang Dao** , located 70 km (45 miles) from Chiang Mai. Chiang Dao is a quiet wooden town supplying surrounding villages. At the far end of town, a simple road leads off west and to the left for 5 km (3 miles) to caves at **Tham Chiang Dao**. Guides with lanterns lead visitors deep into high caverns containing Buddha statues. Further down in a deeper section of the cave is a large, reclining limestone Buddha. ❑

BELOW: April's Songkran festival in Chiang Mai.

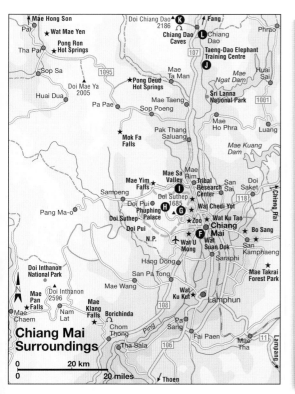

Chiang Mai
Surroundings

CHIANG RAI AND THE GOLDEN TRIANGLE

Map, page 216

Just the mention of "Golden Triangle" suggests uncertain frontiers and illicit smuggling. And, indeed, both are found here. But the area north of Chiang Rai offers escapes for the adventurous

Like other cities of the north, Chiang Rai has undergone rapid development, not only in the town itself but also in the surrounding hills where holiday homes for affluent Thais are springing up. Indeed, for travellers seeking the exclusively historical, Chiang Rai has little of its rich past extant. Capital of Thailand's northernmost province, Chiang Rai lies only about 65 km (40 miles) to the east of Fang. But for most visitors the trip to Chiang Rai begins in Chiang Mai, the focal point for the northern part of the country.

From Chiang Mai

Out of Chiang Mai, Route 107 heads due north past Chiang Dao to **Fang ❽**, located 150 km (100 miles) from Chiang Mai. Fang is another town where development has dulled a reputation for wildness. Established by King Mangrai in the late 1260s, Fang was levelled by the Burmese in the early 1800s and remained uninhabited until the 1880s. During the 1950s, the district witnessed a "black-gold rush" following a minor discovery of crude oil. Production never matched expectations, but "nodding donkey" pumps still groan and grind in the fields to the west of the town. Fang enjoys a reputation for *yaa baa* (amphetamine) smugglers, although nothing in its seemingly benign appearance would suggest as much.

LEFT: ferry on the Mekong.
BELOW: opium poppy.

Dressed in distinctively embroidered clothing, Mien hill tribes live in the mountains east of Fang. The women wear black hats decorated with red or magenta woollen pompoms, while babies carried on their mothers' backs sport little embroidered caps. Young girls may spend an entire year embroidering flowing trousers for their weddings. The government has worked extensively with the Mien, promoting crops as substitutes for the more lucrative opium.

Some 40 km (25 miles) west of Fang is **Doi Angkhang**, which at 1,300 metres (4,625 ft) has nice year-round temperate climate (with temperatures that can become downright freezing in winter). The agricultural station here, supported by the Thai king, specialises in the research of temperate fruit trees, vegetables, herbs and flowers. A few hill tribe communities also make their home in the mountain slopes.

A few kilometres south of Fang, Route 109 cuts east towards Chiang Rai. North from Fang, a rough road leads 25 km (15 miles) to **Thaton ❾**, on the banks of the Mae Kok. Here, rent a boat for an exciting 3-hour journey down the Kok to Chiang Rai. It is now also easy to continue north to the hill town of **Mae Salong ❿**.

The road is dusty but wide and has been paved since 1991. It swiftly climbs a ridge along the Burmese bor-

Northern Akha child.

der, emerging at a small town clinging to the hillsides. At first, it seems one has taken a wrong turn and ended up in a Chinese village. The walls of the houses are decorated by red banners covered in gold Chinese characters; everyone speaks Chinese, while only the young speak Thai.

It quickly becomes apparent that these, too, are the descendants of Guomintang soldiers who were given refuge in Thailand. Unfortunately, many of them soon became involved in the opium trade and and did not convert to other cash crops until quite recently, following conflict with the Thai army. Many of the inhabitants now tend tea plantations and brew potent wines.

Of more recent vintage is Ban Thoet Thai, a few kilometres north. It was only in 1988 that the opium warlord Khun Sa was ousted from this mountain stronghold. A 13-km (8-mile) paved road leads to the village, allowing visits by outsiders. Beyond Thoet Thai lies Burma, and heavily armed soldiers man bunkers labelled with the unreassuring sign, "Tourist Security Post". The road east drops off the ridge, eventually entering the Chiang Rai Valley just above Mae Chan.

From Lampang to Chiang Rai

The standard routes to Chiang Rai are Route 1, which continues north from Lampang, or the highway, Route 118, that leads northeast from Chiang Mai via Doi Saket, cutting travel time by half over the older route via Lampang.

Route 1 twists around and over mountains on its way to Ngao, 80 km (50 miles) northeast of Lampang. At the highest point in the road, below twin rocky peaks, drivers usually stop – or if in a hurry, blow their horns – to pay respects to the *phi* (spirits) believed to inhabit the pass. Spirit houses, some simple, others as elaborate as small palaces, cluster along the side of the road.

BELOW: lush northern landscape.

Northwest of Lampang on the highway to Chiang Mai, between Km 28 and Km 29, the royally sponsored **Thai Elephant Conservation Centre ⓫** (tel: 0 5422 8035, open daily 9am–6pm; admission fee) celebrates the culture of the Asian elephant in Thailand with public shows as well as *mahout* training programmes. The thrice-daily elephant shows include a segment in which elephants play over-sized drums and other instruments in a musical ensemble. Elephant rides are also available. In addition, an elephant hospital treats sick or injured pachyderms from all over Thailand.

North of Lampang about 20km (15 miles) before Ngao, a left turn leads in less than 1 km (½ mile) to a small grove of teak trees, and a refreshment stand that marks the entrance to **Tham Pha Thai ⓬** (open daily 8am–6pm; admission fee), probably the most interesting cave in Thailand. Climb the 283 steps up the hill, then drop down into the huge arched entrance, above which stands a gleaming white *chedi*.

Inside the main cave is a large bronze Buddha, an object of great veneration judging from the number of garlands and candles. Most striking, however, is the colossal stalagmite rising like a white explosion from a sea of limestone. Often a young novice monk will lead visitors down into the cave and point out bizarre limestone formations, which, with a little imagination, can resemble a throne, a rabbit or a turtle. Within the cave, slithering green snakes wrap themselves around electric wires or coil up in crevices. The guide explains that these snakes are protected and have never bitten anyone. The 400-metre (440-yard) walk into the cave ends at a small mound of bat guano. Light streaks down from a jagged opening in the cave roof, silhouetting flying bats onto the cavern walls.

About 10 km (6 miles) before Ngao, on the left of Route 1, the Burmese-style

Cave entrance.

BELOW: carrying a load, and entrance of Tham Pha Thai.

Map:
e 216

GLE ◆ 235

Chong Kram exudes charm in the face of alarming decrepitude. The building is gradually becoming crooked as its supporting pillars sink into the mud. Route 1 continues through **Ngao** ⑬, another typical northern Thai town, and 50 km (30 miles) further north to **Phayao** ⑭. Although quite small and recently undistinguished, Phayao holds great interest for archaeologists, as the town was rebuilt in the 11th century on a more ancient site. Judging from the remains of a moat and eight city gates that enclose an area of about 2 sq km (1 sq mile), scholars believe the older site may predate the Bronze Age. **Wat Li**, on the left of the road, has a fine collection of terracotta Buddha heads from Phayao's own early, distinctive and unique school, which were unearthed in the surrounding fields and land near the *wat*.

The cultivation of opium was first introduced to northern Thailand in the late 1800s by hill-tribe people from southern China.

Between the lake and the road, leaving Phayao, sits **Wat Si Khom Kham**, considered by scholars to be the area's most important temple because of its 400-year-old, 16-metre (55-ft) high Buddha image inside a *viharn*. In a new *ubosot* on the edge of the lake, modern Thai artist Angkarn Kalayanapongsa has created a beautiful set of murals.

Chiang Rai

From Phayao, Route 1 continues north 100 km (65 miles) to the provincial capital of **Chiang Rai** ⑮, located in Thailand's northernmost province, at an elevation of about 580 metres (1,900 ft). King Mangrai, who also established Chiang Mai as a walled city, founded Chiang Rai in the late 1200s.

Legend claims that the king, then ruler of Chiang Saen, decided to conquer regions to the south after his favourite elephant ran away in a southerly direction. The search for the elephant led to the banks of the Kok River, where the king decided to build Chiang Rai. A much-venerated statue of King Mangrai stands in northeastern Chiang Rai, by a reconstructed stretch of the old city wall.

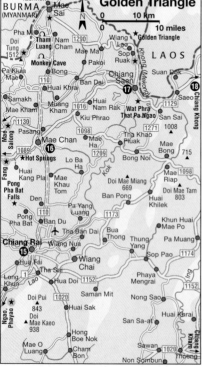

Like much of northern Thailand, lengthy wars with Burma inflicted suffering on the town and its residents; for much of the 1800s, it was almost uninhabited. In recent years, in large part due to both drug money and tourism, Chiang Rai has regained some of its prosperity, reflected in the existence of new hotels and shops.

Despite its exotic location, the city itself lacks both ambience and historic ruins. Near the busy streets are two of the town's most important temples: Wat Phra Singh and Wat Phra Kaew. Both share the distinction of having once sheltered famous images. The chedi and viharn at **Wat Phra Singh**, where legend holds that an important Buddha image was located, have been restored too many times to allow accurate dating, but documents suggest the 15th century or earlier.

Founded in the 13th century, **Wat Phra Kaew**, situated behind Wat Phra Singh, was the original residence of the Emerald Buddha that is now housed in Bangkok at the royal temple of the same name. (Apparently, the chedi in Chiang Rai was struck by lightning in the 1430s, revealing a simple stucco Buddha image, later discovered to be jadeite in nature.)

To the west of Wat Phra Kaew rises **Ngam Muang**. Atop the hill, **Wat Ngam Muang** is believed by local people to contain some remains of King Mangrai.

From Chiang Rai, Route 110 continues 30 km (20 miles) north to **Mae Chan** . Formerly a centre for silverwork, the tiny district town serves mostly as a trading post for Akha and Mien hill people.

Maps on pages 216 & 236

Northern border and Golden Triangle

The **Mekong River** – the name conjures up images of another time, another place, another world. It is the 12th-longest river in the world at 4,000 km (2,500 miles) in length, passing through six countries on its way to the South China Sea. It also defines much of the border between Thailand and Laos. Only during the last 15 years has the border opened to modern trade and travel.

The ancient capital of **Chiang Saen** nestles near where Burma, Laos and Thailand meet. This area, known as the Golden Triangle, has for years produced a considerable part of the world's opium supply. Thailand's contribution has dropped greatly in the past 25 years, but both Laos and especially Burma continue to produce opium in major quantities.

Scholars believe Chiang Saen was founded around the end of the 13th century and strongly fortified about 100 years later by a grandson of King Mangrai. The Burmese captured it in the 16th century, but Rama I of Thailand recaptured it in the early 1800s. Fearing history would repeat itself with another Burmese invasion, however, Rama I ordered the town abandoned. It remained deserted for nearly a century. In 1957, the revived town became a district seat.

Chiang Saen's lovely setting on the Mekong River strongly enhances the charm of its old temples. Moreover, it is one of the few ancient towns in Thailand to have retained most of its lovely old trees, giving it a rare claim to tranquillity. The remains of its stout wall and moat can clearly be seen at its perimeter, and ruins of ancient monuments are scattered everywhere, popping up when one least expects them.

Just west of town stands **Wat Pa Sak**, whose name derives from the use of 300 teak, or *sak*, trunks for the original enclosure. The temple's foundation was laid in 1295 during the reign of King Mangrai. Earlier Srivijaya and Dvaravati influences, along with the then-prominent Sukhothai style, are evident in the *that* (reliquary), the clothing worn by the deities and the walking Buddhas.

Located about one kilometre west of the town gate, **Wat Phra That Chom Kitti** occupies a hill commanding a good view of Chiang Saen. Chronicles suggest that the old *that,* with a leaning top, was first built around the 10th century and subsequently restored at least twice. Below this temple lies a ruined chedi in **Wat Chom Chang**. From here, a staircase leads further downhill and back towards the town.

Close to the main street stand **Wat Chedi Luang** and a branch of the **National Museum**. The 60-metre (200-ft) tall, 13th-century chedi stands out in style as well as size; its bricks rise from an octagonal base to a bell-shaped top. In the grounds of the museum, one can see a good assortment of bronze Buddhas and other Chiang Saen art.

The most scenic return trip from Chiang Saen to Chiang Rai is via water in a long-tail boat down the Mekong River, as far as **Chiang Khong** , a three-

BELOW: limestone landscape.

hour trip after the rainy season when the river is high. The river follows an approximately S-shaped course, first flowing southeast to the mouth of the Mae Nam Kok River, then curving north between beautiful hills and mountains, then finally south again for a thrilling 20 km (12 miles) down deep and narrow sections, through stomach-churning rapids and swirling eddies beneath steep, jungled mountain sides.

At Chiang Khong, the river widens slightly. Set on left-bank hills, the Laotian town of **Houei Sai** lies opposite the Chiang Khong district seat. Lao government officials still work in Fort Carnot, built by the French. A ferry boat carries visitors across the river to the customs post on the Lao side. Visas for Laos are now available on arrival in Houei Sai.

Heart of the Golden Triangle

Returning to Chiang Saen and heading north for around 9 km (6 miles) brings the visitor to the small town of **Sop Ruak**, which proudly promotes itself as the "Heart of the Golden Triangle". In recent years, the town has heavily cashed in on the wild mystique of the area that most Westerners hold, and now Sop Ruak is home to several high-quality resorts and hotels, which entice people to stay longer than they would have a few years ago. The main street of Sop Ruak is lined with souvenir shops that sell a variety of local textiles and plastic kitsch, as well as numerous food stalls and sit-down restaurants providing welcome refreshment to those passing through the town; the quality of culinary offerings is rather variable, however.

BELOW: a black giant squirrel.

In reality, the town of Sop Ruak has little to hold the traveller's attention, aside from the views of neighbouring Burma (Myanmar) and Laos. Worth a visit, though, is the impressive **Hall of Opium** (Moo 1, Ban Sop Ruak; open Tue–Sun 10am–3.30am; tel: 0 5378 4444; www.doitung.org), which is located opposite the **Anantara Resort and Spa** to the southwest of town. This huge museum houses multimedia displays relating to the history, cultivation and trade of the *Papaver somniferum* – the opium poppy from which heroin is extracted, and for which the area of the Golden Triangle is famous.

Several boat trips are currently available from Sop Ruak, including ferries to Chiang Saen and Chiang Khong, as well as round trips on the Mekong and Ruak rivers skirting the Burmese and Lao frontiers. Occasional trips depart for the long journey to China's province of Yunnan, but these are not yet regular.

Continuing north and east from Sop Ruak, the road finally reaches **Mae Sai**, the most northerly town in Thailand. This busy border town, with Tachilek clearly visible on the Burmese side of the small Sai River, has a real frontier feel to it. In the shops and stalls along the main streets, Burmese, Thai, Shan and hill-tribe traders sell a heady mix of gems, lacquerware and antiques – both new and old – along with imported whisky, cigarettes and medicinal herbs.

Visitors are usually allowed to cross the small bridge to Burma for up to three days, for a quick stroll around **Tachilek** – which, like Sop Ruak, really has little to offer except for the claim of visiting Burma – or for a longer journey as far as Kengtung, midway between Thailand and China. Frontier regulations between Thailand and Burma are prone to change, so check before crossing. And note that the bridge closes in the evening, so be sure not to be stranded on the wrong side of the river.

In the 1990s, the area around Tachilek was a site of the Burmese army's campaign against the Shan guerrilla movement, which was concentrated around here. As many as 3,000 refugees fled into Thailand near Mae Sai to escape the fighting. (Later in the year, the infamous drug warlord, Khun Sa, long the kingpin of the opium trade in the Golden Triangle, surrendered to the Burmese junta, only to take up residence in Rangoon.) The Shan are ethnically related to Thais and Laos, and have long had considerable autonomy from the Burmese government. Opium cultivation has financed the Shan independence movement against the Burmese government.

To the west of the main street, close to the border, there is a flight of steps ascending a small hill to **Wat Phra That Doi Wao**. This temple was purportedly constructed in memory of several thousand Burmese soldiers who died fighting members of Chiang Kai-shek's Guomintang army, which was fighting against Mao Zedong's communists for control of southern China, here in 1965. The temple grounds afford splendid views over Mae Sai and Burma.

About 6 km (4 miles) south of town, **Tham Luang** (Great Cave), on a turn-off to the west of Route 110 heading back to Chiang Rai, burrows for several kilometres into the hills. Gas lanterns are available for hire at the entrance. The first cavern is impressive in its size alone. Thereafter, a series of short, sometimes fairly restricting passages lead to caverns of varying magnitude, where the roof formations and crystalline deposits become more magnificent. ❏

Maps
on pages
216 & 236

BELOW: Lisu women in traditional attire.

MAE HONG SON

Map, page 216

Perhaps long the most ignored part of Thailand, Mae Hong Son's isolation leaves it feeling rather unfettered by modern contrivances. Still, people have lived here for over 10,000 years

Mae Hong Son

THAILAND

Bangkok

Secluded by jungle ridges and framed on the north and west by Burma, the Mae Hong Son area has benefited from years of benign neglect by the outside world. (Access was difficult until the mid 1960s, when a paved road opened up the town.) Mae Hong Son's years of human occupation, however, are rather lengthy. In a cave, an archaeologist found tools, and seeds from betel nut, cucumber and black pepper, all apparently cultivated by early people. Analysis dates these between 10,000 and 6,000 BC. Other items include cutting tools from around 7,000 BC.

To reach Mae Hong Son by road, head south from Chiang Mai on Route 108. Just before the 57-km marker, turn right and drive 10 km (7 miles) past the entrance of **Doi Inthanon National Park** ⓳ (open daily 8am–6pm; tel: 0 5331 1608; admission fee), a popular retreat named after its prime attraction, Doi Inthanon, the highest mountain in the country at 2,596 metres (8,517 ft). Girls rush out to visitors to sell bead necklaces, whilst cold beer and soft drinks are served in small shops along the river's edge, below Mae Klang Falls.

From the shops, walk up a bit to see this powerful cataract and its spectacular fusion of muddy brown water and white spray. Clearly marked footpaths branch into the rocky hills; one leads around a corner of boulders to a full view of a wider fall, Pakauna, which slides over its broad, craggy slopes for 120 metres (400 ft) like a liquid carpet.

The road continues to climb a further 25 km (16 miles) to the peak of **Doi Inthanon**, whose summit is dominated by an off-limits radar station. Another spectacular waterfall, Mae Ya, is in the southern part of the park, dropping more than 250 metres (820 ft).

The limestone mass of Doi Inthanon is a comparatively modest foothill in the southern extension of the Himalayan range, which stretches southeast from Yunnan in southern China. Although less than a giant, Doi Inthanon has a majesty of its own conveyed by its steep, forest-clad slopes and mist-enshrouded summit. Karen and Hmong tribespeople still live nearby in isolated villages but are slowly being relocated, as the mountain is now a national reserve. On its summit the ashes of Chiang Mai's last king are enshrined.

By making prior arrangements with park authorities in Chiang Mai, it is possible to take a 3- to 5-day hike on foot or by pony up the mountain. Several campsites afford simple accommodation for trekkers. During the climb, one can observe rare birds and enjoy nature under a broad canopy of trees.

At the 58-kilometre marker on Route 108, 1 km (½ mile) south of the park turn-off, is **Chom Thong** ⓴. The town's pride is the elegant **Wat Phra That Si Chom Thong**, where glints of subdued light accentuate a beautiful collection of bronze Buddhas. The

BELOW: Shan child.

monastery creaks with old age, as do the slumping boughs of trees scattered about its courtyard. The brilliantly gilded *chedi* dates from 1451, and the sanctuary only 50 years later.

A large cruciform *viharn* built in 1516 – deeply incised with a profusion of floral patterns entwined with birds and *naga* serpents – dominates this temple compound. Four standing Buddhas, clothed like celestial kings, flank the viharn. Although much of the decoration in the temple reflects the Burmese penchant for elaboration, the central Buddha image, with its protective naga, seems eminently Thai, and resembles the famed image at Wat Phra Singh in Chiang Mai. On either side of the viharn are enshrined miniature gold and silver Buddha images, some bejewelled and metallic, others carved of crystal.

Further south on Route 108 are many northern touches: rambling, stylised elephants carved on the backs of bullock carts; *lamyai* trees and green beanpatches; giant plaited baskets, in which farmers thresh harvested rice; and shady, thatched-roof *sala* dotting the extensive rice fields.

Hot ㉑, 90 km (50 miles) southwest of Chiang Mai on Route 108, once lay 15 km (9 miles) further south at the mouth of the Ping River, until the rising reservoir behind the Bhumibol Dam submerged it. Today, it has evolved into a fully fledged town that seems to have been there forever. Further south on Route 1012 lies the original site of ancient Hot. Cracked, rain-washed chedi dot the landscape – dignified relics from the time when Hot was part of the early kingdoms of the north. Excavations have unearthed gold jewellery, amulets and lively stucco carvings, which are now on display in the Chiang Mai Museum.

Route 1012 continues south to **Wang Luang**, a tiny village that earns its keep by selling dried fish caught in the reservoir created by Bhumibol Dam. Karen

TIP

A boat can be hired at Wang Luang for an hour's voyage among the islands at the estuary of the Ping River, and out onto the expanse of water at the upper end of the reservoir. Reflections of ruined chedi and strange, eroded cliffs enliven remote mountain scenes.

BELOW: falls at Mae Klang, Doi Inthanon National Park.

people have settled much of this area. Their necks hidden by a profusion of black beads, and their bodices covered with thick, coloured patchwork, Karen tribeswomen walk into the tiny town to buy provisions.

From Hot, Route 108 strikes out west across the Chaem River, following its right bank towards Mae Sariang. About 20 km (15 miles) from Hot, the road passes **Ob Luang Gorge**, sometimes referred to as Thailand's version of the Grand Canyon, though this requires a considerable stretch of the imagination. Stop at the sala for a look into the deep, ragged incisions in the rock.

The drive towards Mae Sariang is more exciting than the town itself. The road runs like a roller coaster over the mountains. Not even motorbikes can reach some of the small leaf-and-bamboo huts tucked away in these hills.

Hill-tribe farming

Most of the villages belong to the largest hill-tribe group in Thailand, the Skaw Karen, who have settled along the Thai-Burmese frontier as far south as Chumphon. In the moist valleys they plant wet rice on steep terraces. On the slopes, black tree stumps stand out like whiskers on a green background of rice sprouts; nomadic Karen burn away the forest to make clearings to plant new crops. This slash-and-burn technique has scarred the mountain sides and caused extensive erosion; today many Karen have taken to sedentary farming.

In places, the road skirts high banks of red earth. Fresh mounds of mud on the asphalt show that landslides are not uncommon – the steep banks cannot always hold back the run-off. A solution to this problem may be the pine tree. Though it is not a tree one normally associates with tropical Thailand, the pine is well suited to rebuilding the soil. Its roots form an extensive earth-holding network,

Because northern Thailand is on a bird migratory flyway, nearly 10 percent of the world's species can be seen here at some time during the year. The Chiang Mai area alone offers around 400 species.

BELOW: hill-tribe woman bottle-feeding cattle.

Map,
page 216

and its seeds are not easily destroyed by fire. Hemmed in by mountains, **Mae Sariang ㉒** itself lies 100 km (65 miles) west of Hot, at the point where Route 108 bends to the north. A few Burmese-style temples, a small, white mosque and a few Karen handicraft shops distinguish this small district administrative centre and border trading post.

Route 108 continues north on a rough track from Mae Sariang, through mountain scenery that is among the most breathtaking in Thailand, reaching Mae Hong Son 170 km (100 miles) later.

Mae Hong Son ㉓ lies in a valley between deep-green mountains, which accounts for its early-morning fogs. The forest valley is buttressed by mountains that separate Thailand from Burma. Mae Hong Son has for years been a destination for seekers of old-world serenity. (Nonetheless, like most of Thailand, it is gradually being developed, including major new hotels.) The presence of Karen, Hmong, Lawa, Shan, Lisu and Lahu, who, taken collectively, easily outnumber the ethnic Thais, adds intrigue to an ill-kept secret: Mae Hong Son is smack in the middle of border-smuggling routes.

A commanding view of the town of Mae Hong Son and the surrounding countryside is afforded from **Doi Kong Mu**, a hill that rises 250 metres (820 ft) above the town. At night, the two tall chedi of **Wat Phra That Doi Kong Mu** atop the hill light up like timid beacons of civilisation in this corner of Thailand. Erected in the 19th century, the wat reflects Burmese influences. A pond and a park at the centre form a core of beauty and peace that few other Thai towns possess. On the edge of the lake, across from a fitness park, are the intertwined temples of **Wat Chong Klang** and **Wat Chong Kum**. These Burmese-style temples, with their pristine, white chedi, look moving when reflected in the waters of the lake. ❑

Unusual chedi of Wat Chong Kum.

BELOW: street front, Mae Hong Son.

Map, page 216

THAILAND

Bangkok

BELOW: gilded images facing the four cardinal points, Wat Phumin.

NAN VALLEY

Untainted by tourism, and with some superb outdoor activities, the area around Nan was once the capital of a small kingdom which later formed part of the first Lanna empire

The Nan Valley may be Thailand's last great undiscovered tourist territory. It has lovely mountain scenery, the full complement of hill tribes, a new national park, and a friendly population not yet jaded by exposure to foreign travellers. The principal roads make for excellent mountain biking and motor-cycling, since they are sealed, hilly rather than mountainous, and not often disrupted by traffic. The drawback is that very few people speak English, many signs are not romanised, and there is barely any accommodation outside of Nan.

With its cement-block and egg-carton architecture, the town of **Nan** ❷ initially appears to be yet another nondescript upcountry town, with a population of around 25,000. A stroll or spin beyond the downtown area, however, will soon reveal plenty of old wooden houses, which come in three upraised styles. There are exhibits of the three styles at the local branch of the **National Museum** (open Wed–Sun 9am–4pm; admission fee), which should be a first stop on any tour. Located in the former airy residence of the last two Nan princes, the museum also provides introductions to tribes, textiles, crafts and history. The 300-year-old black elephant tusk on display is reputed to have magical powers.

The first Nan dynasty emerged in the mid 1300s. By the end of the 14th century, Nan was among ten Thai-Lao states that joined to form the first Lanna

empire. The town was later conquered by the Burmese and the next few hundred years were tumultuous, but in 1788 Nan finally allied with the Rattanakosin, or Bangkok, kingdom. Because Nan's rulers fully cooperated in the drive by Bangkok's King Chulalongkorn to unite a crazy quilt of vassal states into a modern nation, the province was allowed to retain its special status as a semi-independent principality until the death of the last Nan prince in 1931.

The allegiances and influences of the past 600 years are evident in Nan temples, which display the styles of Lanna, Sukhothai, northern and southern Laos, the Thai Lu people, and combinations thereof. Styles of the Sukhothai period are prominent at **Wat Chang Kham**, which is across the street from the museum and located within the old city walls. The elephants, seven on each side, supporting the second tier of the square *chedi* are a Sukhothai motif. The standing Buddhas in the 15th-century *viharn* are also Sukhothai style and very common in Laos. The *wat* library, with its high ceiling, was at one time the largest in Thailand, although it is now empty.

Next door to the National Museum is the even older **Wat Hua Khuang** with a wooden verandah in the Luang Prabang (that is, northern Lao) style. Although it's often closed, visitors may be lucky to catch the weekend painter who for years has been restoring the murals. The town's most famous murals, however, are found a short walk south at **Wat Phumin**, which was first constructed in 1596. The building in question has a highly unusual cruciform layout that combines viharn and *bot*. If the great carved doors of the viharn wing are fully open, make sure to peek behind them to see the murals that decorate this front wall: there are rowing boats loaded with bearded foreigners, who smoke pipes and wear naval caps, among them a few heavily dressed *farang* (European) women,

From the 1960s to the 1980s, Nan Valley was a stronghold of communist insurgents, who filtered through the border with Laos. Later, Thai communists took advantage of government amnesties.

BELOW: dragon-boat race in Nan, and mural detail, Wat Phumin.

Map, page 216

TIP

Nan's best shop for local crafts is run by the Thai Payap Development Association. This co-operative exports to North America and Europe; the quality of textiles is superior. The crafts are made by Hmong, Mien, Htin and Khmu people.

BELOW: Sao Din.
RIGHT: Akha tribeswoman.

and there's a great three-masted sailing ship. The murals depict an episode from the *Jataka Tales*, the chronicle of Buddha's previous incarnations. The scenes of Asian characters engaged in war, torture and all-around mayhem on the other walls convey one hellish life. Since the murals were painted in the late 19th-century, shortly after the cession to the French, it has recently been proposed that the murals may also have intended to express how Nan people regarded their long history of betrayals and abandonment.

Wat Phra That Chae Haeng is located on a hill about 3 km (2 miles) south-east of town and across the Nan River – where the large "dragon boats" race for a week every autumn. You'll recognise the wat by the lengthy *nagas* snaking down the hill in greeting. The square gilded chedi is Lao-style. The bot, how-ever, has many Thai Lu influences, such as the sweeping, five-layered wooden roof, the low ceilings and the dog-like dragons guarding the entry. A minority, but not a hill tribe, Thai Lu are ethnic Thai people that immigrated to the Nan Valley about 150 years ago. On the return trip to town, turn left before crossing the river and watch how thick, rough *saa* paper is made from mulberry bark in a factory that resembles someone's backyard.

One can arrange one- to three-day hill treks in Nan, but it's also easy to visit tribal (and Thai) villages on the approximately 80-km (50-mile) journey to **Doi Phu Kha National Park ㉕** (open daily 8am–6pm; tel: 0 5470 1000; admis-sion fee). Few of the tribal villages are long standing. During the insurgency some decades ago, many people were relocated from the uplands to remove them from communist temptations. They were joined by tribal people fleeing war-torn Laos. After a decade or more in refugee camps, they have been dis-persed to new villages throughout the province.

Trails meander through tribal villages. Like most of the forests that visitors will spy elsewhere in Nan, these here are the fruit of reforestation projects. The national park does have some undisturbed areas, but they are not served by trails. Park rangers or US Peace Corps vol-unteers can direct you to some pretty spots, such as the 1300-metre (4,300 ft) peak of Don Khao and Ton Tong waterfall. Continue for about 20 km (12 miles) along Route 1256, the windy, steep road running east of park headquarters, and you'll reach the Htin village of Ban Bor Kleua, where the salt wells still function.

On the return trip to Nan town, take the eastern branch of Route 1080, which sprouts off south of the town of Pua. About 6 km (4 miles) along the way is **Ban Pa Klang**, a veritable town of Hmong, Htin and Mien people. Mien make and sell silver jewellery here. The views of majestic mountains along this route are stun-ning, though it's difficult to pick out **Doi Phu Kha**, the province's highest at 1,985 metres (6,512 ft).

As for the area south of Nan, the top sights are the eerie Hom Chom and **Sao Din** rock pillars. Carved by the wind, these bare, pointed projectiles form desolate canyons. Nan, both the town and the province, are usu-ally entered from the southwest via Route 101, a sooth-ing ride through tobacco, cotton and rice fields and gently rolling, reforested hills.

The next substantial town south is **Phrae ㉖**, capital of the like-named province. ❑

CRAFTS AND CLOTHING OF THE HILL TRIBES

Each hill tribe of Thailand has its own customs, dress, language and spiritual beliefs that are reflected in the crafts they produce.

Textiles and silver jewelry play a very important role in the ceremonial activities of Thailand's hill-tribe communities. Hill-tribe women are defined by what they wear, and their choice of clothing and adornment can reveal not only what tribe they are from, but also their social status, age and even where their home town is located. However, the way of life of Thailand's hill-tribe people is changing as they are slowly assimilated into mainstream Thai society, abandoning many features of their traditional culture. This may be sad for visitors in search of traditional hill-tribe culture, but the process is inevitable and has distinct advantages for these ethnic minorities, since they can now benefit from educational opportunities and medical facilities.

THE CRAFTS INDUSTRY

Hill-tribe craft items started to be made commercially in the mid-1970s when small craft centres were set up in refugee camps. Authentic items are now rare and expensive, but good quality, modern crafts can be found in craft shops.

◁ **HMONG EMBROIDERY**
Women from the Hmong hill tribe used to hand-weave cloth, but today they use ready-made fabrics for their intricately embroidered clothing. The Hmong are skilled in making indigo-dyed batik which is then embroidered with appliquéd layers of geometrically-shaped fabric to make up their skirts.

BRASS NECK COILS▷
Padaung women wear brass coils around their arms, legs and necks. The coils compress the collarbone and upper rib cage and gives the impression that the neck has stretched. Removal of the coils is not dangerous.

▽ **LISU TEXTILES**
Lisu women make distinctive clothing. In the past, the cloth was woven by hand but the Lisu now use machine-made material that they run up on sewing machines.

AKHA COTTONS

Women of the Akha hill tribe spin cotton into thread with a hand spindle, then weave it on a foot-treadle loom. The cloth is dyed indigo and is then appliquéd and decorated with shells, seeds, silver or buttons and made into clothing for the family. The men make a variety of baskets and other items from wood, bamboo and rattan.

LISU CEREMONIAL WEAR ▷

On special occasions, Lisu men wear turbans and the women don large amounts of hand-crafted silver jewelry, chunky necklaces and colourful tunics with silver buttons. Men of the tribe are skilled blacksmiths. The sale of crafts means they no longer need to grow opium poppies to make a living.

▽ **AKHA HEADDRESS**
Married Akha women are famous for their head-dresses decorated with silver coins, which they wear all the time. Unmarried women from the tribe attach small gourds to their head-dresses.

HOW THE KAREN MAKE *IKAT*

The White Karen tribe (above) produce striped warp *ikat* textiles woven on back-strap looms. Ikat is a technique used to pattern cloth that involves the binding of the cloth with fibre or strips of material, so in places it becomes resistant to dyeing. Before the cloth is dyed, the weft (yarns woven across the width of the fabric) or the warp (lengthwise yarns) is pulled tightly over a frame and then threads are bound tightly together singly or in bunches. The cloth is then dyed several times using different colours. As a result, complex and beautiful patterns are built up with soft, watery edges on the parts of the cloth not completely covered by the binding materials.

The dyeing process is complex, with the dominant colour of the ikat dyed first. Cotton yarns are the most suitable for making warp ikat, and the dyes used to produce these textiles are natural dyes that are easily absorbed by cotton. The most popular colours for warp ikat are indigo and red. Weft ikats, usually made from silk, use mainly yellow dyes (made from turmeric), diluted indigos and a deep crimson red extracted from the lac insect. Orange, green and purple are created by an overdyeing process.

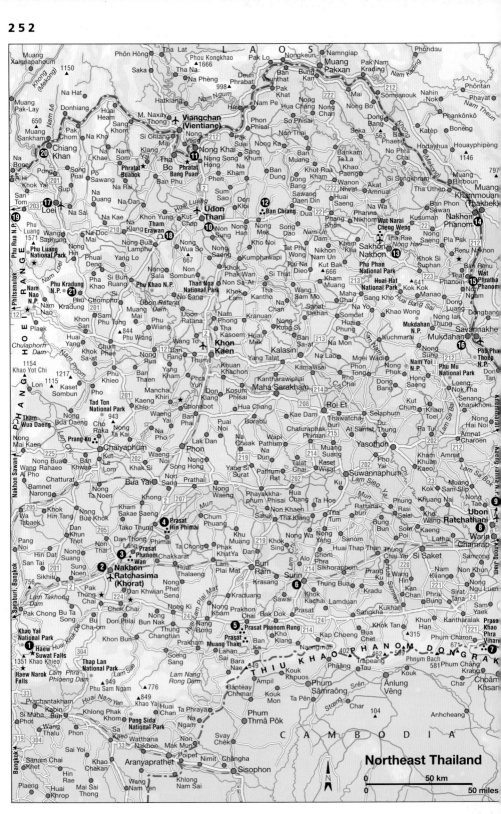

Northeast Thailand

THE NORTHEAST

The days of a dirt-poor, arid northeast are in the past. And its historical ruins are among Thailand's most impressive

The northeast does not usually figure prominently on anybody's list of travel destinations in Thailand. This is a pity, for the northeast is a treasure trove of ancient monuments. Parts of the region were ruled by the Khmers, during the great period when they built Angkor Wat and colonised large areas of northeastern Thailand, building temples in key cities. Outside of Angkor itself, the northeast is certainly the best place in Asia to view the remains of the Khmer culture.

The northeast of Thailand is a high plateau upon which about one-third of the country's population lives. Many northeasterners' ancestors migrated from Laos across the great Mekong River, which forms the natural border between Laos and Thailand. Today, Thais of the northeast retain the Lao quality of sweet passivity in the face of adversity. The quality is useful, for the northeast is not always an easy place to live. The soil is often thin and infertile, there is either not enough rain, or too much, and the Mekong can be unforgiving when it floods – many northeasterners go to Bangkok, filling unskilled jobs in the capital. Small wonder that the northeast also has a tradition of dissident politicians whose demands for social reform have been louder than those from other parts of the country.

The basic agricultural products of the northeast are poor-soil staples like cotton and tapioca. Mulberry trees, too, are grown to feed the worms that spin silk. In the late 1950s, the Friendship Highway, a joint Thai-American undertaking, opened the region. In the 1960s, large American military bases during the Vietnam War pumped money into the region and made boom-towns out of places like Nakhon Ratchasima (also called Khorat), Udon Thani and Ubon Ratchathani. In 1994, the first road bridge from Thailand into Laos, crossing the Mekong River at Nong Khai, opened.

For several years now, there has been a fairly successful effort to develop the northeast. Numerous development projects have been initiated by the royal family and the government to improve production, processing and transport for agricultural products.

Because the northeast isn't on the agenda of most foreign travellers, this reason alone, perhaps, is the major lure of the region. ❏

PRECEDING PAGES: sorting out raw silk, a product of Khorat, that has been spun.

KHORAT PLATEAU

With Cambodia to the south, it's not surprising that northeastern Thailand retains a Khmer texture to its history, whether in the architecture of ancient sanctuaries or in old tales

Map, page 252

The good roads of northeast Thailand – an area called *Isaan* by the Thais – invite travel by car, which undoubtedly is the best way to see the many out-of-the-way sights in this part of the country.

The Friendship Highway, or Route 2, the main road through the northeast, begins about 100 km (60 miles) from Bangkok, branching off Route 1 just before the town of **Saraburi**. About 20 km (15 miles) after the Saraburi turn-off on Route 2, a dirt road on the right leads to an experimental farm run by the Kasetsart Agricultural University of Bangkok, and then beyond to **Phra Ngam** (Beautiful Buddha Image), a cave where a Dvaravati-era image may be seen. There are numerous other caves nearby, many as yet unexplored.

Another 15 km (10 miles) leads to **Muaklek**. Once known mainly for malaria, Muaklek has been transformed from an unhealthy jungle into dairy land that features a small arboretum garden, where a wonderful variety of roses bloom alongside a stream.

About 50 km (30 miles) east of Saraburi is **Wat Teppitakpunnaram**, where a monumental white Buddha sits on a green mountain, like an alabaster relic. The countryside in this area belongs to **Khao Yai National Park ❶** (open daily 8am–6pm; tel: 0 3731 9002; admission fee), hidden 40 km (25 miles) to the south (*see Outside of Bangkok, page 177*).

LEFT: Prasat Hin Phimai.
BELOW: young Phimai girl.

Route 2 continues northeast up the Khorat Plateau, passing the reservoir of **Lam Takhong**. Soon the blue lake disappears and scrub brush, typical of the drier areas of the northeast, begins to dominate the scenery. About 150 km (100 miles) from Saraburi is the provincial capital of **Khorat**, now officially called **Nakhon Ratchasima ❷**. The richest and largest city in the northeast, and once an air base for American bombers during the Vietnam War, Nakhon Ratchasima now serves as a trade, communications and military centre for the entire northeast region. It is also the capital of the most densely populated upcountry province in Thailand, with over 1.5 million residents.

Although a busy and important commercial centre, Nakhon Ratchasima has not forgotten its past. A statue of national heroine Khunying Mo (Thao Suranari) presides over the town square and the whitewashed old city wall, which dates from around the 10th century. Khunying Mo was the wife of an assistant provincial governor in the early 19th century, when Prince Anou of Vientiane led his army to Khorat.

After taking the city, the prince threatened to enslave its residents. Khunying Mo rallied the women of Khorat, who enticed many of the Laotian soldiers to a drunken revelry and then killed them whilst they slept. Prince Anou, who meanwhile had gone to attack Saraburi, was forced to withdraw his depleted forces to

Vientiane, to the north. Outside the walls and moat is the offbeat **Wat Sala Loi**, erected in 1973 in the shape of a Chinese junk. The symbolism is clear – it will convey the faithful believer of Buddha to *nirvana*.

Silk is one of the region's most important industries. To visit a nearby silk production centre, take Route 304 south towards Kabinburi. After 30 km (20 miles) is the town of **Pak Thong Chai**, where the Jim Thompson silk company has established a weaving cooperative to produce Thai silk. It is, in fact, the world's largest hand-woven silk enterprise.

There are 1,000-plus Khmer ruins in Thailand, most of them in the northeast. There has been a concerted effort since the 1920s to restore many of them.

Excursions from Nakhon Ratchasima

The main attractions outside Nakhon Ratchasima are two sites created nine centuries ago by Khmer architects, both northeast of town on Route 2.

The peaceful monastery of **Prasat Phanom Wan** ❸ (open daily 8am–6pm) has heavy stone galleries, revealing the Khmer penchant for false windows with stone mullions, a method adopted to compensate for the soft stone. Elaborate zig-zag patterns cover the carved stones.

An uncommon stillness pervades this 11th-century retreat, broken only by the footsteps of resident monks. Unlike the majority of Khmer ruins, this one contains an active temple. Behind its well-preserved vaulted entrance, the original, dark sanctuary is filled with many more recent Buddha images of different styles, most of them covered with patches of gold leaf. Full-grown trees sprout from the oldest chambers. The presence of older monks in residence reminds visitors that donations are needed to help with the upkeep of the site.

BELOW: differing Buddha styles, Prasat Phanom Wan.

Further north are the ruins of **Prasat Hin Phimai** ❹ (open daily 8am–6pm; tel: 0 4447 1167; admission fee), 50 km (30 miles) from Nakhon Ratchasima

on the Mae Nam Mun, a tributary of the Mekong. Renovated with the help of the same expert who restored Angkor Wat in nearby Cambodia, it has been suggested that Phimai may have been a prototype for Angkor Wat itself.

Map, page 252

The last of the great Angkor monarchs, King Jayavarman VII, who replaced Hinduism with Mahayana Buddhism as the official religion, could easily travel from his palace along a 240-km (150-mile) road to Phimai, which was at the western extent of his expanding kingdom. A string of 112 rest houses was constructed along the route to shelter pilgrims and government officials making the long journey to Phimai. During the king's reign (AD 1181–1201), Phimai prospered within a walled rectangular area of 1,000 by 560 metres (3,300 by 1,840 ft), on an artificial island created by linking the Mun River and one of its tributaries via a canal. There were four entrances, with serpents, or *naga,* guarding each. The primary entrance faces south. Like the shrines at Angkor, the monuments at Phimai were never inhabited. Shops, libraries and houses were built of wood, and therefore have disintegrated centuries ago.

However, the old city gate, most likely the main entrance to the sanctuary, still stands at the end of Phimai's present main street. Near the bridge over the Mae Nam Mun, the government maintains an open-air museum displaying some of the more beautifully carved lintels and statues found in the area.

Detail from Prasat Hin Phimai.

Before leaving Phimai, visit Sai Ngam, or "Beautiful Banyan Tree", a kilometre east of the temple near an irrigation reservoir. It has an umbrella of dense leaves and roots that locals revere as a shelter for special spirits, and it is claimed to be the largest banyan tree in the world.

From Phimai, one can continue north on Route 2 to **Khon Kaen** and directly to the Mekong River town of Nong Khai. But for a better look at the rural north-

BELOW: old ruins at Phimai.

Khmer Legacy

Between the 10th and 14th centuries AD, a large part of mainland Southeast Asia, from the Mekong Delta in the east to around Phetchburi in the west, lay under the control of the Khmer Empire. Administered at the height of its power by god-kings, the empire's capital at Angkor was connected to the outlying reaches of the empire by a system of highways and religio-political strongpoints such as Prasat Khao Phra Viharn, Wat Phu, Phanom Rung, and Phimai.

By the mid-19th century, when the frontiers of present-day Indochina were effectively fixed by French colonialism, the Khmer Empire had long since disappeared, leaving Cambodia much reduced in size. It is true that the crowning glory of the Khmer past, Angkor Wat, still lay within Cambodia's confines, as did the magnificent "lofty sanctuary" of Phra Viharn, albeit only just. Yet many other symbolic relics of the Khmer past now lay outside Cambodia, most notably Wat Phu in southern Laos, and a

series of magnificent sites across Thailand's Tung Kula Rong Hai, the "Weeping Plain" of the lower Northeast.

Thailand has long valued these unique historic treasures, yet only very recently have concerted efforts been made to preserve and promote them. Over the past three decades, several of the most important sites have been painstakingly and successfully restored by the government's Department of Fine Arts. Moreover, the Tourism Authority of Thailand has publicised a "Khmer Culture Trail" in lower Isaan which offers the visitor an unparalleled opportunity to explore the glories of the Khmer past.

Khorat and Buriram provinces host the major Khmer complexes: Prasat Hin Phimai, Prasat Phanom Rung and Prasat Muang Tam. All three have been carefully restored, though Phanom Rung is perhaps today the most impressive. Like Angkor Wat itself, these temples were all originally constructed as Hindu temples, dedicated to Vishnu and Shiva, and as such the ruins demonstrate, particularly in their carvings, a deistic diversity and Indic sensuality not evident in more recent, Buddhist structures. It was under Jayavarman VII that Hinduism was replaced by Buddhism, and the temples were converted to *wat*. Until today, their significance to Thai Buddhists remains strong, weakened neither by memories of foreign powers on what is now Thai soil nor by the slightly unfamiliar iconography. Phanom Rung is indeed a regular and important place of Buddhist pilgrimage.

Even as far away as Lopburi, Khmer influence is easily recognisable in the three ruined *prang* of Phra Prang Sam Yot, which are often attributed to Jayavarman VII. And in the vicinity of Phanom Rung are various Khmer *kuti*, or meditation retreats, as well as several other unrestored temple complexes, languishing in the forests and undergrowth. All bear testimony to the fact that this area, far from being an outpost of the Khmer empire, was very much in its heartland. Indeed, as recently as 1976, Democratic Kampuchea's despotic regime was staking a claim to the region, promising to "liberate" lost Khmer territories in Thailand. Fortunately, whilst the local Khmer-speakers are conscious of, and justly proud of, their cultural links with Angkor, they are also loyal Thai citizens. ❑

east, Khmer temples, and Isaan atmosphere, journey along Route 24, southeast of Khorat, running roughly parallel to the Cambodian border.

Three full ponds – essential elements of Khmer monumental architecture – and pretty farmland surround **Prasat Phanom Rung ⑤** (open daily, 9am–4pm; tel: 0 4463 1746; admission fee). Historians believe this temple was an important station between Angkor and Phimai during the 11th and 12th centuries. Many generations must have elapsed during its construction, since several of the stone lintels resemble the early Baphuon style, while the naga date from the later Angkor Wat period. A stone inscription in Sanskrit mentions King Suryavarman II, the ruler behind the construction of Angkor Wat.

The temple includes a stolen lintel spirited out of Thailand by art thieves in the early 1960s. Later it surfaced in the United States, in a museum collection. After negotiations, the lintel was returned to Thailand in the early 1990s and put back in its original position over a temple entrance. The main *prang* of Phanom Rung, and its galleries and chapels, reflect the geometric precision of Angkor architecture: symmetrical doors and windows face the four cardinal points. The monumental staircase, relieved by landings, exudes a sense of mass and power typical of Khmer design. Look for the sandstone bas-reliefs of elephants and enthroned Hindu deities. Monks of the Dharmayuti sect maintain the temple.

Further east a couple of kilometres is **Prasat Muang Tham**, or Lower Temple, sitting on a mossy lawn like an art historian's daydream. Older than Prasat Phanom Rung, its cornerstones were laid in the 10th century, with the temple finished about a hundred years later. Thick jungle surrounded Muang Tham until recently, when several families moved there from Ubon and established a village.

Five prang – surrounded by galleries, protected by walls, and now shaded by trees – constitute Muang Tham, which has recently been beautifully restored. Once crazily leaning blocks of masonry and fallen lintels are now back in place, the monumental tank rebuilt and filled with lilies. The huge rectangular stone blocks that form the outer walls contain drilled circular holes, probably used for stone figures shaped like lotus buds. The outer rims of the ponds are lined with naga, whose many heads rise at the corners, marking the outer boundary of the temple.

Surin and Si Saket

Located on an old Khmer site, **Surin ⑥** was known primarily for silk production until the government tourism authority began organising an annual elephant roundup each November. The people of Surin are famed for their skill at training elephants. (In the early 1900s, there were around 100,000 working elephants in Thailand; now there are only 4,000.) During the well-publicised roundup, *mahout* put their pachyderms through a variety of acts. Special buses and a train from Bangkok take tourists to the popular event.

A direct rail line connects Surin to the next main town, **Si Saket**, which borders on Cambodia. Travelling by car is less direct.

The province of Si Saket's former main attraction no longer lies in Thailand. In the early 1960s, the World

Map, page 252

Elephants are a common element not only in modern-day Surin, but also in the ornamentation of ancient Khmer ruins.

LEFT: example of Khmer design in Thailand's Khorat. **BELOW:** guardian image, Wat That Phanom.

Map, page 252

Khmer image of a garuda, the mythological creature.

Court awarded to Cambodia the splendid temple complex of **Prasat Khao Phra Viharn** ❼ (open daily 7.30am–4.30pm; tel: 0 4561 9214; admission fee), about 100 km (60 miles) southeast of Si Saket and easily reached from the Thai side of the border. It is, however, almost inaccessible from Cambodia. Prasat Khao Phra Viharn sits on a 500-metre (1,650-ft) high perch encompassing the Dongkrak Mountains overlooking Cambodia, and was re-opened in 1992 after being closed for decades because of danger from the Khmer Rouge insurgency. From Si Saket, it is a 60-km (40-mile) drive to Kantharalak, then another 40-km (25-mile) leg through jungle to the border.

Its construction starting sometime in the early 11th century, Prasat Khao Phra Viharn stretches almost a kilometre in length. Its stairs alternate between hewn bedrock and imported stones placed there perhaps 100 years before the days of Angkor Wat. Each layer is marked by an increasingly large *gopura,* or gate, and ends at the topmost sanctuary that honours the god Siva.

To the east of the first gopura, a precarious trail descends through the jungle to the Cambodian plains. Before the second gopura, a sacred pond cut in the rock was found to contain a 45-kg (100-lb) fish, which is now displayed in Cambodia's National Museum, in Phnom Penh.

The second gopura, shaped like a Greek cross, is superbly carved in the Khmer style of the 11th century. Its lintels show Vishnu in a scene from the Hindu myth of creation. The stairs continue in a symbolic ascent to heaven, past another purificatory basin, to the first courtyard with its two palaces and gopura, and finally up to the second and third courtyards and the main sanctuary. At the end of the long ridge is a breathtaking precipice, 600 metres (2,000 ft) above the Cambodian countryside, a stunning achievement of turning a natural site into a work of exquisite art.

Ubon Ratchathani ❽, Royal Town of the Lotus Flower, lies 700 km (430 miles) east of Bangkok and about 60 km (40 miles) east of Si Saket. Its size and wealth indicate the increasing prosperity of the region. In fact, much of the town's early growth coincided with the American build-up during the Vietnam War in the 1960s. Office buildings, construction sites, and some of the best-endowed temples in the northeast rise abruptly behind the banks of the Mun, which flows eastwards into the Mekong 100 km (65 miles) from Ubon.

In the 1100s, the area surrounding Ubon Ratchathani was part of the Khmer kingdom, until the Ayutthayan empire supplanted the Khmers. Ubon Ratchathani itself is a rather young urban centre, founded in the late 1700s by Lao immigrants. Established by King Rama III, **Wat Thung Si Muang** is noted for its library made of teak wood. The **National Museum** (open Wed–Sun 9am–4pm; admission fee) in Ubon Ratchathani is Khorat's finest and is well worth a stop. Housed in the former country residence of King Vajiravudh, the museum displays a number of fine artefacts, including exhibits of Khmer, Lao and Hindu origin. The highlight of Ubon's festival year is the Wax Candle Procession each July, when huge mythical animals and legendary figures are carved from beeswax and paraded through the streets.

A decent excursion out of Ubon is **Kaeng Tanna National Park** ❾ (open daily 8am–6pm; admission fee) to the northeast near Laos and the Mekong River, and noted for its prehistoric cave paintings and a series of rapids where the Mae Nam Mun is squeezed through a gorge before entering the Mekong.

If planning to travel north from Ubon Ratchathani, allow a full day for the trip from Ubon to Nakhon Phanom. In the dry season the fields along Route 212 look barely arable, but after the rains they produce the rice that turns golden brown in late October, and the tapioca piled in great mounds for export as animal feed throughout the region. ❑

RIGHT: Prasat Phanom Rung.

NORTHERN KHORAT

In the northeast, there are archaeological finds suggesting that not all technological advances came south from China. But if you're not interested in anthropology, consider the region's modern country life

Map, page 252

THAILAND

Bangkok

T he Thais call northeastern Thailand, *Isaan*. It is a poor part of the country, but its cuisine, as an off-the-wall example, dismisses any notions of poverty in creativity or initiative. Typically overlooked by both Thai and foreign travellers, northeastern Thailand makes up for its lack of awesome scenery with a number of fine nature preserves and ancient archaeological sites.

From just north of Bangkok, Route 2 heads northeast to **Udon Thani ⑩** via Khorat (Nakhon Ratchasima) and Khon Kaen. Udon Thani is a town that grew quickly with the arrival of American airmen during the 1960s. Today, instead of military convoys, noisy motorcycles and packed pick-up trucks fill city streets that are punctuated by increasing numbers of traffic lights.

From Udon Thani, Route 2 continues north for some 50 km (31 miles) to **Nong Khai ⑪**, on the southern bank of the Mekong River. In 1994, the 1.2-km (mile) long Friendship Bridge opened, connecting Nong Khai with the Laotian capital of Vientiane, on the other side of the Mekong River in Laos. This first bridge across the lower Mekong may well mean that Nong Khai's days as a quiet town are numbered. Fancy hotels have already opened to cater for the increased tourism and business.

LEFT: Friendship Bridge.
BELOW: Ban Chiang pottery.

East of Udon Thani

The people of **Ban Chiang ⑫**, long used to encountering fragments of pots, beads, and even human bones when digging around their houses or working on their farms, paid little attention to these finds in this area 50 km (31 miles) east of Udon Thani. Then, in 1966, a young American anthropology student showed some of his finds to the archaeology authorities in Bangkok. His discoveries led to more comprehensive analysis of the artefacts found around Ban Chiang, leading to some surprising, if not controversial, conclusions. Not only were the finds older than believed – between 4,500 and 5,700 years old – but bronze artefacts found around Ban Chiang were dated at around 3,600 BC.

If accurate, this would put the appearance of bronze in Thailand centuries earlier than in the Middle East, until then thought to be the earliest location of such bronze manufacture. Equally intriguing is that this dating of Ban Chiang bronze would suggest that bronze manufacture may have been transmitted from Thailand to China, rather than from China to Thailand, which has long been the received wisdom. Still, many experts maintain that the dating of 3,600 BC for the appearance of bronze remains too early, suggesting that 2,000 BC, or even 2,500 BC, is more accurate. This would put the appearance of bronze in Southeast Asia later than the Middle East, but at around the same time as China. Even were the claims of antiquity not authenticated, the

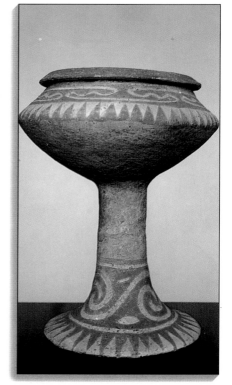

Rock inscriptions found in the northeast reflect Khmer influence over 1,000 years ago.

BELOW: traditional ceremony in the northeast.

beautiful whorl designs of the pottery and the intricacy of the bronze jewellery and implements would earn Ban Chiang culture high marks among the early peoples of the earth. Many of these artefacts can be seen in Ban Chiang's National Museum (open daily 8.30am–4.30pm; admission fee), established with the help of the US-based Smithsonian Institute.

About 120 km (75 miles) further east on Route 22, **Sakon Nakhon** ⑬ is spread out along a low plain that borders Nong Han, Thailand's largest natural lake. (Visitors should avoid going for a swim, however, as the waters are infested with liver fluke.) Although the site was one of the Khmer's important regional centres, the ancient Khmers left monuments whose significance is so minor that only those with keen archaeological interest should make a special effort to see them. In the town centre, the white *prang* of Wat Choeng Chum hides a 10th-century laterite prang; you must peer through a crack in the door to see it. West of town is Wat Narai Cheng Weng, built in the Khmer Baphuon style by a princess in the 11th century.

Further east on Route 22 is **Nakhon Phanom** ⑭. On a fresh morning, a chain of jagged, powder-grey mountains can be seen behind the small Laotian town of Thakhek, across the wide Mekong. Over 25,000 Vietnamese refugees crossed the river during the 1950s and 1960s to settle in this province. Although security precautions long complicated their resettlement, many Vietnamese have prospered financially in the town's markets, perhaps matching the Chinese in business acumen. During the Vietnam War, American rescue and reconnaissance missions flew from the Royal Thai Air Force Base hidden behind grassy mounds west of town. The base was also a listening post filled with sophisticated radios and electronic sensors. Nowadays few signs of the base's past remain. The town is quiet, attractive and relaxed.

Fifty km (30 miles) south is **That Phanom** . The road, which is straight and flat, stays close to the Mekong River all the way up to the village and temple of That Phanom. Uncultivated brush interspersed with rice fields rushes by. Blue-shirted farmers balance produce-laden baskets from the ends of long poles.

Thousands of pilgrims from northeast Thailand and southern Laos used to make an annual pilgrimage to **Wat That Phanom**, making offerings at the base of the spire, which was built around the 9th century and restored several times. In mid 1975, the spire collapsed after four days of torrential monsoon rains. But in 1979, the temple was restored, again making it well worth a visit for those interested in history or simply seeking a beautiful setting. For a short and pleasant side trip into the countryside, north of That Phanom and inland is **Renu Nakhon**. Like several small weaving villages in northern Thailand, Renu Nakhon is famous for textiles. The people are friendly and welcome visiting bargainers.

Continuing south on Route 212 leads to the district town of **Mukdahan** , on the right bank of the wide Mekong River and opposite the Laotian town of Savannakhet. Mukdahan is, in fact, a trading centre for Laotian timber, agricultural products and gems. Take the road to the river, turn right, and visit Wat Sri Nongkran, a temple built by Vietnamese refugees in 1956. The gates present a curious mixture of Thai contours, Vietnamese writing and Chinese-inspired dragons. A bridge spanning the river between Mukdahan and Savannakhet will open in 2006, replacing the ferry service. Southward on Route 212 will lead to Ubon Ratchatani.

West of Udon Thani

Route 210 runs 150 km (100 miles) west of Udon Thani to the ruggedly beautiful province of **Loei** , and the town of the same name. Midway en route, stop

Map, page 252

BELOW: Phu Kradung National Park.

Map, page 252

TIP

The Thai government prohibits the illegal excavation and sale of artefacts, but near archaeological sites, villagers may approach visitors offering to sell artefacts. If they are fakes, you'll not know unless you're an expert.

BELOW: wreathed hornbills in flight. **RIGHT:** typical Isaan headscarf.

at the **Tham Erawan** ⑱ (Elephant Cave), about 50 km (30 miles) before Loei and a couple of kilometres off the road. Despite its isolation, the monastery there is well organised. A life-size statue of Erawan, the triple-headed elephant of Thai mythology, marks the steep stairway and rocky path to the cave's entrance. The climb up is rough. Prehistoric artefacts have been found here, but apart from its size and an occasional cobra emerging from the rocks, all that distinguishes the cave is an elephant's skull.

An ongoing agricultural boom is slowly changing Loei's shy simplicity. The usually placid Mae Nam Loei flows through the centre of town. Until the 1980s, communist insurgents hid amid the surrounding forests. What is now the traveller's delight was once the civil servant's nightmare. In the Thai bureaucracy, being assigned to Loei was like going to Siberia: Loei was a jungle outpost that meant fever, cold weather, little comfort, isolation and poor security. Not so today – Loei has hotels, restaurants, and even a street full of karaoke bars.

Route 203 plunges west into the wilderness, to **Phu Rua National Park** ⑲ (open daily, 8am–6pm; tel: 0 4288 1716; admission fee). The road slices through heavy banks of red laterite, past a sawmill and fields of *kenaf* and cotton, the latter being the area's primary source of income. In December, the mountains lie under thick blankets of smoke as farmers burn the forest undergrowth. Phu Rua itself is about 1,370 metres (4,500 ft) high. A rough road to the top affords a view of the national forest.

To reach the Mekong, near where it once again becomes the border between Thailand and Laos, drive 50 km (30 miles) north from Loei to the charming riverside town of **Chiang Khan** ⑳. A boat can be hired for the short ride downstream to the Kaeng Khut Ku rapids, worthwhile both for their beauty and for the sheer sense of being in the deep heart of Southeast Asia.

No experience in the Loei area can match the crisp beauty of **Phu Kradung National Park** ㉑ (open daily, 8am–6pm; tel: 0 4287 1333; admission fee), the most memorable escape in northeast Thailand, and just 100 km (60 miles) south of Loei. The area came to public attention only during the reign of King Rama VI. Phu Kradung, a 60-sq-km (24-sq-mile) plateau lying between 1,200 and 1,500 metres (4,000–5,000 ft) in elevation, beckons the naturalist-at-heart to try some of its 50 km (30 miles) of marked trails.

The entrance is on Route 201. About 3 km (2 miles) from this is the park office, where one can arrange for porters, storage for excess equipment, and parking. The park provides bedding and blankets in cabins that hold up to eleven people. It is by no means an easy climb, but ladders enable visitors to negotiate the steepest boulders, and it is well worth the effort.

Atop Phu Kradung, clear and mostly level paths crisscross the tableland. Rare birds, including hornbills, woodpeckers and pheasants, may be seen. Even wild elephants and the occasional panther make their homes on the mountain. Most of the wildlife is quite shy, however. The park's cabins and upper offices are located 3 km (2 miles) from a small radar station and helicopter pad. The government closes the park in the summer months to permit the ecology to recover. In the past forests were cut indiscriminately, but times have changed a little. ❑

THE GULF COAST

It was Thailand's eastern gulf coast that first lured travellers to the country's beaches several decades ago. It still does

The eastern coast along the Gulf of Thailand is an almost unbroken stretch of sand that runs to Trat, the narrow finger of land that abuts the neighbouring country of Cambodia.

Closer to Bangkok, towns like Si Racha and Chonburi, if somewhat lacking in visual charm, are nonetheless important commercial centres, with factories for processing and canning the region's agricultural produce. Si Racha, in particular, is noted as the home of a fiery hot chilli sauce bearing its name that is a prominent feature of Thai dinner tables.

Few areas in Asia have undergone such a precipitous rise to fame and, some say, a plummet in popularity and integrity, as the beach resort of Pattaya. This huge resort was once a beautiful and quiet beach, a graceful, 4-km (2-mile) long crescent of golden sand lapped by gentle waves and balmy breezes. By the 1980s, the visitors came flowing in from all directions, making it one of the great success stories in Asian tourism. By the late 1980s, there were dozens of high-rise hotels lining the beach. Pattaya's lustre had begun to dull, however, with a lack of planning that robbed the resort of the very qualities that made it so popular. It also gained a reputation as a seaside Patpong crawling with paedophiles and Western men looking for cheap sex.

Nevertheless, tourism brought the Eastern Gulf new prosperity. While mainstream travellers are avoiding Pattaya, more pristine islands along the coast like Ko Samet and Ko Chang are luring visitors aplenty. Ko Chang especially is set to be Thailand's hot new beach destination. Roads are being widened and private entrepreneurs are rushing to build a string of new resorts on its white sand beaches.

Still, tourism is far from being the region's sole source of income. Older industries in the area have long played an important part in the Thai economy. Much of the seafood consumed or exported by Thailand comes from Eastern Gulf ports, and some of the largest fruit orchards are between Rayong and Chanthaburi. The area around Chanthaburi is also noted for its gem mining, such as for sapphires.

All this industry notwithstanding, the Eastern Gulf's main lures for the average foreign visitor are its sun and sand, and its plentiful tourist facilities. Despite the naysayers, Pattaya and its sisters continue to thrive, and maybe even improve. ❑

PRECEDING PAGES: fruit stand stacked with offerings; boat on gulf harbour.
LEFT: seller of Southeast Asia's popular durian.

SOUTH TO PATTAYA

*Both far away and close at the same time, the coastal road south of
Bangkok along the Gulf of Thailand offers a little of everything to
travellers, whether hot beach, hot sex or hot sauce*

Map,
page 277

THAILAND

Bangkok

T he main route from Bangkok to the pretty eastern Gulf Coast is the unappealing Bangna-Trad highway, lined by nondescript concrete buildings. The views pick up when Bangna joins with the older Sukhumvit highway from Bangkok, Route 3, just outside Chonburi, and the landscape gradually starts to become green and hilly.

Chonburi ❶ is a sprawling and industrious town of about a quarter million merchants, traders and craftsmen. Filled with Bangkok-style traffic, it is also the accident capital of Thailand. Nevertheless, its attractions include **Wat Buddhabat Sam Yot**, Buddha's Footprint Mountain of Three Summits, just outside town. Built amid green trees by an Ayutthayan king and renovated during the reign of King Chulalongkorn, this hill-top monastery was once used to conduct the water oath of allegiance, when princes and governors drank the waters of fealty, pledging loyalty to the throne.

Near the centre of Chonburi, a colossal gold-mosaic image of Buddha dominates **Wat Dhamma Nimitr**. The largest image in this region, and the only one in the country depicting the Buddha in a boat, the 40-metre (135-ft) high statue recalls the story of the Buddha's journey to the cholera-ridden town of Pai Salee. On the same hill is the local Chinese Buddhist Society, with the burial shrines of prominent members.

Those interested in the historical arts could stop near the old market, at the oldest and most important *wat* in the province, **Wat Intharam**, a mix of architectural styles and one of the best examples of Ayutthayan architecture in the southeast. In the 18th century, this wat was the rallying point for soldiers recruited by King Taksin to drive the Burmese from Ayutthaya.

South of Chonburi

Seven km (4 miles) south of Chonburi on a back road is the town of **Ang Sila**. Once favoured by Thai royalty as a resort, the town takes its name of Stone Basin from the chain of rocks that form an oval protrusion into the sea. The roads are lined with shops selling the sculpted wares of local craftspeople. Fishing beds line the shallow waters around the village, and the small pier is full of activity.

Further south sits an unusual monastery on a hill, **Rua Sam Pao**. Facing seaward and recently expanded, its walls are shaped like the huge hull of a Chinese junk, which some say points to a shipwreck in which emigrants from China were lost. In fact, it represents a vessel carrying the faithful to *nirvana*. The 300-plus meditation cells arranged around the main ship are also in the shape of small boats.

Many of the residents are very old and believe that to die at Rua Sam Pao brings good fortune; many of the older Chinese women believe that, when they die, their

LEFT: waiting for the show, Nong Nooch Village.
BELOW: Pattaya resort.

souls will be carried on the sea back to China. Pilgrims share the hill with hundreds of monkeys, and some excellent seafood restaurants make this a popular spot with day-trippers.

On the road past Ang Sila, the long straight beach at the slightly rundown **Bang Saen** comes alive each weekend as hordes of Thai tourists descend in buses. A profusion of beach umbrellas, inner tubes and wrinkled watermelon rinds quickly cover the sandy beach, the surf filled with bobbing people. Under the casuarina trees lining the sand, picnickers enjoy vendor food and pick up souvenirs. The south end of the beach runs into a messy, garbage-strewn fishing and factory district and is best avoided. Bang Saen's main street on Thanon Sukhumvit is lined with hundreds of stalls selling local produce.

There are many spicy if not hot sauces to be tried in Thailand. The town of Si Racha is known for a local version called naam phrik see raachaa.

At the Bang Saen Reservoir bird refuge, with permission it is possible to sit in a blind and observe waterfowl. Chinese graves dot the countryside outside the town – the hills and sea make this a favourite burial spot for Bangkok's Chinese. Up the hill behind the bird reserve is the **Khao Khieo Open Zoo** (open daily 8am–6pm; tel: 0 3829 8187; admission fee), which has animals in relatively natural settings. A huge aviary built over a natural hill allows visitors to stroll around and relax among plants and waterfalls in the company of hundreds of species of birds. On the hill are simple bungalows that can be reserved from the Dusit Zoo in Bangkok.

Si Racha ❷, further south, descends from the hills and extends into the sea on tentacle-like piers. Its famous hot sauce can be enjoyed at waterfront restaurants, where fresh shrimp, crab, oyster, mussel or abalone are dipped into the thick, tangy red liquid. An offshore rock supports a picturesque wat with Thai and Chinese elements. A footprint of the Buddha cast in bronze graces the wat, as do pictures of the goddess of mercy, Kuan Yin, and the Monkey God.

BELOW: transvestite show and beach high-rise in Pattaya.

The **Sriracha Tiger Zoo and Resort** (open daily 9am–6pm; tel: 0 3829 6556; admission fee), about 7 km (4 miles) outside of town in the Surasak precinct, boasts the most successful tiger breeding programme in the world. Here visitors will find Thailand's largest concentration of Bengal tigers, along with other animals.

From the longest pier at Si Racha, boats ferry passengers to a nearby island, **Ko Si Chang ❸**. On the southern end of Ko Si Chang are deserted beaches and the attractively overgrown remains of a former royal palace once used by King Chulalongkorn as a summer retreat. A few modest bungalows past the Chinese temple overlooking the main town offer good sea and cliff views. Ko Si Chang also has the Yai Phrik Vipassana Centre, a meditation retreat.

Pattaya

A few kilometres south of Si Racha is the beach resort of **Pattaya ❹**. Few areas in Asia have undergone such a precipitous rise to fame and, soon after, a plummet into notoriety as Pattaya. This huge resort was once a quiet village and beach known only to a handful of foreigners and Thais from Bangkok. By the 1970s, others were starting to discover its charms. Large hotels began to rise along the seashore. By the 1980s, Europeans and American sailors flocked to its beaches, and those of **Jomtien**, the neighbouring beach just south.

Then Pattaya's sheen began to fade. There were disturbing signs that problems lurking beneath the surface were emerging: polluted beaches and water, as well as crime. The town had gained a seedy reputation, a waterfront Patpong-like rest-and-recreation holdover from the Vietnam War. Visitors started going elsewhere, to Phuket and Ko Samui. Pattaya today is still primarily known as a sex resort – the go-go bars are the most noticeable feature of the main tourist

Map, page 277

TIP

No matter how much effort some Pattaya businesses have made to make Pattaya respectable, the place has a backdrop of sex tourism, high crime, and drug abuse. It's impossible to ignore.

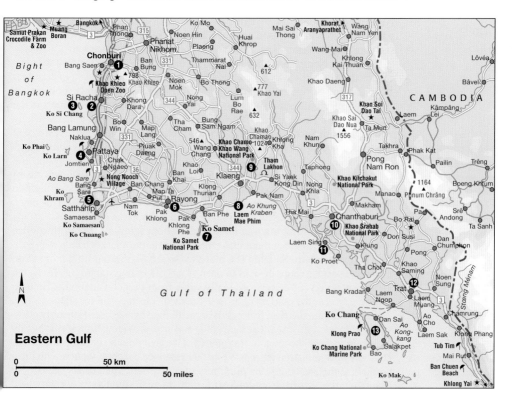

Eastern Gulf

0   50 km

0   50 miles

Map,
page 277

Golf swings south of
urban Bangkok.

areas. South Pattaya is the main tourist and bar area, though bars and shops are increasingly moving into the quieter northern section of town.

Pattaya is making attempts to change its reputation from that of party town to family resort, but it has a long way to go. Several resorts have tried to publicise their family attractions, but with limited success. These days, some hotels have resorted to attracting a new clientele from Russia and eastern European countries. The larger hotels are well equipped with water sports and activities. A local English-language paper, *The Pattaya Mail*, keeps visitors and foreign residents well-informed about things to do, services and special offers and excursions. But the backdrop of sex tourism, a high crime rate and obvious drink and drugs abuse is impossible to ignore in Pattaya.

The angler can test skills at landing grouper and red snapper, mackerel and bonito, sailfish and barracuda. Fishing expeditions can be arranged at Pattaya shops, and at Bang Sare further down the coast. Offshore, **Ko Larn**, whose name translates as Bald Island, has the wide, soft-sand beaches that Pattaya lacks and it is a pleasant place to spend a leisurely day. The shore is filled with good seafood restaurants, and there are water-sports facilities for those who may be inclined to stir from their beach chairs. The island also has a golf course. Ten km (7 miles) east of Pattaya is the Siam Country Club, which boasts one of the finest golf courses in the kingdom.

South of Pattaya

Excursions can be organised to visit sapphire mines, orchid farms and an elephant kraal, and boat trips to local islands are also easily arranged. Year by year, visitors have been exploring further and further south of Pattaya, discovering new resort areas with less noise and crowds. One popular resort for Thais is **Nong Nooch Village** (open daily 8am–6pm; admission fee), a complex of bungalows situated in park land around a lake, and offering a variety of activities, including an elephant show, an orchid nursery and a cactus garden.

Just before Nong Nooch, a quiet resort at the end of Soi Sunset offers wonderful coastal and hill views past a quiet beach, which is almost always deserted. Beyond Nong Nooch are a number of resorts fronting waters known for deep-sea fishing, both commercial and sport. The area is one of the premier spots in the world for marlin and sailfish. The winding, busy streets of the untouristy fishing village of **Bang Sare**, cosily sheltered under a forested hill, are in great contrast to the resorts of the area. Food stalls, schoolchildren, motorbikes, dogs and cottage-industry shophouses bump up against each other in a scramble of activity and life.

Six km (4 miles) past
Sattahip, a broad
road leads to a large
Thai military base,
which once served
the American air
force as its only B-52
airstrip on the Asian
mainland during the
Vietnam War.

Overlooking a scenic bay sprinkled with small islands, the fishing town of **Sattahip ❺**, about 20 km (15 miles) south of Pattaya, blossomed overnight to become a busy deep-water port. It now acts as a headquarters for the Thai navy, which owns much of the surrounding land and many of the small islands off the coast. In the heart of town, a large and modern temple rests on turquoise pedestals, while in the commercial centre, a boisterous market teems with fish, fruit and vegetables. Sattahip is a place to de-stress, offering little more to do than stroll past the shops or sit in an open-front coffee shop sipping an *oliang,* the great sweet iced coffee that originally came from French Cambodia. Enjoy a spicy curry near the market, or browse over teak elephants in the shops.

RIGHT: motorcycle taxi and young passenger.

From Sattahip, the road follows the coastline eastward, but offers only occasional glimpses of the sea. The land is flat and arid, providing little scenic beauty until approaching the town of **Rayong ❻**. This area is being developed as Thailand's newest industrial region. While there are nice beaches popular with local workers at the weekends, the proximity of oil refineries and heavy industry at Maptaput make seafront alternatives further down the road more attractive. ❏

EASTERN GULF

Map, page 277

Extending down to the rough Cambodian border, this part of Thailand is rich in both gems and island beaches. Gems take some knowledge to recognise, but picking the beaches is intuitive

A t the busy market town of **Rayong ❻**, 220 km (140 miles) from Bangkok, an attractive local tourism office is well stocked with information on the east coast as far as the Cambodia border. A right turn in the centre of town leads to an old, but busy, fishing village that occupies land between the beach and the estuary. Rayong is famed for its *naam plaa*, or fish sauce, the source of salt in the Thai diet and the *sine qua non* of Thai condiments. Nam plaa is made from a small silver fish that abounds in the Gulf; it is left to decompose for about seven months in order to produce a ruddy liquid, which is filtered and bottled on the spot.

About 20 km (15 miles) past Rayong is a turn-off to **Ban Phe**, on the coast. Dressed in weathered black shirts, straw hats and sarongs, women carpet the ground with tangerine-coloured shrimp, drying them in the sun.

This busy fishing port is sheltered on the west by a rocky outcrop, and by the 6-km (4-mile) long island of **Ko Samet ❼** to the south. The island is remembered by students of Thai literature as the place where Sunthorn Phu, a romantic court poet, retired to compose some of his work. Born in nearby Klaeng, Sunthorn Phu called the island "Ko Kaew Phisadan" or "island with sand like crushed crystal". Ko Samet's sand is reputed to be the finest in Thailand. The island has gained popularity as a superb resort for its pristine waters and secluded coves, but not without controversy: cheap bungalow complexes are being razed to build small hotels; rubbish and noise have increased on the larger beaches. Ko Samet is, in fact, part of a national park, which means that much of the development is actually illegal and is periodically half-heartedly tackled by local authorities.

The coastal road leading east from Ban Phe passes fishmongers and barber shops before entering the kilometre-long pine forest of **Ban Pha Phrae National Park**, a refreshing change in scenery from the scrubland preceding it, and a popular picnicking spot with Thai tourists and locals.

Attractive resorts line the 10 km (6 miles) from Wang Kaew to the peninsula of **Laem Mae Phim ❽**, an underrated part of the Thai coast. Suan Wang Kaew is a landscaped garden on a hill stretching into the sea and a favourite Thai picnic spot. It has bungalows and rooms for rent on the west side. A couple of good restaurants jutting out to the sea provide views of the long stretch of sand in front.

This stretch of coast has seen little of the commercialisation that has developed at most Thai resorts. Vendors offering cheap goods and traditional massage are notable by their absence. It's not unusual for visitors to have the beaches (which could be cleaner) almost to themselves when weekend holidaymakers from Bangkok have departed. Further along is Laem Mae Phim, a popular Thai resort where excellent seafood

LEFT: popularity threatens Ko Samet.
BELOW: coral reef off Ko Samet.

restaurants line the top end of the beach. A few kilometres on, the charming, untouristy fishing village of **Ao Khai** is a restful place to watch the loading and unloading of all sorts of fish from old, gaily coloured wooden fishing boats.

Just offshore are a number of jagged islands. Many local resorts offer day-trips to the nearby islands, one of which has been set aside as a reserve for turtles. On the way to Chanthaburi from Laem Mae Phim, the village of Ban Krum has a small park dedicated to the poet Sunthorn Phu, with statues of the poet and some of his most famous characters.

The town of **Klaeng** is quietly busy, its streets lined with numerous and attractive old-style Thai wooden houses. The imposing Wat Saranat Thammaram is located at the market. At Klaeng, a new double-lane highway leads directly to Chonburi and Bangkok.

Khao Chamao – Khao Wong National Park ❾ (open daily 8am–6pm; tel: 0 3889 4378; admission fee), 12 km (8 miles) to the north off Route 3 a few kilometres past Klaeng, has a long waterfall with eight levels. Ascent is relatively easy with the aid of special bridges and walkways. Soro brook carp cluster in the pools by the hundreds. The fish scrabble to grab green leaves that drop from trees overhead or from the hands of helpful visitors to the falls. When eaten, this carp is said to induce stomach aches or a mild "high" due to its diet of a special fruit.

Nearby are the **Khao Wong caves**, about 60 in all, many of which are occupied by Buddhist monks. One cave has been turned into a shrine with a replica of the Buddha's footprints. **Wat Khao Sukim**, a large meditation temple set high in the mountains further down the coast (turn left off Route 3), has stunning views, tranquil shady spots and strangely lifelike wax figures of Buddhist monks. There are displays of fine jade, furniture and antiques. A funicular takes

Chanthaburi's history began as much as 6,000 years ago. But historical pages are mostly blank until the 17th century, when Ayutthaya's King Narai moved people from Chiang Mai and Laos to Chanthaburi to defend it against incursions and attacks by Khmer and Vietnamese forces.

BELOW: unloading supplies during a downpour.

visitors to the top, or else it's an energetic walk up hundreds of steps on the adjacent stairway, lined with two colourfully decorated stone-and-ceramic serpents.

From Wat Khao Sukim to Chanthaburi, the mountain road has few surprises, except for an understated, official-looking sign for "Paradise", which is an invitation that may be hard to pass up. "Paradise" is a Catholic religious retreat, with a church and little bungalows clustered around a small lake and waterfalls.

Map, page 277

Chanthaburi

The area between **Chanthaburi** ❿ and the Cambodian border lies in a climate pattern somewhat different from the rest of Thailand, receiving the southwest monsoon that makes it wetter, but greener. The rains nurture rubber plantations, a luscious *rambutan* crop, and what are reputedly the best durians in the kingdom. (Try one, but don't bring it back to your hotel.) Gems, delicious fruits, handicrafts, beaches, an air of quiet antiquity, and relics of the past make this area a prime spot.

Chanthaburi itself sits amid rolling hills, beside the winding Chanthaburi River. Its residents are a mix of Thai, Burmese, Chinese and Vietnamese faces. The lake in the town centre, built by the French, is a favourite meeting and exercise spot, and is an unusual feature in Thai towns. Motorcycles clog Chanthaburi's streets. Shops along the river and elsewhere open out onto the street, revealing rows and rows of grinding stones, where artisans patiently cut facets on precious stones that are mined nearby.

Chanthaburi's recent history is contained on a hill, and in a jail. About 5 km (3 miles) south of town stands **Khai Noen Wong**, the "Camp on a Small Circular Hill." King Taksin retreated here after the fall of Ayutthaya in 1767 to regroup his

Khmer lintel from the early 7th century found in the Chanthaburi area.

BELOW: coastal fishing trawlers.

Thailand's Gems: Crystal Power

Thais have turned a national passion for gems and jewellery into one of the country's largest export industries. Rubies, sapphires and jade are among the best bargains, while gold, silver and diamond products, finished by master craftsmen, are also popular buys.

Rubies, the name given to red, gem-quality corundum stones, vary in shade from pinkish or purplish to the brownish-red found in Thailand, depending on the stone's chromium and iron content. A really fine ruby can appear to glow like hot coal. Since prehistory, rubies have been associated with a range of spiritual and supernatural beliefs. The Burmese thought rubies conferred invulnerability, and that they could foretell danger by loss of colour or brilliance. Most of the rubies in Thailand traditionally originated from the Chanthaburi region, and from the Pailin area of

Cambodia, which together account for around two-thirds of the world's supply of rubies. A small number come from Vietnam and parts of Africa.

Thailand's ruby mines were known in early times, with the first known reference coming from a Chinese traveller, Ma Huan, in AD 1408. Now they are close to depletion. At Bo Rai, once the king of Thai ruby-mining towns, abandoned equipment litters the landscape. Where there used to be hundreds of traders, just a few remain. Supplies from the Cambodian side of the border have become more sporadic. Rubies from the remote Mogok and Mong Hsu mines in upper Burma, where primitive, back-breaking extraction methods still apply, are relatively rare and highly sought-after for the international market when they get to Thailand.

An important distinction is made between prime-quality unheated stones, most of which come from Mogok, and less valuable heat-treated samples, originating primarily in Mong Hsu. The latter tend to look like bad garnet before treatment, after which they turn into bright red gems.

Sapphires, also composed of corundum, come in different colours, from the highly prized rich blue to orange, green, yellow, pink and colourless varieties. Sapphire was traditionally believed by Buddhists to produce a desire for prayer, to help ward off negative energies, and to promote calm. Thailand's sapphires now come mainly from Sri Lanka, Australia and Africa. Locally mined sapphires in Kanchanaburi and Phrae, and Cambodian stones from the Pailin area are increasingly limited in number and quality.

In recent years, Thailand has also become a major centre for processing diamonds, catering to a large foreign as well as thriving domestic jewellery scene.

Shopping for gems and jewellery in Thailand is easy and rewarding, so long as one sticks to reputable stores. (If in doubt, contact the local Tourism Authority of Thailand office for authorised gem and jewellery establishments.) Innumerable scams involving gullible tourists have been reported in the Thai press. They often take the form of an individual with a "special offer", backed up by a convincing story. A polite but firm refusal will deflect the scam. ❑

forces, recruit new soldiers and construct a fleet of warships. From this staging point, he returned to Ayutthaya to rout its Burmese occupiers. On the same hill are the remains of a fortress built by King Rama III. At several points around the hill, derelict cannons point at the now-silent jungle. Several of the pieces are of great size; locals claim they protect the mouth of the Chanthaburi River, over 10 km (6 miles) away.

Across the river is the French-style **Church of the Immaculate Conception**, the largest Catholic church in Thailand. Built around 1880, its congregation is comprised of Vietnamese who migrated to Thailand over the past two centuries. The descendants of these immigrants engage in a number of businesses, foremost of which is the weaving of reed mats, handbags and purses in attractive shapes and patterns. Many items are made in family homes. Some excellent products can be ordered from the nuns of the church.

Nearby is **Laem Sing** ⓫, site of a Thai confrontation with European powers. Around the turn of the 20th century, the Thais were embroiled in a territorial dispute with the French occupiers of Cambodia. The French invaded, and for 11 years stationed a garrison at Laem Sing. The Tuk Daeng (Red Building) Customs House and the Kook Khi Kai (Chicken Dung Prison) attest to their presence.

Since the 15th century, the area's prime activity has been mining for sapphires and other precious stones, especially rubies. The red soil of the rubber plantations is pitted with holes up to 12 metres (40 ft) deep, each miner staking a claim and hauling out the muck by the bucket-full. It is backbreaking work, with meagre rewards. But occasionally a giant gemstone is found.

The nearest gem-mining area is at **Khao Ploi Waen** (Hill of the Sapphire Ring). To reach it, return to Khai Nern Wong, the old fort ruins. Just past it is a

Map,
page 277

Gem dealer displays a blue-sapphire ring.

LEFT: a precious sapphire find.
BELOW: tattoos protect from evil.

Map,
page 277

junction where the gemstones are traded and purchased. Another kilometre on is Khao Ploi Waen. The open pits in the hillside are up to 10 metres (33 ft) deep.

Consider a side trip to the north: from **Sa Kaew**, 200 km (125 miles) to the north of Chanthaburi, drive 60 km (40 miles) east on Route 33 to **Aranyaprathet** on the border with Cambodia. The area is now free of the huge refugee camps that once stood here. Back in Chanthaburi, head down the road to its waterfalls. At the 324-km marker of Route 3, opposite the Chanthaburi turn-off, a small road leads inland for 20 km (13 miles), through orchards of rambutan, durian, oranges and lychees. **Nam Tok Krating** (Bull Waterfall) is a cascade of small falls tumbling 400 metres (1,300 ft) across a granite face. Further down Route 3, near the 347-km marker, is another popular waterfall, **Nam Tok Praew**. Beyond makeshift stalls, where women sell sticky rice and durian jam, is an oddity: a pyramidal *chedi* overlooking the falls. The chedi commemorates a consort of King Chulalongkorn who drowned while being rowed up the Chao Phraya River. Her death was particularly tragic, since her attendants could have saved her, had they not been forbidden to touch the body of a royal person. Today, falls and pools are seldom deserted in daylight.

Trat and Ko Chang

The road to **Trat ⑫**, 400 km (250 miles) from Bangkok and the last major town before the Cambodian border, passes through rubber plantations, paddies and marshlands. A gem-trading centre, Trat itself is undistinguished, but serves as a starting point for trips to 47 beautiful offshore islands which make up the **Ko Chang National Marine Park**. Head from the town clock tower to the port of **Laem Ngop**, about 20 km (15 miles) southwest. There, boats leave in the morning for **Ko Chang ⑬**. Some 8 km (5 miles) wide and 30 km (20 miles) long, Thailand's third-largest island is famed for its pristine beaches, rare wildlife and scenic waterfalls like **Than Mai Yom Falls**. Off the northern tip of Ko Chang, some of the largest sharks in the gulf cruise near a rocky outcrop. Nearby, **Ko Mak**, **Ko Kut** and **Ko Wai** islands offer clear lagoons and excellent diving and snorkelling.

Most of the accommodation on Ko Chang is found along the western coast where the best beaches are found. Up till recently, most visitors to Ko Chang have been Thai, and lodgings mainly simple cottages and a few modest resorts. In 2002, however, realising the tourism potential of the island, Thai authorities pumped in more than US$10 million for the construction of tourism-related infrastructure, including a new airport. In anticipation of a tourist boom, land is being cleared for a string of new beachfront resorts.

From Trat, drive down the scenic narrow finger of Thailand to the town of **Khlong Yai**, built over the water. From the main street, rows of houses run into the sea. Between them, parked like cars on a side street, are moored fishing trawlers that earn the inhabitants their income. The road, with unspoilt, sometimes dramatic sea views, continues to **Hat Yai**, a tiny fishing (and smuggling) village on the Cambodia border, which is an interesting spot from which to watch life, and trucks of whiskey and cigarettes, go by. ❏

BELOW: Nam Tok Praew waterfall.
RIGHT: finely worked tattoos.

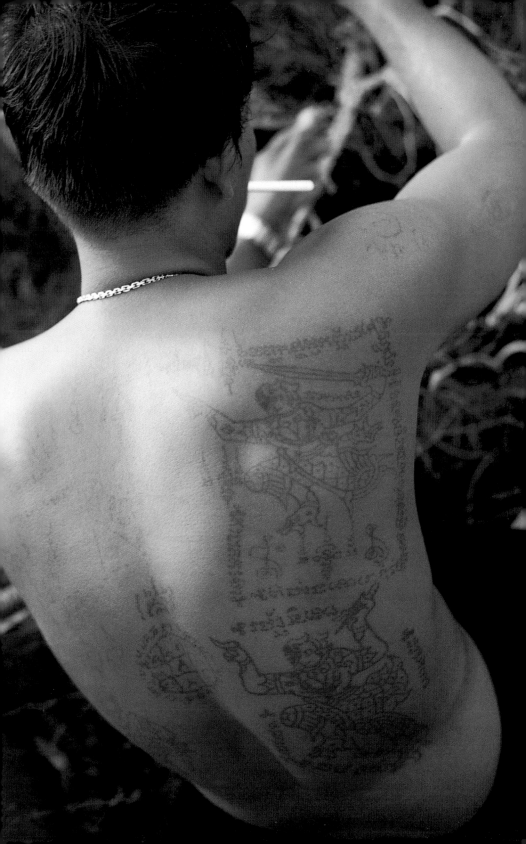

A FEAST OF FRUITS

There is a sizeable range of fruits in Thailand, many of which may be unfamiliar. As well as bananas and pineapples, there are all kinds of brilliantly coloured and strangely shaped fruits for the adventurous traveller.

Thai people love food, and during the afternoon they snack on an incredible variety of fruits. For visitors who are in need of a boost, fruit can be a great source of refreshment and energy. Traditional fruit sellers have glass-fronted carts stacked with blocks of ice and pealed pieces of seasonal fruits. Choose a selection of what you want to eat and the vendor will pop it into a bag for you along with a toothpick for spearing the slices. Some fruits, like pineapple, are eaten with a little salt and ground chilli, a twist of which is supplied separately. Don't be afraid of this combination – the natural sweetness of the pineapple is enhanced by this bitter condiment, surprisingly enough.

One of the best ways to cool down is to drink a delicious fruit juice or *naam phon-la-mai*. To order, say the Thai word for water (*naam*) in front of the name of the fruit, or just point to your selection from the fruits on display. Another favourite drink is fruit juice blended with ice – known as a *naam pan* or "smoothie". You can have syrup mixed in to sweeten your juice (*namm pan*) or salt added (as the Thais like it) to bring out the flavour of the fruit.

CONTROVERSIAL DURIAN

People either love or hate durian. Ask any visitor in Thailand to recall the first time they came across it and they will describe, in detail, its "perfume". To most *farang* (Europeans or Caucasians), the durian's odour is repugnant, but for the Thais the fruit commands the utmost respect. According to devotees the rewards of eating durian far outweigh any objections to its smell. The only way to enter the great durian debate is to try it for yourself. If you can't face eating the fruit *au naturel* there is durian cake, ice-cream and chewing gum.

◁ **JACKFRUIT** *(KHANUN)*
The ripe, rich yellow sections of the jackfruit are waxy-textured and semi-sweet. When green they are used in curries, and the flowers and young shoots are eaten in salads.

RAMBUTAN *(LUUK NGOH)*▷
The hairy rambutan (*rambut* means hair in Malay) is a close relative of the lychee, and its translucent, sweet flesh has a similar taste. There is a technique to squeezing it open to avoid squirting yourself with its juices; any Thai can demonstrate this.

▽ **STAR FRUIT** *(MA FEUANG)*
This sweet, yellow fruit is native to India. It has a thin waxy skin with a crisp texture and sweet-tart juice. It can be found in fruit salads or can be candied and eaten as a confection. The unripe fruit is bright green and is sometimes added to dishes that require an acidic taste.

CROPS: A GROWING CONCERN

△ **CUSTARD APPLE** *(NOI-NA)*
The custard apple looks like a small, light green hand-grenade and can be pulled apart by hand. The pulp is soft, often mushy, very sweet and very tasty. It is best to eat it with a spoon.

▽ **MANGOSTEEN** *(MANGKHUT)*
Thais believe durian requires the cool, refreshing sweet taste of the mangosteen as a chaser. See if you can guess how many sections your mangosteen has before you break it open.

Farming and fishing have always been at the centre of Thai life. Despite rapid industrialisation, this is still the case. Thailand is self-sufficient in food, and agribusiness is an important pillar of the Thai economy, claiming nearly a quarter of GDP and making Thailand the only net food exporter in Asia. Thailand is the world's leading exporter of canned pineapple and has big overseas markets in canned logans and rambutans.

Fruit production is expected to increase as available land and labour resources dwindle and farmers switch from producing staple crops, such as rice and cassava, to cash crops like soya beans, fruits, sugar cane and rubber. Large fruit farmers are starting to process their products before they reach the consumer, and many are now applying for loans to invest in equipment to dry and freeze their produce. Although some of this produce will be sold to Thailand's neighbours, much of it will end up in the snack food departments of Japanese supermarkets – Japanese businesses have already set up factories in Thailand to process fruits, vegetables and nuts for their home market.

◁ **DURIAN (** *TURIAN***)**
The most expensive of Thai fruits has mushy flesh that tastes good with sticky rice and coconut milk. Ignore the smell and you will be rewarded.

JAPANESE PEAR ▷
This crunchy and slightly dry fruit is usually eaten raw. Its semi-sweet flavour can be enhanced by dipping it into slightly salted water.

THE SOUTH

*From carefree beaches and rubber-tree plantations to curries
and mosques, surprises abound in Thailand's south*

Southern Thailand, a long arm of land sometimes likened to an
elephant's trunk, consists of 14 provinces and is rich in stunning scenery. Wild jungles alternate with rocky mountains and
broad beaches of powdery sand. While a few select areas are increasingly world-class destinations, other parts of the region are still being
discovered by the outside world.

Countless islands, large and small, are scattered down this narrow
strip of land that leads to Malaysia. The eastern coast of the Isthmus
of Kra faces the Gulf of Thailand, while the other shore lies on the
Andaman Sea and Indian Ocean.

In many ways, the south of Thailand is a world far removed from
the rest of the country, especially in the deep south. A different climate, religion and type of farming make it unique among Thailand's
regions. Groves of rubber trees are more common than fields of rice.
The gilded dome of a Muslim mosque becomes a more familiar sight
than the sloping orange roof of a Buddhist temple. In the provinces
near the border, the people speak Malay as well as Thai, and throughout the region, there is a distinctive southern dialect, as well as a
cuisine resembling that of Malaysia.

From time to time there is talk – as there has been since 1793 – of
building a 100-km (60-mile) long canal, like the Panama and Suez
canals, across the Kra Isthmus, from outside Songkhla to north of
Satun. Alternative "land bridge" proposals include from Songkhla
to Penang, in Malaysia, and from near Surat Thani to Krabi. Any of
these routes would minimise the need to use Singapore as a shipping
transit point, but the environmental concerns are monumental.

Rich in natural resources, the south is Thailand's most prosperous
region after Bangkok. Rubber, the country's second-largest agricultural export product after rice, thrives so well that Thailand is the
world's largest exporters, as with tin, which is mined in southern
provinces. Tourism has become a major foreign exchange earner, so
it is unfortunate that the decades-old separatist struggle has led to
increasing violence in the region. In addition to the unrest, the earthquake-generated tsunami at the end of 2004 caused massive damage
to life and property along Thailand's Andaman coast. Fortunately,
most tourist destinations in the six Andaman provinces were back to
near-normal conditions within six months.

For many years, access to the south's secluded areas was a major
undertaking. Only the really adventurous attempted it. While getting
around the southern areas is easy these days, there is still a sense of
adventure and remoteness to one's travels here. ❏

PRECEDING PAGE: isolated beach in northwestern Phuket. **LEFT:** boats at rest in Phang
Nga Bay, on the western coast of peninsular Thailand.

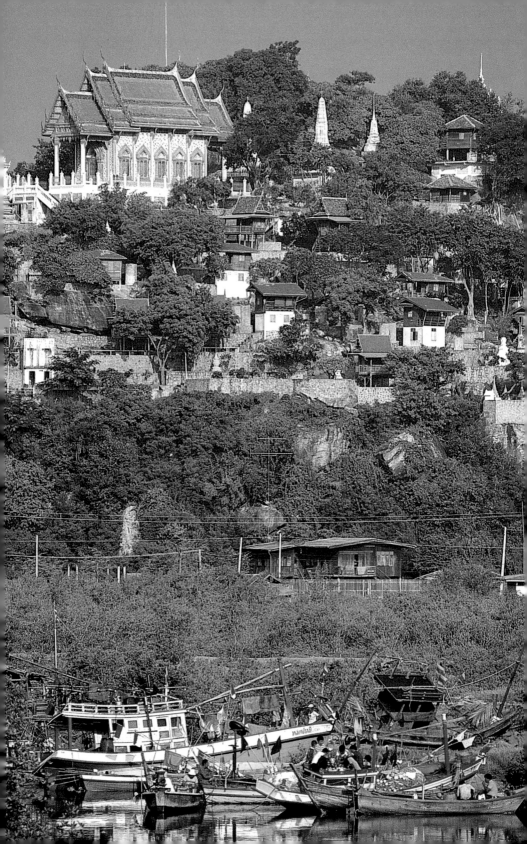

NORTHERN ISTHMUS

Looking like the trunk of an elephant, the Isthmus of Kra is Thailand's overland link to the Malaysian peninsula. Both sides of this narrow isthmus offer some of the world's finest beaches

Map, page 297

THAILAND

Bangkok

There is little to distinguish **Ratchaburi ❶**, but in recent years, it has become a ceramics centre, manufacturing everything from large brown rainwater storage jars decorated with dragons and known as *ong*, to exquisite *benjarong* wares – small porcelain vessels with intricate, five-coloured designs. One can spend a day wandering from shop to shop in Ratchaburi, contentedly browsing among a wide variety of styles and types. Prices are generally very reasonable, and outlets will be only too pleased to arrange shipping.

Phetchburi ❷, 160 km (100 miles) south of Bangkok, has far more to offer. Approaching the town on Route 4, take the left fork and continue past a rocky hill on the right. Cross the railroad tracks and stop under the shady trees for a visit to the cave at **Khao Luang**. Around midday, huge stalactites and dozens of Buddha images are bathed in a soft light that pours through the cave roof.

Entering Phetchburi, *naga*-topped walls frame the pathway to **Khao Wang**, a palace built by King Mongkut in the 1860s. Ascend by foot or miniature railway the fragrant frangipani-fringed path, past the royal stables, to the restored palace at the summit. The gleaming – sometimes blindingly – white palace is dominated by an observatory, which the king constructed to pursue his favourite pastime of astronomy. The view from the parapet is superb; one can survey the entire city, its river, the rice fields and the mountains along the Burmese border to the west.

Four temples are worthy of a visit. **Wat Yai Suwannaram** is east of the river, and **Wat Kamphaeng Laeng**, just southeast of it. Wat Yai Suwannaram, built in the 17th century, has murals that are among the oldest in the country. Wat Kamphaeng Laeng, a Khmer temple, is thought to delineate the most western frontier of the Angkorian empire. **Wat Ko Kaew Sutharam** contains fading, but beautiful, Ayutthaya-period murals dating from 1734. **Wat Mahathat**, in the middle of town, is marked by a huge *prang* that towers over it. Much of the decor is new, but it nevertheless acts as a magnet for Buddhists, and visitors will find that festivals are often in progress there.

About 20 km (15 miles) southeast of Phetchburi is **Kaeng Krachan Dam**, which is a part of the **Kaeng Krachan National Park**, the largest in Thailand. Visitors may stay at bungalows overlooking the scenic reservoir, and take boats up the reservoir to the river.

Some 40 km (25 miles) south is **Cha-am**, the first of several beach resorts along the peninsula. Better known is the sister resort of **Hua Hin ❸** further south, Thailand's oldest major beach resort. It was put on the map in 1910 by the brother of King Rama VI, Prince Chakrabongse, who led a party of European and Thai royalty down the peninsula to hunt game. King Prajadhipok (1925–1935) built a palace here called **Klai**

LEFT: wat and dwellings, Hua Hin.
BELOW: Khao Luang.

Klangwon, meaning "far from worries". Ironically, he was on holiday here in 1932 when a bloodless coup toppled him, replacing 700 years of absolute monarchy with a constitutional one. Unfortunately, the palace is not open to the public. Remnants of the 1920s and 1930s linger at the **Sofitel Central Hua Hin Resort**, better known by its former name, the **Hua Hin Railway Hotel**. Renovated, it retains its air of gentility, with ceiling fans and gardens filled with a menagerie of animal topiary. The tea room is, in fact, a museum collection of domestic Thai artefacts from the 1920s and 1930s. Because of its old-world atmosphere, this hotel stood in for the French Embassy in Phnom Penh in the film *The Killing Fields*.

Hua Hin beach is wide and flat, and shelves very slowly. Horses can be rented for a gallop, or a trot, along the sand. As a booming weekend resort for Bangkok residents, Hua Hin's modern development generally lacks the charm lingering in the old Railway Hotel. A string of new resort hotels have opened in recent years, with both international brands like Hyatt, Hilton and Marriott as well as local (but expensive) concerns like Dusit, Anantara and Chiva Som. The town has a thriving night market with a range of food stalls, restaurants and shops that are open late to satisfy the appetite of visitors. For some lively local colour, stroll down to the pier in the morning, or else in the evening, to watch fishermen unload their catches, while women examine and bargain for a wide variety of fresh seafood, including an occasional catch of shark or stingray.

South of Hua Hin

Leave Hua Hin by heading south again on Route 4. Some 20 km (15 miles) from the town, the highway by-passes vast pineapple fields, crosses a river, then enters sleepy **Pranburi**, where isolated beach luxury resorts like the Evason and the

boutique Aleenta Resort have recently opened at **Paknampran** beach.

Further south, the jagged outline of the **Khao Sam Roi Yot National Park** ❹ (open daily 8am–6pm; admission fee) comes into view. The caves here once sheltered bandits who robbed unwary travellers; their haunts were cleared out long ago. Now, deer, monkeys and numerous species of birds roam the park, the coastal areas of which have been badly denuded by prawn farms.

The sky above Khao Sam Roi Yot (Three Hundred Peaks Range) is fondly remembered in the annals of the Chakri dynasty. In 1868, King Mongkut, an astute mathematician and astronomer, brought the governor of Singapore and members of the Bangkok court here to view a total eclipse of the sun, which he had foretold. The king's prediction, to the astonishment of local astrologers, was only four minutes off. News of this event helped to discredit the superstition that an eclipse occurred when a giant swallowed the sun and disgorged it only when impelled by gongs and general noise-making. (Unfortunately, King Mongkut contracted a fever and died a week after his return to Bangkok.)

About 90 km (55 miles) south of Hua Hin, **Prachuap Khiri Khan** ❺ faces a scenic little harbour enclosed by knob-like hills. A natural arch at Khao Chong Krachok frames the sky. Steps – 404 in all – lead up the hill to a small monastery surrounded by frangipani trees. Within the *chedi* are Buddha relics bequeathed to the state by Rama I and Rama IV, and used in the coronation of Chakri kings.

From Prachuap, continue to **Huay Yang**. The waterfall here cascades over 120 metres (400 ft) of boulders, in a forest setting not far from the Burmese border. Beyond lies **Bang Saphan** ❻, divided in two by the tracks of the south-bound railway. A wide bay is rimmed by a pretty beach. A green hill, Khao Mae Pamphung, is to the north; Ko Thalu is to the south. Seafood and drinks are served on wooden tables right on the beach.

South of Bang Saphan, the countryside becomes lush and mountainous. Rubber

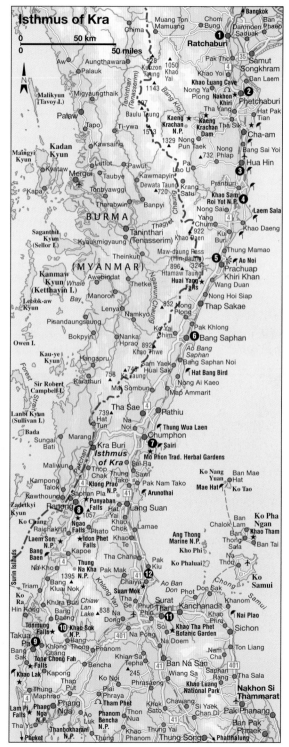

plantations are laid out beneath dramatic limestone cliffs that erupt from the Kra Isthmus, and further south down the Malay Peninsula.

Around 500 km (300 miles) south of Bangkok, Route 4 comes to an important junction, where it branches right and heads west to the Andaman Sea, on the west coast. The left branch leads to Chumphon, Lang Suan and the east coast towns of Surat Thani, Nakhon Si Thammarat and Songkhla. Turn left at this junction to reach **Chumphon ❼**, noted for its inexpensive bird's-nest soup. East of it lies **Paknam Chumphon**. Situated at the mouth of the Mae Nam Chumphon, this fishing port rents boats by the hour for trips to nearby islands, where swallows build their nests. The island of **Lanka Chio** is especially famous. The island-dotted coastal waters make for exciting sailing, too, for those so inclined.

To the west coast

South on Route 41 is Surat Thani. A longer way, and more scenic, is Route 4, which strikes west across the narrowest point on the Kra Isthmus, then veers south, following the Pakchan River through **Kraburi** on the way to Ranong.

About 12 km (8 miles) beyond Kraburi, turn left just before the 504-km marker to reach **Tham Prakayang**, a temple in a cavern. If you lack a torch, the monks may lend you one for the dark ascent into the image-filled cave. One completely black Buddha gazes upon visitors through mother-of-pearl eyes. A limestone-and-wooden staircase leads up and out of the cave to well-worn paths, trodden by monks who meditate amid the solitude atop the outcrop.

South of Tham Prakayang, the highway winds through jungled hills and crosses a wide river. Punyaban Falls appears next to the road. Truck drivers stop, don sarongs, and take a quick dip in the cool water. This is a popular spot for

TIP

During the swallow mating season, from March to late August, collectors climb high up the cliffs to fetch the swallows' nests. Merchants bid for nest concessions; gunmen are hired to guard the claim.

BELOW: southern street market.

Thai tourists, who stop for snacks at the teahouse near the falls. Climb a path to the left of the falls for a good view of the Pakchan estuary, nearby islands, and the contours of mountains on the southern tip of Burma.

Further down the road, turn right near the Thara Hotel to enter **Ranong ❽**. The hotel itself holds one of Ranong's main attractions: hot mineral water piped from nearby thermal springs. A well encloses the main outlet, which pours forth 500 litres (880 UK pints) per minute of sparkling mineral water, at 70°C (160°F). Cross a suspension bridge to a little park, or climb the hill behind the shrine to a small wat enclosed in a secluded grove.

The road past the hot springs leads to the village of **Hat Supin**. This is tin-mining country; stark landscapes of white silt, bamboo scaffolding, deep and dark pits, and gouged-out cliff faces are everywhere. In open-cast mining, water from high-pressure hoses carves holes in the earth. The mineral-laden water is filtered through a sieve, which separates the tin ore from the mud and sand. One of Thailand's major exports, tin is mined all along the Indian Ocean coast of the isthmus. Much of the ore comes from private holdings, like those around Hat Supin. A small sign with fish painted on it points the way to **Wat Hat Supin**, where children rush up to sell sweet popcorn, which is fed to hundreds of carp that swarm in a pool located by the side of the temple.

Drive back to Ranong, then take the 3-km (2-mile) road to **Saphan Pla**, on the sea where boats unload fish at a modern wharf and trucks dump tons of crushed ice on emptied decks. From this port, some boats sail the Indian Ocean as far as Bangladesh in search of fish. Directly opposite Saphan Pla is **Ko Pak Nam**, with its stilt houses and fishing boats. Boats can be rented for trips to the island. Ferries make frequent trips from Saphan Pla to the Burmese town of

Map, page 297

Spirit house.

BELOW: across the Kra Isthmus.

Kawthoung (known as "Victoria Point" under British rule), for which you need a valid tourist visa for Burma. Continuing south past Kapoe and Khuraburi for 160 km (100 miles), the road meets the junction of Route 401, near the town of Takua Pa. From here, the highway heads east towards Surat Thani.

The indifferent appearance of **Takua Pa ⑨** belies its rich past. In the 3rd century BC, Emperor Ashoka of India sent troops to conquer Klingkarach, in the southeast of his country. Natives of that region fled overseas and resettled in Takua Pa and Takua Tung. Later, the area became a significant port for Indian traders, who settled along the Malayan coast when the region was called Suvannabhumi, Land of Gold, over 1,500 years ago. Three statues of Brahma, Siva, and Vishnu – all four-armed and larger than human size – found in nearby hills, and two 7th-century Dvaravati statues, discovered on an island in the mouth of the yellowish Mae Nam Takua Pa, add to the archaeological evidence. By the 16th century, Portuguese merchants were buying and selling goods on this coast, especially at Phuket and Malacca.

Today, Takua Pa has little to claim except as the district centre of a rich tin-mining area. South of Takua Pa, a road branching off Route 4 leads to **Bang Sak**, a beach that rims a scenic, wide bay. The 2004 Indian Ocean tsunami devastated villages and resorts at or near the beach in Bang Sak and neighbouring Bang Niang. While the beach itself is back to normal, it will be another three or four years before the local tourism infrastructure will be completely rebuilt.

Forty km (25 miles) south of Takua Pa, at **Khao Lak**, about 30 families live most of the year in the natural shelter of this cove. The men do not fish, but rather dive for tin, with the aid of air pumps and goggles. Like nautical prospectors, they stay underwater one or two hours at a time, loading tin-bearing sand into buckets. Work-

Some scholars think Indian traders sought short cuts across Thailand to the South China Sea. Unearthed statues are evidence of caravan routes across the Kra Isthmus to Surat Thani. Takua Pa is thought to have been a major centre for the spice trade.

BELOW: coconut-hunting patrol.

ers hoist the full buckets onto bamboo rafts and sieve their contents. Every June, the powerful monsoons churn up the ocean and halt the tin diving. The mining families abandon their huts to the destructive lashing of wind and sea until the monsoon relents. Parts of Khao Lak were heavily damaged by the tsunami, and the properties on the beach will take a few years to rebuild. If continuing south from here, one will reach the island of Phuket and the Phang Nga Bay area.

Return to the eastern seaboard

Back at Takua Pa, Route 401 cuts east across the isthmus, a great drive full of ups, downs and challengingly sharp corners, zigzagging over and around the cloud-cloaked limestone pinnacles of the Kra Isthmus. First the road enters the hills, plunging through a remarkable series of streaked limestone precipices and splintered rocks. Then it traverses the wide valley of the Takua Pa River, passing tin mining camps flanked by mountains. For a midway rest, stop at **Wat Thamwaran**, just to the left of a small river. The wat provides a simple shelter for monks who often meditate near a cave.

Nature-oriented travellers have the pleasure of stopping at the well-marked **Khao Sok National Park** ❿ (open daily 8am–6pm; tel: 0 7739 5139; admission fee). The park, in combination with Klongsang Wildlife Sanctuary and the Ratchaprapha Dam (sometimes called Chiaw Lan lake), covers 123,600 hectares (300,000 acres) of mostly virgin rainforest, with surrounding peaks rising to over 1,000 metres (3,300 ft). Although poaching is rife, the sheer size of the forest has helped protect sizeable populations of elephant, bison, langur, bear, Asiatic wild dogs, and even brilliant-beaked hornbills, as well as tiger, leopard and other jungle cats. The world's largest flower, the 80-cm (2.6-ft) wide *Rafflesia*

Map, page 297

The Rafflesia is a real stinker, with the intent of attracting pollinating insects. Parasitic and lacking leaves, it grows in the roots of host trees. Once a year it surfaces and blooms, smelling foul and hoping for a passing insect. Days later, the flower withers.

BELOW: the banteng, a wild cattle species found in the south of Thailand.

Map, page 297

Ancient votive tablet from the Srivijaya empire.

BELOW:
Suan Mok art.
RIGHT: Wat Mahathat, in Chaiya.

(known in Thai as *bua phut*), was recently found in the park, one of the few places in the world where it occurs. A number of Spartan, but clean, bungalow resorts along the Khlong Sok River act as a base for guided treks and canoeing excursions, and trips to floating villages on the lake.

The road leaves the hills and enters dense rubber plantations before entering the town of **Surat Thani** ⓫. This busy shipbuilding, fishing and mining centre lies on the bank of the Tapi River. Surat itself has little worth seeing, but is a point of departure for several interesting side trips, not to mention for Ko Samui.

Ancient empire

Twenty km (12 miles) north of Surat Thani is **Chaiya** ⓬, a small and sleepy town of unpainted wooden buildings. The area is the subject of a debate about whether or not it was the capital of a once-great empire.

Some historians now believe that the capital of the Srivijaya empire – described by the wandering Chinese monk, I Ching, in AD 671 – was not Palembang, in Sumatra, but rather Chaiya. In fact, they claim, the date previously accepted as the founding of the empire in Palembang was actually the date it was conquered by Chaiya. The name Chaiya may be a contraction of Srivijaya.

In any case, only a few traces remain of this mighty empire, which once stretched from Java through Malaysia, and into Thailand. Less than 2 km (1 mile) out of town stands **Wat Borom That**, one of the most revered temples in Thailand. Its central chedi is thought to be over 1,300 years old, and is a direct visual link between Chaiya and the Srivijaya period. A small museum adjoining the wat displays some interesting relics found in the vicinity.

Closer to town is **Wat Wieng**, where an inscription dated AD 755 is ascribed to a King Vishnu. It was the erroneous attribution of this inscription, 50 years ago, to a different location that led to the hypothesis that Nakhon Si Thammarat was an important local Srivijayan centre. Two other wats, Wat Long and Wat Kaew, equidistantly spaced from Wat Wieng, mark the sites of Srivijaya edifices. Today only Wat Kaew holds a dim reminder of a forgotten past in the crumbling wall of a once-great chedi. All that's known is that it commemorates a victory in battle.

A few kilometres west of these historic remains, a small hillock rises from the flat countryside. Here stands a Buddhist retreat named **Suan Mok**, as new as Chaiya's past is old. The walls and columns inside the central building are covered with an eclectic series of paintings, which run the gamut from the history of Buddhism in Asia to Aesop's fables from Europe.

Suan Mok owes a surrealistic touch to a wandering Zen Buddhist, Emanuel Sherman, whose search for enlightenment led him from the United States to Japan and Thailand, eventually ending on the island of Pha Ngan, off the Thai coast.

After his death, local artists covered one wall with illustrations to portray Sherman's epigrams. Bas-reliefs telling the story of the Buddha decorate the outer walls. They were modelled locally from photos of the Indian originals. Suan Mok's quirky touch continues into its adjoining structures. The *bot* is a large concrete ship that serenely sails the sea of suffering to eventual *nirvana*. ❑

KO SAMUI AND KO PHA NGAN

Savvy travellers need little introduction to the appeal of Ko Samui, once a backpacker's retreat but now an international resort. A few of the other islands nearby, however, are not as well-known

Sometime during your stay in Thailand you will probably meet a few entrenched expatriates or ageing tourists who will be unable to resist waxing nostalgically about the Ko Samui they discovered a generation ago. They camped under the stars on powdery Chaweng Beach. They explored coral reefs from fishermen's boats. And they shared the simple meals of coconut farmers by the light of flickering kerosene lamps. That island is long gone.

Nowadays, about 4 million tourists descend upon Ko Samui every year. There are luxury hotels, fancy restaurants, a modern airport, easy transport, and the full panoply of water sports and other diversions. Despite that, the 250 sq km (100 sq miles) of archipelago retain much natural beauty. The interior is still the preserve of coconut farmers and forested hills. Unlike high-rise Phuket, buildings are prohibited from surpassing the height of palm trees on Samui. Hire a motorbike or hop on a circulating *songthaew* – pick-up trucks with benches in the back – and follow the paved, well-fringed rolling road that rings the island.

Aside from attendance at the Catholic church or immigration office, there's no reason to linger among the drab cement blocks of Samui's biggest town, the western port of **Na Thon ❶**. Ferries to Ko Pha Ngan and Ang Thong National Marine Park depart from Na Thon, however.

PRECEDING PAGES: island silhouette. **LEFT:** a boring Ko Samui beach. **BELOW:** waterfall at Na Muang.

The choice of beach or diving spots, nonetheless, should take into consideration the monsoonal wind factor. From May to October, the southeast monsoon blows on the western and northern coasts. From October to January, unleashing the heaviest rains in November, the northeast monsoon can disrupt the eastern coast. Usually you can still swim during these periods, if not read on the beach.

The original beachcombers and today's tasteful hotels were drawn to Ko Samui by a 6-km (4-mile) long swath of soft, silky sand at **Chaweng ❷**. The sand at its half-sized southern neighbour, **Lamai ❸**, is slightly lower-grade. Behind each beach runs a treacherous road – pitted, potted and often swamped – that barely supports a sprawl of all the traveller's necessities: post office, Internet access, banks, money exchanges, travel agencies, clothing shops, tailors, gyms and body piercers. Not to mention all manner of restaurants, bars and music clubs, with old rock and reggae prevailing over techno. Samui never approaches the sleazy excesses of Pattaya and Phuket, but Lamai has a conspicuous share of open-air hostess bars, go-go girls and transvestite shows.

South of Lamai, the small beaches of **Ban Hua Thanon ❹** and **Ban Bangkao ❺** are nothing to write home about, but the coral reef is healthy near the former, and the latter is a charming, wooden Muslim village. From either, make a day trip inland and swim at the two-tiered waterfall at **Na Muang ❻**.

Coming up the western side of the island, **Ban Taling Ngam** ❼ offers a couple of rather deluxe resort retreats. Further north, just before the road juts east along the northern coast, is Na Thon.

For panorama, head along the north shore to **Maenam** ❽. The sand is coarser than that of the east, but the 4-km (2-mile) stretch is little developed. East of Maenam, **Bo Phut** ❾ is much narrower, but relatively protected, whichever way the wind blows. Popular with French and Italian families, it's a short walk from the cute little fishing village of Ban Bo Phut. As for **Bangrak** ❿ (better known as **Big Buddha Beach**), it's a mystery why anyone stays here unless they enjoy the din from the adjacent road or the airplanes roaring overhead. Or perhaps it's the view of the indisputably large Buddha statue and its complement of especially garish souvenir shops. Quieter **Choeng Mon** ⓫, on the island's northeastern spur, has decent sand and is within quick access of Chaweng's facilities.

In addition to all the outlets for water sports, in the island's interior are several waterfalls descending from the heights of **Khao Phlu**, the island's highest point at 635 metres (2,080 ft). Sprinkled elsewhere around the island are a go-kart track, snake farm, butterfly farm and lots of snooker parlours. With 10 stadiums and counting, water-buffalo fights are Samui's newest entertainment. The bulls don't draw blood, but the high-stakes betting is fast and raucous. The numerous signs for "monkey shows" are actually opportunities to see pig-tailed macaques engaged in their usual jobs on coconut farms. They twist coconuts from the tree tops, then retrieve and deposit them in burlap bags. Copra, the dried coconut flesh, will eventually be pressed to produce coconut oil.

Last but not least are the attractions of 41 brilliant isles comprising **Ko Ang Thong National Marine Park** ⓬ (open daily 8am–6pm; tel: 0 7728 0222;

The gold-gilded Buddha near Big Buddha Beach is actually on a small island, Ko Faan. The Buddha statue is 12 metres (40 ft) high.

BELOW: Bo Phut, on Ko Samui.

admission fee). Day-long package trips go to Ko Wua Talab, park headquarters, and Ko Mae Ko. But these tours allow little time to investigate any more than a viewpoint and a cave on Wua Talab and the clear, pea-green saltwater lake on Mae Ko. On both, the designated swimming spots have negligible coral and fish. It's better to take the standard tour out, but stay a few days on Wua Talab. Visitors can rent park bungalows or tents, or set up their own. The island is teeming with macaques, langurs, otters, birds and other wildlife. Hire one of the resident fishermen to take you to a smaller isle with virgin coral.

Ko Pha Ngan

If Ko Samui is the land of package tours and brief holidays, its neighbour 15 km (9 miles) to the north, **Ko Pha Ngan**, is a refuge for backpackers on leisurely world tours and Europeans whiling away winter-long holidays. Smaller, rustic and rugged, and with horrible roads, Pha Ngan lacks Samui's spectacular beaches, but has plenty of secluded, craggy bays sheltering small sandy jewels adorned with coral. At the last count, over a dozen of these host a bungalow resort or two (or 40, in the case of Hat Rin), where US$5 will get you a sturdy roof, a cold-water bath and electricity at least until midnight.

Ah, yes, about the roads... From the cacophonous southern port town of **Thong Sala** ⑬, a ferry port for Ko Samui and Ko Tao (except for e-mail and mountain bike rentals, there's little call to hang around Thong Sala), there is a paved 10-km (6-mile) stretch that runs due north to the village of **Cha Loak Lam** ⑭, a favourite stopover on the north coast for trawlers. This route is plied by *songthaew* "taxis," which can drop you off for the short walk to Pang waterfall, followed by a challenging 400-metre (1,300 ft) climb to the island's

Map,
page 309

TIP

Many people prefer Chaweng and Lamai in a stiff wind – usually in winter between November and February – because it forces jet-skiing and water-skiing, and the incessant droning of motors, to a halt.

BELOW: statue of Buddha, near Big Buddha Beach.

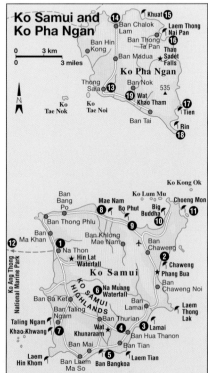

Another sunset on Ko Pha Ngan.

stellar viewing point. The dirt trails branching off to the western coast lead to about a half-dozen beaches and are navigable by motorbike if it hasn't rained recently. These are not Pha Ngan's premier beaches, although there's fine snorkelling coral at Hat Yao (West) and Mae Hat to the north. The rutted trails meandering around the eastern quadrant, however, are always hazardous and should not be attempted by novice cyclists, whether on motorbike or mountain bike.

East of Cha Loak Lam, the justly prized beach of the moment is **Hat Khuat** ⑮ (Bottle Beach), which can only be reached by sea. The quickest jump there is from Ban Cha Loak. Continuing eastward and down the coast, one could enjoyably argue the merits of **Hat Sadet** (with a waterfall and jumbo rocks bearing the graffiti of Thai royalty) or **Thong Nai Pan** ⑯, with wonderful cliff viewpoints, a double-barrelled bay and a coral reef. Eventually you will reach the pretty southern cove of **Hat Tien** ⑰, which offers an additional choice of beaches on either side. One of the two bungalow resorts here is The Sanctuary, with an arresting central building constructed amidst enormous boulders and outcroppings. From September to late May, it sponsors alternative health and New Age courses. Hat Tien forswears videos, noise and mind-altering drugs.

Not coincidentally, the next sign of habitation, a mere 10 minutes away by long-tail boat, is **Hat Rin** ⑱, better known internationally than Pha Ngan itself. The fame, or notoriety, stems from the monthly all-night "full-moon" party. The biggest bashes of the year take place in December and January, when leading British DJs fly in with cutting-edge sounds and hordes of young clubbers. Together with the island's semi-permanent foreign residents and the charters from Samui, the numbers can swell to 15,000. Even in the slowest months, when the ambience is more akin to a US frat party, 3,000 people may dance into the

BELOW: manta rays in formation.

wee small hours. Poopers gripe that the party has become detached from its pagan roots; others say that undercover policemen have put a damper on the chemical enhancements. Of the two beaches that comprise Hat Rin, the eastern side of the headland, known as Sunrise Beach, is far superior with a wide bay of sand, good swimming and a bit of coral. West of the headland, Sunset is scraggy and usually strewn with flotsam, but it's so quiet that you can fall asleep to the waves. Besides, it's only a 10-minute walk to Sunrise. In between, there's a grid of dirt lanes lined with clothing, jewellery and dive shops, as well as two banks, a clinic, a post office, pharmacies, tattooists and overseas telephones. Besides the usual video cafes and unusual MSG-free zones, there are genuine Italian restaurants.

There's even a thrice-daily boat connection between Hat Rin and Samui. Nonetheless, the roller-coaster road joining Hat Rin and Thong Sala is now paved and has further opened up the intervening villages and so-so beaches of Ban Tai and Ban Khai.

An easy stroll up a hill from Ban Tai brings you to **Wat Khao Tham ⑲** (open daily; admission fee). During most months of the year, Australian and American teachers run recommended 10- to 20-day Buddhist meditation courses here.

Ko Tao

Alone in the middle of the ocean, flung a good 40 km (25 miles) northwest of Ko Pha Ngan, tiny **Ko Tao** is the third principal island of the 80-strong Samui archipelago. The home of fewer than 800 fisher folk, it was colonised in the past decade or so by backpackers on a tireless search for "somewhere quiet." Ko Tao is quiet. The brief strip of paved road supports only one or two trucks. There's no place to race motorcycles. There are no bars, nightclubs, banks or jet skis. No go-karts. You can fall asleep listening to the waves.

Arriving by boat from either Chumphon or Ko Pha Ngan at **Ban Mae Hat**, the only proper village, you will be greeted by long-tail touts proclaiming the virtues of their often isolated bungalow resorts. Be wary. Those located on the northern and eastern coasts probably do provide fine snorkelling sights surrounding garage-sized boulders, but there is no beach or sand.

To the left (north) of Ban Mae Hat, the long beach of **Sai Ree** is deceptive, since the water is too shallow for anything more vigorous than the breast stroke. Likewise with Coral Beach on the right. Better to heed the touts from the southern coast. Or walk the few kilometres to **Ao Chalok** and **Hai Sai Daeng**.

Once settled, nature lovers can happily explore the island's 21 sq km (8 sq miles) on foot. Rough trails criss-cross the uninhabited, thickly forested interior. Although you may never glimpse the gibbons, you will probably hear their distinctive *whoop-whoop* signalling their presence in nearby tree tops.

For a cooling drink and a swim, follow the obvious signs for those boulder-strewn bungalows dotted around the coast. Ko Tao's strongest attraction, though, is its proximity to about 25 excellent scuba-diving sites. In fact, these are where many diving trips originating in Ko Samui or Ko Pha Ngan head each day. At Ban Mae Hat, at least a dozen foreign-managed dive shops fiercely compete. Certified instruction is available. ❑

Map, page 309

TIP

Diving services operate year-round, but January until late May offers the best visibility, reaching up to 30 metres (98 ft). Visibility drops markedly from June to September, as well as in November, when the monsoonal winds shift.

BELOW: macaques are often heard, not seen, aloft.

PHUKET

Long before Ko Samui hit the limelight, Phuket was the prime beach destination in Thailand. It still is, and unlike Pattaya, which has sunk into sleaziness, Phuket retains its tropical charms

Map,
page 313

Phuket's physical beauty is even greater than its exquisite beaches. This beauty stems from its picturesque villages, coconut groves and rubber plantations, as much as from its patchwork of wild flowers presented against a backdrop of forested hills. Seaward from the beaches, coral reefs teem with marine life. It can be a dangerous beauty. During the monsoon season, May to October, rough surf and high winds can make swimming unsafe. The eastern shore is comprised primarily of rocky shoals, mud flats and mangroves. Nearly all of Phuket's decent beaches are located on the western side of the island. Landward, Phuket people exude the confidence of islanders who have prospered from an island rich in natural resources.

For centuries Phuket was a backwater. The long road south from Bangkok to reach it, the lack of a bridge across to the mainland, bad roads on the island itself, and a seeming lack of interest in developing it for recreation meant that it languished in relative isolation for decades despite natural resources of tin, rubber and coconut. Indeed, Phuket airport was only upgraded to international status in the 1970s to let tin and rubber merchants travel easily to Penang, Kuala Lumpur and Singapore. No one thought about tourism back in those days.

In the late 1970s, Phuket began appearing on the maps of budget backpackers. They stayed in fishermen's bungalows or camped out on the beach at Patong. Word spread, and developers descended on the island. The airport was expanded to handle long-haul jets from Europe. Dirt roads were paved. As tourist dollars flowed towards the beaches, the island grew to become the richest province in Thailand, second only to Bangkok.

The lion's share of Phuket's wealth now comes from tourism. The boom has had a social knock-on. Although there are only 10,000 native Phuket inhabitants, an estimated 240,000 migrant Thais, drawn from all 76 provinces in the kingdom, now live and work on the island, mostly in tourism-related activities.

The Indian Ocean tsunami of 2004 sent a series of huge waves crashing onto Phuket's western and south-western beaches, damaging many resorts, restaurants, and other businesses. The worst-hit beaches were those at Kamala and Bang Thao, while close on the heels of these two were Patong and Nai Han. By mid 2005, however, most places had been repaired and re-opened, and tourism was returning to normal levels.

LEFT: yet another typical Phuket sunset.

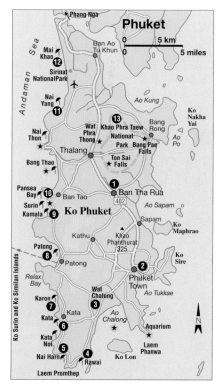

Urban Phuket

The road from Phang Nga crosses the 600-metre (2,000-ft) Sarasin Bridge to Phuket, an island about the same size as Singapore. The sojourn to Phuket town, 30 km (19 miles) to the south, soon reaches the emotional heart of the island. The intersection at **Ban Tha Rua ❶**, leading to Surin Beach and Khao Phra Taew National Park, is dominated by a bronze statue of two women warriors, swords in hands. The pair are sisters: Chan and Muk. In 1785 they led an army of villagers against Burmese invaders.

Unlike many provincial centres, **Phuket** ❷, a town on the island's southeast coast, has a rich identity of its own. The style is set by the beautiful colonial-style houses built by tin and rubber barons at the end of the 19th century. The construction followed a disastrous fire that destroyed the downtown area. Thanon Thalang, Thanon Phang Nga, and some of the smaller surrounding streets are still lined with Sino-Portuguese-style shophouses. Three storeys high, the rowhouses were built by middle-income Chinese to house their extended families. The ground floor normally serves as a shop and reception hall; the upper floors are the living quarters. Huge signs with large Chinese characters etched in gold are hung over, or alongside, the doors to identify the family residing within. The Chartered Bank building, Thai Airways office and others, with their arched loggias, resemble buildings of colonial Singapore and Penang.

The charm of Phuket's old buildings is complemented by the many Chinese shrines that accent the town with bright splashes of colour. Of note is the brightly painted temple of **Jui Tui** and its smaller companion Put Jaw next door, which sit just past the market on Thanon Ranong. Like many similar Chinese shrines elsewhere in Asia, their central altars are dedicated to Quanyin (Kuan Yin), the goddess of mercy.

Outside of town, the only noteworthy building is **Wat Chalong** ❸ (open daily). It lies 6 km (4 miles) further south on the Phuket Bypass, a ring road that runs west of Phuket. The opulently decorated temple is famed for its gilded statue of Luang Pho Chaem, the *wat*'s abbot and famous lay physician.

In 1786, Capt. Light of the East India Company sought to secure Phuket for England. Thai claims and England's desire for a more strategic island to guard the Straits of Malacca led Light to drop the plan. So he founded Penang, which became the chief British colony on the Malay peninsula until the 1819 founding of Singapore.

BELOW: offering at a Chinese temple, Phuket town.

Southern Phuket

South along the coast from the town of Phuket is **Rawai** ❹, whose foreshore is a mass of rocks that lie exposed during low tide. It is then that clam hunters venture out, turning over the stones in search of dinner. Rawai offers many tasty seafood snacks sold along the beach. Rawai also holds one of the island's handful of *chao lay* (sea gypsy) villages. The sea gypsies were once nomadic fishing families, roaming from island to island. They are skilled fishermen both above and below the water. From a young age, they learn to dive to great depths in search of lobsters, prawns, and crabs, staying below for up to three minutes. However, diminishing stocks and environmental and tourism concerns have robbed the sea gypsies of traditional fishing grounds.

Because the sea gypsies are not allowed to own the land they live on, they cannot install permanent facilities, such as brick houses or even septic tanks. Their villages are effectively shanty towns, impermanent shacks reflecting their lack of spiritual attachment to terra firma. The gypsies are not materialistic. Even as fish stocks dwindle, they are reluctant to take up waged employment. They fear complicated involvement with government officers or business people. Proposals have been made to enhance the sea gypsies' standards of living, but lacking strong collective will, the placid gypsies are losing their identity. The youngsters speak Thai instead of Urak Lawoi, their indigenous tongue.

From Rawai the coastal road continues over the north-south ridge of hills, offering great views of Ko Phi Phi, 45 km (30 miles) away. Continuing south around the point at **Laem Prom Thep**, you come to one of the island's prettiest beaches. Nestled between two hills, fronted by a calm sea and backed by a lagoon, **Nai Han** ❺ is a serene setting. The surrounding headlands are lashed by salty breezes.

Map,
page 313

TIP

Prom Thep Cape is a well-visited vantage point for viewing the sunset. The gold-and-green promontory plunges into the hissing sea.

BELOW: Kata Noi.

The more picturesque bays of **Kata** ❻ and **Kata Noi** have a more intimate feel due to their smaller size. There is fine snorkelling at the southern end of Kata Noi beach. Relax Bay, with its single hotel, Le Meridien Phuket, offers some snorkelling along its northwestern rocks. **Karon Beach** ❼ is a long and quiet strip of sand backed by hotels and restaurants at its top, middle and bottom, with empty plots of former rice paddy in between. Both Karon and Kata are much less frenetic than Patong, but with a growing choice of hotel, dining and watersport facilities.

The most developed beach is **Patong** ❽, due west of the town of Phuket and north of Karon. In the early 1970s, Patong was little more than a huge banana plantation wedged between the mountains and a wide crescent of sand. The plantation is now a tourist city-by-the-sea, with multi-storey condominiums and hotels rising above night markets, seafood emporiums, beer bars, discos and tour shops. The beach itself is dotted with colourful parasols.

In the calm weather from November to May, the bay is peppered with visiting yachts. Unlike most other Phuket beaches, Patong has a wide range of water-sports facilities, including scuba diving, windsurfing, waterskiing, parasailing, jetskis, sailing and boogie boards. Dive shops offer trips to Racha and Phi Phi islands, or 80 km (50 miles) northwest to the Similan Islands Marine National Park, considered one of the best diving areas in Asia. Patong also has the most developed land-sports facilities on the island. Most large hotels have pools and many have tennis courts. There are four 18-hole golf courses in Phuket, and one 9-hole.

Patong is a gourmet's delight; seafood is a speciality. The legendary Phuket lobster, however, each weighing up to 3 kg (6 lb), is now caught in Burmese or Indonesian waters. Patong is also a great place to eat Western, Indian, Mexican, Italian, Japanese and Korean cuisines.

BELOW: Le Meridian Phuket, one of several world-class resorts on Phuket.

Map, page 313

After dark, Patong has many open-air bars along Soi Bangla in the middle of the resort. These barbeers, as they are called, lure customers with a heady mix of female company, rock music, and an ocean of booze. Within a few steps you can eat great seafood, barter your price for a silk shirt, go bungy jumping, join some Thai boxing, or buy real estate. Patong is all things to all people. At any major beach you can rent cars, jeeps or motorcycles to explore the island. A valid driver's licence is all that is necessary. The town itself is reputed to have had the first paved road in the kingdom. Phuket also has the highest road fatality statistics in Thailand. Usually only vehicles rented by the large international firms carry insurance, despite signs and verbal promises to the contrary.

Travelling cheaply means relying on the blue-and-white *songthaew* – two-row, wooden buses that leave the Phuket town market for every point on the island. Alternatively, small cramped red vehicles called *tuk-tuk* function as taxis. Barter for the fare before starting off.

Northern Phuket

Some 3 km (2 miles) north of Patong, quiet **Kamala Bay ❾** retains charm around its Islamic hamlets, with their well-kept gardens against a backdrop of forested hills rising to over 500 metres (1,640 ft). The tranquillity has been broken at the northern end of Kamala, where a giant Disney-like theme park has been built, called Phuket Fantasea.

The attractive coastal road north to **Surin Beach** passes the compact Singh Beach, its sandy cape hedged by verdant headlands. Larger Surin Beach with its seafood shacks soon gives way to idyllic **Pansea Bay ❿**, dominated by two proprietary resorts, the Chedi and the Amanpuri. The long beach at **Bang Thao** is dominated by the immense Laguna Phuket Resort, housing five hotel complexes. Much of the land around here used to be a tin mining wasteland. In 1785, the Burmese invaded here, seeking to take over the island.

Nai Yang ⓫ beach, just south of the airport, is now under the jurisdiction of Sirinat National Park. It is a pleasant hangout where local people and tourists come to eat seafood and spicy papaya salad under the casuarina trees. An offshore reef allows year-round swimming in the shallow bay. There are a few Spartan bungalows for rent in the national park. With a good map, you can drive along Phuket's scenic west coast, all the way from Nai Yang to the island's southern tip, Laem Prom thep.

North of Nai Yang is Phuket's longest beach, **Mai Khao ⓬**. The 9-km (6-mile) long beach is undeveloped except for a solitary JW Marriott resort, and is a haven for beachcombers and giant sea turtles that come ashore from December until late February to lay their eggs.

The last main outpost of the island's monsoon evergreen forest can be inspected on an organised hike through **Khao Phra Taew National Park ⓭** (open daily; tel: 662-01 968 2874; admission fee). Wild bears and cats still live in the park, all of them keen to avoid human contact. The park is fringed by two pretty waterfalls: Ton Sai on the west, and Bang Bae on the east.

The sheltered waters off the northeast coast around **Ao Po** contain numerous pearl farms, which you can visit on informative guided tours. ❑

BELOW: pearls.

Map,
page 319

PHANG NGA AND KRABI

*The traveller couldn't ask for a more exquisite, seductive
and resplendent retreat than the islands and bays of Phang Nga.
Increasingly popular – and threatened – is Ko Phi Phi*

THAILAND

Bangkok

In the waters east of the island of Phuket, the spectacle of towering limestone massifs reaches its zenith with 300-metre (1,000-ft) peaks crowding together in close proximity. The same unlikely topography imposes itself throughout Phang Nga Province, making it the most spectacular and visually opulent province in Thailand. The ingenious ways people have adapted to such surroundings also make Phang Nga and its bay one of the wonders of the world.

On the mainland north of the island of Phuket, the town of **Phang Nga ❶** is a lovely, docile township left behind in Thailand's development surge. The main source of employment seems to be in sleepy government offices. Several small hotels provide simple accommodation. The main objective of any first-time tripper, however, should be to the geological wonderland of **Phang Nga Bay**. A long-tail boat trip from near the Phang Nga Bay Resort Hotel reveals Andaman mangrove culture at its best, with mussel farms, floating fish traps, and Brahminy kites circling overhead looking for scraps. The mangroves are fertile breeding, spawning, and feeding grounds for mud skippers, crabs, prawns, and an assortment of fish, like sea bass. Hungry dolphins penetrate the upper reaches of the channels at high tide. Mangrove wood also feeds the long-established charcoal-making industry, a feature of the Andaman coast from Ranong to Malaysia.

BELOW: one of
Phang Nga Bay's
many caves.

Note: Areas of Krabi Province affected by the 2004 tsunami included Ko Phi Phi, Ao Nang, and Ko Lanta. Ao Nang and Ko Lanta quickly recovered, but some parts of Ko Phi Phi remain closed, including the twin beaches of Ao Lo Dalam and Ao Ton Sai, which were flattened and will be reconstructed as a public park.

Just before the mouth of the Mae Nam Phang Nga, an excursion boat approaches the base of the mountain of **Khao Kien**, where a cavern contains primitive paintings depicting human and animal forms. Such cave daubings are quite common in the limestone caves in the area, and were painted around 2,000 years ago. The strange forms depicting sea creatures, six-fingered hands, and semi-human shapes are thought to have played a religious-shamanistic role for the cave dwellers. Prior to hunting expeditions or battles, primitive people would make sacrifices to placate spirits in front of the paintings. The floors of many caves in Phang Nga and Krabi are still scattered with the discarded sea shells left by prehistoric man. Tide fluctuations have compromised archaeological evidence. Forty thousand years ago it was possible to walk to Phi Phi. Five thousand years ago sea levels were higher than at present.

On what seems a collision course with a huge limestone outcrop, the boat then slips into the barely discernible, overgrown cave entrance of **Tham Lot**. For more than 50 meters (165 ft), the boat slides under giant stalactites. Rocks protruding from the water appear to have been sliced by a sword-wielding god. In **Tham Nak**, a twisted stalagmite at the cave's entrance resembles a *naga* serpent, giving this cave its name. Green stalactites burst from the ceiling like a frozen waterfall. The whole mountain-island drips with streaked limestone.

Ko Talu receives its name from *talu*, meaning to pass from one side to the other – in this case, not over the mountain, but under it as the boat squeezes

Ancient cave paintings of the Phang Nga Bay region.

BELOW: limestone, or karst, pillar.

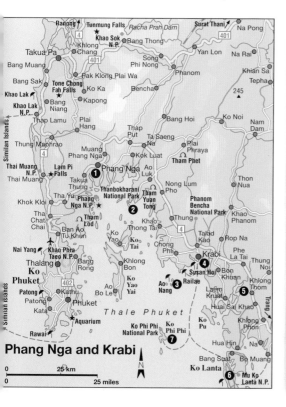

Phang Nga and Krabi

through a cave filled with stalactites. **Ko Ping Kan** is perhaps the most spectacular of Phang Nga's islands. Behind the beach, the mountain seems to have split in two, the halves leaning against each other. Locals say they are two lovers. This area was the setting of part of the James Bond film *The Man with the Golden Gun*. A small beach overlooks another island, Ko Tapoo, or Nail Island, which looks like a thorny spike driven into the sea.

Further south in Phang Nga Bay, the towering islands hold natural treasures hidden from passing boats. Far from being impregnable, a few of the sheer islands allow cave access by canoe when the tide is right. By squeezing in through minute gaps at the correct tidal window, canoeists paddle into a lost world, an open-top sea chamber, its sheer walls covered with vines and ferns. It's like entering the hole in the middle of a doughnut through a side door. These are ecological time capsules where eagles, macaques, and other mangrove species have dwelled for millennia unfettered by people. The chambers are caused by acidic rainwater percolating into the limestone peaks. The soluble limestone island becomes addled with hidden chasms, causing the roof to cave in.

To the south

South of Phang Nga, the journey south on the mainland coast takes the traveller further into the heart of limestone country. At times, the horizon resembles the graph line of a seismic tremor, with jutting rocks thrusting out of the forests.

About 50 km (30 miles) southeast of Phang Nga, **Than Bokkharani National Park** ❷ (open daily 8am–6pm; tel: 0 7568 1071; admission fee) is one of the most beautiful in Thailand. Like a scene from *Lost Horizon*, the park is dominated by lofty cliffs. In one spot, an underground stream rises amid lush vege-

TIP

A small number of sea canoe companies in Phuket arrange superlative day trips into the hidden *hong* of Phang Nga Bay. Of the operators, the pioneering SeaCanoe Thailand has the best safety, service, and environmental track record.

BELOW: rocky retreat near Krabi.

tation at the base of a mountain. Footpaths wind beneath cliff faces covered in green vines, punctuated with brilliant hibiscus.

At **Ao Nang ❸**, near Krabi and 3 km (2 miles) eastwards along the coast road, comfortable resorts act as a base for exploring nearby islands and hidden coves. The Ao Nang area, with its low-key bungalow developments, seafood restaurants, scuba diving, sea canoeing and mountain bike options, makes a refreshing alternative to brassier beach resorts on Phuket.

The town of **Krabi ❹** is a small but bustling service centre built opposite mangrove swamps along the Krabi River. From here, long-tail boats sail out to Railae Beach; larger ones leave for Ko Phi Phi daily, and for Ko Lanta, from November to May. From town, the Krabi River mangroves can be explored by renting a long-tail boat, first stopping off to visit the huge cavern inside the Kanab Nam twin peaks, which flank the river. Traditionally, the leaves, bark, fruit and mosses of the surrounding mangroves provided folk cures for the alleviation of lumbago, thrush, kidney stones and menstrual pains. The trees also provided a source of weak alcohol and leaves in which to wrap tobacco. Two rare bird species inhabit the mangroves: the mangrove pitta and the brown-winged kingfisher.

Southeast from Krabi the land gradually flattens. Dyke-enclosed rice fields appear on both sides of the road. Seemingly abandoned suitcases and boxes on the roadside designate bus stops; passengers wait under banana trees nearby.

Forty km (25 miles) south of Krabi, a hot spring and nature trail make **Klong Thom ❺** a rewarding stop. The small museum at Wat Klong Thom displays artefacts such as beads, pots and religious icons, purportedly from the 5th to 7th centuries AD, when the area was a port for traders, monks and diplomats crossing the peninsula. A bumpy laterite trail eastwards from the main intersection

Map, page 319

BELOW: busy beach on Ko Phi Phi.

Map, page 319

leads to a hot spring suitable for bathing. Further on, the Tung Tieo nature trail starts and finishes at an inviting emerald pool. Southwest of Klong Tom, and also accessible by boat from Krabi, quiet **Ko Lanta** ❻ offers some rustic bungalow accommodation as well as a few comfortable resorts along its 19 powdery beaches. At low tide there is as much chance of finding monkey or lizard tracks as human, although one might prefer the former.

Ko Phi Phi

Turquoise waves caress a beach so dazzlingly white it is almost painful to the eye. The water is so crystalline that colourful fishing boats seem suspended in mid-air. With palm-fringed beaches and lofty limestone mountains as a backdrop, **Ko Phi Phi** ❼ arguably surpasses Phuket as one of the most beautiful islands in Asia. Where Phuket is undulating, physically sociable and with a sizeable population, Phi Phi, like the karst islands of Phang Nga, is geologically dramatic, its population confined to low-lying sand bars below towering rocks.

The underwater grinding you hear while snorkelling is the sound of hungry parrot fish munching their way through the 12 kg (26 lbs) of coral reef they consume each year. The coral is digested and excreted as fine sand.

Phi Phi lies equidistant, about 45 km (28 miles), from both Phuket and Krabi. The island is in fact two islands: the smaller **Phi Phi Ley**, a craggy limestone monolith similar to the other shrub-covered peaks of Phang Nga Bay, and **Phi Phi Don**.

Ironically, it is the unprotected Phi Phi Ley that remains environmentally pristine. It even escaped the 2004 tsunami relatively unscathed. The island's famous beach on the western flank, Ao Maya, where scenes for the Leonardo DiCaprio's The Beach was filmed, has grown in size and reportedly looks better than ever. Ao Lo Samah, near the island's southern tip, has lost some of its sand to the tsunami, so the beach looks smaller than before, but the bay itself is said to be more pristine than usual.

By contrast, the island of Phi Phi Don, previously a cheap and cheerful tourist destination consisting of resorts and shops, was completely devasted by the tsunami. All beachfront properties suffered extensive damage and most were simply swept away by the massive waves. It is likely that a public park will be erected in the place of the former resort.

To enjoy the best of Phi Phi, take a long-tail boat ride around both islands. The boat stops at Viking Cave on Phi Phi Ley first. The cave is renowned as a site for swallows that build their nests on the ceilings of rocky caverns. A web of bamboo scaffolding reaches up, disappearing into the gloomy upper recesses of the cave. Sinewy young men climb up these precarious ladders to collect the swallow nests, which are sold as delicacies to Chinese restaurants. However, there is no demonstration of nest gathering in any cave that still hosts swallows. The nests are more valuable, ounce by ounce, than pure gold, so no concessionaire is going to publicise the location of a productive site.

Tropical fish find sanctuary in the coral reefs of Ko Phi Phi.

Viking Cave is named after its wall painting of long boats with sails. How old these pictures actually are, and who painted them, remains in dispute. What is certain, of course, is that before the 19th century, no Norsemen ever visited the Andaman Sea. It is likely the cave painting here is of later origin than others in Phang Nga and Krabi.

At **Maya Bay**, the long-tail boat stops for snorkelling in a horseshoe bay of corals surrounded by steep cliffs and a deserted white beach. After circumnavigating much of both Phi Phi islands, the boat stops at Bamboo Island for more snorkelling. The reefs at Bamboo are bigger, with more branch and seafan forms. Fish life is more diverse, including groupers lurking in the nooks and crannies. Should the diving bug bite, Phi Phi has dive shops where visitors can earn their open-water diving card. The deeper waters of Ko Bida and Hin Muang, with their barracudas, manta rays, and whale sharks, can then be explored. ❑

RIGHT: Ko Phi Phi.

THE DEEP SOUTH

South of the resort islands of Samui and Phuket, the peninsular character of Thailand takes on subtle changes as it approaches Malaysia. Mosques replace wats, and curry appears in the cuisine

Map, page 327

THAILAND
Bangkok

Lower peninsular Thailand is where Thai-speaking Buddhism meets Malay-speaking Islam. It's a land of verdant jungle and limestone peaks, azure seas and rich, coconut-flavoured cuisine. Southern peninsular Thailand is criss-crossed by a network of excellent roads that connect the Andaman Sea with the Gulf of Thailand. Once troubled by insurgent guerrillas of the People's Liberation Army of Thailand in the north, and by guerrillas of the Communist Party of Malaysia in the south, the region is now completely safe for the traveller. True, a handful of Muslim separatists still hide in the jungled hills that straddle the Thai-Malay frontier, but these regions are well off the beaten track, and the problem is rapidly disappearing. The deep south is an area of pristine beaches, friendly, predominantly rural communities, and markets overflowing with exotic fruits and other native produce. Amongst Thais elsewhere in Thailand, the people of the deep south have a reputation for quickness of thought and swiftness to anger – though this is far from apparent to the foreign visitor. It's a land where travellers can revel in the sun or explore ancient Srivijayan sites.

Trang ❶ is a commercial centre inhabited primarily by the descendants of Teochew-speaking Chinese immigrants, who originally sought work here panning tin but wound up running the region's rubber trade.

Trang's Chinese heritage is reflected in monuments at the northern approach to the city. At **Ban Bangrok**, 3 km (2 miles) north on Route 4, a shrine honours Kwan Tee Hun, a red-faced, bearded god believed to have the power to prevent or start war. Some of Thailand's best beaches are found near Trang: **Jao Mai** and **Yong Ling** beaches to the south, and **Chang Lang** and **Pak Meng** to the north. There is also excellent snorkelling and diving at some of Trang's offshore islands. Accomodations are simple except for a five-star Amari resort at **Chang Lang beach**.

The port of Pak Bara, on the opposite coast of the isthmus in Satun province, around 150 km (90 miles) southwest of Hat Yai, serves as the port for remote **Ko Tarutao Marine National Park ❷** (open daily, 8am –6pm; tel: 0 7478 3485; admission fee). The 51-island archipelago, with a mixed Thai and sea gypsy population, is known for its extensive corals, unpopulated sandy beaches, and simple beach huts. After the monsoon abates, small tour and supply boats link the islands between November and May each year.

Note: Since Thaksin came to power in 2001, the south-eastern-most provinces of Yala, Pattani and Narathiwat have seen an escalation of decades-old Muslim nationalism. Bombings and attacks in these provinces, usually targeting police, army, or government installations, have taken the lives of over 800 Thai nationals during this period. So far tourists have not been targeted, but visitors to these areas should nevertheless travel cautiously.

LEFT: painted prow of Muslim *korlae*, or fishing boat.
BELOW: Songkhla girl.

Nakhon Si Thammarat

Continuing northeast from Trang through Huay Yot, a beautiful and winding valley threads its way to **Nakhon Si Thammarat ❸**. Nakhon may well have been the capital of the elusive kingdom of Tambralinga, mentioned in Chinese annals. A large hoard of silver coins of a type sometimes attributed to Funan, dating from the fifth or sixth century AD, was discovered near Moklan village. Nakhon later became a regional centre of the Sumatra-based Srivijaya empire, at least until the 10th century. Trade and ecclesiastical links between Nakhon and southern India and Ceylon flourished. Around this time, the city's name evolved to the Sanskrit Nagara Sri Dhammaraja, or City of the Glorious Dharma-Observing King, and numerous Indian migrants settled in an area known as Hat Sai Kaew, or Beach of Crystal Sand, where the city's most sacred site, Wat Phra Mahathat, still stands. Later, the city became an important regional centre, whose governors ruled the entire south. From the 16th century it was known to Europeans by the Malay name of Ligor.

While Wat Phra Mahathat may be up to 10 centuries old, the chedi dates from the 1400s.

The human legacy of Nakhon's rich history is evident in the surviving traditions of the *nang thalung* shadow-puppet play, and also in exquisite classical dance-dramas called *lakhon* and *manohra* performed to acclaim by the city's fine-arts school. At **Suchart House**, on Si Thammasok Soi 3, it is possible to watch puppets for shadow-puppet plays being made from leather, and perhaps enjoy an impromptu performance by a master puppeteer.

BELOW: interior and exterior, Wat Phra Mahathat.

The physical aspects of Nakhon's history are extensively displayed in the **National Museum** (open Wed–Sun 9am–4pm; admission fee), at the southern end of Thanon Ratchadamnoen and housing one of the most important collections in Thailand outside of Bangkok. **Wat Phra Mahathat** is Nakhon's most

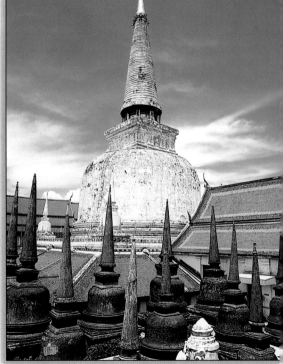

Map,
page 327

revered temple, and one of the country's oldest. The *wat*'s prime attraction is a 77-metre (250-ft) high *chedi,* the top of which is covered by an estimated 270 kg (600 lbs) of gold. To the right of the chedi, a temple museum houses an assortment of delicate gold and silver offerings. South of the chedi, the Viharn Luang, with its inward-leaning columns, is a fine example of Ayutthayan design.

In the city centre, the outdoor **Boworn Bazaar** near the Thai Hotel presents a pleasant environment for Thai dining and drinking, especially at the Ban Lakhon wooden restaurant, built round a mature takian tree. Nakhon comes alive during the Festival of the 10th Lunar Month, usually in October, when spirits of ancestors return in response to donations of food at temples by devotees.

The road north leads to the gulf coast town of **Sichon**, which offers scenic views and southern-style handicrafts. Nearby, it is also possible to visit the cave that some believe sheltered King Taksin after he was deposed by Rama I. (More orthodox histories hold that Taksin was tied up in a velvet sack and beaten to death with a sandalwood club in the manner reserved for royalty.) Take the road across the railway tracks to the village of Lan Saka, then right at the first fork and it is 9 km (6 miles) to the cave, with magnificent views of the countryside.

Heading south

The mostly coastal Route 408 links Nakhon to Songkhla, running south through extensive shrimp farms, lime orchards, dusty training arenas for fighting bulls, and the village of Sathing Phra, where many ancient artefacts have been found.

An alternative to the coast road are the inland routes 403 and 41, leading to **Phatthalung ❹**, which offers rather basic hotels, though one may wish to continue without stopping. If so, head back to Route 4 and turn south for Hat Yai.

Phatthalung may be where nang talung – shadow-puppet plays of local folklore – was first performed in Thailand.

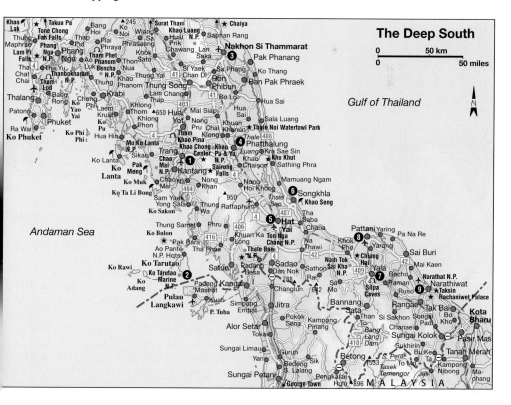

The Deep South

0   50 km
0   50 miles

Gulf of Thailand

Andaman Sea

MALAYSIA

In Khuan Khanun district, just north of Phatthalung, Route 4048 leads to **Thale Noi**, the largest waterfowl reserve in Thailand. Around 150 species of birds make up a population of about 100,000 during the peak migratory period, from December to April. The average depth of the lake is just 1.5 metres (16 ft).

Westwards from the main Phatthalung intersection along Route 4, motorists were sometimes relieved of their cash and valuables in the past by highway robbers, but this is no longer the case. You will likely only see Thai soldiers camped in tents between rows of rubber trees.

About 35 km (20 miles) west of Phatthalung, the **Khao Chong Centre of Wildlife and Nature Study** encompasses jungle, a rocky creek and a number of waterfalls. Drive into the reserve, but do not panic if you encounter soldiers brandishing weapons; the reserve hosts a military camp.

Khao Chong represents part of Thailand's developing conservation and ecology movement. Students at its Nature Education Centre study local flora and fauna in their natural rainforest environment. The small zoo houses local wildlife such as the *binturong*, Prevost squirrel, Brahminy kite, hog badger and endangered species, including the white-handed gibbon, which poachers usually capture at a young age by killing the mother.

The hog badger has a curious connection with southern Thai bullfighting, which draws gamblers from far and wide. The long-clawed mammal is occasionally shot for the fat of its nose. It is claimed that a bull with this wild-smelling fat rubbed on its horns can intimidate and defeat any opponent. The use of this fat is regarded, understandably, as cheating.

From Khao Chong, the return drive to Phatthalung zigzags under towering trees, past pink rocky outcrops, and up and down the mountainous watershed along the spine of the isthmus. About 3 km (2 miles) before Phatthalung, the highway branches south to Hat Yai.

Continue straight on, past the provincial administrative offices, and then bear left on a road to Khuan Khanun (Jackfruit Hill) and **Wat Kuha Sawan**. This antiquated temple was recently renovated, but behind its yellow buildings a staircase climbs up to a large grotto lighted by a natural arch. A delightfully obese and laughing Buddha marks the entrance. Around a copper-leafed bodhi tree are dozens of Buddha images. Light from the arch glints off the statues' gold leaf.

To the right of Wat Kuha Sawan lies another cave, formerly inhabited by a hermit monk. His personal collection of Buddha images is kept there.

To visit another temple and the northern end of the Thale Luang inland sea, take the road leading east from here. **Wat Wang** (Palace Temple) is 8 km (5 miles) from the city. An attractive chedi graces the temple courtyard. Inside the temple proper are unrestored frescoes dating back about two centuries.

Down the road is Ban Lampam, where the waters of the inland sea, 70 km (40 miles) from its entrance to the Gulf of Thailand, are fresh.

A short boat trip from Phatthalung leads to **Tham Malai**, a cave lying between the province's two famous peaks: Broken-Hearted Mountain and Broken-Headed Mountain. Legend says these represent two women turned to stone as punishment for jealousy, perhaps shar-

BELOW: Muslim women at prayer.

ing a common and lasting interest in the same man. To reach the cave, it is best to catch the boat behind the Phatthalung train station for the 15-minute ride to Tham Malai. A monk caretaker will turn on a generator to light up the stalactites.

Map, page 327

Hat Yai

The commercial capital of south Thailand, **Hat Yai ❺** is a boom town. Rubber and tin have been its traditional income earners, but they are rapidly being over-shadowed by an entertainment and commercial centre geared towards thousands of sybaritic Malaysians, who pour over the border each month to enjoy illicit pleasures denied at home. Nightclubs with singers, massage parlours and broth-els are the magnets for some single men, whilst women and families come for the wide range of shops and reasonably priced restaurants.

Hat Yai has several cultural points of interest, nonetheless. **Wat Hat Yai Nai**, in the middle of town, has the third-largest reclining Buddha in the world. One can do more than just admire the exterior of this giant atop its 3-metre (10-ft) high base. Ascend the pedestal and enter the Buddha's innards, where lungs and shrines are displayed side by side.

Sunday is usually the day for bullfights. The TAT office will confirm dates and fight locations, which rotate around the city's handful of arenas. Do not envisage a Spanish-style corrida with matadors and picadors; Thai-style bull fighting is a contest that pits one bull against another. Two animals are brought face to face. They lower their heads, clash horns and paw the ground, each pushing against the other like sumo wrestlers. The fight may last minutes or a couple of hours. It ends when one bull "bulldozes" the other to the edge of the ring, or when one simply turns and takes flight.

For those with more gastronomic interests, the shark's-fin soup at Hat Yai's restaurants draws people all the way from the reaches of Bangkok and Kuala Lumpur. Other specialities are poached duck and fried pigeon. Several large open-air restaurants serve superb seafood to the accompaniment of live music.

From Hat Yai, there are two rail and three road routes to Malaysia. The more frequently used railway line runs southwest, crossing the border to Alor Setar and But-terworth, the connection port for Penang island.

The second heads southeast through Yala and ends at the border town of Sungai Kolok. From there, it is a short walk and taxi ride to Kota Bharu on Malaysia's east coast.

The **Rubber Research Centre** on the outskirts of Hat Yai, en route to Songkhla, serves all of Thailand. It experiments with new grafting and tapping methods, and with how to induce the rubber trees to be more bountiful in their production of latex. Smallholding farmers study at the centre, where there is a rubber pro-cessing laboratory. Next to the research centre is the **Songkhla Nakharin University**, a splendid complex set on a 120-hectare (300-acre) campus. A pumpkin-shaped building containing the auditorium and labora-tories is surrounded by a moat. Arched windows in the pumpkin-shaped building catch breezes from all direc-tions and funnel them through the building to provide natural air-conditioning. An exhaust pump in the cen-tre sucks the warm air out.

Tapping the latex from a rubber tree.

BELOW: Songkhla harbour.

Image from Wat Matchimawat.

Songkhla

If Hat Yai is brash, then **Songkhla** ❻ is discreet, a well-kept secret from the pleasure-seekers who visit Hat Yai. Trains, buses and taxis cover the 25 km (15 miles) between the two towns. Located at the tip of a quiet peninsula, Songkhla is an old city showing clear signs of Chinese influence. Only the seaward (eastern) shore is suitable for sunbathing and swimming. The north portion of the beach is backed with lush casaurina trees, and here one finds monks in saffron robes walking past humpbacked bulls being prepared for the bullfights. The focal point of the beach is a bronze statue of a little mermaid, perched on a rock and looking wistfully seaward.

Immediately northwest of the mermaid, a score of seafood restaurants occupy the sandy strand. Select your ingredients from fresh seafood displayed on ice, including 35-cm (15-inch) long tiger prawns.

Across the road from the mermaid is **Khao Noi**, a topiary garden with realistic fighting bulls, birds in flight and an elephant sculpted out of a living yew tree. Around the corner, on Thanon Sukhum, a group of monkeys gathers in the late afternoon to scratch, screech and scowl. They sit, hands on knees, looking like crotchety members of a debating society.

Songkhla boasts two museums. The dusty museum in **Wat Matchimawat** is in marked contrast to the spick-and-span **Songkhla National Museum** (open Wed–Sun 9am–4pm; admission fee), set in a beautifully proportioned Chinese mansion built in 1878. The latter contains an excellent collection of ceramics and documented relics, recovered from an ancient wreck in the Gulf of Thailand. The Wat Matchimawat museum collection includes early Thai Bencharong (five-colour) pottery, 200-year-old shell boxes, and oddities like a gas-powered fan.

Map,
page 327

The 200-year-old marble Buddha gracing the altar inside the *viharn* is minus its gold lotus crown, which is now preserved in a vault to protect it from thieves. Stone lions, a gift of a rich 19th-century Chinese merchant, guard the doorway that opens onto a set of interesting murals. Some show scenes of Songkhla's history, while others depict European sailors and a steamboat.

Lift your eyes as you walk along Thanon Nakhon Nawk and Thanon Nakhon Nai; old Chinese families living in these lovely Sino-Portuguese shophouses are reputed to be extremely rich and conservative.

Continue towards the lake to Thanon Vichianchom. A steep path leads, 20 minutes later, to the summit of **Tangkuan** and the ruins of an ancient chedi. The panorama is superb, and the bustle at the wharves along the lake bear witness to Songkhla's status as a busy fishing port.

A pleasant excursion can be made to **Ko Yo**, situated in **Thale Sap** or Songkhla Lake, one of the largest lakes in Southeast Asia. The lake is, in fact, a deep ocean inlet, and its waters are rather brackish. En route to Ko Yor, stop at the fisheries station, where enormous white *plaa kapong* (white snappers) are bred. Ko Yor is renowned for its locally woven cotton, ancient Buddhist monuments and its simple tranquillity. The lake is also home to tens of thousands of water birds, which migrate here to settle among the rushes. With special permission, it is possible to take a boat onto the lake to observe their habits. The water, even in the middle of the lake, is no more than 1 metre (3 ft) deep, making the grassy bottom with its darting fish easy to see.

Another excursion by boat is to the offshore islands of Maew and Nuu (Cat and Mouse). Nuu is the larger of the two and has some pleasant picnic spots and swimming beaches.

Three km (2 miles) south of the town is a small, extremely active fishing village, inhabited mainly by Muslims. It is the fishing boats, rather than the people, however, that are the most colourful. It would be difficult to beat these brightly painted *korlae* for imaginative themes and execution.

Beyond the fishing village lies the rocky beach of **Khao Seng**, whose fame rests on an apparently precariously poised giant boulder called Nai Bang's Head. Legend says that if you succeed in pushing it over, you will uncover the millionaire's treasure buried beneath it. Inland from the beach is the Banloa Coconut Plantation, where you can watch monkeys trained to climb trees and toss down selected coconuts.

Wat Kho Tham is built among enormous boulders on a nearby hilltop. The cave contains the inevitable Buddha's footprint, and a reclining Buddha sheltered by an overhanging rock. Around the corner is **Wat Mae Chi**, a charming sandy spot inhabited by Buddhist nuns. The shaven-headed nuns, often quite young, dress in white robes, grow flowers and, like monks, rise at 4am to meditate before setting out to collect alms.

To Malaysia

Down the east coast from Songkhla are the provincial capitals of Yala, Pattani and Narathiwat. Many of the residents of **Yala ⑦** are ethnic Chinese, whilst Pattani and Narathiwat are fascinating centres of southernmost

BELOW: mosque.

Map, page 327

Thailand's Malay Muslim culture. **Pattani ❽** is home to a large fishing fleet and the 400-year-old Kreuse Mosque, built in 1578 by a Chinese settler, To Khieng, who converted to Islam. In fact, construction seems never to have been fully completed. According to legend, this is because To Khieng's sister, Lim Ko Niaw, sailed from China and begged her brother to renounce Islam and return to their ancestral home. When he refused, she cursed the mosque, saying it would never be completed, then hanged herself from a nearby cashew nut tree.

Today, the mosque is maintained by the faithful in its original state. No attempt is made to complete it, because local Muslims believe lightning will strike anyone who makes the attempt. Meanwhile, Lim Ko Niaw has acquired a certain religious status herself – her shrine at San Jao Leng Ju Kieng is always packed, and in February it is the site of an important ceremony featuring fire walking and a vegetarian food festival. In 2004 Kreuse Mosque was bloodied by a Thai police massacre of 108 machete-wielding Muslim militants.

Of interest near Yala are the Silpa caves. The large cave of Tham Koo Hu Pimuk contains a 25-metre (80-ft) high Buddha, considered a holy pilgrimage site by southern Thai Buddhists.

All the way south

Narathiwat ❾ is markedly distinguished by its rural charm, prized songbirds and succulent mangoes. Next stop further south is Malaysia, accessible by ferry from the small town of Tak Bai. Yet before moving on, the traveller should linger a while in Narathiwat, which offers fine swimming at the beach at Narathat, a delightful and pleasant stretch of all-but-deserted white sand shaded by tall casuarina trees.

Hat Narathat is reached by walking north along Thanon Pichitbamrung, the town's main street, and towards the green dome of the provincial mosque. Here a bridge leads right across a branch of the Mae Nam Bang Nara to the beach. A fascinating and informative glimpse of the life of southern Thai Muslim villagers can be gleaned at this point by walking through the fishing village at the mouth of the Bang Nara. Brightly painted fishing vessels jostle for space in the clear waters, and everywhere fish of all sizes and species are laid out on racks to dry in the sun. While the people are welcoming to visitors, they are conservative and Islamic, and female travellers should take care that their clothing does not offend local sensibilities, with skimpy tops or shorts a definite no-no.

Satun is an overwhelmingly rural province with the largest Muslim population – over 80 percent – in Thailand. A tiny, riverside town, it's a pleasant place to overnight if en route to Malaysia by sea. Boats to the Malaysian province of Perlis, just south of Thailand, have very low fares, and depart either from Khlong Bambang, which is directly in the centre of Satun, or at Tammalang Pier, at the estuary just south of the town.

Boats also leave Tammalang four times daily for Malaysia's fabled Langkawi Island, costing around US$5 each way. Travellers exiting Thailand for Malaysia via Satun should remember to get their passport stamped at the immigration office in town; otherwise there may be bureaucratic delays and perhaps even a bureaucratic nightmare on arrival in Malaysia. ❑

BELOW: Diard's trogon. **RIGHT:** climbing for the boss.

INSIGHT GUIDES
Travel Tips

☆ INSIGHT GUIDES Phonecard

One global card to keep
travellers in touch.
Easy. Convenient. Saves
you time and money.

It's a global phonecard

Save up to 70%* on international calls
from over 55 countries

Free 24 hour global customer service

Recharge your card at any time via customer
service or online

It's a message service

Family and friends can send you voice
messages for free.

Listen to these messages using the phone*
or online

Free email service - you can even listen
to your email over the phone*

It's a travel assistance service

24 hour emergency travel assistance –
if and when you need it.

Store important travel documents online
in your own secure vault

For more information, call rates, and all
Access Numbers in over 55 countries,
(check your destination is covered) go to
www.insightguides.ekit.com or call
Customer Service.

JOIN now and receive
US$ 5 bonus when you
join for US$ 20 or more.

Join today at

www.insightguides.ekit.com

When requested use ref code: **INSAD0103**

OR SIMPLY FREE CALL
24 HOUR CUSTOMER SERVICE

UK	0800 376 1705
USA	1800 706 1333
Canada	1800 808 5773
Australia	1800 11 44 78
South Africa	0800 997 285

THEN PRESS 0

For all other countries please go to "Access Numbers" at
www.insightguides.ekit.com

* Retrieval rates apply for listening to messages. Savings based
on using a hotel or payphone and calling to a landline. Correct
at time of printing 01.03

(INS001)

powered by **ekit**

"The easiest way to make calls and receive messages around the world"

CONTENTS

Getting Acquainted

The Place

Area approximately 514,000 sq km (198,000 sq miles)
Capital Bangkok
Population 64,865,000 million
Language Thai
Religion Buddhism (95 percent)
Time Zone GMT plus 7 hours
Currency baht
Weights and Measures Metric
Electricity 220 volts, 50 cycles. Use either flat-pronged or round-pronged plugs
International dialling code 66

Geography

Lying between 7 degrees and 21 degrees latitude, Thailand has a total area almost the size of France, and is said to resemble an elephant's head with its trunk forming the southern peninsula. Bangkok is sited at its geographic centre, approximately at the elephant's mouth. The country is bordered by Malaysia to the south, Burma to the west, Laos across the Mekong River to the northeast and Cambodia to the east.

The north is marked by low hills and contains the country's tallest peak, Doi Inthanon, standing 2,590 metres (8,500 ft) tall. A range of hills divides Thailand from Burma and forms the western boundary of the broad alluvial central plains, the country's principal rice-growing area. To the east, the plains rise to the Khorat Plateau, which covers much of the northeast.

The spine of the southern peninsula is the same range of hills that separates Thailand from Burma, sloping down to the Andaman Sea on the west and the Gulf of Thailand on the east. Thailand has a total of 3,219 km (2,000 miles) of coastline.

Bangkok is situated at 14 degrees north latitude. It is a city divided into halves by a river, the Chao Phraya, which separates central Bangkok and Thonburi. The city covers a total area of 1,560 sq km (602 sq miles) of delta land, of which no natural area is more than 2 metres (7 ft) above any other.

Chiang Mai lies 686 km (426 miles) north of Bangkok. It sits 300 metres (1,000 ft) above sea level, and is crowned by Doi Suthep, which rises to a height of 1,676 metres (5,499 ft). The city is home to over 160,000 people.

Phuket, an island in the Andaman Sea, lies 867 km (539 miles) or a 70-minute flight south of Bangkok. Measuring 48 km (30 miles) long by 21 km (13 miles) wide, it is approximately the size of Singapore.

Climate

There are three seasons in Thailand: hot, rainy and cool. But to the tourist winging in from anywhere north or south of the 30th parallel, Thailand has only one temperature: hot. To make things worse, the temperature drops only a few degrees during the night and is accompanied 24 hours by humidity above 70 percent. Only air-conditioning makes Bangkok and other major towns tolerable during the hot season. The countryside is somewhat cooler, but, surprisingly, the northern regions can be hotter in March and April than Bangkok.

Adding together the yearly daytime highs and the nighttime lows for major world cities, the World Meteorological Organization has declared Bangkok to be the world's hottest city. When the monsoon rains fall, the country swelters.

Chiang Mai enjoys a cooler, less humid climate. In the cool season, temperatures range between 13° and 28°C (55° and 82°F) and are lower in the hills. As in Bangkok, the heaviest rain falls in September.

In Phuket, the monsoon begins in early May, and generally ends late in October. Temperatures range from 36°C (96°F) in the hot season to nighttime temperatures of 21°C (70°F) in the cool season. The water temperature never drops below 20°C (67°F).

Seasons

Hot season
March to mid-June
22°–41°C (72°–100°F)
Rainy season
June to October
23°–37°C (73°–98°F)
Cool season
November to February
13°–37°C (55°–98°F), but with less humidity.

The Economy

Nearly 49 percent of the population are farmers, who till alluvial land so rich that Thailand is the world leader in the export of tapioca, rice, rubber and canned pineapple. The country is also a major exporter of tuna, shrimp, sugar, maize and tin.

Increasingly, Thailand is turning to manufacturing, especially in clothing, machinery and electronics, while 37 percent of the work-force is in the service industry.

Government

Thailand is a constitutional monarchy headed by His Majesty, King Bhumibol Adulyadej. The royalty's power has been reduced considerably since the period before the 1932 revolution. However, the present king can, by the force of his moral authority, influence important decisions merely by a word or two.

Although he no longer rules as did the absolute monarchs of previous centuries, he is still regarded as one of the three pillars of the society – monarchy, religion and the nation. This concept is represented in the five-banded national flag: the outer red bands symbolizing the nation; the inner white bands the purity of the

Buddhist religion; and the thick blue band at the centre, the monarchy.

Along with Her Majesty Queen Sirikit and other members of the royal family, the king has long been active in promoting the interests of Thais in the lower economic strata, earning the royal family genuine respect from their people.

The structure of the government is defined by the constitution and its enabling ordinances. A new constitution, designed to place power in the hands of the people, was passed in 1997. Despite its frequent revisions, it has remained true to the spirit of the original. The exercising of it, however, has often favoured certain groups over others, especially the military, which has sometimes abused its power.

Modelled loosely on the British system, the Thai government consists of three branches: legislative, executive and judiciary, each in theory acting independently of the others in a system of checks and balances. The legislative branch is composed of a senate and a house of representatives. The senate consists of 200 leading members of society, including business people, educators and many high-ranking military officers. Members have traditionally been selected by the prime minister and approved by the king. However, under the 1997 Constitution, they were elected in 2000. The house of representatives comprises 500 members elected by popular vote.

The executive branch is represented by a prime minister, who must be an elected member of parliament. He is selected by a single party or coalition of parties and rules through a cabinet of ministers, the exact number dependent on his own needs. They, in turn, implement their programmes through the very powerful civil service.

The judiciary consists of a supreme court, an appellate court, and a pyramid of provincial and lower courts. It acts independently to interpret points of law and counsels the other two branches on the appropriateness of actions.

Planning the Trip

What to Bring

Bangkok, Chiang Mai, Pattaya and Phuket are modern destinations with most of the amenities found in Europe or North America.

Lip balm and moisturizers are needed in the north during the cool season. Sunglasses and hats are useful items to protect eyes and sensitive skin from tropical glare.

What to Wear

Clothes should be light and loose; natural blends that breathe are preferable to synthetics. The cool season in the north can be chilly; a sweater will be welcome, especially when travelling in the hills.

Suits are worn for business and in many large hotels but, in general, Thailand lacks the formal dress code of Hong Kong or Tokyo. Open shoes (sandals during the height of the rainy season, when some Bangkok streets get flooded) and conservative dresses (with sleeves) for women or short-sleeved shirts for men are appropriate It is not appropriate for men to walk around cities and towns without a shirt.

The clothing code for Buddhist temples and Muslim mosques is more conservative than on the street. Shorts are taboo for both women and men wanting to enter some of the important temples. Those wearing sleeveless dresses may also be barred from certain temples. Improperly dressed and unkempt visitors will be turned away from large temples like the Wat Phra Kaew (Temple of the Emerald Buddha) and from the Grand Palace in Bangkok. Dress properly in deference to the religion and to Thai sensitivities.

Entry Regulations

VISAS AND PASSPORTS

Travellers should check visa regulations at a Thai embassy or consulate before starting their journey. All foreign nationals entering Thailand must have valid passports. At the airport, nationals from most countries will be granted a free transit visa valid up to 30 days, provided that they have a fully paid ticket out of Thailand.

Tourist visas allow for a 60-day stay from the date of entry into the kingdom. People who are waiting for a work permit to be issued can apply for a non-immigrant visa, which is good for 90 days, from their Thai embassy or consulate at home. A letter of guarantee is needed from the Thai company you intend to work for.

Visa Extensions

Visas can be extended before they expire by applying at the Immigration Bureau on Soi Suan Plu, Thanon Sathorn Tai, tel: 0 2287 3101, ext. 205 (Mon–Fri 9am–noon, 1–4.30pm, Sat 9am–noon). Visitors wishing to leave Thailand and return before their visas have expired can apply for a re-entry permit prior to their departure at immigration offices in Bangkok, Chiang Mai, Pattaya, Phuket and Hat Yai. An exit visa is not required.

CUSTOMS

The Thai government prohibits the import of drugs, dangerous chemicals, pornography, firearms and ammunition. Attempting to smuggle heroin or other hard drugs may be punishable by death. Scores of foreigners are serving long prison terms for drug-related offences.

Tourists may freely bring in foreign banknotes or other types of foreign exchange. For travellers leaving Thailand, the maximum amount permitted to be taken out in Thai currency without prior authorization is 50,000 baht.

Foreigners are allowed to import, without tax, 200 cigarettes and one litre of wine or spirits.

Health

HYGIENE

Thais place high value on personal hygiene and are aware of the dangers of germs and infections. Establishments catering to foreigners are generally careful with food and drink preparation. They do not, however, place such a high priority on keeping the environment clean.

Bangkok water is clean when it leaves the modern filtration plant; the pipes that carry it into the city are somewhat less than new, however, and visitors are advised to drink bottled water or soft drinks. Both are produced under strict supervision, as is the ice used in large hotels and restaurants. Most streetside restaurants are clean; a quick glance should tell you which are and which are not.

DISEASE

Sexually transmitted diseases

With its thriving nightlife and transient population, Bangkok is a magnet for sexual diseases. The women (and men) in the sexual service industries are aware of the consequences of carelessness and of not insisting that their partners take precautions, but economic necessity, coupled with a Thai reluctance to offend anyone, means that there is a great risk of infection from unprotected sex.

Aids and other sexually transmitted diseases are not confined to "high risk" sections of the population in Thailand, and visitors are at risk from sex without condoms (see also Medical Services, page 348.)

Malaria

Malaria is still a high risk in some regions of Thailand. The best protection is to avoid being bitten. Mosquitoes are most active at night, so after dark, wear long trousers,

Heat Exposure

Most first-time visitors experience a degree of heat exhaustion and dehydration that can be avoided by drinking lots of bottled water and slightly increasing the amount of salt in the diet. Sunblock is essential.

long-sleeved shirts, shoes and socks. Hands and neck should be protected with an insect repellent, and you should sleep in rooms with mosquito screens on the windows and under a mosquito net.

If using anti-malarial tablets, remember that mosquitoes in many areas are resistant to many of the proprietary brands of medication. Seek advice from a tropical institute before your departure. Should you nonetheless contract malaria, there is a network of malaria centres and hospitals throughout Thailand.

It is important to remember that the most dangerous form of malaria often appears disguised as a heavy cold. If you contract what appears to be influenza, you should consult a doctor immediately. This also applies during the weeks after your return from the tropics.

Vaccinations

Visitors are no longer required to show evidence of vaccination for smallpox or cholera. Cholera vaccination is of limited effectiveness and is no longer recommended for travellers. Before you leave home, check that **tetanus** boosters are up to date. **Dengue fever** persists in rural areas.

Money Matters

The baht is the principal Thai monetary unit. It is divided into 100 units called satang. Banknote denominations include 1,000 (tan), 500 (purple), 100 (red), 50 (blue), 20 (green) and 10 (brown) baht. The 10-baht banknotes are being removed from circulation and have become rare.

Thai coins have no Roman script on them but are marked with Arabic

numerals denoting denomination. There are 10-baht coins (brass centre with a silver rim), two different 5-baht coins (silver pieces with copper rims), three varieties of 1-baht coin (silver; usually only the small size will fit in a public telephone), and two small coins of 50 and 25 satang (both are brass-coloured).

EXCHANGE RATES

The once-stable Thai currency was devalued in mid-1997. Since then, the exchange rate, which for years hovered at 25 baht to the US dollar, has risen to an average of around 40 baht to the dollar. There is no currency black market.

BANKING SYSTEM

Thailand has a sophisticated banking system with representation by the major banks of most foreign countries. Money can be imported in cash or traveller's cheques and converted into baht. It is also possible to arrange telex bank drafts from one's hometown bank. There is no minimum requirement on the amount of money that must be converted. Both cash and traveller's cheques can be changed in hundreds of bank branches throughout the city; rates are more favourable for traveller's cheques than for cash. Banking hours are 8.30am–3.30pm Mon–Fri, although some banks near major tourist areas are open longer for foreign exchange. Hotels generally give poorer rates than banks.

ATM/Debit Cards

Most banks now have ATM machines outside, open around the clock. Currency is dispensed in baht only. ATM machines can also be found in malls, department stores, airports, as well as at major train and bus stations.

Occasionally, an ATM card may not work at one machine for some unspecified reason; try another branch of the same bank and results may be different. Alternatively, MasterCard and Visa debit cards (as distinct from credit cards) are also accepted at many ATM machines and an increasingly large number of local merchants. Most banks have signs with an array of symbols indicating which cards are accepted at the machine. Periodically, cards are accepted at machines in spite of the fact that no related sign appears out front. When in doubt, give it a try, but be prepared to be flexible.

Credit Cards

American Express, Diners Club, MasterCard and Visa are widely accepted in tourist areas. In provincial destinations, it is better to check that plastic is accepted, and not to count on using cards.

If you lose your credit card, notify the relevant company at one of the following offices:

Bangkok
American Express (Thai) Co. Ltd.
S.P.s Building, 388 Thanon
Phaholyothin
Tel: 0 2273 5500 (office)
0 2273 5222 (global assist)
0 2273 5544 (cardmember hotline)
Fax: 0 2273 0309
www.americanexpress.com/thailand
/en/homepage.shtml
Open 8.30am–5pm Mon–Fri.
Diners Club
Silom Complex, 12th Floor,
191 Thanon Silom
Tel: 0 2238 3660 (24-hour service)
Fax: 0 2234 4523
www.citibank.co.th/global_docs/
dinersclub/index.htm
Open 8.30am–5pm, Mon–Fri.
MasterCard International
Sermmitr Tower, 11th Floor,
Soi 21 (Soi Asoke),
159 Thanon Sukhumvit
Tel: 0 2260 8572-3
Fax: 0 2260 8574
Global service centre 001-800-118
887 0663
www.mastercard.com/sea
Visa International (Asia-Pacific) Ltd.
Sindhorn Building, 15F, Tower 3,
130–132 Thanon Withaya,
Pathumwan
Tel: 0 2263 2091
Fax: 0 2263 2093
www.visa-asia.com

Chiang Mai
American Express
Bangkok Bank,
2/3 Thanon Prachasampan
Tel: 053-821 089-91

Phuket
American Express
Phuket International Airport
Tel: 0 7632 8324

Credit Card Fraud

Credit card fraud is a major problem in Thailand. Do not leave credit cards in safe deposit boxes.

Getting There

BY AIR

The **Bangkok International Airport** at Don Muang is a major transport hub for Southeast Asia. Several airlines fly direct from destinations in Australasia, Europe and the US. A free shuttle bus service connects the international and domestic terminals, for those transferring to a domestic flight. The airport will be replaced in 2006 by the **New Bangkok International Airport** (NBIA) (www.bangkokairport.org), also known as **Suvarnabhumi Airport**, approximately 30km (19 miles) east of Bangkok. Thailand has four other international airports: Chiang Mai, Chiang Rai, Phuket and Hat Yai.

Thai Airways International (THAI) flies to more than 50 cities on four continents. **Bangkok Airways** is an excellent regional airline with exclusive routes within Asia. Flying time from the UK is about 12 hours; from the west coast of America, about 21 hours; from Australia and New Zealand about 9 hours. Visit: www.thaiairways.com, www.bangkokair.com.

BY SEA

The days when travellers sailed up the Chao Phraya River to view the golden spires of Bangkok are long gone. Luxury liners now call at

Pattaya and Phuket but have ceased serving Bangkok. Check with a travel agent or shipping company to find those which depart from your city.

BY RAIL

Trains operated by the State Railways of Thailand (Tel: 0 2220 4334, 0 2222 0175; www.railway.co.th/eng) are clean, cheap and reliable, albeit a little slow. There are only two railroad entry points into Thailand, both from Malaysia on the southern Thai border. The trip north to Bangkok serves as a scenic introduction to Thailand.

A daily train leaves **Butterworth**, the port opposite Malaysia's Penang Island, at 2.10pm, crossing the border into Thailand and arriving in Bangkok at 10.05am the next day. There are second-class cars with seats which are made into upper and lower sleeping berths at night. There are also air-conditioned first-class sleepers and dining cars serving Thai food. Prices from Butterworth to Bangkok are US$30 or less, depending on class.

Trains leave Bangkok's **Hualamphong Station** daily at 2.40pm for the return journey to Malaysia. If you want to take a more adventurous, but less convenient route, another train travels from Kuala Lumpur up Malaysia's east coast to the northeastern town of Kota Bharu. Take a taxi from here across the border to catch the SRT train from the southern Thai town of Sungai Kolok. Trains leave Sungai Kolok at 11.30am and 1.35pm, arriving in Bangkok at 9.15am and 9.45am the following day.

If you like to travel in style and prefer not to fly, try the Eastern & Oriental Express, Asia's most exclusive travel experience (www.orient-express.com). Travelling several times a month between Singapore, Kuala Lumpur, Chiang Mai and Bangkok, the 22-carriage train with its distinctive green-and-cream livery passes through spectacular scenery. It's very expensive, but worth it.

BY ROAD

Malaysia provides the main road access into Thailand, with crossings near Pedang Besar and Sungai Kolok. It is possible to cross to and from Laos from Nong Khai by using the Friendship Bridge across the Mekong River, as well as Nakhon Phanom and Mukdahan by ferry. There are also crossings into Laos at Chong Mek (in Ubon Ratchathani province) and Chiang Khong (in Chiang Rai province). Visas on arrival are only available at the Friendship Bridge crossing. The Cambodian border town of Aranyaprathet is now open for travel as well. Visas for Cambodia can usually be bought at the border here but it is best to check at the Cambodian embassy in Bangkok first. Drivers will find that most Thai roads are modern and well maintained, so the going should be smooth and comfortable.

Special Facilities

LEFT LUGGAGE

There are two left luggage facilities at Bangkok International Airport, one in each terminal. The fee is 20 baht (US$0.50) per bag per day and there is a three-month limit (tel: 0 2535 1250).

RESERVATIONS

Hotel reservations can be made in the airport arrival lounge once you have passed through customs, though many of these hotels are poorly situated – choose carefully. It is recommended that you book a room in advance during the Christmas, New Year and Chinese New Year holidays and, for destinations outside of Bangkok, during Songkran in mid-April.

Travelling with Kids

Bangkok

Children may enjoy the animals of **Dusit Zoo** on Thanon Ratchawithi, off Thanon Rama V (open daily

Public Holidays

New Year's Day 1 January
Magha Puja February full moon
Commemorates the spontaneous gathering of 1,250 disciples of the Lord Buddha
Chakri Day 6 April
Commemorates the establishment of the Royal House of Chakri
Songkran 13–15 April
Thai New Year
Coronation Day 5 May
Ploughing Ceremony May (variable)
Visakha Puja May (full moon)
Commemorates the birth, enlightenment and death of the Lord Buddha
Asalaha Puja July (full moon)
Commemorates the Lord Buddha's first sermon
Khao Phansa July
Beginning of the Buddhist rainy season retreat
Queen's Birthday 12 August
Chulalongkorn Day 23 October
King's Birthday 5 December
Constitution Day 10 December
New Year's Eve 31 December
Chinese New Year January/ February depending on the lunar cycle. Not an official public holiday, but many businesses are closed for several days.

9am–6pm; tel: 0 2282 7111; adult 30 baht and children 5 baht). Alternatively, there are paddling boats on the lake at the zoo, as well as in **Lumphini Park** (open daily 6am–9pm; no fee) and **Chatuchak Park** (open daily 5am–9pm; free). **Safari World**, Thailand's only drive-through wildlife park, is at 99 Thanon Ramindra, Minburi, 40 km (25 miles) east of Bangkok (open daily 9am–5pm; adult 400 baht and children 300 baht; tel: 0 2518 1000-19; www.safariworld.com). In addition to elephants, lions, giraffes and other mammals, look for dolphin and sea lion shows at Marine Park, and monkey shows and white pandas at the Panda House. An afternoon at one of Bangkok's many amusement parks is also guaranteed fun: **Yoyoland**, Seacon Square, 904

Thanon Si Nakharin. Tel: 0 2721 8888. Open Wed–Mon 12.30pm– 6pm. Upside-down roller coaster, go-karts, roller blade rink.
Dream World, Km 7 on Thanon Rangsit-Ongkharak, north of Bangkok International Airport. Tel: 0 2533 1152, www. dreamworld-th.com. Weekdays 10am–5pm, weekends 10am–7pm. Admission: 250 baht. Four different themes, largest water log slide in Asia and live shows.
Siam Park, 101 Thanon Sukhapiban 2, Bangkapi. Tel: 0 2919 7200. Weekdays 10am–6pm, weekends 9am–7pm. Admission: adults 400 baht, children 300 baht. Amusement park, water park and small zoo. Note: The park prohibits the wearing of T-shirts in the swimming areas, so take plenty of suntan oil for tender young skins.

Pattaya

In Pattaya, children may enjoy a number of attractions, including go-karts, miniature golf, or a visit to **Ripley's Believe It or Not Museum** (open daily 10am–midnight; tel: 0 3871 0294–8; www.ripleys.com; adults 280 baht, children 230 baht) at the Royal Garden Plaza.

Samut Prakan

Head for the **Crocodile Farm** and **Elephant Land** on Thanon Taiban (open daily 7am–6pm, tel: 0 2703 4891-5; www.paknam.com/ crocodile.html; admission 300 baht). Shows are held regularly throughout the day.

Gay Travellers

Gays quickly discover that Thailand is one of the most tolerant countries in the world. In Bangkok, most gay bars are on Patpong 3 or the upper end of Thanon Silom, especially Silom Sois 2 and 4. Transvestites and transvestite shows are common in Bangkok, as well as in Phuket and Pattaya. There are also quite a number of small eateries all around the city where the clientele is almost totally gay. **Utopia Tours** (Tarntawan Place Hotel, 119/5-10 Thanon Surawong; tel: 0

2238 3227; www.utopia–asia.com) offers gay-oriented guided tours of Bangkok and Thailand.

Disabled Travellers

To say that facilities for the handicapped in Thailand, even in Bangkok, are underdeveloped is something of an understatement. Paths are uneven, riddled with potholes and studded with obstructions; ramps are non-existent. (It's no accident that on many street corners sit cobblers repairing damaged shoes.) To cross major streets in Bangkok without using the pedestrian bridges (steep flights of stairs on either side of the street linked by an overhead walkway) is to court disaster, even for the non-disabled. Few buildings in Bangkok have ramps, although upscale hotels throughout Thailand, especially international chains, are wheelchair-accessible.

While there is no taxi service specifically geared towards the disabled, and ordinary taxis often do not have enough storage room for a wheelchair, some of the newer taxis are modified station wagons with ample room in the back. Hiring a private car, however, may be the most reliable alternative. The capital's new Skytrain has disabled facilities at several of its major stations.

In spite of this somewhat disheartening picture, disabled travellers can visit and enjoy the wonders of Thailand. Forethought and flexibility are key. Some organizations to contact for further information include:

Association of the Physically Handicapped of Thailand, 73/7-8 Soi 8, Thanon Tivanon, Talaat Kawan, Nonthaburi 11000. Tel: 0 2951 0445, 0 2951 0569; fax: 0 2951 0567; e-mail: apht@loxinfo.co.th
Mobility International, Post Office Box 10767, Eugene, OR 97440, USA. Tel: 541-343 1284; www.miusa.org
Society for Accessible Travel and Hospitality, 347 Fifth Avenue, Suite 610, New York, NY 10016, USA. Tel: 212-447 7284; www.sath.org.

Useful Addresses

DOING BUSINESS

Most hotels have business centres with communications and secretarial services in several languages. Elsewhere in Bangkok, it is possible to lease small offices with clerical staff.

Chambers of Commerce in Bangkok

Canada
9th Floor, Sethiwan Tower,
139 Thanon Pan
Tel: 0 2266 6085–6
Fax: 0 2266 6087
tccc.or.th
Open 8.30am–4.30pm.

Great Britain
7th Floor, 208 Thanon Witthayu
Tel: 0 2651 5350–3
Fax: 0 2651 5354
www.bccthai.com
Open Mon–Fri 8am–4.30pm.

Japan
15th Floor Amarin Tower,
500 Thanon Ploenchit
Tel: 0 2256 9170–3
Fax: 0 2652 0931
www.jcc.or.th
Open daily 9am–5.30pm.

Singapore
193/8 Lake Rachada Complex,
Thanon Rachadapisek, Khlong Toey
Tel: 0 2264 0680–4
Fax: 0 2264 0688
www.singaporethaicc.or.th
Open 8am–6pm Mon–Thur,
8am–5pm Fri.

Thailand
150 Thanon Rachabophit
Tel: 0 2622 1860
Fax: 0 2225 5475
www.iccthailand.or.th
Open Mon–Fri 8.30am–5.30pm.

USA
18th Floor, Kian Gwan Building
140/1 Thanon Witthayu
Tel: 0 2251 9266–7
Fax: 0 2651 4472
www.amchamthailand.org
Open Mon–Fri 8am–noon, 1–5pm.

Special Clubs

Alliance Française, 29 Thanon Sathorn Tai. Tel: 0 2670 4200; fax: 0 2670 4270; www.alliance-francaise.or.th. Open 10am–7pm Mon–Fri, 10am–6pm Sat. Library, bookshop and caféteria; open to all. In Chiang Mai: 138 Thanon Charoen Prathet. Tel: 0 5327 5277.
American University Alumni (AUA), 179 Thanon Ratchadamri. Tel: 0 2252 8170–3. Open daily 7am–7pm. Library open to all. US films, monthly newsletter, caféteria. In Chiang Mai: 24 Thanon Ratchadamnoen. Tel: 0 5321 1377; www.auathailand.org.
British Council, 254 Chulalongkorn, Soi 64, Siam Square, Thanon Phaya Thai. Tel: 0 2652 5480-9; fax: 0 2253 5312; www.britishcouncil. or.th. Open daily 8am–7pm. Members-only library. British films, monthly newsletter. In Chiang Mai: 198 Thanon Bamrungrat. Tel: 0 5324 2103; fax: 0 5324 4781. Open Mon–Fri 9am–7pm, Sat–Sun 8am–5pm.
Foreign Correspondents Club of Thailand, Maneeya Centre, Penthouse, 518/5 Thanon Ploenchit (next to Amarin Plaza). Tel: 0 2652 0580–1; fax: 0 2652 0582; www.fccthai.com. Non-members may browse in the small library with the purchase of something at the bar.
Goethe Institut, 18/1 Soi Goethe, Sathorn 1. Tel: 0 2287 0942-4; www.goethe.de/bangkok. Open Mon–Thur 8am–4.30pm, Fri 8am–2pm; info centre closed on Mondays. German films, restaurant, monthly newsletter. Open to all.
Lions Club Bangkok Muang-Ek, 149/16 Thanon Surawong. Tel: 0 2235 9075; www.muang-ekbkk. lionwap.org. There are numerous Lions Clubs in Bangkok and this one welcomes foreign members. Meetings are held on the third Thursday of the month at 6pm at the Sofitel Hotel on Thanon Silom.
Rotary Club, Bangkok South. Tel: 0 2632 9160; fax: 0 2632 9161; www.bangkok-south.com. Meets for luncheon, meeting every Friday at 12.30pm in the Pan Pacific Hotel, 21st floor, on Thanon Rama IV.

Tourist Offices

The **Tourism Authority of Thailand** (**TAT**) offer brochures, maps and videotapes of the country's many attractions. The head office in Bangkok has information on the whole country. Other offices in Bangkok are at 4 Ratchadamnoen Nok Avenue, tel: 0 2504 2701; and Bangkok International Airport, tel: 0 2504 2701–3.

TAT has its own travel information site on the Internet: www.tourism thailand.org, a general information telephone number (open 8am–8pm) on 1672, a hotline (open 24 hours) on 1155, and offices worldwide:

Asia and the Pacific
Australia
2F 75 Pitt St, Sydney 2000

Tel: 0 29247 7549
Fax: 0 29251 2465
www.thailand.net.au
Hong Kong
1601 Fairmont House,
8 Cotton Tree Drive, Central
Tel: 2868 0732
Fax: 2868 4585
e-mail: tathkg@pacific.net.hk
Japan
Yurakucho Denki Building, South Tower 2F, R 259, 1-7-1, Yurakucho Chiyoda, Tokyo 100-0006
Tel: 03-3218 0337
Fax: 03-3218 0655
e-mail: tattky@tattky.com; and Technoble Yotsubashi Building,

3F 1-6-8 Kitahorie, Nishiku, Osaka 550-0014
Tel: 06-6543 6654
Fax: 06-6543 6660
e-mail: info@tatosa.com
Malaysia
Suite 22.01, Level 22, Menara Citibank, 165 Jalan Ampang, 50450 Kuala Lumpur
Tel: 03-216 23480
Fax: 03-216 23486
e-mail: sawatdi@po.jaring.my
Singapore
c/o Royal Thai Embassy, 370 Orchard Road, Singapore 0923
Tel: 65-6235 7694, 65-6235 7901
Fax: 65-6733 5653
e-mail: thaisgp@singnet.com.sg
South Korea
Room 604, 6F, Coryo Daeyungak Centre Building, 25-5, 1-ka. Chungmu-ro, Chung-ku, Seoul
Tel: 0 2779 5417
Fax: 0 2779 5419
e-mail: tatsel@kornet21.net
Taiwan
13F Boss Tower, 111 Sung Chiang Road, Taipei 104
Tel: 0 225 502 1600
Fax: 0 225 502 1603
e-mail: tattpe@ms3.hinet.net

Europe
France
90 Avenue des Champs-Elysées, 75008 Paris
Tel: 01-5353 4700 (+33)
Fax: 01-4563 7888
e-mail: tatpar@wanadoo.fr
Germany
Bethmannstrasse 58, D-60311, Frankfurt
Tel 069-138 1390 (+49)
Fax: 069-138 1395
e-mail: info@thailandtourismus.de
www.thailandtourismus.de
Italy
Via Barberini 68, 4th Floor, 00187, Rome
Tel: 06-420 14422 (+39)
Fax: 06-487 3500
e-mail: tat.rome@id.it
United Kingdom
Brook House, 98-99 Jermyn Street, London SW1Y 6EE
Tel: 207-925 2511 (+44)
Fax: 207-925 2512
e-mail: thaiduto@btinternet.com
www.thaismile.co.uk

Embassies in Bangkok

Australia, 37 Thanon Sathorn Tai. Tel: 0 2287 2680; www.austembassy.or.th Visas are processed at a separate office: **Australian Visa Application Centre**, 34 Floor, Thai CC Tower, 889 South Thanon Sathorn Tel: 0 2672 3476-9; www.vfs.co.th Open: 8.30am–4.30pm Mon–Fri
Brunei, 154 Soi 14, Soi 63 (Soi Ekamai), Thanon Sukhumvit. Tel: 0 2381 5914–6; fax: 02-381 5921. Visas: 8.30am–noon.
Canada, No. 990 Abdulrahim Place, 15th Floor, Thanon Rama IV, Bangrak. Tel: 0 2636 0540; fax: 02-636 0565; www.dfait-maeci.gc.ca/bangkok/embassy-en.asp. Visas: 8am–noon.
China, 57 Thanon Ratchadapisek. Tel: 0 2245 7032, 0 2245 7044, 0 2247 7554; fax: 0 2246 8247; www.chinaembassy.or.th/eng. Visas: 9am–noon.
Germany, 9 Thanon Sathorn Tai. Tel: 0 2287 9000; fax: 02-287 1776; www.german-embassy.or.th. Visas: 8–11am.
Indonesia, 600–602 Thanon Phetburi. Tel: 0 2252 3135-40; fax: 0 2255 1267; www.kbri-bangkok.com. Visas: 9am–noon, 2–3pm.
Israel, Ocean Tower II, 25th Floor, 75 Soi 19, Thanon Sukhumvit. Tel: 0 2204 9200 (general); 0 2204 9226–7 (visa section); fax: 0 2204 9221; bangkok.mfa.gov.il. Visas: 8.30am–2pm.

Laos, 520/502/1–3 Soi Sahakarnpramoon, Soi 39, Thanon Ramkhamhaeng. Tel: 0 2539 6667–8, fax: 0 2539 6678; www.bkklaoembassy.com. Visas: 8am–4pm.
Malaysia, 33-35 Thanon Sathorn Tai, Tungmahamek, Sathorn, Bangkok 10120. Tel: 0 2679 2190, fax: 0 2679-2208; e-mail: malbangkok@klngov.my. Visas: 8.30–11.30am.
New Zealand, MThai Tower, 14 Floor, All Seasons Place, 87 Thanon Witthayu, Lumphini. Tel: 0 2254 2530; fax: 0 2253 9045; www.nzembassy.com. Visas: 9am–noon, 1–2.30pm.
Singapore, 129 Thanon Sathorn Tai. Tel: 0 2286 2111, 0 2286 1434; fax: 0 2286 6966, 287 2578; www.mfa.gov.sg/bangkok. Visas: 9–11am.
United Kingdom, 1031 Thanon Witthayu. Tel: 0 2305 8333; fax: 0 2253 7121; www.britishemb.or.th. Visas: 7.30–9.30am Mon–Thurs, 7.30–10.30am Fri.
United States, 95 Thanon Wireless. Tel 0 2205 4000; fax: 0 2254 1171; bangkok.usembassy.gov. Visas: 7–9am.
Vietnam, 83/1 Thanon Witthayu. Tel: 0 2251 5836, 0 2251 5838; fax: 0 2251 7203, 0 2254 4730; www.vietnamembassy.co.th. Visas: 8.30–11am and 1.30–4.30pm.

USA

Los Angeles
1F, 611 North Larchmont
Boulevard, Los Angeles, CA 90004
Tel: 323-461 9814 (+1)
Fax: 323-461 9834
e-mail: tatla@ix.netcom.com
New York
61 Broadway, Suite 2810,
New York, NY 10006
Tel: 212-432 0433
Fax: 212-269 2588
e-mail: info@tatny.com
www.seeyouinthailand.com

(Call toll-free from anywhere in the
USA: 1-800-THAILAND)

Thailand

Bangkok
1600 Thanon New Phetburi (Thanon
Petchaburi), Makkasan,
Rachathewi, Bangkok 10400
Tel: 0 2250 5500
Fax: 0 2250 5511
e-mail: center@tat.or.th
Ayutthaya
108/22 Moo 4, Thanon Phratoochai
Tel: 0 3524 6076–7
Fax: 0 3524 6078
e-mail: tatyutya@tat.or.th
Chiang Mai
105/1 Thanon Chiang Mai-Lamphun
Tel: 0 5324 8604
Fax: 0 5324 8605
e-mail: tatchmai@tat.or.th
Chiang Rai
448/16 Thanon Singhakhlai
Tel: 0 5371 7433
Fax: 0 5371 7434
e-mail: tatchrai@tat.or.th
Hat Yai
1/1 Soi 2, Thanon Niphat Uthit 3
Tel: 0 7424 3747, 7423 8518
Fax: 0 7424 5986
e-mail: tatsgkhi@tat.or.th
Kanchanaburi
Thanon Saeng Chuto
Tel: 0 3457 7200, 0 3451 2500
Fax: 0 3451 1200
e-mail: tatkan@tat.or.th
Khon Kaen
15/5 Thanon Prachasamoson
Tel: 0 4324 4498–9, 0 4323 6634
Fax: 0 4324 4497
e-mail: tatkhkn@tat.or.th
Lopburi
Thanon Ropwat Phrathat
Tel: 0 3642 2768–9

Fax: 0 3642 4089
e-mail: tatlobri@tat.or.th
Nakhon Phanom
184/1 Thanon Sunthornvichit
Tel: 0 4251 3490–1
Fax: 0 4251 3492
e-mail: tatphnom@tat.or.th
Nakhon Ratchasima
2102–2104 Thanon Mittraphap
Tel: 0 4421 3666, 0 4421 3030
Fax: 0 4421 3667
e-mail: tatsima@tat.or.th
Nakhon Si Thammarat
Sanam Na Muang,
Thanon Ratchadamnoen
Tel: 0 7534 6515–6
Fax: 0 7534 6517
e-mail: tatnksir@tat.or.th
Pattaya
609, Moo 10, Thanon Pratamunk
Tel: 0 3842 8750, 0 3842 7667
Fax: 0 3842 9113
e-mail: tatchon@tat.or.th
Phitsanulok
209/7–8 Thanon Boromtrailokanat
Tel: 0 5523 1063
e-mail: tatphlok@tat.or.th
Phuket
73–75 Thanon Phuket
Tel: 0 7621 1036, 0 7621 7138
Fax: 0 7621 3582
e-mail: tatphket@tat.or.th
Rayong
153/4 Thanon Sukhumvit
Tel: 0 3865 5420–1
Fax: 0 3865 5422
e-mail: tatyong@tat.or.th
Surat Thani
5 Thanon Talat Mai, Ban Don
Tel: 0 7728 8818–9
Fax: 0 7728 2828
e-mail: tatsurat@tat.or.th
Trat
100 Moo 1, Thanon Trat-Laem
Ngop, Laem Ngop District, Trat
(opposite pier at Laem Ngop)
Tel: 0 3959 7259–60
Fax: 0 3959 7255
e-mail: tattrat@tat.or.th
Ubon Ratchathani
264/1 Thanon Khuan Thani
Tel: 0 4524 3770
Fax: 0 4524 3771
e-mail: tatubon@tat.or.th
Udon Thani
16/5 Thanon Mukmontri
Tel: 0 4232 5406–7
Fax: 0 4232 5408
e-mail: tatudon@tat.or.th

Websites

www.tourismthailand.org
Tourism Authority of Thailand's
comprehensive site.
www.thaistudents.com
A noncommercial website with
thousands of pages of information
about Thailand and Thai culture.
Possibly the best Thailand website
on the Internet.
www.farangonline.com
On line version of the popular
Thailand travel, listings and events
magazine.
www.bangkokpost.com
The *Bangkok Post* is one the best
source of news about Thailand and
Bangkok.
www.mahidol.ac.th
Mahidol University.
www.boi.go.th
Thailand Board of Investment.
www.customs.go.th
Customs Department.
www.bot.or.th
Bank of Thailand.
www. travel-online.to/srt
State Railway Authority of Thailand.
www.ethailand.com
A wealth of useful information on
Thailand.
www.atta.or.th
Association of Thai Travel Agents.
www.thailandhotels.com
Hotel booking service operated by a
private travel company.

Banks

Bangkok

Most Thai institutions as well as
foreign banks are equipped to handle
telegraph and telex money transfers
and a wide range of money services.
In the provinces, the services are
much more restricted. If you have
overseas business to conduct with a
bank, it is better to do it while you
are in Bangkok. Most banks are
open from 8.30am–3.30pm.

Thai Banks
Bank of Asia, 191 Thanon Sathorn
Tai. Tel: 0 2285 1555; fax: 0 2287
2973-4; www.bankasia4u.com.
Bank of Ayudhya, 1222 Thanon
Rama III. Tel: 0 2296 3000; fax: 0
2683 1304; www.krungsri.com/eng.

Bangkok Bank, 333 Thanon Silom. Tel: 0 2231 4333; fax: 0 2231 4742; www.bbl.co.th.
Kasikorn Bank, 1 Thanon Ratburana. Tel: 0 2888 8888; www.kasikornbank.com.
Krung Thai Bank, 35 Thanon Sukhumvit. Tel: 0 2255 2222; fax: 0 2255 9391; www.ktb.co.th.
Siam City Bank, 1101 Thanon New Phetburi. Tel: 0 2208-5000; www.scib.co.th.
Siam Commercial Bank, 9 Thanon Ratchadapisek, Chatuchak Area. Tel: 0 2777 7777; www.scb.co.th.
Thai Military Bank, 3000 Thanon Phaholyothin. Tel: 0 2299 1111, call center: 1558; fax: 0 2273 7121-4; www.tmb.co.th.

Overseas Banks
Bank of America, 2/2 Thanon Witthayu, CRC Tower, All Seasons Place. Tel: 0 2251 6333; fax: 0 2253 1905; www.bankofamerica.com.
Bank of Tokyo-Mitsubishi, Harindhorn Tower, 2nd Floor, 54 Thanon Sathorn Nua. Tel: 0 2266 3011; fax: 0 2266 3055.
Banque Nationale de Paris, BNP Paribas, Abdulrahim Building, 29th Floor, 990 Thanon Rama IV. Tel: 0 2636 1900; fax: 0 2636 1933; www.bnpparibas.co.th.
Citibank, 82 North Thanon Sathorn, Silom. Tel: 0 2232 2000; call centre: 1588; fax: 0 2639 2560; www.citibank.co.th.
Deutsche Bank (Deutsche Bank AG), 208 Thanon Witthayu. Tel: 0 2651 5000; fax: 0 2651 5151; www.deutsche-bank.de.
HSBC, HSBC Building, 968 Thanon Rama IV. Tel: 0 2614 4000; fax: 0 2632 4818; www.hsbc.co.th.
Standard Chartered Bank, 90 North Thanon Sathorn. Tel: 0 2724 6330-8; fax: 0 2724 6121; www.standardcharterednakornthon. co.th.

Chiang Mai
Bangkok Bank, 53–59 Thanon Ta Pae (Tha Pae). Tel: 0 5328 2100-2; fax: 0 5327 4734.
Bank of Asia, 149/1–3 Thanon Chang Klan. Tel: 0 5327 0029-30; fax: 0 5328 2015.

Bank of Ayudhya, 222-6 Thanon Ta Pae (Tha Pae). Tel: 0 5325 1130-1, 0 5325 1811-2.
Krung Thai Bank, 298/1 Thanon Ta Pae (Tha Pae). Tel: 0 5323 2535-6; fax: 0 5323 2537.
Siam Commercial Bank, 17 Thanon Ta Pae (Tha Pae). Tel: 0 5327 6122, 0 5327 2501; fax: 0 5327 2465.

Phuket
Bangkok Bank, 22 Thanon Phangnga. Tel: 0 7621 6256; fax: 0 7621 6895.
Siam City Bank, 33/124 Thanon Patak, Karon. Tel: 0 7622 2838; fax: 0 7621 1355.
Siam Commercial Bank, 66 Moo 7, Thanon Ratsada. Tel: 0 7621 2254–5; fax: 0 7621 4341 and 72/63 Moo 1, Thanon Ratuthit, Patong. Tel: 0 7634 0467–8; fax: 0 7634 2594.

Airlines

Bangkok
Air Asia (regional), 18th Floor, Block B, Elephant Tower, 3300/98–99 Thanon Phaholyothin, Latyao, Chatuchak. Tel: 0 2515 9999; www.airasia.com (online booking available).
Air France, Vorawat Building, 20th Floor, 849 Thanon Silom. Tel: 0 2635 1191 (reservations & ticketing); fax: 0 2635 1204; airport: 0 2523 2112; www.airfrance.com/th.
Air New Zealand, c/o Airlines Agency Ltd., 130–132 Sindhorn Building, 14th Floor Tower 3, Thanon Witthayu. Tel: 0 2254 8440–9, fax: 0 2253 0268; airport: 0 2535 3981; Arrivals/Departure: 0 2535 1111; www.airnz.com.
All Nippon Airways, C.P. Towers, 2nd Floor, 313 Thanon Silom. Tel: 0 2238 5121 (reservations & ticketing), 0 2238 5143 (mileage); fax: 0 2238 5137; airport: 0 2535 8899; www.anaskyweb.com/th/e.
Bangkok Airways, 99 Moo 14, Thanon Viphavadee Rangsit, Chom Phon, Chatuchak. Tel: 0 2265 5678; fax: 0 2265 5500; Tel: 0 2265 5555; fax: 0 2265 5556 (reservations); call centre: 1771; www.bangkokair.com.
British Airways, Charn Issara, Tower

1, 21F, 942/160–163 Thanon Rama IV. Tel: 0 2636 1747; fax: 0 2636 1749 (reservations); airport: 0 2535 2220; www.british-airways.com.
Cathay Pacific, Ploenchit Tower, 11th Floor, 898 Thanon Ploenchit. Tel: 0 2263 0606; fax: 0 2263 0622 (reservations); tel: 0 2263 0616; fax: 0 2263 0631 (ticketing); airport: 0 2535 2155-6; www.cathaypacific.com.
Dragonair, 191 Silom Complex Building, 15th Floor, Thanon Silom. Tel: 0 2266 2651–4; fax: 0 2266 2655; www.dragonair.com.
Garuda Indonesia, Lumphini Tower, 27th Floor, Thanon Rama IV (opposite Lumphini Boxing Stadium). Tel: 0 2679 7371–2 (reservations & ticketing); fax: 0 2285 6474; airport: 0 2535 2170–1; www.garuda-indonesia.com.
Japan Airlines, Nantawan Building, 12th Floor, Thanon Ratchadamri, Lumphini. Tel: 0 2649 9500 (reservations); 0 2649 9520 (ticketing); fax: 0 2274 1460 (reservations & ticketing); airport: 0 2535 2135-6; www.th.jal.com/en.
KLM, Thai Wah Tower II, 19th Floor, 21/133–134 South Thanon Sathorn. Tel: 0 2679 1100 (reservations & ticketing); fax: 0 2679 1416; airport: 0 2535 2190; www.klm.co.th.
Korean Air, Klongboonma Building, 699 Thanon Silom. Tel: 0 2635 0465-72 (reservations & ticketing); fax: 0 2267 0992; airport: 0 2523 7320; www.koreanair.com.
Lufthansa, Q House Building, 18th Floor, 66 Soi 21, Thanon Sukhumvit. Tel: 0 2264 2400 (reservations); fax: 0 2264 2399; airport: 0 2535 2211; www.lufthansa.com.
Malaysia Airlines, Ploenchit Tower, 20th Floor, 898 Thanon Ploenchit. Tel: 0 2263 0565–71 (reservations), 0 2263 0520–33 (ticketing); fax: 0 2263 0577 (reservations), airport: 0 2535 2288; www.malaysiaairlines.com.
Myanmar Airways, Unit 3803, BB Building, 8F 54 Thanon Asoke, Sukhumvit 21, Wattana. Tel: 0 2261 5969; 0 2630 0334–8; fax: 0 2261 5075; airport: 0 2535 2266, 0 2535 2484; www.maiair.com.
Nok Air (domestic), 11th Floor, One Pacific Place, 140 Thanon

Sukhumvit. Tel: 1318 (call centre); www.nokair.co.th (online booking available).

Northwest Airlines, Peninsula Plaza, 4th Floor, 153 Thanon Ratchadamri. Tel: 0 2652 1010 (reservations), 0 2254 0789 (ticketing); fax: 0 2254 0741; airport: 0 2535 6200; www.nwa.com/th/en/home.html.

Orient Thai Airlines (domestic), Jewelry Center, 17th Floor, 138/70 Thanon Nares. Tel: 0 2267 3210–5 (reservations & ticketing); fax: 0 2267 3216–17; airport: 0 2535 2021-5; call centre: 1126; www.orient-thai.com.

Philippine Airlines, 12th Floor Manorom Building, 3354/47 Thanon Rama IV. Tel: 0 2633 5713–4; fax: 0 2671 5470; airport: 0 2535 2338–9; www.philippineair.com.

Phuket Air (domestic & regional), 1168/102 34th Floor, Lumphini Tower Building, Thanon Rama IV, Sathon. Tel: 0 2679 8999; fax: 0 2679 8235–6; www. phuketairlines.com.

Qantas, Charn Issara, Tower 1, 21F, 942/160–163 Thanon Rama IV. Tel: 0 2636 1747; fax: 0 2636 1749 (reservations); airport: 0 2535 2220, 0 2535 2149; www.qantas.com.

Royal Brunei, 968 U Chu Liang Building, 17F Thanon Rama IV, Lumphini. Tel: 0 2637 5151; fax: 0 2637 5885; airport: 0 2535 2626–7; www.bruneiair.com.

SAS, Glas Haus Building, 8th Floor, Soi 25, Thanon Sukhumvit. Tel: 0 2645 8200 (reservations & ticketing); fax: 0 2665 2900; airport: 0 2535 2716, 0 2535 2322; www.scandinavian.net.

Singapore Airlines, Silom Center Building, 12th Floor, 2 Thanon Silom. Tel: 0 2236 0440 (reservations); 0 2236 5301 (ticketing); fax: 0 2236 5294; airport: 0 2535 2260–1; www.singaporeair.com.

Swiss International Airlines, Abdulrahim Place, 21st Floor, 990 Thanon Rama IV. Tel: 0 2636 2160-5 (reservations & ticketing), fax: 0 2636 2168; airport: 0 2535 2371-2; www.swiss.com.

Thai Airways, head office: 89 Thanon Vibhavadi Rangsit,

Chatuchak. Tel: 0 2545 3690–2, 0 2628 2000 (reservations, etc), 0 2232 8000, 0 2628 2000 (ticketing); fax: 0 2545 3832; airport: 0 2535 2081–2 (domestic), 0 2535 2846–7 (international); www.thaiair.com.

United Airlines, Sindhorn Building, 14th Floor, Tower 3, 130–132 Thanon Witthayu. Tel: 0 2253 0558 (reservations); 0 2253 0559 (ticketing); fax: 0 2255 1304; airport: 0 2535 2231, 0 2535 2241; www.unitedairlines.co.th.

Vietnam Airlines, Ploenchit Center Building, Soi 2, Thanon Sukhumvit. Tel: 0 2655 4137–40 (reservations & ticketing); fax: 0 2656 9101; airport: 0 2535 2671; fax: 0 2655 4420; www.vietnamairlines.com.

Chiang Mai

Bangkok Airways, 2nd Floor, Chiang Mai International Airport. Tel: 0 5328 1519, 153 Thanon Sridonchai, Chang Klan. Tel: 0 6327 6176.

Thai Airways, 240 Thanon Phra Poklao. Tel: 0 5321 1644.

Silk Air, Imperial Mae Ping Hotel, 153 Thanon Sridonchai, Chang Klan. Tel: 0 5327 6647, 0 5327 6495; www.silkair.com.

Phuket

Bangkok Airways, 158/2–3 Thanon Yaowarat. Tel: 0 7622 5033–5.

Dragonair, 156/14 Thanon Phang Nga. Tel: 0 7621 5734, 0 7621 7300–1.

Malaysian Airlines, 1/8–9 Thanon Tungka. Tel: 0 7621 6675, 0 7621 3749.

Silk Air, 183/103 Thanon Phangnga. Tel: 0 7621 3891, 0 7621 3895.

Thai Airways, 78 Thanon Ranong. Tel: 0 7621 2946, 0 7621 1195, 0 7621 2499, 0 7621 6678.

Religious Services

Christian

Assumption Cathedral, 23 Oriental Lane, Thanon Charoen Krung. Tel: 0 2234 8556. Sunday Mass: 10am.

Calvary Baptist Church, 88 Soi 2, Thanon Sukhumvit. Tel: 0 2251

8278; fax: 0 2251 0809. Sunday service: 10.45am.

Holy Redeemer Catholic Church, 123/19 Soi Ruam Rudi, Thanon Witthayu. Tel: 0 2256 6157. Sunday Mass: 8.30am, 9.45am, 11am and 5.30pm.

International Christian Assembly, 196 Soi Ekamai, Thanon Sukhumvit. Tel: 0 2391 4387. Services: 10.30am.

International Church of Bangkok, Bangkok Christian College, 35 Soi Pramuan (at Thanon Sathorn). Tel: 0 2258 5821. Sunday service: 10am.

St. Louis Church, 215/2 Thanon Sathorn Tai. Tel: 0 2211 0220. Sunday Mass: 6am, 8am, 10am, 11.15am and 5.30pm.

Hindu

Sri Maha Mariamman Temple, Thanon Silom, 2 Thanon Pan. Tel: 0 2238 4007.

Hindu Dharm Sabha, 050 Soi Tung Wat Don, Yannawa. Tel: 0 2211 3840.

Jewish

Jewish Association of Thailand (Ashkenazi), Jewish Community Center and Beth Elisheva Synagogue, 121 Soi Sai Nam Thip 2 Sukhumvit Soi 22. Tel: 0 2663 0244; fax: 0 2663 0245; www.jewishthailand.com. Services: Friday evening at sundown with meal, Shabbat service 10am.

Even Chen Synagogue, Chao Phya Office Tower, 4th Floor (attached to Shangri-La Hotel), Soi Charoen Krung, 42/1 New Road. Tel: 0 2630 6120–9; fax: 0 2237 3225. Services: daily 8am, Friday sundown, Saturday 9am, Shabbat meals only by appointment.

Ohr Menachem Chabad House, 96 Thanon Rambutri. Tel: 0 2282 6388, 0 2629 2770; fax: 0 2629 1153. Services: daily, Friday evenings with meal.

Muslim

The Foundation of Islamic Center of Thailand, 87/2 Thanon Ramkhamhaeng, Soi 2. Tel: 0 2314 5638; fax: 0 2314 3692.

Haroon Mosque, 25 Soi 36, Thanon Charoen Krung. Tel: 0 2630 9435.

Practical Tips

Emergencies

SECURITY AND CRIME

If you run into trouble in Bangkok, the police emergency number is 191, but unless you speak Thai you won't get far with this number. There are Tourist Police assigned specially to assist travellers, and members of the force speak passable English. They can be reached most quickly by dialing **1155** from anywhere in Thailand. The operator will transfer your call to the nearest Tourist Police office.

The Tourist Police headquarters is at 29/1 Unico House Building, Soi Lang Suan, Thanon Ploenchit, tel: 0 2255 2964. Another office is at the Tourist Assistance Centre at 4 Thanon Ratchadamnoen Nok (www.tourist.police.go.th) or they can be reached by simply dialling 1155.

Tourist police booths can also be found in many tourist areas including Lumphini Park (near the intersection of Thanon Rama IV and Thanon Silom) and Patpong (at the Thanon Silom intersection). Their offices can be found outside Bankok in Chiang Mai, Pattaya and Phuket as well.

In Chiang Mai, they are located below the Tourist Authority of Thailand office at 105/1 Thanon Chiang Mai-Lamphun. Tel: 0 5324 8604, 5324 8607.

In Pattaya, their office is at No 2 Thanon Pattaya, Pattaya Beach, tel: 0 3842 9371. In Phuket, the Tourist Police booth is on Thanon Patong, tel: 0 7621 9947.

Medical Services

First-class hotels in Bankok, Chiang Mai and Phuket have doctors on call for medical

Avoiding Scams

Visitors to Thailand should be aware of the following:

● Overly-friendly, well-dressed Thai men (or women) who speak good English and approach you unbidden with advice or an offer to help you find somewhere. These encounters almost always lead to some scam or another. Often these people will tell you that the place you are going to (Grand Palace, etc.) is closed for the day. Such encounters normally happen in areas where there is a lot of daytime tourist traffic. Don't be afraid of offending a friendly local – the average Thai is too shy to approach foreigners in such a way.

● Touts on Patpong offering upstairs live-sex shows. Once inside, you can be handed an exorbitant bill and threatened with mayhem if you protest. Pay, take the receipt, and go to the Tourist Police to gain restitution, which may or may not be forthcoming. (If you do venture into one of these places, keep track of the number of drinks you order and check your bill carefully before you leave.)

● Tuk-tuk or taxi drivers who offer to take you anywhere for 10 baht (or for free). No matter where you want to go, the destination will always be a gem shop and you will be pressured to buy flawed gems at high prices. If you succumb to any of Bangkok's numerous gem scams, don't expect to get a refund after you've handed over your money or credit card. The police are almost no help whatsoever in such cases.

● People on buses or trains offering sweets, fruits or soft drinks. The items may be drugged and the passenger is robbed while unconscious. This is unfortunate because Thais are generous people and it is normal for them to offer food to strangers. Use your discretion.

emergencies. The hospitals in these three destinations are the equivalent of those in any major Western city. Intensive-care units are fully equipped and staffed by doctors to handle emergencies quickly and competently. Nursing care is generally superb, because there is a high staff-to-patient ratio. Many doctors have been trained in Western hospitals, and even those who have not speak good English.

Most small towns have clinics which treat minor ailments and accidents.

HOSPITALS

Bangkok
(All cover major specialities)
BNH Hospital, 9/1 Thanon Convent. Tel: 0 2632 0550, 0 2632 0560; fax: 0 2632 0577–9; www.bnhhospital.com. Several Western doctors. Near Thanon Silom area.
Bumrungrad Hospital, 33 Sukhumvit Soi 3, Wattana. Tel: 0 2667 1000; emergency tel: 0 2667 2999; fax: 0 2667 2525; www.bumrungrad.com. Staff comfortable with foreigners.
Samitivej Hospital, 133 Soi 49, Thanon Sukhumvit. Tel: 0 2711 8000; fax: 0 2391 1290; www.samitivej.co.th. Popular with expatriates living in the area.
Thai Nakarin Hospital, 345 Thanon Bang Na Trat. Tel: 0 2361 2727; fax: 0 2361 2777; www.thainakarin.co.th. Mostly US-trained doctors, excellent ambulance service.
Vibhavadi General Hospital, 1 Soi 111, 51/3 Thanon Ngam Wongwam, Chatuchak. Tel: 0 2941 2800, 0 2941 2900; fax: 0 2561 1466; www.vibhavadi.com. Staff comfortable with foreigners.

Chiang Mai
Maharaj Nakorn Chiang Mai Hospital, 110 Thanon Suthep. Tel: 0 5322 1122, 0 5322 1075; fax: 0 5321 7144; www.med.cmu.ac.th.
Chiang Mai Ram Hospital, 8 Thanon Boonmuangrit, Tamboon Sripoom, Muang. Tel: 0 5322 4850; emergency tel: 0 5389 5001; fax:

0 5322 4860,
www.chiangmairam.com.
Lanna Hospital, 1 Thanon
Sukkasem, off the super highway
on the north side of town. Tel:
0 5335 7234; fax: 0 5340 8432;
www.lanna-hospital.com.
Nakornpin Hospital, 159 Moo 4,
Thanon Chottana-Mae-rim. Tel: 0
5389 0755–64; fax: 0 5322 2152;
www.nkp-hospital.go.th.

Pattaya
Bangkok Pattaya Hospital, 301
Moo 6, Thanon Sukhumvit, km 143,
Banglamung, Chonburi 20150.
Tel/fax: 0 3825 9999;
www.bph.co.th.
Pattaya International Hospital, Soi
4, Thanon Second. Tel: 0 3842
8374–5; fax: 0 3842 8373;
www.pih-inter.com.
Pattaya Memorial, 328/1 Thanon
Pattaya/Klaeng. Tel: 0 3842
9422–4, 0 3842 7751.
Phyathai Siracha General, 90
Thanon Si Racha Nakorn, Chonburi.
Tel: 0 3877 0200; fax: 0 3877
0213.

Phuket
Bangkok-Phuket Hospital, 2/1
Thanon Hongyok Utit, Phuket town.
Tel: 0 7625 4425; emergencies:
ext. 1060; fax: 0 7625 4597;
www.phukethospital.com.
Patong-Kathu Hospital, Thanon Sai
Nam Yen, Patong Beach. Tel: 0
7634 0444, 0 7634 2633–4.
Phuket International Hospital, 44
Thanon Chalermprakiat. Tel: 0 7624
9400; emergencies: 0 7621 0935;
fax: 0 7621 0936; www.phuket-
inter-hospital.co.th.

Medical Clinics
For minor problems, there are
numerous clinics in all major towns
and cities. Most international hotels
also have an on-premises clinic or
doctor on call.

STD CLINICS

Clinics along Thanon Ploenchit
perform tests for sexually
transmitted diseases; there are
several similar clinics in Patpong.

Bangkok General Hospital, 2
Soi Soonvijai, Thanon New Phetburi,
tel: 0 2310 3344;
www.bangkokhospital.com, is
reputed to offer the most reliable
tests for the presence of HIV,
International Medical Center, tel:
0 2310 3102 and **Anonymous
Clinic** run by Thai Red Cross at the
"Snake Farm", on 1871 Thanon
Rama IV, tel: 0 2256 4109. Open
Mon–Fri noon–7pm, performs
anonymous HIV tests and is a good
source for HIV/AIDS information.

Snake Bites

There is little chance of being
bitten by a poisonous snake in
Bangkok or its environs, but
should it occur, most clinics have
anti-venom serum on hand. If
they cannot acquire any, travel to
the **Saovabha Institute** (Snake
Farm; tel: 0 2252 0161–4) on
Thanon Rama IV. They maintain
sera against the bites of six
types of cobras and vipers.
Provincial clinics maintain a
constant supply of anti-venom
serum supplied by the Institute.

DENTAL CLINICS

Dental clinics are almost as
numerous as medical clinics. Some
hospitals also have dental surgery
facilities.
BNH Hospital, 9/1 Thanon Convent,
tel: 0 2632 0550, 0 2632 0560;
www.bnhhospital.com. Located
between Thanon Silom and Thanon
Sathon, BNH has an excellent dental
clinic with all the latest equipment.
   In Bangkok, one clinic with a long-
standing reputation is the **Dental
Polyclinic**, at 2111–2113 Thanon
New Phetburi, tel: 0 2314 5070, 0
2314 7177. **The Dental Hospital**,
88/88 Soi 49, Thanon Sukhumvit,
tel: 0 2260 5000–15; fax: 0 2260
5026; www.dentalhospitalbangkok.
com, looks more like a hotel than a
dental hospital and has the latest
imported equipment.
   In Chiang Mai, there is
Dentaland, Soi 17, Thanon
Nimmanhemin. Tel: 0 5322 4578;

e-mail: dentaland17@yahoo.com.
   In Phuket town, the **Dental Care
Clinic** is located at 62/5 Rasda
Center. Tel: 0 7621 5025;
fax: 0 7622 3500; www.dentist-
phuket.com.

PHARMACIES

Pharmaceuticals in Thailand are
produced to the highest standards,
and pharmacies must have a
registered pharmacist on the
premises. Most pharmacy
personnel in the shopping and
business areas speak English.
Many prescription drugs in other
countries can be bought, legally,
over the counter in Thailand.
   Pharmacies are everywhere in
Bangkok; look for the sign of the
green cross. Two of the more
common outlets, found in malls and
districts frequented by foreigners,
are **Siam Drugs** and **Pharma
Choice**. In addition, many of the
larger grocery stores have
pharmacy counters with helpful
personnel who generally speak
passable English. Try branches of
Foodland, **Central** or **Robinson**.

Business Hours

Government offices are open from
8.30am–4.30pm Mon–Fri. Business
hours are 8am or 8.30am–5.30pm
Mon–Fri. Some businesses are
open half days from 8.30am–noon
on Sat.
   Banks are generally open from
8.30am–3.30pm five days a week,
but many operate money-changing
kiosks throughout the city, which
are open until 8pm seven days a
week. The Bank of Asia has
pioneered branch banking at
supermarkets and shopping malls
outside of normal hours. Other
banks have followed suit.
   Most department stores are
open 10am–9pm seven days a
week. Ordinary shops open at
8.30am or 9am and close between
6pm and 8pm, depending on the
location and type of business.
Some pharmacies in the major
cities remain open all night.

Small open-air coffee shops and restaurants open at 7am and close at 8.30pm, though some stay open past midnight. Large restaurants generally close at 10pm. Most coffee shops close at midnight; some stay open 24 hours. Twenty-four-hour convenience stores have become increasingly common. It is difficult to find a corner without one nowadays.

Tipping

Tipping is not a custom in Thailand, although it is becoming more common. Although a service charge of 10 percent is generally included in restaurant bills and is divided among the staff, a bit extra for the waitress doesn't go unappreciated.

Do not tip *tuk-tuk* drivers unless the traffic has been particularly bad and he has been especially patient; 10 baht would suffice for a long journey costing more than 60 baht.

Hotel room boys and porters are becoming used to being tipped but will not hover with hand extended.

Media

PRESS

The English language morning newspapers are one of the foreigner's lifelines to the outside world. There are two national English-language dailies – *Bangkok Post* and *The Nation*. The *Asian Wall Street Journal* and the *International Herald Tribune* are both available in Bangkok. News stands in major hotel gift shops carry air-freighted, and therefore expensive, editions of British, French, American, German and Italian newspapers. Newsagents on Soi 3 (Soi Nana Nua), Thanon Sukhumvit also offer Arabic newspapers.

Monthly magazines designed for travellers and foreign residents alike have listings of restaurants and nightlife venues. *Farang* is one of the more well-known and can be found in bookshops. Free listings magazines that rely on advertisements can be found in hotel lobbies. These come and go with each season so it's often

worth seeking out something more credible at a bookshop.

In Chiang Mai, the weekly *Chiang Mai Mail* contains local news and features, as well as information on events, special offers and new facilities and services in the area.

RADIO

AM radio is devoted entirely to Thai-language programmes. FM frequencies include **Radio Thailand** (92.5 FM) with a variety of English-language programmes including a travel show in the late afternoon, and **Chulalongkorn University** (101.5) which plays jazz 5pm–6pm and classical music 8–10pm. Other popular stations can be found at 89 FM (Thai rock); 95.5 FM (English-speaking DJs playing hits from the '70s, '80s and '90s); 105 FM (easy listening with hourly international, local and traffic news); 107 FM (hits from the '50s through to the '90s with hourly **CNN** broadcasts).

In addition, **Voice of America** and **BBC World Service** offer shortwave radio broadcasts in English throughout the day. Check newspapers for current frequencies and programme schedules.

TELEVISION

Bangkok has five Thai language television channels, in addition to a variety of satellite and cable television services: **Satellite Television Asian Region** (STAR), and **UBC**. **BBC World**, **Australia TV**, **CNN**, **HBO**, **Discovery**, **TNT**, **Supersport** and **ESPN**, as well as other news, sports, music and entertainment programmes, are widely available on these networks.

Postal Services

Thailand has comprehensive and reliable postal and post restante services. All major towns offer regular air mail service, and a global express courier service.

In Bangkok, the **General Post Office** (GPO), on Thanon Charoen

Krung (New) between Thanon Suriwong and Thanon Si Phraya, tel: 0 2233 1050-9, 0 2235 2834; www.thailandpost.com, is open 8am–8pm Mon–Fri and 8am–1pm on weekends and holidays. It has a useful and inexpensive parcel packaging service.

A separate building located to the right of the main post office provides telecommunications services around the clock, including telephone, internet, telegram, fax and telex.

There are branch post offices throughout Bangkok, many of which stay open until 6pm. Kiosks along some of the busier streets sell stamps and aerograms and ship small parcels. Hotels will send letters for their guests at no charge.

The main post offices in Bangkok, Chiang Mai and Phuket also have special facilities where stamp collectors can browse and buy from a wide selection of beautiful Thai stamps.

Courier Services

A number of international courier agencies have offices in Bangkok: **DHL International**, Grand Amarin Tower, 22nd Floor, 1550 Thanon New Phetburi. Tel: 0 2658 8000; 24-hour service tel: 0 2345 5000; fax: 0 2207 0630; www.dhl.co.th. **Federal Express**, Green Tower, 8th Floor, 3656/22–23 Thanon Rama IV. Tel: 0 2229 8800; customer service: 1782; fax: 0 2240 1411; www.fedex.com/th. **TNT Express Worldwide**, 599 Thanon Chong Non Si, Khlong Toey. Tel: 0 2249 5702; fax: 0 2672 9850. **United Parcel Service**, 16/1 Soi 44, Thanon Sukhumvit. Tel: 0 2712 3300; customer service: office tel: 0 2712 3090; fax: 0 2712 1818; www.ups.com.

Telecommunications

Thailand has a modern and sophisticated communications system. Most hotels have telephone, e-mail and fax facilities.

TELEPHONE

Most international telephone calls can be dialled direct from Bangkok. International telephone calls can be placed at the **General Post Office** (GPO) 24 hours a day. Most provincial capitals have telephone offices at the GPO; hours are generally 7am–11pm.

A hyphen before the last couple of digits (eg. 392 2520–4) indicates that all numbers between these two can be dialled. Note that any telephone number beginning with **01, 04, 06 or 09** indicates a cellular telephone, and the zero must be dialled. Note, also, that telephone calls to Malaysia do not require a country code; simply prefix the number, including the area code, with **09**.

Operator Assistance

For directory assistance in English in Bangkok and upcountry, dial **1133**.

For operator assistance with a domestic call, plus those to **Cambodia**, **Laos**, **Malaysia** and **Burma (Myanmar)**, dial **101**; for assistance with all other international calls (including collect/reverse charges calls), dial **100**. Operators at these numbers speak English.

International Telephone Calls

The international prefix from Thailand is **001**.

International card phones are widely available in tourist areas, and can be purchased from post offices, convenience stores and supermarkets.

TELEGRAM AND FAX

The main post offices in nearly every city offer telegram, telex and fax services to all parts of the world. Many small shops throughout the country also offer a variety of telephone and fax services, although the prices may be a little steep, particularly for faxes.

ON-LINE ACCESS

Once thin on the ground, internet cafés can now be found on almost every street in Bangkok, and even the least developed provinces have places to check e-mail and surf the web. Many of these places are really more like video arcades (look for a shop full of school kids manning the computers) but there is almost always internet access in addition to the games.

Larger facilities in shopping malls offer a wide range of services, including hot and cold food and drink, laser and colour printing, and other business services, such as photocopying.

Many places of accommodation, from luxury hotels to the cheapest guesthouses, will also have internet access. Thanon Khao San in particular is peppered with internet cafés. A current listing of these can be found at www.khaosanroad.com. If your hotel doesn't have internet access, they will know where the nearest and most convenient facility is located.

Internet Cafés

Big John's@email-café.com
159/12 Sukhumvit Soi 55 (Soi Thonglor)
Tel: 0 2392 6518
www.email-café.com
Open 7am–2am; a wide range of services and some of the cheapest rates in town. They use iMacs that can handle a variety of languages (Chinese, Japanese, Russian, etc.) and have a language library to boot. Staff is friendly, helpful, and can speak decent English. Homemade Aussie pies and burgers are the speciality at Big John's.

Getting Around

On Arrival

BANGKOK AIRPORT

The once nightmarish journey from the Bangkok International Airport (www.airportthai.co.th) into the city centre has vastly improved with the completion of an elevated highway and several linking expressways. It takes about 30 to 45 minutes to get to or from the airport, depending on traffic.

Limousine Service

There are two limousine companies operating at the airport. **Airport Associate Co Ltd** (tel: 0 2982 4900; www.airporttaxithai.com) in Terminal 1 and 2 operates a limousine service (using Mercedes Benz sedans) to the city for 800 baht, an 8-seater van for 1,100 baht; limousine to Pattaya for 2,400 baht and 8-seater van for 2,700 baht. **Thai Airways Limos** (tel: 0 2535 2801; www.thai airways.com) in Terminal 1 and 2 has a premium service (using Mercedes Benz E220) to downtown for 1,500 baht, or a regular service (Mercedes Benz 200) for 800 baht.

Airport Bus

If you don't have much luggage, consider using the Airport Bus, which passes the main hotel locations in downtown Bangkok. Tickets can be bought on the bus or at the booths outside the Arrival Hall of all terminals. Buses depart every 15 minutes from 5.30am to 12.30am, and the fare is 100 baht per person.
Airport Bus Routes:
A-1 to Thanon Charoen Krung (New Road) via Pratunam, Thanon Ratchadamri, Thanon Silom and

Thanon Surawong.

A-2 to Sanam Luang (Banglamphu) via Thanon Phaya Thai and Thanon Lan Luang.

A-3 to Soi Thonglor (Sukhumvit 55) via Thanon Petchaburi and Thanon Sukhumvit.

A-4 to Hualamphong Railway Station via Thanon Ploenchit, Thanon Rama, Thanon Phaya Thai and Thanon Rama IV.

Taxis

Operating 24 hours daily, all taxis officially serving the airport are air-conditioned and metered. The taxi stand is located just outside the Arrival Hall of all terminals. Join the queue and tell the person at the desk where you want to go to. A receipt will be issued, with the licence plate number of the taxi and your destination in Thai written on it. Make sure the driver turns on the meter. At the end of your trip, pay what is on the meter plus a 50 baht airport surcharge. If the driver uses the expressway to speed up the journey, he will ask for your approval first. If you agree, you have to pay the toll fees of 60 baht (20 baht for the first toll booth and 40 baht for the second). Depending on traffic, an average fare from the airport to the city centre is around 200–250 baht (excluding toll fees and airport surcharge).

Train

Another fast and cheap way into the city is to take the train. Don Muang train station is just across the street from the airport (look for the Amari Hotel entrance sign in the Arrival Hall of Terminal 1). It takes roughly 40 minutes to Hualamphong station, not far from Chinatown. There are trains at 15 to 30 minute intervals from 5am–8pm. The fare is 5 baht for ordinary trains and 21 baht for express trains.

CHIANG MAI AIRPORT

Chiang Mai's airport is a 10-minute drive from the city centre. Getting from from Chiang Mai's airport into the city requires hiring an airport

taxi. Destinations within the city, up to the Ping River cost 100 baht. Going east beyond the river is 120 to 150 baht.

For the return journey, if you are staying in a major hotel, the desk can arrange a ride for you. If not, you'll have to take your chances with hailing a *tuk-tuk* (motorised tricycle) or *song tao* (share taxi pick-up truck) from the street. Unfortunately, these are few and far between. Unless you have arranged a ride to the airport in advance, give yourself plenty of time to get there.
Limousines: Major hotels have limousines to ferry guests with reservations (or make a reservation at the airport) to their premises.

PHUKET AIRPORT

Limousines: Thai Airways offers air-conditioned limousines to each beach. The price is calculated per vehicle, and each vehicle holds four people.
Minibus: Major hotels maintain minibuses to ferry guests with reservations (it is possible to make a reservation at the airport) to and from the airport. The Thai Airways minibus runs hourly between the airport and its Phuket town office on Thanon Ranong, but you have to find your own way from the office to your hotel.
Metered Taxis: Air-conditioned taxis, like the ones in Bangkok, are available in the parking lot of the airport.

Domestic Travel

BY AIR

The domestic arm of **Thai Airways International** (THAI) operates a network of daily flights to 14 of Thailand's major towns aboard a fleet of 737s and Airbuses.

The frequency and number of flights changes with the seasons – the peak season being November through February. From Bangkok, there are daily flights to Nakhon Si Thammarat, Surat Thani, Ubon Ratchathani, Udon Thani, Khon

Kaen, Phitsanulok, Hat Yai and Phuket. Connections to Mae Hong Son are made via Chiang Mai.

In addition, **Bangkok Airways** flies from Bangkok to Ko Samui more than a dozen times daily; to Sukhothai and Chiang Mai twice daily; and to Hua Hin at least once daily. It also flies to Phnom Penh and Siem Riep (Angkor Wat) in Cambodia, Luang Prabang in Laos and to Xian, Jinghong and Guilin in China. From Ko Samui, it also connects to Phuket and Singapore.

In recent years, a number of low-cost domestic and regional carriers have appeared in Thailand. The most notable, Nok Air, is actually owned in part by Thai Airways and caters to the budget traveller. Phuket Airlines, Orient Thai and Air Asia also fly domestically within Thailand and to other parts of Southeast Asia including Singapore, Hong Kong and Malaysia. For detailed route information, visit the websites listed for each of these airlines on page 346. In keeping with the times, Nok Air and Air Asia allow passengers to book tickets and pay online via their websites, while Nok Air and Orient Thai have enlisted, easy-dial, four-digit phone numbers within Thailand to streamline booking and reservations.

Note: flights are affordable so where you can fly instead of travelling by road. Flying to the island of Ko Samui from Bangkok for instance takes less than two hours; the same trip by road and boat may take as long as 14 hours.

BY RAIL

From Hualamphong Station

The State Railways of Thailand (see also page 341) operates five principal routes from Bangkok's Hualamphong Station.

The **northern** route passes through Ayutthaya, Phitsanulok, Lampang and terminates at Chiang Mai. The upper **northeastern** route passes through Ayutthaya, Saraburi, Nakhon Ratchasima, Khon Kaen, Udon Thani and terminates at Nong Khai. The lower northeastern route

Train Information

Hualamphong Station, Thanon Rama IV; tel: (information) 0 2233 7010, 0 2233 7020, 0 2621 8701, (reservations) 0 2223 3762, Train Info Tel: 1690; fax: 0 2225 6068; www.railway.co.th/eng.
Bangkok Noi (Thonburi) Station, Thanon Arun Amarin (near Siriraj Hospital), tel: 0 2225 0300, 0 2411 3102.

branches east at Nakhon Ratchasima and passes through Buriram, Surin, Sisaket and terminates at Ubon Ratchathani. The eastern route goes due east from Bangkok to the town of Aranyaprathet on the Cambodian border.

The **southern** route crosses the Rama VI bridge and calls at Nakhon Pathom, Phetchaburi, Hua Hin and Chumphon. It branches at Hat Yai, one branch running southwest through Betong and on down the western coast of Malaysia to Singapore. The **southeastern** branch goes via Pattani and Yala to the Thai border opposite the Malaysian town of Kota Bharu.

From other stations

Another line leaves **Bangkok Noi** (tel: 0 2411 3100–2) station, in Thonburi, on the western bank of the Chao Phraya River, for Kanchanaburi and other destinations in western Thailand.

Express and rapid services on the main lines offer first-class, air-conditioned or second-class, fan-cooled cars with sleeping cabins or berths and dining cars. There are also special air-conditioned express day coaches that travel to key towns along the main lines. Rail passes valid for 20 days are available. Reservations can be made at the station or with any travel agent within 60 days of departure.

Make certain you know from which station your train leaves, particularly if you are travelling to Kanchanaburi.

BY ROAD

Bus services are reliable, frequent and very affordable to most destinations in Thailand. Rest stops are regular, and in some cases limited refreshments are available on the bus.

Fan-cooled buses, painted orange, are the slowest, since they make stops in every village along the way. For short distances, they can be an entertaining means of travel, particularly in the cool season when the fan and the open windows make the trip reasonably comfortable. Blue air-conditioned buses, however, are generally a faster, more comfortable way to get to your destination. VIP buses are available on some of the longer routes; these usually have larger seats, more leg room and toilets.

Private bus companies also run the same routes, sometimes at cheaper rates than government buses. The bad news is that the vehicles are often substandard and drivers are either poorly trained or overworked. When given a choice, always opt for the government bus services that depart from public bus terminals.

Coach Stations

For bus and coach journeys to destinations outside of Bangkok, the major terminals are:
Eastern
Thanon Sukhumvit, opposite Soi 63 (Soi Ekamai)
Tel: 0 2391 2504, 0 2391 8097
Departures for Pattaya, Rayong, Chanthaburi.
Northern and Northeastern
Moh Chit Mai (meaning new, as it is a new terminal)
Tel: 0 2936 2853–5
Departures for Ayutthaya, Lopburi, Nakhon Ratchasima, Chiang Mai.
Southern
Thanon Phra Pinklao (western bank of Chao Phraya)
Tel: 0 2435 1199, 0 2434 7192
Departures for Nakhon Pathom, Kanchanaburi, Phuket, Surat Thani.

To reach a small town from a large one, or to get around on some of the islands, *song tao* (meaning two benches), pick-up trucks with benches along either side of the bed, function as taxis.

Public Transport

BANGKOK

Taxis, Tuk-Tuks & Motorcycle Taxis

Taxis are abundant in Bangkok. They are metered, air-conditioned, inexpensive, and comfortably seat 3 to 4 persons. Taxis can be hailed anywhere along the streets; there are no taxi stands on the streets but you can expect to find them outside hotels and the shopping centres.

The flag fall charge is 35 baht; after the first 2 km (1 mile), the meter goes up by 4–5.50 baht every kilometre, depending on distance travelled. If stuck in traffic a small per minute surcharge kicks in. If your journey crosses town, ask the driver to take the expressway. The network of elevated two-lane roads can cut the journey by half. The toll fare of 20–50 baht is given to the driver at the payment booth, not at the end of the trip.

Seatbelts must be worn in the front seat. A 10 percent tip is suggested; it's not a must.

Before starting any journey, check that the meter has been reset and turned on. On seeing a foreign face, some drivers may quote a flat fee instead of using the meter. Unless you're desperate, don't use these. Fares, however, can be negotiated for longer distances outside Bangkok: for instance, Pattaya (1,200 baht), Koh Samet (1,500 baht) or Hua Hin (1,500–2,000 baht).

These taxi companies will pick up for a 20 baht surcharge: **Siam Taxi** (hotline tel: 1661); **Julie Taxi** (tel: 01 846 2014; www.julietaxi.com).

Tuk-tuks are the brightly coloured three-wheeled taxis whose name comes from the incessant noise their two-stroke engines make. Few tuk-tuk drivers speak English, so make sure your destination is written down in Thai. Unless you bargain hard, tuk-tuk fares are rarely lower than metered taxi fares.

Expect to pay 30–50 baht for short journeys of a few blocks or around 15 minutes or less, and 50–100 baht for longer journeys. A 100 baht ride should get you a half-hour ride across most parts of downtown. Be sure to negotiate the fare beforehand.

Motorcycle taxi stands (with young men in fluorescent orange vests) are clustered at the mouth of most *soi* (small sidestreets) and beside any busy intersection or building entrance. The drivers are experts at weaving through Bangkok's heavy traffic and may cut travel time in half, but do so at your own peril, as drivers tend to weave precariously in and out of traffic. If the driver is going too fast, ask him to slow down in Thai: *cha-cha*.

Hire only a driver who provides a passenger helmet. Fares must be negotiated beforehand, and they are rarely lower than taxi fares for the same distance travelled. Females wearing skirts must also cope with sitting side-saddle.

A short distance, such as the

Street Names

Note that **Wireless Road** (a street full of embassies and hotels) is more commonly known by its Thai name, **Thanon Witthayu**. Similarly, **Sathorn Road**, a main thoroughfare divided into north and south which runs between Lumphini Park and the river, is often referred to as **Sathorn Nua (north)** and **Sathorn Tai (south)**. With no standard translated English spellings for the Thai language, it is common to find a street or area spelt with several variants and broken or joined syllables.

Skytrain station names often differ from the street sign spelling, so **Chidlom district** becomes **Chit Lom station**, **Thanon Asoke** becomes **Asok station**, and **Soi Thonglor** becomes **Thong Lo**.

length of a street, will cost 10–20 baht; longer rides are between 50–100 baht. During rush hours (8–10am and 4–6pm), prices are higher. A 80–100 baht ride should get you a half-hour trip across most parts of downtown.

Buses

Bus transport in Bangkok is very cheap but can also be equally arduous, time-consuming and confusing. Municipal and private operators all come under the charge of the **Bangkok Mass Transit Authority** (tel: 0 2246 0973; www.bmta.co.th).

With little English signage and few conductors or drivers speaking English, boarding the right bus is an exercise in frustration. Public buses come in four varieties: microbus, Euro II bus, air-conditioned and non-air-conditioned "ordinary". In theory, the routes of both air-conditioned and ordinary buses appear on standard bus maps. In practice, however, routes change and many air-con bus routes have been added in recent years, rendering bus maps out of date.

Skytrain

The Bangkok Transit System's (BTS) elevated train service (BTS Tourist Information Centre: tel: 0 2617 7340; Hotline: tel: 0 2617 6000; www.bts.co.th), better known as Skytrain, started operations in December 1999. It is the perfect way of beating the city's traffic-congested streets.

The Skytrain consists of two lines. The Sukhumvit Line runs from Mo Chit station in the north to On Nut in the southeast. The Silom Line runs from National Stadium, near Siam Square, south to Saphan Taksin station near Tha Sathorn (or Central Pier). Both lines intersect at Siam station.

The Skytrain is fast, frequent and clean, but suffers from overcrowding during peak hours. Accessibility too is problem for the disabled and aged as there aren't enough escalators or lifts.

Trains operate from 6am to midnight (3 minutes peak; 5

minutes off-peak). Single-trip fares vary according to distance, starting at 10 baht and rising to 40 baht. Self-service ticket machines are found at all station concourses. Tourists may find it more useful to buy the unlimited ride 1-day Pass (100 baht) or the 30-day Adult Pass (which comes in three types: 250 baht, 10 rides; 300 baht, 15 rides and 540 baht, 30 rides) – all available at station counters.

BTS Tourist Information Centres are found on the concourse levels of Siam, Nana and Saphan Taksin stations (daily 8am–8pm).

MRTA

Bangkok's metro line (Customer Relations Centre tel: 0 2624 5200; www.mrta.co.th or www.bangkokmetro.co.th) was launched in July 2004 by the Mass Rapid Transit Authority (MRTA). The line has 18 stations, stretching 20km (12 miles) between Bang Sue in the northern suburbs of Bangkok and the city's main railway station, Hualamphong, at the edge of Chinatown. The line hasn't secured a popular name among the city's commuters yet, and is variously referred to as the MRT, metro or subway.

Three of its stations – Silom, Sukhumvit and Chatuchak Park – are interchanges, and passengers can transfer to the Skytrain network at these points. More lines and extensions to both rail networks are planned.

Operating from 6am to midnight, the air-conditioned trains are frequent, with never more than a few minutes wait (2–4 minutes peak, 4–6 minutes off-peak). Fares start at 14 baht, increasing 2 baht every station, with a maximum fare of 36 baht.

Unlike the Skytrain, which uses cards, coin-sized plastic tokens are used. There are self-service ticket machines at all stations. Also available at station counters are the unlimited ride 1-day Pass (150 baht), 3-day Pass (300 baht) and the stored-value Adult Card (200 baht, which includes a 50-baht deposit).

Boats

The most common waterborne transport is the Chao Phraya River Express Boat (tel: 0 2623 6001), which travels from Tha Nonthaburi pier in the north and ends at Tha Wat Rachasingkhon near Krungthep Bridge in the south. Boats run every 15 minutes from 6am to 6.40pm, and stop at different piers according to the coloured flag on top of the boat. Yellow flag boats are fastest and do not stop at many piers, while the orange flag and no flag boats stop at most of the marked river piers. If unsure check before boarding. Fares cost 6 baht to 15 baht and are purchased from the conductor on board or at some pier counters.

The Chao Phraya Tourist Boat (www.chaophrayaboat.co.th) operates daily from 9.30am to 3.30pm and costs 75 baht. After 3.30pm, you can use the ticket on the regular express boats. A useful commentary is provided on board, along with a small guidebook and a bottle of water. The route begins at Tha Sathorn (Central Pier) and travels upriver to Tha Phra Arthit, stopping at 10 major piers along the way. Boats leave every 30 minutes and you can get off at any pier and pick up another boat later on this hop-on-and-off service.

The cross-river ferries are used for getting from one side of the river to the other. They can be boarded at the jetties that also service the Chao Phraya River Express. Costing 2 baht per journey, cross-river ferries operate from 5am to 10pm or later.

The longtail boat taxi plies the narrow inner canals and are used for carrying passengers from the centre of town to the outlying districts. Many of the piers are located near traffic bridges; remember to stand back from the pier's edge to avoid being splashed by foul-smelling water. Choose a seat away from the spray, and be sure to tell the conductor your destination as boats do not stop otherwise. Tickets cost 5–10 baht, depending on distance, with services operating roughly every 10 minutes until 6 to 7pm. While there are routes serving Thonburi's canals and Bangkok's outskirts, tourists will probably only use the main downtown artery of Khlong Saen Saep, which starts from Tha Saphan Phanfah near Wat Saket, and goes into the heart of downtown and beyond to Bang Kapi. It's useful if you are going to Jim Thompson's House, Siam Centre and the Thanon Ploenchit malls to Thanon Witthayu and all the way to Thonglor and Ekamai.

CHIANG MAI

Buses: Chiang Mai has red minibuses known locally as *song tao*. They carry passengers almost anywhere within the town for 10 baht during daylight hours.

Tuk-tuk: They charge according to distance, starting at 20 baht. You must bargain for the price before you get in and the average fare around town is 40 baht.

Samlor: These pedal trishaws charge 5 baht for short distances. Establish a price before you board.

PHUKET

Buses: Picturesque wooden buses ply regular routes from the market to the beaches. They depart every 30 minutes, 8am–6pm, between Phuket town market and all beaches except Rawai and Nai Harn. Buses to Rawai and Nai Harn leave from the traffic circle on Thanon Bangkok. They often prowl the beach roads in search of passengers. Flag one down; 15–20 baht per person. More modern, green microbuses with air-conditioning run along the same routes for 10–20 baht per person.

Tuk-tuk: The small cramped tuk-tuks function as taxis. They'll go anywhere. Barter your fare before getting on. Reasonable fares are: Patong to Karon, 250 baht, Patong to airport, 500 baht. Journeys within town should be around 20–50 baht if shared.

Motorcycle taxis: 20 baht per ride. A convenient if dangerous way to get around.

RENTAL CARS

Thailand has a good road system with more than 50,000 km (31,000 miles) of paved highways, and more being built every year. Road signs are in both Thai and English, and you should have no difficulty following a map. An international driver's license is required.

Driving on a narrow but busy road can be a terrifying experience; right of way is generally determined by the size of vehicle you are travelling in. It is not unusual for a bus to overtake a truck despite the fact that the oncoming lane is filled with vehicles. It is little wonder that, when collisons occur, several dozen lives are lost. In addition, many of the long-distance drivers consume pep pills and have the throttle to the floor because they are getting paid for beating schedules. One is strongly advised to avoid driving at night for this reason. When dusk comes, pull in at a hotel and get an early start the next morning.

Avis, Budget and numerous local agencies offer late-model cars with or without drivers, and with inusurance coverage for Bangkok and upcountry trips. The international companies may be a bit more expensive, but they are also much more reliable.

In the provinces, agencies can be found in major towns like Chiang Mai, Pattaya and Phuket. These also rent four-wheel drive jeeps and minibuses.

When renting a jeep, read the fine print carefully and be aware that you are liable for all damages to the vehicle. Ask for first class insurance, which covers both you and the other vehicle involved in a collision.

Bangkok

Although Avis has a desk at the Bangkok International Airport, the general practice is for car rental agencies to deliver the car to your hotel. Check the brakes and air conditioning, and read the fine print for insurance terms.

Avis
2/12 Thanon Witthayu
Tel: 0 2255 5300–4; Airport:
0 2535 4052 (Terminal 1);
0 2535 4031–2 (Terminal 2)
www.avisthailand.com
Budget
19/23 Building A, Royal City
Avenue, Thanon New Petchburi
Tel: 0 2203 0250
www.budget.co.th

Chiang Mai
Avis
The Royal Princess Hotel
122 Thanon Changklan
Tel: 0 5328 1033, ext. Avis
Chiang Mai International Airport
Tel: 0 5320 1574, 0 5320 1798–9
Budget
(Opposite Central Airport Plaza)
201/2 Thanon Mahidol, Haiya, Muang
Tel: 0 5320 2871–2
North Wheels Rent-A-Car
70-4–8 Thanon Chaiyaphum (east
side of moat)
Tel: 0 5387 4478
www.northwheels.com

Pattaya
Budget
Thip Plaza, 219/1–3 Moo 10,
Thanon Liabchaihat (Beach),
Nongprue, Banglamung
Tel: 0 3871 07177–8
www.budget.co.th

Phuket
Avis
Car Rental Counter
Phuket International Airport
Tel: 0 7635 1244–5
Budget
36/5 Moo 6, Thanon Maikao
Thalang, Phuket
Tel: 0 7629 2389, 0 7620 5396
www.budget.co.th
Good for Suzuki Caribians. Free
delivery.

On Foot/Hitchhiking

There are not many places one
can walk in Thailand, other than
national parks like Khao Yai and
Phu Kradung. Hitching a ride on
ten-wheel trucks is not advisable,
particularly for females.

Where to Stay

How to Choose

Hotel accommodation in all the
major tourist destinations in
Thailand is equal to the very best
anywhere in the world. The facilities
in the first-class hotels may have as
many as 10 or more different
restaurants serving Western and
Asian cuisine, coffee shops,
swimming pools, exercise rooms,
business centres, banqueting halls,
shopping arcades, and cable &
satellite television. Service is also
second to none. Indeed, most of
the moderately priced hotels rival
what in Europe would be considered
first-class hotels. Even the budget
and inexpensive hotels will
invariably have a swimming pool
and more than one food outlet.

Due in part to terrorist attacks in
Southeast Asia and the SARS
epidemic, hotel rates can range
widely, even amongst the top-end
hotels. Depending upon season,
discounts can exceed 50 percent or
more of the published rack rate. It
pays to shop around and try
bargaining – even at the best hotels.

Following the Bangkok listing is a
selection of regional hotels from
among the many available. They
have been chosen to show a range
of facilities and prices and, in a few
cases, because they are unusual.

Note that a resort hotel does not
always have the same connotation
in Thailand that it might in the West;
often it means nothing more than
that the hotel is located in the
countryside. One might be surprised
by excellent service and luxurious
accommodations at a resort hotel,
but to expect it, particularly in the
smaller areas, is to court
disappointment in many cases.
Hotels also charge a value added

tax (VAT) of 7 percent and often, a
service charge of 10 percent.

During peak holiday periods
(holidays, Christmas, New Year,
etc.), accommodation is at a
premium rate, as it is during high
season, from November through
April. But the rest of the year, it is
always worth asking for a discount.

ABOUT ROOM RATES

Relative price categories are used
in this section because hotel rates
can be quite elastic in Thailand. In
Bangkok there is a glut of rooms,
and rates can often be highly
discounted. Moreover, in Bangkok
especially, some luxury hotels
quote prices in baht, while others,
such as the Oriental, quote only in
dollars. Even if a room rate is
quoted in dollars, it may be billed
on the credit card in baht, and so
can vary depending upon the
prevalent exchange rates.

The hotels are listed by price
range (see tinted boxes) and by
alphabetical order within the range.
Remember to include the area code
even when dialling local calls.

Bangkok

$$$$
Amari Airport
333 Thanon Chert Wudthakas
Tel: 0 2566 1020-1, 0 2566 1941
www.amari.com/airport
Reasonably good hotel, connected
to the airport by an air-conditioned
walkway. A bit costly for what it is,
but you can do plenty worse,
particularly if you have a late night
arrival or early morning departure.
Reduced rates for stays of less
than six hours.
Amari Watergate
847 Thanon Petchburi, Pratunam
Tel: 0 2653 9000
Fax: 0 2653 9045
www.amari.com/watergate
Another good hotel under the Amari
management. Location is a bit out of
the way, in the older section of
Bangkok. Close to Pantip Plaza,
home to computer outlets, and the
sprawling Pratunam shopping district.

Price Categories

Prices are for one night in a double room during the high season:

$$$$ – over 4,000 baht
$$$ – 2,500–4,000 baht
$$ – 1,000–2,500 baht
$ – less than 1,000 baht

Bangkok Marriott Resort and Spa

257/1 Thanon Charoen Nakorn
Tel: 0 2476 0022
Fax: 0 2476 1120
www.marriott.com
If your friends have told you that you must stay on the river but you can't afford the Oriental, this is the place for you. Located on the "other" side of the river: an oasis of tranquility in a sea of madness. Self-contained, with six restaurants, three bars, and a full-service business centre, the hotel is also part of a shopping complex complete with fast-food restaurants, pharmacies, and barber shops. A complimentary water taxi ferries guests across the river.

Banyan Tree Bangkok

21/100 Thanon South Sathorn
Tel: 0 2679 1200
Fax: 0 2679 1199
www.banyantree.com
The second-tallest hotel in Bangkok features 216 suites geared for the business traveller. Separate living and working areas, plus in-room faxes and on-demand room services. The restaurant on the roof of the tower, and the Banyan Tree Spa, offer spectacular views of the city.

Conrad Bangkok

All Seasons Place, 87 Thanon Witthayu
Tel: 0 2690 9999
Fax: 0 2690 9000
www.conradbangkok.com
A top-notch hotel located near embassies and next door to a swanky shopping mall. A free shuttle bus (every 10 minutes from 7am–10pm daily goes to Phloenchit BTS Station, a 10-minute walk away). Spacious rooms are furnished with Thai silk and woods, and data ports for high-speed Internet access. Excellent choice of eateries, plus the chic 87 nightclub/restaurant and jazzy Diplomat Bar.

Dusit Thani

946 Thanon Rama IV
Tel: 0 2200 9000
Fax: 0 2236 6400
www.dusit.com
The first high-rise hotel in Bangkok, this classic example of fashionably "retro" 1950s architecture is located near many corporate headquarters and the nightlife of Patpong, as well as Lumphini Park.

Emporium Suites

622 Thanon Sukhumvit (Soi 24)
Tel: 0 2664 9999
Fax: 0 2664 9998
www.emporiumsuites.com
Convenically located above the upmarket Emporium shopping mall and close to the Phrom Pong BTS station, this stylish service apartment complex offers a range of accommodations – from studio and one-bedroom suites to 3-bedroom apartments. Full range of in-house facilities: gym, pool, business centre and restaurant/bar. Ideal for long-term guests.

Four Seasons Hotel Bangkok (formerly Regent Bangkok)

155 Thanon Rajadamri
Tel: 0 2250 1000
Fax: 0 2253 9195
www.fourseasons.com
From the magnificent lobby, with hand-painted silk ceilings, to the best hotel swimming pool in Bangkok and the highest staff-to-guest ratio in the city, the Four Seasons is consistently excellent. Recently voted number one by *Business Traveller Asia Pacific* readers. The staff's attention to detail helps set it apart from other luxury establishments.

Grand Hyatt Erawan

494 Thanon Rajadamri
Tel: 0 2254 1234
Fax: 0 2254 6308
www.bangkok.grand.hyatt.com
Not your run-of-the-mill Hyatt, the Erawan has a great location, an excellent health club, video conferencing, and a helipad on the roof. The hotel's location is hard to beat – in the heart of modern Bangkok and close to big shopping malls – yet there are no less than four major Hindu shrines within easy walking distance of the hotel.

Hotel Plaza Athenee Bangkok

Thanon Witthayu
Tel: 0 2650 8800, 0 2650 8855
Fax: 0 2650 8500–1, 0 2650 8844
www.hotel-plaza-athenee.com
Sister property to the famed Plaza Athenee in New York, this is on the site of the old Imperial Hotel, it is convenient to the Skytrain and several diplomatic missions, most notably the US Embassy.

InterContinental Hotel

973 Thanon Ploenchit
Tel: 0 26560 444
Fax: 0 26560 555
www.ichotelsgroup.com
New InterContinental with the standard luxury and business facilities you'd expect from this hotel chain. Good location, fine views of the cityscape and about 30 minutes away from the airport by cab.

The Oriental

48 Soi Oriental, Thanon Charoen Krung
Tel: 0 2659 9000
Fax: 0 2659 0000
www.mandarin-oriental.com/bangkok
The Oriental is part of the history of East meeting West, as for more than a century it has been the most famous hotel in Bangkok. Always at or near the top of the list of best hotels in the world. While service has become a little uneven in recent years, even a bit snooty, the Oriental is still a top-level hotel. Don't bother with trying to do a little sightseeing in the lobby or on grounds however, polite but very firm guards ensure that only guests get as far as the hotel's driveway.

JW Marriott

4 Sukhumvit Soi 2
Tel: 0 2656 7700
Fax: 0 2656 7711
www.marriott.com
A classy five-star hotel in the middle of Bangkok. All the usual amenities, plus Bangkok's largest fitness centre, an efficient business facilities and spacious rooms make this one of the best hotels in the city.

The Peninsula

333 Thanon Charoennakorn, Klongsan
Tel: 0 2861 2888
Fax: 0 2861 1112
www.peninsula.com
Standing proud on the opposite

bank of the Chayo Phraya to The Oriental, this new kid on the block has already earned a reputation for its attention to service and detail. Food and service are impeccable. Has already been voted as one of Bangkok's best even though it has been opened only since 1999.

Royal Orchid Sheraton
2 Captain Bush Lane
Tel: 0 2266 0123
Fax: 0 2236 8320
www.royalorchidsheraton.com
Located on the river, this hotel was once considered one of the top in town. This is no longer the case, indeed, it is not even the best Sheraton in town. Most of the guests these days are package tourists who are herded onto and off of a long queue of tour buses that seem to constantly block the pedestrian entrance. Still, the hotel does offer some great views of the Chao Phraya River.

Shangri-La Hotel
89 Soi Wat Suan Plu
Tel: 0 2236 7777
Fax: 0 2236 8579
www.shangri-la.com
With 799 spacious guest rooms, recently refurbished and all facing the river, the Shangri-La is the largest of the five-star hotels located on the river, and consistently ranks among the top five hotels in Asia. Restaurants, particularly Angelini's and the Maenam Terrace barbeque are top notch.

Sheraton Grande Sukhumvit
250 Thanon Sukhumvit
Tel: 0 2649 8888
Fax: 0 2649 8000
www.sheratongrandesukhumvit.com
Terrific location on Thanon Sukhumvit, not far from the Queen Sirikit National Convention Center. First-rate services across the board, ranging from health and business centres to video-conferencing. Extra large rooms contain all the "bells and whistles" you expect from a five-star property.

Sofitel Central Plaza
1695 Thanon Phaholyothin
Tel: 0 2541 1234
Fax: 0 2541 1087
www.accorhotels-asia.com
www.sofitel-centralplaza.bangkok.com

Located midway between the airport and city, this rebranded hotel (formerly known as the Central Grand Plaza) is a bit out of the way for the average visitor. French package tourists who booked from home seem to make up the majority of the guests.

Sofitel Silom
188 Thanon Silom
Tel: 0 2238 1991
Fax: 0 2238 1999
www.accorhotels-asia.com
In the banking and insurance district, conveniently located for business, shopping and nightlife. Good service at a good price.

The Sukhothai Bangkok
13/3 Thanon South Sathorn
Tel: 0 2344 8888
Fax: 0 2344 8889
www.sukhothai.com
This is one of the top five hotels in Bangkok and, arguably, the number one business hotel in town. It has well appointed guest rooms, an excellent restaurant, tropical gardens and a reflecting pool. Its Sunday buffet is popular and generally considered the best in town, albeit the most expensive.

$$$

Amari Boulevard
2 Soi 5, Thanon Sukhumvit
Tel: 0 2255 2930, 0 2255 2940
Fax: 0 2255 2950
www.amari.com
Located in the middle of bustling Thanon Sukhumvit, with the Nana Skytrain station, street vendors and nightlife nearby. Certainly above average, but would not make too many Top 10 lists.

Ambassador
171 Thanon Sukhumvit
Tel: 0 2254 0444
Fax: 0 2253 4123
www.amtel.co.th/bangkok
Tour operators fill the majority of the more than 1,000 rooms. Food mall and fast-food on property, and street vendors all around.

Arnoma Hotel
99 Thanon Ratchadamri
Tel: 0 2255 3410
Fax: 0 2255 3456
www.arnoma.com
Good location for shopping, adjacent

to Gaysorn Plaza and Narayana Phand, the government's handicrafts store, opposite the Central World Plaza. A solid, dependable hotel at a reasonable price.

Baiyoke Sky Hotel
222 Thanon Rajaprarop
Tel: 0 2656 3000
Fax: 0 2656 3555
www.baiyokehotel.com
At 94 stories, the hotel is Bangkok's tallest landmark, and on a clear day you can see forever. It's surrounded by countless garment shops and street vendors.

Bangkok Palace Hotel
1091/336 Thanon New Petchburi
Tel: 0 2253 0510
Fax: 0 2253 0556
www.bangkokpalace.com
The good news is that it is close to the expressway. The bad news is that it is very close to the expressway. 650 rooms. Near shopping, but not really close to anything of interest.

Bel-Aire Princess
16 Soi 5, Thanon Sukhumvit
Tel: 0 2253 4300–45
Fax: 0 2255 8850
www.bel-aireprincess.com
One of a growing number of small boutique hotels in Bangkok. Personalised service and location of nearby shopping and nightlife make it one of the better hotels in the price range and is run by the Dusit Group.

Evergreen Laurel Hotel
88 Thanon North Sathorn
Tel: 0 2266 9988
Fax: 0 2266 7222
www.evergreen-hotels.com
A true boutique hotel, small but elegant; European atmosphere and personal service. Close to embassies, foreign banks and Patpong.

Holiday Inn Crowne Plaza
981 Thanon Silom
Tel: 0 2238 4300
Fax: 0 2238 5289
www.bangkok-silom.holiday-inn.com
Large (700 rooms), full service, in interesting location adjacent to the Jewelry Center, and not far from the river and the expressway.

Imperial Queen's Park
199 Sukhumvit Soi 22
Tel: 0 2261 9000
Fax: 0 2261 9530–4

www.imperialhotels.com/queenspark 1,400-room high-rise situated half way down a *soi* (lane) that is difficult to access. The hotel is enormous: guests must walk long distances to reach many in-house facilities. A full-service hotel, complete with state-of-the-art health club, and butler service. Good promotions are often available to help fill its rooms.

Indra Regent Hotel
120/126 Thanon Rajaprarop
Tel: 0 2208 0022–33
Fax: 0 2208 0388–9
www.indrahotel.com
Surrounded by old markets and eating places that are gradually being replaced, the hotel is still adequate, with decent restaurants. Popular with tour groups.

Landmark
138 Thanon Sukhumvit
Tel 0 2254 0404
Fax: 0 2253 4259
www.landmarkbangkok.com
Good location on Thanon Sukhumvit, with easy access to the airport and Skytrain and the Nana Entertainment Plaza. A very comfortable hotel at a reasonable price. Good facilities for business travellers and good shopping nearby.

Montien Hotel Bangkok
54 Thanon Surawong
Tel: 0 2233 7060
Fax: 0 2236 5218–9
www.montien.com
One of the older hotels in downtown Bangkok, it is close to Patpong.

Novotel Bangkok on Siam Square
Siam Square, Soi 6
Tel: 0 2255 6888
Fax: 0 2255 1824
www.accorhotels-asia.com
French run (Accor) hotel in the middle of Siam Square, a shopping area with numerous movie theatres, restaurants and traffic jams. Ballroom dancing available.

Novotel Lotus
1 Soi Daeng Udom, Sukhumvit 33
Tel: 0 2261 0111
Fax: 0 2262 1700
www.accorhotels-asia.com
Very nice guest rooms in this recent addition to the Accor network of hotels in Bangkok. It is located close to shopping and the Siam Skytrain station, and on a street

with many watering holes and restaurants. Surely one of the best in this price range.

Siam City Hotel
477 Thanon Sri Ayutthaya
Tel: 0 2247 0123
Fax: 0 2247 0178
www.siamhotels.com
Relatively new hotel in an out-of-the-way location offering good restaurants and typical four-star amenties. Good value for money.

Windsor Hotel
8-10 Sukhumvit Soi 20
Tel: 0 2262 1234
Fax: 0 2262 1212
www.windsorbkk.com
This former Embassy Suites property is still an all-suite hotel but without the high price tag. Located on a relatively quiet *soi* off a major artery. You can do a lot worse.

Price Categories

Prices are for one night in a double room during the high season:
$$$$ – over 4,000 baht
$$$ – 2,500–4,000 baht
$$ – 1,000–2,500 baht
$ – less than 1,000 baht

$$

Asia Hotel Bangkok
296 Thanon Phaya Thai
Tel: 0 2215 0808
Fax: 0 2217 0109
www.asiahotel.co.th
Many extra facilities available, possibly to offset the non-stop traffic at its doorstep. Home to a cabaret show performed by transvestite dancers.

Bangkok Center
328 Thanon Rama IV
Tel: 0 2238 4980
Fax: 0 2236 1862
www.bangkokcentrehotel.com
If you're on an early train to Malaysia or upcountry, you can do worse than this 2–3 star hotel. Walking distance from both Chinatown and the Hualampong Railway Station.

Emerald Hotel
99/1 Thanon Ratchadapisek
Tel: 0 2276 4567
Fax: 0 2276 4555

www.emeraldhotel.com
Huge hotel located in one of Bangkok's newest business, shopping and recreation areas. Not close to downtown or the airport, but a good hotel for the price, especially its promotional packages.

Euro Inn
249 Soi Sukhumvit 31
Tel: 0 2259 9480–87
Fax: 0 2259 9490
e-mail: euroinn@loxinfo.co.th
Not a bad choice for those on a budget. Modern hotel with swimming pool, business facilities, and reasonably appointed rooms not far from Thanon Sukhumvit.

Golden Dragon
20-21 Thanon Ngamwong-Wan
Tel: 0 2589 0130–41
Fax: 0 2589 8305
Old Chinese-style hotel which has seen better days. Not up to contemporary Western standards, but quite inexpensive and not too far from the airport.

Jim's Lodge
125/7 Soi Ruamrudi
Thanon Ploenchit
Tel: 0 2255 3100–3
Fax: 0 2253 8492
Nothing fancy, but a convenient location for good restaurants and shopping.

Maruay Gardens Hotel
1 Thanon Phaholyothin
Tel: 0 2561 0510–47
Fax: 0 2579 1182
Located over 30 km (20 miles) from the heart of the city, but well served by taxis and the expressway. Over 300 rooms. The hotel is often used for minor conventions.

New Trocadero
343 Thanon Surawong
Tel: 0 2234 8920–8
Fax: 0 2234 8929
e-mail: newtroc@ksc.th.com
Nothing new about the New Trocadero, except its name, but it is inexpensive. Once the favourite of journalists during the 1960's, the hotel's clientele is now almost exclusively from Africa and the Middle East.

Park
6 Sukhumvit Soi 7
Tel: 0 2255 4300
Fax: 0 2255 4309

Smallish hotel with reasonable range of amenities, not far from the Skytrain and Nana Plaza entertainment.

Tai-Pan
25 Thanon Sukhumvit, Soi 23
Tel: 0 2260 9888
Fax: 0 2259 7908
www.tai-pan.com
150 rooms situated close to the business, shopping and entertainment areas along the Sukhumvit corridor.

Tarntawan Place
119/5-10 Thanon Surawong
Tel: 0 2238 2620
Fax: 0 2238 3228
www.tarntawan.com
Located off a quiet *soi*, close to the business area and shopping. Excellent service, multilingual staff.

Outside of Bangkok

KANCHANABURI

$$$
Felix River Kwai Resort
9/1 Moo 3 Thamakham
Tel: 0 3451 5061
Fax: 0 3451 5095
www.felixriverkwai.co.th
Comfortable hotel in a pretty garden setting near the bridge.

$
Apple Guest House
52 Thanon Saeng Chuto
Tel: 0 3451 2017, 0 3451 3457
This friendly and well-run place has quiet bungalows just a stone's throw from the river, and is locally famous for it's outstanding food and Thai cooking courses. The guesthouse also runs a tour company that specialises in bicycle tours of the province's national parks.

KHAO YAI NATIONAL PARK

A campsite and some simple dormitories are available within the park, and camping out on one of the observation towers may also be a possibility. Policy changes are not uncommon, so it is best to inquire at the TAT office or the Royal Forestry Department in Bangkok or at park headquarters for further details before heading out. There is a 200 baht entrance fee for foreigners.

$$$–$$$$
Kirimaya
1/3 Moo 6, Thanon Thanarat
Tel: 0 4442 6099
www.kirimaya.com
The Kirimaya is one of the plushest hotel options in the Central Plains. Draws inspiration from African safaris with four luxury tented villas nestled among plantation-style buildings, all overlooking lush foliage of the national park. There's an infinity pool, spa and golf course.
$$$$

Price Categories

Prices are for one night in a double room during the high season:
$$$$ – over 4,000 baht
$$$ – 2,500–4,000 baht
$$ – 1,000–2,500 baht
$ – less than 1,000 baht

Khao Yai Garden Lodge
Thanon Thanarat, Km 7, Pak Chong
Tel: 0 4436 5178, 04436 5167
Fax: 0 4436 5179
www.khaoyai-garden-lodge.de
Popular with German tour groups. 35 rooms ranging from 100 baht (fan-cooled, shared toilet) to 1,400 baht (air-conditioned, traditional Thai decor, private bath). Spacious grounds include a bird garden, a 40-year old tortoise, and many botanical wonders; herbal sauna and swimming pool with waterfall. Offers a range of tours, not only of Khao Yai, but throughout the northeast as well. Will pick up from Bangkok by arrangement.

$
Green Leaf Guest House
Thanon Thanarat, Km 7.5, Pak Chong
Tel: 0 4436 5024
This excellent-value place of accommodation is friendly and offers imaginative tours of the park including birdwatching and moonlight tours to view the park's many nocturnal creatures. The accommodation is basic but comfortable and the food is excellent.

Central Plains

SUKHOTHAI

$$$
Wang Neua
43 Thanon Singhawat
Tel: 0 5561 1193–4
Fax: 0 5561 2038
A modern provincial hotel with swimming pool.

$$
River View
92 Thanon Nikhornkasem
Tel: 0 5561 1656, 0 5561 1516, 0 5561 3371
Fax: 0 5561 3373
As the name implies, this hotel offers rooms with a river view but not much else.

North and Northeast

CHIANG MAI

$$$$
Four Seasons Resort Chiang Mai (formerly Regent Chiang Mai)
Thanon Mae-Rim-Samoeng
Tel: 0 5329 8181
Fax: 0 5329 8190
www.fourseasons.com
When this resort was built in the early 1990s, locals laughed at the idea that anybody would pay US$200+ a night to stay in Chiang Mai. Well, the owners are having the last laugh. The Four Seasons is a true world-class resort and you need to plan early if you want to stay there during the high season. The 64 suites are all a minimum of 70 sq metres (750 sq ft), with teak floors, Thai cotton furnishings and CD sound systems standard. The swimming pool overlooks a working rice paddy and the new health spa features seven treatment rooms.

Sheraton Chiangmai Hotel
318/1 Thanon Chiangmai–Lamphun
Tel: 0 5327 5300
Fax: 0 5327 5299
www.starwoodhotels.com

Currently the poshest digs in Chiang Mai city, this large, luxurious hotel is situated on the banks of the Mae Ping River near the shopping and business centre and only 10 minutes from the airport. Deluxe amenities include swimming pool, fitness centre, three restaurants and a nightclub.

$$$
Amari Rincome
1 Thanon Nimmanhemin
Tel: 0 5322 1130
Fax: 0 5322 1915
www.amari.com/rincome
Once one of the best hotels in Chiang Mai, the Amari has been surpassed by the Regent resort and Westin. Situated on the edge of town, it is quiet, with a superb swimming pool.

Empress Chiang Mai
199/42 Thanon Changklan
Tel: 0 5327 0240
Fax: 0 5327 2467
www.empresshotels.com
A first-class hotel with amenities at reasonable prices. Good location near the night bazaar. Offers attractive rates.

Pornping Tower Hotel
46–48 Thanon Charoen Prathet
Tel: 0 5327 0099
Fax: 0 5327 0119
www.pornpinghotelchiangmai.com
Centrally situated tower housing the famous Bubbles disco.

Rachamankha Chiang Mai Hotel
6 Rachamankha 9, Th. Phra Singh
Tel: 0 5390 4111
Fax: 0 5390 4114
www.rachamankha.com
Located inside the Old City of Chiang Mai, this is a true boutique hotel, with only 23 rooms, modelled after Lanna temple architecture. Gourmet restaurant, bar, swimming pool and culture gallery on the grounds.

Royal Princess
112 Thanon Chang Klan
Tel: 0 5328 1033
Fax: 0 5328 1044
www. royalprincess.com
Managed by the Dusit group, this first-class hotel is well known for its service. The hotel is located in the night market.

$$
Galare Guest House
7 Thanon Charoen Prathet, Soi 2
Tel: 0 5381 8887, 0 5382 1011
Fax: 0 5327 9088
www.galare.com
Attractive and inexpensive location by the river.

Top North Guest House
Thanon Moon Muang, Soi 2
Tel: 0 5327 8900, 0 5327 8684
Fax: 0 5327 8485
www.topnorthgroup.com
Quiet, central, cheap and with pool; one of the most attractive offers in town.

CHIANG RAI

$$$
Dusit Island Resort
1129 Thanon Kraisorasit
Tel: 0 5371 5777
Fax: 0 5371 5801
chiangrai.dusit.com
The best hotel in town lies on an island in the Kok River.

Wiang Inn
893 Thanon Phaholyothin
Tel: 0 5371 1533
Fax: 0 5371 1877
www.wianginn.com
No pool, but a disco and a central location.

$
Ben Guest House
35/10 Thanon Sankhongnoi, Soi 4
Tel: 0 5371 6775
e-mail: bengh@infothai.com
Awarded "Best Guest House" in Chiang Rai by the TAT and the Tourist Police. It has everything – teak wood buildings, great food, tours and vehicle rentals.

CHIANG SAEN

$$$$
Anantara Resort & Spa
Golden Triangle, 229 Moo 1
Tel: 0 5378 4084
Fax: 0 5378 4090
www.anantara.com
Located at the confluence of the Ruak and Mekong rivers and an hour's drive from Chiang Rai

airport, this is the most luxurious resort in this area of north Thailand. Charming Thai-style architecture with fine views and good restaurants. The hotel can arrange tours and activities. Coveniently located directly opposite the newly-opened Hall of Opium museum.

$$$
Imperial Golden Triangle Hotel
222 Golden Triangle
Tel: 0 5378 4001/5
Fax: 0 5378 4006
www.imperialhotels.com/goldentriangle
An attractive resort offering 73 well-appointed rooms with great views over the Mekong to Burma and Laos. Good inhouse restaurant and bar.

$$
Gin's Guest House
Thanon Golden Triangle
Small and quiet establishment with a pleasant atmosphere by the banks of the Mekong River.

$
Chiang Saen Guesthouse
45 Tambon Wiang
18 rooms. Reasonably priced, basic, clean and close to the Mekong.

MAE HONG SON

$$$
Imperial Tara Mae Hong Son
149 Mu 8 Pang Mu
Tel: 0 5361 1021–5
Fax: 0 5361 1252
www.imperialhotels.com/taramaehongson
104 rooms. Without doubt the best accommodation in Mae Hong Son. Full facilties with restaurants, bar and pool.

Rooks Holiday Hotel & Resort
114/5–7 Thanon Khunlum Prapas
Tel: 0 5361 2324
Fax: 0 5361 1524
114 rooms. First class hotel with splendid mountain views. Facilities include pool, tennis court, disco and restaurants.

MAE SAI

$$$

Wang Thong
299 Thanon Phaholyothin
Tel: 0 5373 3388–95
Fax: 0 5373 3399
Comfortable hotel with Chinese decor
and a view of the bridge at the border.

$$

Mae Sai Hotel
Tel: 0 5373 1462
Located next to the ruby market.

MAE SALONG

$$$

Khum Naiphol Resort
Tel: 0 5376 5001–3
Fax: 0 5376 5004
Built by General Tuan's family and
still run by them.

NAN

$$

Dhevaraj Hotel
466 Thanon Sumonthewaraj
Amphur Muang
Tel: 0 5471 0094–6, 05471 0212
Fax: 0 5477 1365
Standard plastic-and-tile provincial
hotel, circa 1980. Air-conditioning,
TV, elevator. Central location.
Doi Phu Kha National Park
Tel: 0 1472 6720, 1224 0789
Budget accommodation (100–200
baht) in bungalows on edge of park.
Visitors can set up tents. Small
restaurant. Bring extra supplies.
There is a 200 baht entrance fee
for foreigners.
Nan Fa Hotel
440 Thanon Sumonthewaraj
Amphur Muang
Tel/fax: 0 5471 0234
Central location. Air-conditioning,
TV, dubious plumbing. Clean, well
maintained old wooden building.
Unfortunately, recent renovation
and the installation of air-
conditioning have left the hotel's
wooden veranda glassed in. On
ground floor, craft store and Thai
restaurant, which features live folk
music in early evening.

Papua Bhuka Hotel
141 Pua-Namyao Street, Moo 4
Tambon Xilalang, Amphur Pua
Tel: 0 5479 1156, 5379 1166
Fax: 0 5479 1166
About 6 km (4 miles) south of the
town of Pua on Route 1080, this is
the only option outside of Nan town.
Air-conditioning, satellite TV, small
restaurant. Lovely views of misted
mountains, handy for jaunts to tribal
villages and Silaphet waterfall.

Price Categories

Prices are for one night in a
double room during the high
season:
$$$$ – over 4,000 baht
$$$ – 2,500–4,000 baht
$$ – 1,000–2,500 baht
$ – less than 1,000 baht

N. RATCHASIMA (KHORAT)

$$$

Royal Princess
1137 Thanon Suranarai
Tel: 0 4425 6629–35
Fax: 0 4425 6601
korat.royalprincess.com
On the edge of town. Decorated in
northeastern Thai style and run by
the Dusit Group.
Sima Thani
2112/2 Thanon Mittraphap
Tel: 0 4421 3100
Fax: 0 4421 3121
www.simathani.com
Best hotel in Nakhon Ratchasima
with a beautiful lobby dotted with
Khmer-style figures.

KHON KAEN

Hotel Sofitel Raja Orchid
9/9 Thanon Prachasumran
Khon Kaen
Tel: 0 4332 2155
Fax: 0 4332 2218
www.accorhotels-asia.com
Huge luxury hotel in what was once
touted as the business centre of
the northeast. Plethora of themed
entertainment and food outlets, as
well as the local Thai Airways
office.

Gulf Coast

CHANTHABURI

$$$

Maneechan Resort & Sports Club
110 Moo 11, Plubpla, Chanthaburi
Tel: 0 3934 3777-8
Fax: 0 3934 4123
A complex with private homes and a
resort with excellent sports facilities.

PATTAYA/JOMTIEN

$$$$

Dusit Resort
240/2 Thanon Pattaya Beach
Tel: 0 3842 5611–7
Fax: 0 3842 8239
pattaya.dusit.com
Top-class service and all the
requisite amenities plus a good
range of water sports.
Pattaya Marriott Resort & Spa
218/2-4 Moo 10, Thanon Beach
Tel: 0 3841 2120
Fax: 0 3842 9926
www.marriott.com
Operated by the group that owns the
Bangkok Marriott Resort & Spa and
the JW Marriott. First-class facilities,
with 293 rooms, restaurant, café,
bar and pool. Excellent location for
shopping, dining and nightlife.
Royal Cliff Beach Resort
353 Thanon Phra Tamnuk
Tel: 0 3825 0421
Fax: 0 3825 0511–13
www.royalcliff.com
One of Pattaya's top addresses,
ostentatiously built into a cliff with
a good private beach.

$$$

Amari Orchid Resort
Thanon Pattaya Beach
Tel: 0 3842 8161
Fax: 0 3842 8165
www.amari.com/orchid
A welcoming beach hotel with a
luxuriant garden.

$$

Cosy Beach Hotel
400 Moo 12, Thanon Pratamnuk
Pattaya
Tel: 0 3825 0800–3
Fax: 0 3825 0193

www.cosybeachhotel.com
Lush gardens, good facilities, quiet beach.
Diana Inn
216/6-20 Thanon Pattaya 2 (Between Soi 11 and 12) Pattaya Beach, Chonburi
Tel: 0 3842 9675
Fax: 0 3842 4566
www.dianapattaya.co.th
A pleasant hotel with an attractive swimming pool and very friendly service.

Northern Isthmus

HUA HIN

$$$$
Anantara Resort & Spa
43/1 Thanon Petchkasem
Tel: 0 3252 0250
Fax: 0 3252 0259
www.anantara.com
Located in Hua Hin not far from Klai Kangwan Palace, where His Majesty King Bhumibol spends much of the year, the classy Anantara is a self-contained property spread over 6 hectares (14 acres) of land, and includes a freeform pool, outdoor fitness centre, tennis courts, and the luxury Mandara spa.
Chiva-Som
73/4 Thanon Petchkasem
Tel: 0 3253 6536,
Bangkok Sales Office: 0 2711 6905
Fax: 0 3251 1154
www.chivasom.com
Located south of Hua Hin about 2½ hours from Bangkok, Chiva Som – translated as "haven of life" – is Thailand's only dedicated health spa, and one of the best in the world to boot. The combination of Thai hospitality, the full range of both traditional and modern health spa services, and a menu of delicious low-calorie food are what make it such a special place.
Hilton Hua Hin Resort & Spa
33 Thanon Naresdamri
Tel: 0 3251 2888
Fax: 0 3251 1135
www.hilton.com
An elegant resort hotel on the beach at Hua Hin. Features over-sized ocean-view rooms and a spectacular pool plus spa facilities.

Hua Hin Marriott Resort & Spa
107/1 Thanon Petchkasem
Tel: 0 3251 1881
Fax: 0 3251 2422
www.marriott.com
A low-rise resort on Hua Hin's long, white sand beach. Formerly known as the Royal Garden Resort until it was re-branded as a Marriott. Uncrowded retreat; full service.
Hyatt Regency Hua Hin
91 Thanon Hua Hin-Khao Takiap
Tel: 0 3252 1234
Fax: 0 3252 1233
www.huahin.regency.hyatt.com
This new low-rise property with 204 rooms is set amid tropical gardens and fronts a nice white sand beach. Three restaurants (Mediterranean, Thai and a café), two bars and a spa provide diversion from the vast free-form swimming pools with waterfalls and a giant slide. Ideal for families.
Sofitel Central Hua Hin Resort & Village
1 Thanon Damnoenkasem
Tel: 0 3251 2021–38
Fax: 0 3251 1014
www.accorhotels-asia.com
The former Railway Hotel, this establishment is full of Old World splendour. Enclosed by tropical gardens and faces one of the best stretches of sand in the Hua Hin area. The Village part of the property, opposite the resort, has a collection of tranquil and well-appointed bungalows.

PRANBURI

$$$$
Aleenta Resort
Paknampran Beach, Pranburi
Tel: 0 3257 0194
Fax: 0 3257 0220
www.aleenta.com
This brand new boutique property (opened in January 2003) is a gem of a resort. Small and intimate with only 10 villas, the Aleenta is big on style: rooms are spacious, most come with private plunge pools, and all have their own distinguishing character. Forget about room numbers; the villas bear charming names like Ylang Ylang, Jasmine and Cumin, and are furnished

simply yet elegantly with king-size beds, and come with robes and slippers and designer toiletries. The main clubhouse has a restaurant and bar, spa and an infinity pool, all of which more than make up for its somewhat isolated position on quiet Paknampran beach, about 30 minutes by car from Hua Hin. This is the perfect honeymoon getaway.
Evason Hua Hin
9 Paknampran Beach, Pranburi
Tel: 0 3263 2111
Fax: 0 3263 2112
www.six-senses.com
The former Club Aldina was taken over by the Six Senses group and given a new lease of life. This luxury resort features contemporary, almost minimalist design and is set among landscaped gardens. Its 185 rooms, studios and villas (with private pools) all feature open-plan bathrooms and outdoor terraces. Three restaurants, bar, huge swimming pool, a spa and other recreational facilities complete the idyllic picture. Air shuttle now available from Bangkok.

CHUMPHON

$$$
Chumphon Cabana Resort
69 Moo 8, Thung Wua Laen Beach
Tel: 0 7756 0245–7
Fax: 0 7756 0247
www.cabana.co.th
A bungalow complex with a famous diving school. Guests will be met in Chumphon on request.

$$
Jansom Chumporn
188/138 Thanon Sala Daeng
Tel: 0 7750 2502
Fax: 0 7750 2503
e-mail: jansombeach@yahoo.com
Large central business hotel with popular coffee shop and disco.

SURAT THANI

$$$
Saowaluk Thani
99/99 Thanon Surat-Kanchanadit
Tel: 0 7721 3700–30

Fax: 0 7721 3735
The best hotel in Surat, located in eastern end of the city.
Wang Tai Hotel
Thanon Talad Mai
Tel: 0 7728 3020
Fax: 0 7728 1007
e-mail: wangtai@loxinfo.co.th
On the edge of town. Pool and excellent coffee shop with good food to match the live (Thai) music.

Ko Samui/Pha Ngan

KO SAMUI

$$$$
Le Royal Meridien Baan Taling Ngam
295 Moo 3, Baan Taling
Ngam Beach
Tel: 0 7742 9100
Fax: 0 7723 4241
www.meridien-samui.com
The beach on this secluded western coast is mediocre with coarse sand, but the views are stunning from the rooms perched on the hill. Pools at beachside and hilltop. Ideal when the northwest monsoon is blowing.
Santiburi Resort
12/12 Moo 1, Maenam Beach
Tel: 0 7742 5031
Fax: 0 7742 5040
www.santiburi.com
Located at the northern tip of the island, on Maenam Beach, this luxury resort features suites and villas which resemble an elegant Thai home. Its Thai restaurant is one of the best in the island.

$$$–$$$$
Imperial Boat House
83 Moo 5, Choengmon Beach
Tel: 0 7742 5041
Fax: 0 7742 5460–1
www.imperialboathouse.com
North of Chaweng and a quieter alternative. Luxury rooms in two-storey converted rice barges.
Laem Set Inn
110 Moo 2, Hua Thanon
Tel: 0 7742 4393, 7723 3299
Fax: 0 7742 4394, 7723 3301
www.laemsetinn.com
Chinese-style hardwood houses have been transplanted and restored to form this boutique hotel. This southeast beach is

unremarkable, but there is good snorkelling available. Excellent for children.

$$$
Amari Palm Reef Resort
Chaweng Beach
Tel: 0 7742 2015–9
Fax: 0 7742 2394
www.amari.com
On the northern end of Chaweng beach but within walking distance to restaurants and shopping, it features both rooms and cottages and a nice free-form pool.
Chaweng Regent Resort
1554 Central Chaweng Beach
Tel: 0 7742 2389–90
Fax: 0 7723 1013, 0 7742 2222
www.chawengregent.com
Three swimming pools, meeting facilities. Smack in the middle of Chaweng Beach, backs onto the nightlife scene.
Poppies Samui
PO Box 1, Chaweng Noi
Tel: 0 7742 2419
Fax: 0 7742 2420
www.poppiessamui.com
Twenty-four cottages hidden among greenery, Balinese style. Near the southern end of the beach. Known for its restaurant.
The Princess Village
101 Moo 3, Central Chaweng Beach
Tel: 0 7742 2382
Fax: 0 7742 2383
www.samuiprincess.com
South-central location. Pretend you're back in Ayutthaya in these period-style bungalows. Traditional furnishings and all mod-cons.
Samui Euphoria Resort
101/3 Bo Phut Bay
Tel: 0 7742 5100–6
Fax: 0 7742 5100
Tennis, billiards, badminton, putting green, pétanque, fitness club, pool. Popular with French and Italian families.

$$
Samui Palm Beach Resort
175/3 Thanon Thaveerat-Pakdee
Tel: 0 7742 5494
Fax: 0 7742 5358
www.samui-hotels.com/spbhotel
Situated in tropical gardens on Bo Phut Bay, this lovely resort offers

both cottages with beach view and Mediterranean-style villas, along with two sparkling pools.
Spa Samui Resort
North Lamai Beach
Tel: 0 7723 0976
Fax: 0 7742 4667
www.spasamui.com
A hotel and New Age health centre. Fasting regimes, herbal saunas, colonic irrigation as well as traditional Thai massage, hikes and mountain-biking trips. Health services are also offered to non-guests.

KO PHA NGAN

$$
Panviman Resort
22/1 Moo 5, Thong Nai Pan Noi Bay
Tel: 0 7744 5100–9
Fax: 0 7744 5100
www.panviman.com
The island's most upmarket resort straddles a steep headland with views of two fine, secluded beaches. Excellent snorkelling and fishing, air-conditioned cottages and hotel-style rooms.
The Sanctuary
PO Box 3, Hat Tien Beach
Tel: 0 1271 3614, 0 1899 2269
www.thesanctuary-kpg.com
A low-budget, attractively designed bungalow resort, 4 km (2 miles) from Hat Rin Beach. Between September and May, hosts a series of New Age courses ranging from massage and tai chi to past-life regression and "cranial sacral" and colonic irrigation.

KO TAO

$$
Black Tip Dive Resort
Tanote Bay, Ko Tao
Tel: 0 7745 6489 (resort)
0 7745 6488 (dive school)
www.blacktipdiving.com
Family resort with budget bungalows through air-con deluxe cottages. Dive school and water sports centre on premises.
Koh Tao Cottage Resort
Ao Chalok Ban Kao Beach

Tel: 0 7745 6134
Fax: 0 7745 6420
www.kohtaocottage.com
One of the island's poshest
resorts. Rooms with fan, fridge and
air-conditioning. Get ready to sign
up for a dive course – there may be
no vacant rooms unless you do.

Price Categories

Prices are for one night in a
double room during the high
season:
$$$$ – over 4,000 baht
$$$ – 2,500–4,000 baht
$$ – 1,000–2,500 baht
$ – less than 1,000 baht

Phuket

PHUKET TOWN

$$$
Metropole
1 Soi Surin, Thanon Montri
Tel: 0 7621 5050
Fax: 0 7621 5990
www.metropolephuket.com
Modern and elegant high-rise hotel.
Staff wear Thai traditional garb.
Popular with business travellers as
well as tourists. Very good food and
beverage outlets, particularly the
coffee shop's buffet lunch. This is
a four-star hotel at three-star prices.
Thavorn Grand Plaza
40/5 Thanon Chanacharoen
Tel: 0 7622 2240–50
Fax: 0 7622 2284
www.thavorngrandplaza.com
Located approximately 35 minutes
from the airport, this is a well-
appointed modern hotel situated in
the heart of town and with all the
necessary amenities.

$$
Thavorn Hotel
74 Thanon Rasda
Tel: 0 7621 1333
Fax: 0 7621 5559
One of the first hotels in Phuket.
Lobby displays historical pictures
of local culture. Rooms fronting
Thanon Rasda are noisy but
otherwise comfortable. This has a
central location.

BEACHES

$$$$
Amanpuri
118/1 Moo 3, Thanon Srisunthon,
Pansea Beach
Tel: 0 7632 4333
Fax: 0 7632 4100
www.amanpuri.com
If you have to ask the price, you
can't afford it. Amanpuri is luxury
with a capital L. Only 40 pavilions
and 30 villa houses are set in the
midst of a coconut grove
overlooking the Andaman Sea. Food
and service are exquisite, which is
what keeps bringing back the
celebrities who frequent the place.
The Banyan Tree
33 Moo 4, Thanon Srisoonthorn,
Choeng Talay District. Bang
Thao/Laguna, Amphur Talang
Tel: 0 7632 4374
Fax: 0 7632 4375
www.banyantree.com/phuket
Individual bungalows encircling a
larger lagoon; some are garden
bungalows, the more expensive
ones come with private outdoor
pool. Full range of spa facilities.
Low key, discreet, romantic and
luxurious. The perfect getaway.
The Boathouse
182 Thanon Kaktanod, Kata Beach
Tel: 0 7633 0015–7
Fax: 0 7633 0561
www.boathousephuket.com
Situated on the quiet end of Kata,
this small and elegant beach-front
hotel prides itself on attentive and
personalized service. Main building
built in the Ayutthaya style with
steep sloping roofs. Famous for its
sophisticated Boathouse Wine &
Grill restaurant, and for its wine list.
The Chedi
118 Moo 3, Choeng Talay,
Pansea Beach
Tel: 0 7632 4017–20
Fax: 0 7632 4252
www.ghmhotels.com
Isolated and elegant hillside resort of
cottages linked by wooden walkways.
Finding your room can sometimes be
a nightmare as the walkways take a
circutous route to your cottage.
Faces a fairly isolated white sand
beach. Rooms are furnished simply
with sundeck, queen-size beds, a

safe and hairdryer. Known for its
French-inspired seafood dining.
Dusit Laguna
390 Thanon Srisoontorn
Tel: 0 7632 4324
Fax: 0 7632 4174
phuket.dusit.com
Part of the Dusit chain of deluxe
hotels, this five-star resort reflects
its Thai heritage, apparent in the
decor, staff costumes and the
acclaimed Ruen Thai restaurant.
Broad, sweeping Bang Thao Bay is
exposed and unsafe to swim in the
monsoon season.
JW Marriott Resort & Spa
Moo 3, Mai Khao
Tel: 0 7633 8000
Fax: 0 7634 8348
www.marriott.com
A five-star property with 265
oversized rooms, it is the only hotel
on remote white sand Mai Khao
Beach. Set in landscaped gardens,
the low-rise resort is just adjacent to
a national park and a turtle nesting
sanctuary. Full facilities including a
spa and three restaurants.
Le Méridien Phuket Beach Resort
8/5 Moo 1 Karon Beach, Relax Bay
Tel: 0 7634 0480–5
Fax: 0 7634 1583
www.meridien-phuket.com
Huge 470-room 5-star hotel filled
with activities year-round, including
a glitzy variety show every night.
Mega-sized swimming pools.
Guests have access to what is
effectively the hotel's own private
beach, in a small bay midway
between Patong and Karon.
Le Royal Méridien Phuket Yacht Club
23/3 Thanon Viset, Nai Harn Beach
Tel: 0 7638 1156–63
Fax: 0 7638 1164
www.yacht-club.phuket.com
Now part of the Le Méridien chain,
the Club has undergone an overhaul
and is, once again, deserving of the
international awards it has
received. Located at the southern
tip of the island, it offers some of
the most spectacular views
imaginable, particularly at sunset.
Elegant rooms and superior service
make it a true luxury destination.
Sheraton Grande Laguna
10 Moo 4, Thanon Srisoonthorn,
Choengtalay, Talang

Tel: 0 7632 4101–7
Fax: 0 7632 4108
www.sheraton.com
A 355-room deluxe hotel built around fresh water lagoons reclaimed from an old tin mining site. Numerous dining outlets. The star attraction is the unique winding swimming pool with piped-in music underwater.

The Racha
Racha Island
Tel: 0 7635 5455
Fax: 0 7635 5240
www.sanctuaryresorts.com/racha
This luxury retreat is not found on Phuket but on idyllic Racha Island, south of Phuket, about an hour away by boat from Ao Chalong. Opened in January 2004, this 69-villa resort is fast making a name for itself among the well-heeled cognoscenti. If you can afford it, splurge on the pool villa, if not settle for one of its spacious deluxe villas (all with open-air bathrooms) right on its white sand beach. Snorkel just offshore, have a massage at its spa, or lie back and soak in the pristine surroundings.

$$$

Amari Coral Beach Resort
2 Thanon Meun-Ngern, Patong Beach
Tel: 0 7634 0106–14
Fax: 0 7634 0115
www.amari.com/coralbeach
Well-run remote hotel on its own site, about 10 minutes' walk from the southern tip of Patong Beach. Uninspiring beach front. Trips to nearby Paradise Beach are popular. First-rate Kinaree Thai restaurant.

Cape Panwa Hotel
27 Moo 8, Thanon Sakdidej,
Cape Panwa
Tel: 0 7639 1123–5
Fax: 0 7639 1177
www.capepanwa.com
Located in a secluded bay overlooking the Andaman Sea, the hotel is an overlooked gem, or was until Leonardo Di Caprio stayed there while filming *The Beach* some years ago. All rooms are elevated from the beach, providing excellent views of the Phi Phi islands from the balconies.

Club Andaman Beach Resort
Patong 2 Thanon Beach, Patong

Tel: 0 7634 0530
Fax: 0 7634 0527
www.clubandaman.com
Large hotel in manicured gardens close to the beach. Cottage accommodation in addition to hotel wing. Tennis courts, gym, pool. Video, fridge and safe deposit box.

Club Med Phuket
7/3 Thanon Patak, Kata Beach
Tel: 0 7633 0455–59
Fax: 0 7633 0461
www.clubmed.com
Large resort in front of Kata Beach. Caters to the young-at-heart with lots of organised activities. Excellent French and international cuisine.

Holiday Inn
52 Thanon Thaviwong, Patong
Tel: 0 7634 0608–9
Fax: 0 7634 0435
www.holidayinn.phuket.com
Right beside the beachfront action. Very popular large resort hotel that attracts families on long vacations. Swimming pool and the Pirate's Cove minigolf for the children. Superlative steaks at Sam's Steak House.

Karon Beach Resort
27 Thanon Rasada, Karon
Tel: 0 7633 0006–7
Fax: 0 7633 0529
www.katagroup.com
Small, motel-type resort located at the quiet end of Karon beach. There are a restaurant, snack bar, pool and tour counter on site with the facilities of both Kata and Karon beaches a short walk away.

Kata Bhuri Beach Resort
14 Thanon Kata Noi
Tel: 0 7633 0124–6
Fax: 0 7633 0426
www.katathani.com/bhuri
Part of the Katathani Resort and Spa complex, this wing has open access to Kata Noi Beach. Rooms are spacious and comfortable, and the pool, shaded by coconut palms, is almost enough to make you shun the nearby beach.

Marina Phuket Resort
47 Thanon Karon, Karon Beach
Tel: 0 7633 0625, 0 7633 0493–7
Fax: 0 7633 0516, 7633 0999
www.marinaphuket.com
Thai-style cottages exquisitely landscaped into a hilly coconut

plantation. Dino Park crazy golf appeals to adults as well as kids. Two excellent restaurants: Sala Thai (central Thai cuisine) and On the Rock (mainly seafood).

$$

Baan Krating Jungle Beach
11/3 Thanon Viset, Nai Harn
Tel: 0 7638 1108, 0 7628 8264,
0 7628 8341
Fax: 0 7638 8108
www.baankrating.com
Fan-cooled and air-conditioned rooms in a tourist-class bungalow resort tastefully melded into its surroundings. Good place for nature-oriented relaxation on the remote southern tip of Phuket.

Krabi/Phang Nga

KRABI

$$$$

Rayavadee Resort
214 Moo 2, Ao-Nang
Tel: 0 7562 0740–3
Fax: 0 7562 0630
www.rayavadee.com
Sumptuous resort discreetly landscaped alongside Phra Nang and Railay beaches. Water sports, tennis courts, sauna, gym. Two restaurants: Thai/seafood and international.

Sheraton Krabi Beach Resort
155 Moo 2, Klong Muang Beach
Tel: 0 7562 8000
Fax: 0 7562 8028
www.sheraton.com/krabi
Newly opened beach front property (February 2003) on Klong Muang Beach, located some 8km (5 miles) west of popular Ao Nang Beach. Three restaurants, two bars and pool.

$$$

Meritime Park & Spa Resort
1 Thanon Tungfah
Tel: 0 7562 0028, 7562 0046
Fax: 0 7561 9929
www.krabi-hotels.com/meritime
Krabi town's most luxurious hotel 2 km (1 mile) from the town centre. Each room has a balcony overlooking limestone karsts, mangrove forests and the township. Satellite TV, coffee shop, pool.

Phra Nang Inn
Thanon Ao Nang Beach
Tel: 0 7563 7130–3
Fax: 0 7563 7134–5
www.phrananginn.com
Conveniently located hotel fronting
Ao Nang beach. The old wing is
more sociable than the new.
Owners organise nature and culture
tours. Has its own sea canoe
facility for guests. Beachside
restaurant and sunset bar.

$$
Krabi City Seaview Hotel
77/1 Thanon Kongkla
Tel: 0 7562 2885–8
Fax: 0 7562 2884
www.krabidir.com/krabicityseaview
Newly built and well-run, this place
has rooms with a view of the river
and is just far enough away from
the city centre to be tranquil.
Viengthong Hotel
155-7 Thanon Uttarakit
Tel: 0 7562 0020–3
Fax: 0 7561 2525
e-mail: viengthong2001@hotmail.com
Centrally located hotel overlooking
the river. Fan and air-conditioned
rooms and a popular coffee shop
and convenient internet facilities in
the lobby.

Price Categories

Prices are for one night in a
double room during the high
season:
$$$$ – over 4,000 baht
$$$ – 2,500–4,000 baht
$$ – 1,000–2,500 baht
$ – less than 1,000 baht

PHANG NGA

$$$
Phangnga Bay Resort Hotel
20 Thanon Tha Dan, Pansea
Tel: 0 7641 2067–9
Fax: 0 7641 2070
Long-established hotel built right on
the mangrove waterside in majestic
Phang Nga Bay. Excellent location
beside the river, ideal as a base for
the exploration of nearby islands.
Quality of service and dining fails to
match the setting.

PHI PHI

$$$$
Holiday Inn Phi Phi Island Resort
Laemthong Beach, Phi Phi
Tel: 0 1676 7317–8, 0 7562 1334
Fax: 0 1476 3787
www.phiphi-palmbeach.com
Designer award-winning bungalows
on isolated beach facing Bamboo
and Mosquito islands. Desert
island setting. Varied water sport
facilities, including scuba diving.
Internationally run.

Deep South

HAT YAI

$$$
Novotel Central Sukontha
3 Thanon Sanehanusorn
Tel: 0 7435 2222
Fax: 0 7435 2223
www.centralhotelsresorts.com
The most upmarket hotel in town,
right in the centre of city.
The Regency
23 Thanon Prachathipat
Tel: 0 7435 3333–47
Fax: 0 7423 4102
Modern tower in the middle of the
market with a view.

$$
Laemthong Hotel
44 Thanon Thamamoonviti
Tel: 0 7423 3413, 0 7424 5235,
0 7435 2301–4
Fax: 0 7435 2307
e-mail: laemthonghotel@hotmail.com
Large, simple and clean Chinese
hotel in a central location.

SONGKHLA

$$$
Haad Kaew Resort
Km 5, Tambon Chingkoh, Songkhla
Tel: 0 7433 1058
Fax: 0 7433 1220
The only beach resort situated in
Songkhla. Suitable for families.
Located 30 minutes' drive from
town on the road to Sathing Phra.
Samila Beach Hotel
8 Thanon Ratdamnoen
Tel: 0 7444 0222

Fax: 0 7444 0442
e-mail: bphtlsuwara@yahoo.com
Ideally situated at the crossing
between the two beaches. With
garden and pool.

$$
Lake Inn
301 Thanon Nakhon Nok
Tel: 0 7432 1044, 0 7432 5050
Fax: 0 7443 7275
High-rise with lake views.

Guesthouses

If you are on a limited budget, there
are numerous guesthouses offering
clean, economical accommodation.
Once of primary interest only to
backpackers, many have now been
upgraded to include fans, air-
conditioning and bathrooms in the
rooms rather than down the hall.
They afford a viable alternative to
the frugal traveller. Prices range
from 80 to 400 baht.

Generally possessing no more
than a dozen rooms, they are more
like pensions than hotels, and
appeal to travellers who like
personalized service, friendly staff
and a more relaxed pace.

Their numbers are legion, and to
list them would fill several books. In
Bangkok guesthouses are found in
Banglamphu, particularly along
Thanon Khao San, and in the Soi
Ngam Duphli area off Thanon Rama
IV. In Chiang Mai, check along the
river and in the area of Thanon
Chaiyaphum. In Pattaya and Phuket,
guesthouses are much less
common.

In other towns, guesthouses are
generally family-run establishments
and so are scattered around town,
but look in the vicinity of bus and
railway stations, and along main
streets. The smaller the town, the
more likely they are to be found on
the main street.

BANGKOK

Bangkok International Youth Hostel
25/2 Thanon Phitsanulok
Tel: 0 2282 0950
Fax: 0 2628 7416

www.tyha.org
70–300 baht. A range of
accommodation from dorm rooms
to rooms with bath, choice of fan or
air-conditioning. Caféteria. Hostel
members only; temporary
membership may be purchased.

Chart Guest House
61 Thanon Khao San
Tel: 0 2282 0171
200–300 baht. Some air-conditioned
rooms available for 450 baht.

Khao San Palace
139 Khao San Road
Tel: 0 2282 0578
Among the best guesthouses here,
though rates are slightly high for the
area. Clean rooms, and some have
windows, ensuite showers and air-
conditioning.

Lee 4 Guest House
off Soi Si Bamphen, Soi Saphan
Khu Duphli, Thanon Rama IV
Tel: 0 2286 7874
120–180 baht. Said to be the best
of the three Lee guesthouses in the
vicinity. Clean, large rooms.

Peachy Guest House
10 Thanon Phra Athit
Tel: 0 2281 6471, 0 2281 6659
85–150 baht, extra for air-
conditioning. Garden restaurant.

Shanti Lodge
37 Thanon Sri Ayutthaya
Tel: 0 2281 2497
50–150 baht. Clean rooms, friendly
service, coffee shop.

Sukhumvit 11
1/33 Soi 11, Sukhumvit Road
Tel: 0 2253 5927
www.suk11.com
Located in the heart of Sukhumvit
and within walking distance of the
Nana BTS, this is a personable,
family-run guesthouse, built in
traditional Thai-house style.

Tavee Guest House
83 Thanon Sri Ayutthaya
Tel: 0 2280 1447, 0 2282 5983
50–150 baht. Clean and fairly quiet
guesthouse.

White Lodge
36/8 Soi Kasem Suan 1,
Thanon Phra Ram I
Tel: 0 2216 8867
Fax: 0 2216 8828
Centally located near Siam Square
and National Stadium. Basic, clean
rooms with an outdoor café.

Where to Eat

What to Eat

The dramatic rise in the number of
Thai restaurants around the world
says something about the cuisine.
It is no surprise that when
gourmets arrive, they fall into a
feeding frenzy that lasts their
entire stay.

The base for most central Thai
curry dishes is coconut milk.
Ginger, garlic, lemon grass and fiery
chilies give Thai dishes a piquancy
that can set tender palates aflame.
While many of the chilies are mild,
their potency is inverse proportional
to their size; the smallest, the *prik
kii no* or "rat dropping chilies", are
guaranteed to dissolve your sinuses
and cloud your vision with tears. For
those averse to spicy food, chefs
can tone down the curries or serve
one of the dozens of non-spicy
curries.

Where to Eat in Bangkok

In Europe, the best restaurants are
not usually to be found in hotels. In
Thailand, the reverse is true. There
are, of course, exceptions to both
these generalities. All the following
restaurants contribute to making
Thailand a gourmet's paradise.

THAI

Central Thai

Baan Kanitha
36/1 Soi 23 (Soi Prasanmit)
Thanon Sukhumvit
Tel: 0 2258 4181
Tel/fax: 0 2260 9601;
also at 49 Soi 2 Ruam Rudee
Tel: 0 2253 4638-9
Consistently rated one of the best

Thai restaurants in Bangkok, Baan
Kanitha lives up to its billing.
Innovative food, including the best
pomelo salad in town, and gracious
service make Baan Kanitha a
popular choice with old Bangkok
hands and a great place to bring
out-of-towners. The original location
(Sukhumvit Soi 23) in an old Thai-
style house has proven so popular,
that the owners opened a second
branch on Soi Ruam Rudee
(occupying the premises of the
former Egyptian Embassy) not far
from Embassy Row on Thanon
Witthayu. **$$**

Basil
Sheraton Grande Sukhumvit
250 Thanon Sukhumvit
Tel: 0 2649 8366
Fax: 0 2649 8888
www.sheratongrandesukhumvit.com
Multi-award winning Thai restaurant
serving home-style dishes in a five-
star hotel. On Sundays, try its
lavish buffet-style lunch which
allows you to sample a huge range
of Thai specialities. **$$$**

Blue Elephant Bangkok
233 Thanon South Sathorn
Tel: 0 2673 9353
Fax: 0 2673 9355
www.blueelephant.com
Easily the city's most elegant. Royal
Thai cuisine restaurant set in a
colonial building with spectacular
service. Forget the set menus and
go for à la carte.

Bussaracum
139 Sethiwan Tower, Thanon Pan
Tel: 0 2266 6312–6
Fax: 0 2266 6317
www.bussaracum.com
Extremely popular with local
connoisseurs of classical Thai
cuisine; pleasant, informal
atmosphere. **$$**

Cabbages and Condoms (C&C)
8–10 Soi 12, Thanon Sukhumvit
Tel: 0 2229 4611, ext. 222
Fax: 0 2229 4610
Value for money and first-class
cuisine. If you are not familiar with
Thai food, this should be among
your first choices. The profits
support various family planning and
HIV awareness programmes and
other charitable projects.
Entertaining gift shop adjacent. **$**

Celadon
Sukhothai Hotel
13/3 Thanon Sathorn Tai
Tel: 0 2344 8888
www.sukhothai.com
Exceptional Thai cuisine in the
setting of an exotic water garden.
This will be an expensive affair but
worth every cent you pay. **$$$**

D'Jit Pochana
1082 Thanon Phaholyothin (near
Chatuchak Park)
Tel: 0 2272 0661-6, ext. 38
Fax: 0 2272 0661
A long-established Thai restaurant
with a diverse menu. The wild boar
curry is one of its specialities. **$**

Lemongrass
5/21 Soi 24, Thanon Sukhumvit
Tel: 0 2258 8637
Fax: 0 2258 3888
Long known for its excellent cuisine,
prices here are quite reasonable. **$$**

Mango Tree
37 Soi Tan Tawan, Thanon Surawong
Tel: 0 2236 2820
www.coca.com/mango-tree
A traditional Thai house is the
setting for this popular restaurant.
Seating in the garden outside
features a traditional Thai orchestra.
Inside the restaurant is tastefully
decorated with antiques and period
photos. The food is superb (try the
yam thua phu wing bean salad) and
reservations are recommended. **$$**

Sorn Daeng
78/2 Thanon Ratchadamnoen
(at the Democracy Monument)
Tel: 0 2224 3088, 0 2224 3178
One of the oldest restaurants in
town, known for good Thai food. **$**

Thanying
10 Thanon Pramuan
(Silom/Soi 17–19)
Tel: 0 2236 4361
Fax: 0 2635 0113
www.thanying.com
Royal Thai cuisine at its finest.
Converted Thai *sala* set well-back
from main roads is an oasis of calm
in the frenzy that is Bangkok. Food is
consistently good, whether you order
from the set menu or à la carte, and
the service and surroundings are
superb. The Second branch at the
Central World Plaza (tel: 0 2255
9838) shopping centre is slightly less
formal, but no less enjoyable. **$$$**

Isaan/Lao and Northern Thai
Ban Chiang
14 Soi Srivieng, Thanon Pramuan
(off Thanon Silom)
Tel: 0 2236 7045, 0 2266 6994
Fax: 0 2630 2205
Pleasant surroundings, good
selection of central Thai and *Isaan*
dishes, with fine wines. **$**

Bua Luang
116 Soi Rambutri, Banglamphu
A long-standing restaurant with
good Northern dishes. **$**

Khing Klao
61/1 Soi 22, Thanon Sukhumvit
(just beyond Washington Square,
near Queen's Imperial Park)
Tel: 0 2259 5623
Interesting decor, great Chiang Mai
sausage dishes. **$**

Seafood
Lord Jim's
Oriental Hotel, 48 Oriental Avenue
Tel: 0 2659 9000, ext. 3202
Fax: 0 2659 0000
www.mandarin-oriental.com
Top-quality restaurant noted for its
good atmosphere; excellent food
and service. **$$$**

Sea Food Market
89 Soi 24, Thanon Sukhumvit (look
for the large neon lobster sign)
Tel: 0 2261 2071–5, 0 2261 1255
Fax: 0 2259 4601
www.seafood.co.th
Novel grocery store layout; pick out
the seafood of your choice from a
vast variety on ice and have it
cooked to suit your taste. Great
selection of wines. Can be
expensive if you succumb to the
temptation of ordering too much.
$$–$$$

Witch's Oyster Bar & Restaurant
20/20-21 Soi Ruam Rudi Village,
Thanon Ploenchit
Tel: 0 2255 5354–5
Fax: 0 2650 7629
www.witch-tavern.com/oyster

Price Categories

Prices are for dinner for two
excluding drinks:
$$$ – over 1,000 baht
$$ – 500–1,000 baht
$ – under 500 baht

A plush English-style oyster bar
with a wide selection of seafood
appetisers and entrees. **$$**

Outdoor Thai Restaurants
When giving instructions to the taxi
driver, tell him "Suan Aahaan"
(which means garden restaurant)
before giving him the name of one
of the restaurants below.

Harmonique
22 Thanon Charoen, Soi 34
Tel: 0 2237 8175, 0 2630 6763
e-mail: harmoniquebkk@yahoo.com
Gracious dining, whether inside or
on the terrace of a converted Thai
shophouse that is full of antiques.
The spiciness of the food may be
a little toned down for foreigner's
tastes, but still done with flair.
A thoroughly pleasant dining
experience. **$$**

Koong Luang
1756 Thanon Pinklao-Nakorn
Chaisri
Tel: 0 2423 0748, 0 2424 8367
Koong Luang (Royal Shrimp) has a
well earned reputation among locals
for serving up first-rate fresh
seafood; as in many seafood joints
in Thailand, you can select your
dinner right out of the tank. **$**

Royal Dragon Restaurant
35/222 Thanon Bangna-Trad
Tel: 0 2398 0037–43
www.royal-dragon.com
Once the largest restaurant in the
world, with 16,000 sq. metres of
space and popular with tourists. All
kinds of Chinese food, especially
seafood, is on the menu (in 7
languages), but the main attraction
is the carnival-like atmosphere,
complete with roller-skating food
servers. Great people watching.
$$$

Ton Pho
43 Thanon Phra Athit
Tel: 0 2280 0452, 0 2281 6899
Named for the Bo tree that stands
in the courtyard as you enter, this
riverfront restaurant offers some
relief from Bangkok's omnipresent
heat and humidity. No reservations,
just good Thai food, prepared the
way it should be. The service can
be a bit slow, but the view of the
bustling river will keep you
occupied. **$**

Hotel Buffets

Many hotels in Bangkok vie with each other to prove that their lunch and dinner buffets surpass that of their competitors, both in quality and value for money. The result is an overwhelming choice of prices. You will not be disappointed wherever you choose to go, and even the least expensive buffets still offer a bewildering variety of dishes. All are highly recommended. In addition, many hotels offer lavish Sunday brunches, with clowns, magicians, games, videos and other diversions to keep children amused.

CHINESE

China House
Oriental Hotel, 48 Oriental Avenue
Tel: 0 2659 9000, ext. 3378
This restaurant is renowned for elegant service and traditional Cantonese specialties, such as Peking Duck (order a day in advance) and abalone. Book one of their six private dining rooms for the ultimate in service and privacy. **$$$**

Coca Suki
8 Soi Tartawan, Thanon Surawong
Tel: 0 2236 9323, 0 2236 0107
Fax: 0 2233 1956
www.coca.com;
branches at Siam Square,
416/3-8 Thanon Henri Dunant
Tel: 0 2251 6337, 0 2251 3538;
1/1 Soi 39; Thanon Sukhumvit
Tel: 0 2259 8188-9
Cantonese hot pot, sukiyaki and noodle dishes. **$$**

Dynasty
Sofitel Central Plaza Hotel
1695 Thanon Phaholyothin
Tel: 0 2541 1234
Fax: 0 2641 1082
www.accorhotels-asia.com
Traditional cuisine with Peking duck, shark's fin and abalone all featured in the extensive menu. **$$**

Evergarden
Evergreen Laurel Hotel
88 Thanon Sathorn Nua
Tel: 0 2266 7223, 0 2266 9988
Fax: 0 2266 7222

www.evergreen-hotels.com
An elegant restaurant with excellent Cantonese cuisine. **$$**

Lin-Fa
Siam City Hotel
477 Thanon Sri Ayutthaya, Phaya Thai
Tel: 0 2247 0123
Fax: 0 2247 0178
www.siamhotels.com
An elegant Chinese restaurant in one of Bangkok's most stylish hotels. **$$$**

Lok Wah Hin
Novotel Bangkok on Siam Square
392/44 Soi 6, Siam Square
Tel: 0 2255 6888
Fax: 0 2255 1824
www.accorhotels-asia.com
Cantonese and Szechuan cuisine at its best. **$$**

New Great Shanghai
648-652 Thanon Sukhumvit
(near Soi 24)
Tel: 0 2258 8746
Fax: 0 2259 6405
Popular with local Chinese, especially for Sunday lunch. Tremendous variety of duck, marvellous rice bread. **$$**

Nguan Lee
101/25-26 Soi Lang Suan,
Thanon Ploenchit
Tel: 0 2251 8366, 0 2252 3614,
0 2250 0936
Covered market; real atmosphere. One of the few restaurants where you can eat the famous Mekong giant catfish. **$$**

Rice Mill
Bangkok Marriott Resort & Spa,
257/1–3 Thanon Charoen Nakhon
Tel: 0 2476 0022
Fax: 0 2476 1120
www.marriott.com
Built on the site of an old rice mill, this luxury riverside hotel has a splendid Chinese restaurant. **$$$**

Royal Kitchen
146 Soi 55 (Soi Thong Lo),
Thanon Sukhumvit
Tel: 0 2391 0252, 0 2391 9634,
0 2391 2581, 0 2391 2080
Fax: 0 2392 7402
Excellent food served in an elegant setting. **$$–$$$**

Scala Shark Fin
218/1 Soi 1, Siam Square,
Thanon Rama I (near Scala Theatre)
Tel: 0 2250 1634, 0 2251 8899,
0 2252 0322, 0 2254 1699

Fax: 0 2254 2891
One of the house specialities is Peking Duck. Adjoining restaurant specialises in shark's fin. **$$**

Shang Palace
Shangri-La Hotel, 89 Soi Wat Suan Plu
Tel: 0 2236 7777, ext. 1205
Fax: 0 2236 8579
www.shangri-la.com
Superb Cantonese and Szechuan specialities. The lunchtime dim sum is a real treat. **$$–$$$**

Cultural Shows

Baan Thai
7 Soi 32, Thanon Sukhumvit
Tel: 0 2258 5403, 0 2258 9517
Pleasant atmosphere in a group of old Thai houses in a tropical garden. Popular with group tours. Thai dancing begins at around 9pm. **$$**

Maneeya Lotus Room
518/4 Thanon Ploenchit
Tel: 0 2251 0382
Fax: 0 2252 6312
Open daily. Lunch 10am–2pm. Nightly 7pm with Thai classical dance performance at 8.15pm. **$$**

Sala Rim Nam
Thanon Charoen Nakhon
Tel: 0 2437 9417, 0 2437 3080
Fax: 0 2439 7590
Located in a beautiful, temple-like building across the river from the Oriental, with particularly good Thai dancing. Free boat service from Oriental Hotel landing. Book ahead. **$$$**

Sala Thai
Indra Regent Hotel,
120/126 Thanon Ratchaprarop
Tel: 0 2208 0022–33
Attractive reproduction of a classic building on an upper floor of the hotel. **$$**

Silom Village Trade Centre
286 Thanon Silom
Tel: 0 2234 4448, 0 2233 9447
www.silomvillage.co.th
Open-air and indoor restaurants, traditional food stalls, Thai cultural show presented every Saturday and Sunday from 12.45pm and Thai classical dance shows daily at 8.30pm. Informal atmosphere. **$$$**

Silom Restaurant
793 Thanon Silom
Tel: 0 2236 4443
One of the oldest Chinese
restaurants in town; northern
Chinese dishes. **$$**
Silver Palace Restaurant
Thanon Silom, Soi 3
Tel: 0 2235 5118–9
Fax: 0 2266 4706
Well known for the variety of its
delicious dim sum menu. Cantonese
cuisine in opulent surroundings. **$$$**
Sui Sian
Landmark Hotel
138 Thanon Sukhumvit
Tel: 0 2254 0404
Fax: 0 2253 4259
www.landmarkbangkok.com
Cantonese and regional delicacies
of the highest standard. **$$$**
Yok Yor Restaurant
762 Thanon Laadya (Thonburi bank
of river, opposite Royal Orchid
Sheraton Hotel)
Tel: 0 2437 1121
www.yokyor.co.th
Cantonese food; one of Bangkok's
oldest and most popular Chinese
restaurants. **$$**

INDIAN/ARABIC/ INDONESIAN

Akbar Restaurant
1/4 Soi 3 (Soi Nana Nua),
Thanon Sukhumvit
Tel: 0 2255 6935, 0 2253 3479,
0 2650 3347
Fax: 0 2655 5097
Tasty northern Indian food. Try the
prawn korma. **$$**
Bali
15/3 Soi Ruam Rudi,
Thanon Ploenchit
Tel: 0 2250 0711, 0 2254 3581
The best of Javanese cuisine in a
peaceful atmosphere. **$**
Himali Cha Cha
1229/11 Thanon Charoen Krung (New)
Tel: 0 2235 1569, 0 2630 6358
Fax: 0 2630 6357
Northern Indian cuisine created by
a master chef. **$$**
Moghul Room
1/16 Soi 11, Thanon Sukhumvit
Tel: 0 2253 4465
Fax: 0 2253 6989

Riverside Restaurants

Baan Khun Luang
131/4 Thanon Khao
(off Thanon Ratchawithi)
Tel: 0 2241 0928, 0 2241 0521
Thai, Chinese and Japanese
cuisine in a riverside setting. **$**
Rim Naam Terrace
Montien Riverside Hotel
Thanon Rama III
Tel: 0 2292 2800
Lovely setting with Thai and
Vietnamese specialties. **$$**
Savoy Seafood Restaurant
River City Complex
23 Thanon Yotha
Tel: 0 2435 0611
Excellent Thai and Chinese
seafood dishes. **$$**

Popular, but more expensive than
some. **$$**
Mrs. Balbir's
155/18 Soi 11, Thanon Sukhumvit
Tel: 0 2651 0498
Fax: 0 2651 0019, 0 2651 3565
www.mrsbalbir.com
Good north Indian cuisine, a
favourite with Bangkok expats. **$$**
Rang Mahal
Rembrandt Hotel
19 Soi 18, Thanon Sukhumvit
Tel: 0 2261 7100
Fax: 0 2261 7017
www.rembrandtbkk.com
First-class Indian cuisine and
impeccable service in this rooftop
restaurant. Excellent samosas. **$$**
Tandoor
Holiday Inn Silom, 981 Thanon Silom
Tel: 0 2238 4300
Fax: 0 2238 5289
www.ichotelsgroup.com
North Indian cuisine of exceptional
quality. **$$**

JAPANESE

Hagi
Sofitel Central Plaza Hotel
1695 Thanon Phaholyothin
Tel: 0 2541 1234, ext. 4081
Fax: 0 2541 1087
www.accorhotels-asia.com
Popular hotel restaurant, with
reasonable prices. **$$**

Hanaya
683 Thanon Si Phraya
Tel: 0 2234 8095
Clean and unpretentious. **$**
Kobe Steak House
460 Soi 7, Siam Square,
Thanon Rama I
Tel: 0 2251 1336, 0 2658 3990
Excellent beef, good service. **$**
Mizu's Kitchen
32 Soi Patpong
Tel: 0 2233 6447
Fax: 0 2238 2434
One of the oldest Japanese
restaurants in the city. The house
speciality is sizzling steak. **$**
Nika-I
Sofitel Silom, 188 Thanon Silom
Tel: 0 2238 1991
Fax: 0 2238 1999
www.accorhotels-asia.com
Sophisticated Japanese dining.
Special family buffet lunches on
Saturday and Sunday. **$$**

KOSHER

Chabad House
108/1 Thanon Rambutri,
Thanon Khao San, Banglamphu
Tel: 0 2282 6388
Fax: 0 2629 1153
e-mail: chabadbangkok@yahoo.com
www.jewishthailand.com
Close to many guesthouses on
Thanon Khao San, popular with
young Jewish travellers. Open
noon–9pm. **$**

PACIFIC

Eat Me
Soi Piphat 2, Soi Convent
Tel: 0 2238 0931
Fax: 0 2630 4566
e-mail: eatmeconvent@hotmail.com
Extremely good value for money.
Run by an Aussie and his Thai

Price Categories

Prices are for dinner for two
excluding drinks:
$$$ – over 1,000 baht
$$ – 500–1,000 baht
$ – under 500 baht

partner. The menu changes regularly. Sticky date pudding must be tried. Bookings advisable. **$$**

Trader Vic's
Bangkok Marriott Resort & Spa
257/1–3 Thanon Charoen Nakhon
Tel: 0 2476 0022
Fax: 0 2476 1120
www.marriott.com
The unique style of oven gives an unusual flavour to the dishes. Delightfully different. **$$$**

VIETNAMESE

Khun Cherie
29 Sukhumvit Soi 31
Tel: 0 2260 2577-8. **$**

Le Dalat
47/1 Soi 23 (Soi Prasanmit),
Thanon Sukhumvit
Tel: 0 2258 4192
Fax: 0 2661 7968
One of the best in town in the moderate price range. **$$**

Le Danang
Sofitel Central Plaza Hotel
1695 Thanon Phaholyothin
Tel: 0 2541 1234
Fax: 0 2541 1087
www.accorhotels-asia.com
A long-established Vietnamese restaurant renowned for its authentic cuisine. **$$**

Saigon
Asia Hotel, 296 Thanon Phaya Thai
Tel: 0 2215 0808, ext. 7402
Luxury in an elegant setting under supervision of a Vietnamese chef. **$$$**

WESTERN FOOD

Le Banyan
59 Sukhumvit Soi 8
Tel: 0 2253 5556
Fax: 0 2253 4560
www.le-banyan.com
Classic French fare and gracious Thai service are the reasons Le Banyan is consistently rated the top French restaurant in Thailand. Reservations are necessary. (No jeans, t-shirt, sandals allowed.) **$$$**

Bed Supperclub
26 Sukhumvit Soi 11
Tel: 0 2651 3537
Fax: 0 2651 3538
www.bedsupperclub.com
An all-white restaurant where guests lounge on huge white beds to the sound of techno – that gets much louder in the club next door. The food is a deliciously great combination of Thai-Western fusion. **$$–$$$**

Bei Otto
1 Sukhumvit Soi 20
Tel: 0 2262 0892
www.beiotto.com
Bei Otto serve up a wide selection of home-made German sausages, both at their restaurant and butchery. **$$**

Biscotti
Four Seasons Hotel Bangkok
155 Thanon Ratchadamri
Tel: 0 2250 1000
Fax: 0 2253 9195
www.fourseasons.com/bangkok
This contemporary Italian restaurant wins accolades every year for its stylish ambience, great Italian food and fine wines. **$$$**

Vegetarian

Alloy
152 Thanon Dinso, Banglamphu
A 5 minute walk from Thanon Khao San, this unassuming vegetarian eatery has been serving authentic vegetarian – and nothing else – for over a decade. **$**

May Kaidee
117/1 Thanon Tanao, Banglamphu
Near the Regal Fashion shop on a small soi opposite the eastern end of Thanon Khao San. Good service. Try the tofu curry. **$**

Veg House
1/6 Soi 3 (Soi Nana Nua),
Thanon Sukhumvit
Tel: 0 2254 7357
Great selection of Indian and Thai dishes, emphasis on fresh ingredients. **$**

Whole Earth Restaurant
93/3 Soi Lang Suan
Tel: 0 2252 5574; branch at 71 Soi 26, Thanon Sukhumvit
Tel: 0 2258 4900
Bangkok's best-known Thai vegetarian restaurant; comfortable and friendly. There is also a tasty menu of non-vegetarian fare with excellent Indian dishes. **$$**

Bourbon Street
Washington Square,
Thanon Sukhumvit, Soi 22
Tel: 0 2259 0328
Fax: 0 2259 4318
www.bourbonstbkk.com
This long-time fixture is popular with the expat crowd, offering authentic Cajun/Creole food, including boiled live crawfish (Bourbon Street breed and raise their own), blackened redfish and jambalaya. **$$**

Greyhound Café
2nd Floor, Emporium Shopping Centre
Tel: 0 2664 8663, and off Thanon Silom, Soi Sala Daeng 1
Tel: 0 2632 4466
Thais love these modern designer-style cafés that have popped up all over town. Great coffees and snacks, but best for relaxing after some serious shopping. **$$**

L'Opera
53 Sukhumvit Soi 39
Tel: 0 2258 5606
Don't be fooled by the out-of-the way location, L'Opera is one of the best Italian restaurants in Bangkok. Reasonable prices. **$$**

New York Steakhouse
JW Marriott Hotel, 4 Sukhumvit Soi 2
Tel: 0 2656 7700
Fax: 0 2656 7711
www.marriott.com
This New York Steakhouse in the Marriot is the genuine article, offering the best fresh-chilled (not frozen) US prime beef and an outstanding wine list. Reserve at least two days in advance; open for dinner only. **$$$**

Zanotti
Saladaeng Colonnade (Silom area)
21 Soi Saladaeng
Tel: 0 2636 0266
Make your reservations early for this restaurant. Top-notch Italian fare including a huge antipasto spread and specialities from the Tuscany region. **$$$**

Chiang Mai

THAI

Aroon Rai
45 Thanon Kotchasan
Tel: 0 5327 6947
This unassuming but long-standing

eatery specialises in spicy Northern Thai fare, but has some standard Thai-Chinese dishes as well. **$**

The Gallery
Thanon Charoenrat
Tel: 0 5324 8601
Fax: 0 5324 8602
Combines an art gallery with a Chinese garden and riverside terrace in a beautifully restored Chinese joss house. **$$**

Dara Steak House
Thanon Ta Pae
Just opposite the Roong Ruang Hotel, this place has been offering a popular Thai and Western menu for over a decade. **$**

Good View
13 Thanon Charoenrat
Tel: 0 5324 1866
Fax: 0 5330 2764
www.goodview.co.th
This riverside restaurant, up river a few hundred metres from the Nawarat Bridge, is very popular with the locals. **$$**

Kafe
127-9 Thanon Mun Muang
Tel: 0 5321 2717
An old wooden building next to the moat. Fine Thai and Western food. **$**

Krua Khun Phan
80/1 Thanon Intrawarorot
Displays a variety of ready-made Thai dishes. **$**

Nang Nual
27/2-5 Thanon Koh Klang
Tel: 0 5328 1961, 0 5328 1955, 0 5328 1962
Fax: 0 5328 1972
A riverside restaurant, down river a few hundred metres off the Thanon Chiang Mai–Lamphun. **$$$**

Phuket Laikhram
1/10 Thanon Suthep
Tel: 0 5327 8909
An excellent southern Thai restaurant serving various curries and tom yam-style noodles. **$**

The Riverside Bar and Restaurant
9/11 Thanon Charoenrat
Tel: 0 5324 3239, 0 5324 6323
Fax: 0 5324 2511
www.theriversidechiangmai.com
Excellent meals served at this restaurant located on the banks of the Ping River. Live music. **$$**

Suandok Vegetarian Restaurant
Thanon Suthep

Lanna Kantoke

At Lanna kantoke dinners, you can dine on northern Thai kantoke cuisine and then sit back to enjoy a programme of northern dances and music.
Khum Khantoke, the Super Highway, behind Carrefour is a spectacle to behold. Aimed at tour groups but also available for individual reservations, northern Thai-style dinner is served at traditional low, round tables, with patrons sitting on cushions surrounding the dance stage. Tel: 0 5330 4212; www.khumkhantoke.net. Daily shows. Dinner at 6.30pm and shows at 7.30pm. **$$**
Old Chiang Mai Cultural Center also presents a Kantoke dinner with a programme of Northern and hill-tribe dances. Offered nightly from 7–10pm in a beautiful Northern Thai style house at 185/3 Thanon Wua Lai. Tel: 0 5320 2993 for reservations. Modest fee, begins at 7pm. Reserve ahead. **$$**

(near Suan Dok Temple)
Has a great selection of Thai vegetarian dishes. It opens very early and closes just after lunch. **$**

Tha Nam Riverfront Restaurant
43/3 Mu 2, Thanon Chang Klan
Tel/fax: 0 5327 5125
A large wooden building with a pleasant riverside terrace. **$$**

Whole Earth
88 Thanon Sri Dornchai
Tel: 0 5328 2463
Vegetarian and non-vegetarian Thai dishes in a garden setting. **$$**

ASIAN

Akamon (Japanese)
Hillside 4 Condotel, Thanon Huay Kaew
Tel: 0 5322 5944
One of the better Japanese restaurants in Chiang Mai features attractive decor, friendly service, and delicious food. **$$$**

Jasmine Chinese Restaurant
Royal Princess Hotel

112 Thanon Chang Klan
(Thanon Night Bazaar)
Tel: 0 5328 1033
Fax: 0 5328 1044
chiangmai.royalprincess.com
Considered by locals to be the best Chinese in town. **$$**

EUROPEAN

Bier Stube (German)
33/6A Thanon Moonmauang (near Tapae Gate)
Tel: 0 5327 8869
German and Thai food at all hours – from early to late. **$**

El Toro Mexican Restaurant
24/5 Thanon Loi Kroh
Tel: 0 5327 3574
eltoro.infothai.com
Excellent fare, pool table, open till late. **$$**

La Villa Pizzaria
145 Thanon Ratdamnoen
Tel: 0 5327 7403
This local favourite has been around for many years, and with good food at reasonable prices, it's easy to understand why. **$**

La Gondola
Rimping Condominium, Thanon Charoenrat at Nakhon Ping Bridge
Tel: 0 5330 6483
Fax: 0 5323 5942
www.lagondolathailand.com
Lovely setting on the Ping River with basic Italian cuisine. The Italian owner sings on Wednesday through Saturday evenings. **$$**

The House Restaurant, Tapas and Wine Bar
199 Thanon Moonmuang
Tel: 0 5341 9011
Fax: 0 5341 9010
e-mail: thehouse@cm.ksc.co.th
Hip, trendy and expensive, with a gourmet fusion menu and Mediterranean style-al fresco tapas bar. **$$$**

Price Categories

Prices are for dinner for two excluding drinks:
$$$ – over 1,000 baht
$$ – 500–1,000 baht
$ – under 500 baht

Pattaya

THAI AND SEAFOOD

La Mer Grill
Montien Hotel, Thanon Pattaya 2
Tel: 0 3842 8155–6
Fax: 0 3842 3311
www.montien.com
Freshly-grilled seafood and steak in a romantic setting. **$$$**

Maela Plaphao
109/9, Moo 6, Soi Siam Country Club
Tel: 0 3871 6181
Well established restaurant featuring grilled seafood cooked over coconut husks. A nice comfortable place to unwind after a round of golf. **$$$**

Thai House
171/1 Thanon North Pattaya
Tel: 0 3837 0579–80
Fax: 0 3837 0581
www.thaihousepattaya.com
Large seafood and Thai Chinese restaurant, complete with cultural shows. **$$$**

OTHER

Akamon
464/19 Thanon Pattaya 2,
North Pattaya
Tel: 0 3842 3727, 0 3842 9598
Fax: 0 3841 0701.
Japanese fare. **$$$**

Greg's Kitchen
370/21–22 Thanon Pattaya 2nd,
North Pattaya
Tel: 0 3836 1227
The real thing: homemade English and international food. Meat pies. **$**

Moon River Pub
Thai Garden Resort, 179/168,
Moo 5, Thanon North Pattaya
Tel: 0 3842 6009
Fax: 0 3842 6198
www.thaigarden.com
Thai and Western food and a selection of Mexican specialities are served in this restaurant and pub. Live band. **$$**

Yamato
Soi Yamato 13/1
Thanon Pattaya Beach
Tel: 0 3842 9685
Japanese fare. **$$$**

Phuket

Phuket Town

Bondeli
Corner of Thanon Rasada and Thanon Thepkasatri
Air-conditioned, with wide windows overlooking a bustling intersection. This is the place to come for great Western breakfasts, sandwiches and pizza. **$$**

Gitano
Opposite Robinson Ocean Plaza Shopping Center, Phuket Shopping Center, Thanon Ong Sim Phai
Tel: 0 7622 5797
Latin food and drink with an incredible selection of Latin sounds on CD. A great place for food or just drinks. **$$**

Ka Jok See
26 Thanon Takua Pa
Tel: 0 7621 7903
Intimate dining in a delightful off-the-wall Thai restaurant. Newspaper table covers, household antiques and a porch with verdant potted plants create a raffish feel underscored by jazz music. **$$**

Metropole Café
Metropole Hotel, Thanon Montri
Tel: 0 7621 5050
www.metropolephuket.com
Upmarket yet very good value lunch venue with a bountiful buffet of Thai cuisine from four regions of the country. Prompt table service. Thai classical music plays in the background. **$$**

Salvatore's Restaurant
15 Thanon Rasada, Dalat Yai,
Phuket Town
Tel/fax: 0 7622 5958
www.salvatorerestaurant.com
Authentic atmosphere, friendly staff, and delicious home made dishes make this one a must during a stay in Phuket town. **$$**

Thai Naan
16 Thanon Wichitsongkhram

Price Categories

Prices are for dinner for two excluding drinks:
$$$ – over 1,000 baht
$$ – 500–1,000 baht
$ – under 500 baht

Tel: 0 7622 6164–7
Fax: 0 7622 5616
www.thainaanrestaurant.com
Mammoth teak-panelled Thai, Chinese and Japanese restaurant which claims to be the largest in southern Thailand. Some small air-conditioned rooms. Live classical music. Good food and service despite size. Sumptuous Srivichai Room specialises in southern fare with show. **$$$**

Tung-ka Café
Top of Khao Rang Hill
Tel: 0 7621 1500
Romantic open-air Thai restaurant with sweeping views of Phuket town and the coast. Small selection of Japanese and Western dishes. At its best by night with views of the town lit up below. **$$**

Phuket Beaches

Albatross Café & Pub
Canal Village, Laguna Phuket
Bang Thao Beach
Tel: 0 7627 0958
Fax: 0 7627 0950
www.albatross-asia.com
Located in the Canal Village in the self-contained and upscale Laguna complex, the Albatross Café is an inexpensive alternative to the restaurants at the five hotel properties in the complex. Good food, ice-cold beer, friendly multilingual service (the owner speaks 8 languages), all at reasonable prices, make the Albatross a great place to relax and watch the sun set. **$**

Baan Rim Pa
110/7 Thanon Kalim Beach
Kathu, Patong
Tel: 0 7634 0789
Fax: 0 7634 2460
www.baanrimpa.com
Royal Thai food served in ambiant teak furnished surroundings. The view of the ocean is spectacular and the food actually matches the atmosphere.**$$$**

Bangla Seafood
82/46 Soi Bangla, Patong Beach
Tel: 0 7634 2436, 7629 2400
The place to go for excellent range of big lobsters, grilled crabs, juicy prawns and crispy-fried fish. Easy to run up a big bill if you choose

lobsters. Fast business-like service in street-side open air café. Great location for watching assorted characters walk by. **$$**

Boathouse Wine & Grill
The Boathouse, 182 Thanon Koktanod, Kata Beach
Tel: 0 7633 0015–7
Fax: 0 7633 0561
www.boathousephuket.com
Refined Thai and European dining on a romantic terrace overlooking the sea. Large wine selection and set menus. **$$$**

The Cliff
Central Karon Village
Karon–Patong coast road
Tel: 0 7628 6300
www.centralhotelsresorts.com
Atmospheric restaurant perched on a cliff overlooking Karon Bay. Specialises in Thai-European fusion cuisine. Thai menu too. **$$$**

Da Maurizio Bar Ristorante
100/9 Thanon Kalim Beach, Kathu, Patong
Tel: 0 7634 4079, 7634 4276
www.damaurizio.com. **$$$**

Gan Eng Seafood
9/3 Thanon Chaofa, Chalong
Tel: 0 7638 1212, 7638 1715
Simple open-air restaurant on the waterfront. Popular with locals and tourists alike. Seafood dishes are a speciality. **$$**

Kampong Kata Hill
112/2 Thanon Patak, opposite Kata Center, Kata Beach
Tel: 0 7633 0103
Fax: 0 7633 0104
Steep flight of stairs leads to quaint Thai restaurant on a wooden balcony in what is effectively an Asian art gallery. Moderately priced food from all areas of Thailand and a few international dishes. **$$**

Little Mermaid
36/10 Thanon Patak, Karon
Tel: 0 7639 6628
Comfortable Scandinavian restaurant in the heart of Karon. The thoughtful menu allows diners to tick options like medium or rare for steaks, with fries or baked potato. **$$**

No. 4
82 Moo 3, Soi Bangla, Patong
Tel: 0 7634 2319
No-frills, brightly lit seafood room at end of a shopping lane. Price

Drinking Notes

Many restaurants catering to western tastes whip up a delicious shake made of pureed fruit, crushed ice and a light syrup. Chilled young coconuts are delicious; drink the juice, then scrape out and eat the tender young flesh. Soft drinks are found everywhere. Try Vitamilk, a health drink made from soya bean milk. For a refreshing cooler, order a bottle of soda, a glass of ice and a sliced lime. Squeeze the lime into the glass, add the soda and enjoy. Sip the very strong Thai coffee flavoured with chicory. The odd orange Thai tea is sticky sweet but delicious. On a hot day, Chinese prefer to drink a hot, very thin tea, believing that ice is bad for the stomach. Try all three over ice anyway.

Beers include Kloster, Carlsberg, Leo, Chang, Singha and Singha Gold. Carlsberg and Heineken are now brewed in Thailand. Of the many Thai cane whiskies, Mekhong is the most popular. It is drunk on the rocks, with soda and lime or with a bit of honey added to it.

advantage does not compromise taste. Extensive Thai and seafood choice. Afterwards you can write your name on the graffiti wall. **$$**

On the Rock
Marina Phuket Resort, Karon Beach
Tel: 0 7633 0625, 0 7633 0493–7
Fax: 0 7633 0516
www.marinaphuket.com
Very popular small restaurant on the rocks overlooking Karon Bay. Strong on Thai food, seafood and international items. Although a bit pricey, the superlative setting and taste compensate. Dinner bookings essential. **$$$**

Pizzeria Napoli
Soi Patong Post Office, Patong
Tel: 0 7634 0674
Fax: 0 7634 1181
e-mail: napoli@pop.samart.co.th
Indoor dining on a wide range of pizzas, pastas and other Italian specialities. **$$**

Red Onion
486 Thanon Patak, Karon
e-mail: redonion@siam.de
Superb Thai food at very affordable prices make this rustic eatery popular among visitors and locals alike. **$**

Regatta Bar & Grill
Le Royal Méridien Phuket Yacht Club
Nai Harn Beach
Tel: 0 7638 0200–19
Fax: 0 7638 0280
www.yacht-club.phuket.com
Colonial feel to an opulent but understated Italian restaurant in one of Phuket's most exclusive hotels. Set menus or à la carte. Eclectic wine list. **$$$**

Ruen Thai
Dusit Laguna Resort
Bang Thao Beach
Tel: 0 7632 4324
Fax: 0 7632 4174
www.dusit.com
Central Royal Thai cuisine served by waitresses in Thai classical costumes to the accompaniment of *kim* music. Romantic candlelit setting beside a lake. **$$$**

Tatonka
382/19 Moo 1, Thanon Srisoonton, Cherngtalay, Talang, just outside Laguna Phuket, Bang Thao Beach
Tel: 0 7632 4349
e-mail: tatonka@e-mail.in.th
Delicate and innovative fusion cuisine combining western, Thai, Mexican and Mediterranean influences in a café setting with wine bar. The kitchen is open for all to see. This is possibly some of the best food in Phuket. Reserve a table, it's quite popular. **$$**

Krabi

Krabi Town
May & Mark
Thanon Ruen Rudee, Krabi town
Tel: 0 7561 2562
e-mail: maymark2544@yahoo.com
Family-run café which serves an excellent range of high-quality pastas, salads, pizza breads, shakes and coffees. Superlative home-made bread. Open daytime only. **$$**

Ruen Mai
Thanon Maharat, Krabi town
Tel: 0 7563 1797

Fax: 0 7563 1796
Shade-dappled outdoor restaurant set among native trees, 1 km (½ mile) out of town. Exclusively Thai menu at competitive prices reflects country cooking from south, central and northeastern Thailand. Open all day. **$$**

Ao Nang
Sala Thai
100 Moo 7, Vichit, behind Beach Terrace hotel, Ao Nang
Atmospheric beachside seafood and Thai curry restaurant a little hard to find, but well worth seeking out. The unpretentious setting on bamboo tables beside lapping waves attracts hotel guests going local. Open all day. Moderately priced. **$$**
Wanna's
Andaman Street Resort
31 Moo 2, Ao Nang Beach
Tel: 0 7563 7484–6
Fax: 0 7563 7322
www.wannasplace.com
Pleasant central rendezvous for all-day dining. Attentive informal service underpins consistently good Thai dishes. Pastas, burgers and imported cheeses are a bonus. **$$**

Leisure

Courses

The Oriental Thai Cooking School, Soi Oriental, Thanon Charoen Krung (New). Tel: 0 2659 9000; www.mandarinoriental.com. Offers five-day classes in Thai cuisine and vegetable-carving.

BUDDHIST MEDITATION

Studying Buddhism is not an uncommon pursuit for visitors to Thailand. The many venues for such study include the following. Call or write first since schedules change and accommodation is often limited.

Bangkok
International Buddhist Meditation Center, Wat Mahathat, Thanon Maharat, Tha Phra Chan. Tel: 0 2623 5881, ext. 1; www.mcu.ac.th/IBMC.
Thailand Vipassana Center, Pathumwan, Bangkok. Tel: 0 2521 0392.
World Fellowship of Buddhists, Thanon Sukhumvit Soi 24. Tel: 0 2661 1284–9; fax: 0 2661 0555; e-mail: wfb_hq@asianet.co.th.

Provinces
Wat Khao Tham, Ko Pha Ngan, Surat Thani Province 84280 www.watkowtahm.org
Wat Pah Nanachat, Ban Bung Wai, Amphur Warin, Ubon Ratchathani 34310
Wat Ram Poeng, Tambon Suthep, Amphur Muang, Chiang Mai 50000
Tel: 0 5327 8620
Wat Suan Mokkh, Amphur Chaiya, Surat Thani 84110
Tel: 0 7639 1851

Health Spas

The Banyan Tree, Banyan Tree Hotel, Thai Wah II Tower, 51st Floor, Thanon Sathorn Tai. Tel: 0 2679 1052/4; fax: 0 2679 1053; www.banyantreespa.com. Hydrotherapy, seaweed masks, Swedish massage. Fabulous view from the tallest building in Thailand.
The Grande Spa, Sheraton Grande Hotel, 250 Thanon Sukhumvit. Tel: 0 2649 8123; fax: 0 2649 8820; www.starwoodspacollection.com. Swedish massage, hydrotherapy, algae and mud wraps.
JW's Health Club and Spa, JW Marriott Hotel, 4 Soi 2, Thanon Sukhumvit. Tel: 0 2656 7700; fax: 0 2656 7711. Offers a flight reviver massage in addition to aromatherapy, Swedish massage, facials, scrubs and body waxing.
The Oriental Spa, on the opposite bank of the river from the Oriental Hotel, 48 Oriental Avenue. Tel: 0 2439 7613; fax: 0 2439 7885; www.mandarinoriental.com. Seaweed treatments, foot massage, aromatherapy, papaya body polish. Special programme to relieve jet lag. Advance booking recommended.

Thai Massage

Massages fall into two categories: "traditional" and "special". Establishments billing themselves as "Traditional Thai Massage" and "Ancient Thai Massage" offer therapeutic services according to age-old traditions, in other words, a legitimate massage.

The best place for traditional massages in Bangkok used to be at Wat Po, though it may have become a victim of its own success – many of the massage therapists watch TV or chat on their mobile phones while giving massage. A more relaxing massage can be arranged through one's hotel – most upscale hotels have a spa with massage therapists on call. Your hotel room is actually the best place to be after a relaxing massage – after the massage you'll probably want to take a nap instead of having to battle Bangkok's traffic. The "special" type of massage is sexual.

Massages in Chiang Mai

Traditional massages are available at **Wangcome Tradition Massage** on Thanon Nimmanhemin (tel: 0 5389 5187–9; fax: 0 5322 2770; www.kalarekspa.com) or at the **Old Medicine Hospital**, 238/8 Thanon Wualai (tel: 0 5327 5085; www.thaimassageschool.ac.th).

Beaches

Beach facilities range from the rustic to the well developed, each attracting a different clientele. We have given them a rating of 1–3.

PATTAYA AND JOMTIEN

Plenty of water activities, but unfortunately the ocean is reputedly none too clean, so fewer people are swimming here. Best bets for water lovers are nearby islands or in hotel swimming pools. Pattaya has extensive services and facilities, excellent restaurants, golf courses, cultural shows, and, of course, the tacky nightlife. **(2/3)**

EAST COAST

The long stretch of sandy, tranquil, tree-lined coast running east of Ban Phe to Laem Mae Phim has numerous quiet resorts and good hotels set in leafy gardens. Water activities are generally confined to swimming and trips to nearby islands. An ideal area for families and those wanting a quiet, relaxing holiday. **(2)**

Ko Samet

This beautiful island has become very popular with Thais from Bangkok over the past few years, and many of the places of accommodation have gone slightly upscale. Even the ones that are still rustic get away with charging more than similar accommodation further south at Ko Samui. Avoid the island on long weekends and during Thai school vacation periods when Ko Samet becomes a crowded (and expensive) place to be. During the week things are more sedate,

though a cluster of bars and discos attracts partiers to the beach known as Hat Sai Kaew. Despite the crowds, Ko Samet is still the best beach option within easy driving distance of Bangkok, and the island gets more days of sunshine than those in the south. Ko Samet is a national park and here is an entrance fee for foreigners. **(2)**

Ko Chang

The size of Phuket, this heavily forested island whose name means "Elephant Island" has boomed over the last year as a new airport has opened in nearby Trat and the threat of violence from neighbouring Cambodia has subsided. Ko Chang is actually a group of islands, some less developed that others. Some of the best diving in Thailand can be found among these lesser-known islands. On Ko Chang itself accommodation ranges from basic to luxurious, but it won't be long before the latter type is the more prevalent. Ko Chang is a national park and here is a 200 baht entrance fee for foreigners. **(2/3)**

HUA HIN AND CHA-AM

In former times, royalty gathered here, and there is still an air of grandeur to its wide beaches. The area generally attracts families and older visitors, but there are young couples as well. Excellent for quiet relaxation, strolling the fishing docks, a leisurely round of golf, riding ponies on the beach, or just sitting in a beach chair. Several international-class hotels and golf courses. **(3)**

PHUKET

Combining natural beauty with a complete range of resort facilities, Phuket is popular with Asians and Europeans alike. Gone is most of the budget accommodation, but there are still low-priced as well as luxury hotels. It has land and water sports, spas, a golf course, nightlife, drives around the island, in short, a fully fledged beach resort. **(3)**

PHI PHI

For years, its natural attractions were muted by its remoteness so that only budget travellers stayed in its thatched bungalows. It is still bungalow accommodation for the most part, but it has moved upmarket. Superb snorkelling, limited water sports, virtually no land sports, limited nightlife, trips to nearby islands, restaurants and surpassing beauty are what it offers. While the scenery is stunning, the rampant development of the island's unnamed "tourist village" with its numerous bakeries, Italian restaurants and Thai massage schools is a bit much for some. Actually, if you visited Phi Phi a decade ago, you might find it all discouraging. If this is your first time, you'll no doubt find it enchanting. **(2/3)**

KRABI

This increasingly popular destination offers first-class hotels, but smaller places and bungalows remain an option. The province is noted for its stunning limestone mountains and caves, and there are plenty of options for the adventurous: from rock climbing to kayaking, to diving. **(2/3)**

KO SAMUI

Wide beaches and a laid-back lifestyle formerly drew only budget travellers. An airstrip has made the island accessible, and first-class hotels make it comfortable for better-heeled tourists. Due to its accessibility from Bangkok by air, Ko Samui is probably Thailand's most convenient and varied island getaway. The options for food and accommodation are also some of the best in the country. There are water sports and cultural activities to keep you entertained if you tire of sunbathing. **(2/3)**

Attractions

Bangkok

After touring the famous attractions like the Grand Palace, Wat Phra Kaew, Wat Pho, and Wat Arun, visit these lesser-known sites:

See Buddhist monks on their morning alms round by visiting **Wat Benjamabophit** at about 6.30am. Here, Buddhists take food to monks waiting silently outside the gates of the temple.

Tour **Vimanmek**, the world's largest golden teak palace, and its superb collection of crystal, gold and silver art objects (open Tues–Sat, 8.30am–4.30pm, admission 100 baht or free with an entrance ticket to the Grand Palace).

Early in the morning, wander through Bangkok's largest wet market, **Pak Khlong Talad**, near the foot of the Memorial Bridge. Then visit the **flower market** on nearby Thanon Chakraphet.

Enjoy a traditional Thai massage in the *sala* (pavilion) near the eastern wall of the **Wat Pho** compound.

Board the Chao Phraya river express from the Oriental Hotel or Tha Chang near the Grand Palace, and ride 45 minutes up river to **Nonthaburi** with its bustling market. Have a drink or a meal at the **floating restaurant** next to the beautiful old provincial office. Alternatively, take the boat downstream to the last stop near the Krung Thep Bridge.

Take a free guided tour of the **National Museum** (Wed–Sun 9am–4pm, admission 40 baht).

Enjoy the educational snake show (where cobras are milked) at the **Snake Farm** (formerly the Pasteur Institute) on Thanon Rama IV (10.30am and 2pm weekdays; 10.30am weekends and holidays, admission 100 baht).

On Saturdays and Sundays, explore the weekend market at **Chatuchak Park**. Start early to avoid the midday heat.

Take the Chao Phraya river express to the Tha Ratchawong landing in Chinatown. Walk down **Thanon Ratchawong** and turn in either direction on Sampeng Lane for a staggering assortment of shops selling everything from gold jewellery to steel wool.

Stroll through a former century of gracious living at the **Jim Thompson House** (www.jimthompsonhouse. com), Soi Kasem San 2, Thanon Rama I (open daily 9am–5pm, admission 100 baht). Or visit the complex of old houses at Wang Suan Pakkad Palace, Thanon Sri Ayutthaya, between Thanon Phaya Thai and Thanon Ratchaprarop (open daily 9am–4pm, admission 100 baht).

Visit the **Ancient City** (*Muang Boran* in Thai) with its miniature replicas of the kingdom's chief architectural masterpieces.

Rent a private boat at the Oriental Hotel and cruise through Khlong Bangkok Noi, stopping at the **Royal Barge Museum** (open daily 9am–5pm, admission 30 baht). Take the long route home, through the smaller canals to Khlong Bangkok Yai and back to the Oriental.

Attend a **Thai boxing** (Muay Thai) match at Lumphini or Ratchadamnoen Stadium.

Watch a free *likay* performance at Lak Muang. (*See Theatre, page 383*.)

Make a wish and an offering at the **Erawan Shrine** at the corner of Thanon Ratchadamri and Thanon Ploenchit.

Take a stroll through **Bangrak Market** (on Thanon Charoen Krung (New), behind the Shangri-La Hotel), to see the splendid array of cut flowers.

Get a traditional herbal cure from a pharmacy in **Chinatown**. Buy a love potion or a Buddhist amulet from the stalls in the covered lanes beside Wat Ratchanadda, off Thanon Ratchadamnoen and across from the Golden Mount.

Try to locate the **gold leaf beater's shop** in a small *soi* behind Thanon Tanao in Banglamphu Market.

Visit the **monks' bowl neighbourhood** *(Baan Baht)*, the only place in Bangkok where the bowls are still crafted by hand, in the small *soi* behind the Golden Mount.

Stroll around the campus of **Chulalongkorn University**, between Thanon Henri Dunant and Thanon Phaya Thai. It is surprisingly cool and peaceful in the midst of Bangkok. Ask where the bookstore is.

Go for a walk or jog in **Lumphini Park** at 6am and watch the *T'ai chi* exercises being performed.

Have cocktails in the rooftop bar at the **Dusit Thani**, or the roof of the **Banyan Tree**. The latter is aptly named Vertigo.

Pay a visit to **Kamthieng House**, a folk art museum, in a traditional northern Thai teak house, at the Siam Society on Soi 21 (Soi Asoke), Thanon Sukhumvit (Tues–Sat, 9am–5pm, admission 100 baht adults, 50 baht children).

Central Plains

Take the train to the **Bridge on the River Kwai**. The State Railways of Thailand offers a day trip each Saturday. If you have several days, stay on one of the raft houses farther up the river.

Ride the *Oriental Queen* up the Chao Phraya River to Ayutthaya, visiting Bang Pa-In along the way.

Enjoy the water sports in **Jomtien** or the nightlife in **Pattaya**.

Take a bus to Phetchaburi to explore **King Mongkut's palace** and observatory on top of the hill.

Drive to **Ratchaburi** to look at the beautiful ceramics crafted and sold there. Visit **King Narai's old palace** at Lopburi.

Take the train to Phitsanulok to see the Phra Buddha Chinaraj image in **Wat Mahathat**. Continue to **Sukhothai** to see Thailand's first capital city, then to **Si Satchanalai** for some quiet beauty. Complete the journey by dropping south to the walled city of **Kamphaeng Phet** before returning to Phitsanulok.

The North

Visit the hilltop temple of **Doi Suthep** at sunset for a panoramic view of Chiang Mai Valley.

Explore the **crafts studios** along the road to Borsang.

Drive the tree-lined road to Lamphun to visit **Wat Phra That Hariphunchai** and **Wat Chamathewi**.

Take a trek to visit **hill tribes** outside of Chiang Mai or Chiang Rai. Attend the demonstration of elephant's skills in moving teak logs at the **Young Elephant's Training School** at Lampang or the **Chiang Dao Elephant Camp**.

Ride a longboat 3½ hours down the **Kok River** from Tha Ton to Chiang Rai.

Visit Mae Sai on the Burmese border and then drive to the **Golden Triangle** where the borders of Laos, Thailand and Burma (Myanmar) meet in the middle of the Mekong River.

Visit the **Hall of Opium**, a newly opened museum detailing the history of opium and its role in the Golden Triangle, as well as a fabulous collection of antique opium-smoking accoutrements.

The Northeast

Drive to the Northeast to see ancient Khmer temples at **Phimai**, **Phanom Wan**, **Phanom Rung** and **Muang Tham** – far flung outposts of Cambodia's famed ancient capital of Angkor. Travel from Ubon along the **Mekong River** to Nong Khai. Stop at Nakhon Phanom and enjoy an unparalleled view of the Mekong River and the jagged mountains of Laos in the distance.

The South

Visit the islands of **Phang Nga Bay**. Take the train from Bangkok to **Penang** in Malaysia. Roam the farm areas and coastal roads of Phuket in a rented jeep. Rent a motorcycle and visit all the beaches of **Ko Samui**. Cruise around Phuket on a Chinese junk. Exlore lesser known beach destinations like **Krabi** and **Ko Lanta**.

Hiking and Camping

Trekking

It's called trekking, but a two- to seven-day hike in the northern Thai hills shouldn't conjure up daunting visions of the Nepalese version. Thailand's tallest mountain, Doi Inthanon, is less than 2,600 metres (8,530 ft) in height. While you should be fit, you need not be excessively so. Retirees trek here, and so do children as young as ten.

Seeing tribal people living and working in their natural settings is the primary reason most people take treks. For those who have been stuck in Bangkok, total immersion in clean air and green things may feel like a physical and mental necessity. Trekkers also tend to have interests in birdwatching, botany, agriculture, opium, herbal medicine or New Age ideas. For wildlife enthusiasts, there's a chance to spot small game, such as antelope, wild pigs, bats and, yes, large snakes.

Most of the walking is on level ground and well-worn paths. The going becomes tough only during the height of the hot season, from March to May. Even then, the nights are cool enough to require a blanket. The best season is from November to March. Second best may be in June and July, before the full onslaught of the rainy season.

No special equipment is required. You carry a change of clothing, toilet articles, a flashlight and mosquito repellent. The guide takes care of the rest, including food, water bottles and transport. You pay for the optional toke of opium, which is, of course, illegal. Water purification tablets should be brought from home, but an adequate substitute, iodine, can be bought in Thailand (one drop to a litre). You can sleep on the hardwood floor of a villager's thatched house while pigs root in the open space below. It's spartan, but no hardship for anyone who is accustomed to camping.

Guides and Tours

The difference between a terrific and a disastrous experience depends greatly on your guide. It's therefore risky to book a tour from a large agency in Bangkok. Besides, whenever you arrive in Chiang Mai or Chiang Rai, it's always possible to join a trek leaving the following day. The choice of trekking tours in the two cities is so huge that it's discouraging. Every agency will promise "new" areas, unjaded villagers, multilingual guides and zero encounters with other groups.

You can narrow the choices by talking to tourists who have just returned from treks. In either city, or anywhere in northern Thailand, it's easy to meet such people, and they will eagerly pass on their recommendations and warnings. Keep in mind that they will recommend an individual guide, not the particular company he or she works for. This emphasis also runs through the books of glowing handwritten customer comments that every self-respecting outfit displays.

You're more likely to hit an uncongested area if you bypass Chiang Mai and Chiang Rai altogether. Start with a small one- or two-person agency in a smaller town, such as Mae Hong Son, Pai, Mae Sai or Mae Sariang. Guesthouses can always direct you to someone. Guides in these places usually have completed a government training course and have previously been employed at low wages by slicker companies. More important, they are often tribesmen themselves or local Thais truly fluent in several tribal languages. Tribal guides usually speak English as well as, or better than, urban Thai guides.

Signing On

Before you sign for any tour, determine how many hours you will walk, what you will eat and which tribes you will visit. As a rule of thumb, treks north of Chiang Mai offer more of the "colourful" tribes, the vividly adorned Akha and Hmong people. To the west, along the Pai river and close to Mae Hong Son, however, there's much less deforestation. Try to meet your companions the night before the trek. The optimum number is between six to ten. The trekking agency will store your luggage and valuables, but credit cards are safer on your person.

A portion, perhaps half, of the tour fee should be paid before setting out, but be sceptical of demands for full payment. If the agency doesn't deliver on the promises, there is no way you will get a refund. A basic three-day, two-night trek costs between 1,000 and 1,500 baht.

River rafting and an elephant ride can add an extra 500 baht. Elephant rides, it must be noted, become uncomfortable very quickly. And rafting means seeing fewer villages. But in the rainy season – from July to October – rafting is a welcome respite from midday heat and leeches.

Getting Along

Many prospective trekkers worry that their presence will contribute to the disintegration of tribal cultures. There is merit in this view. The most zoo-like encounters take place at tribal villages close to major roads and at the chilling, artificial Padaung (Long Necks) villages outside Mae Hong Son. A tour bus will pull up on schedule. Exotically garbed tribal women will envelop the tourists, badgering them to buy clothing or trinkets. The tourists will snap photos for a price. When the bus departs, the women will replace their traditional dress with T-shirts and Thai sarongs.

With a good guide-cum-interpreter, trekkers can humanise interactions by asking villagers about their customs, history and legends. Show respect for their religious beliefs and ceremonies. Play with the children. Via sign language, ask people before taking their photos. Give only adults small gifts, such as soap, bandages and sewing needles, which are the kinds of things for which they need money. It's certainly bad form to bargain for the clothing on a person's back, but it's hard to see why some tourists refuse to buy handwoven clothes or embroidered bags that have been made for sale. Such small sums may keep a village intact, and the purchase indicates a respect for quality workmanship.

It also eliminates the much wealthier Thai middlemen who run the numerous tribal handicraft shops in Chiang Mai. Many tourists say they wouldn't mind overpaying for an item if the money reached the maker. You can maximise the amount that will reach the hill tribes by buying products marketed by charitable organizations, such as the Thai Hill-Crafts Foundation and Thai Tribal Crafts. Another way is to seek out the tribal vendors in Chiang Mai's night market. They are easily recognised by the colourful garments and jewellery they wear.

Nightlife

Bangkok

Many visitors' expectations of Bangkok nightlife extend no further than the much-hyped up Patpong go-go bar scene, but this cosmopolitan city has plenty of options for entertainment once the sun goes down. The Thai craving for *sanuk* (fun) has in recent years seen booms in microbreweries and bars offering everything from Cuban cigars and art on the walls to clubs specialising in music as diverse as jazz, Latin, hip hop, house and mind-numbing techno, often all on the same street. Bangkok really comes alive under the cover of darkness, and never before has it offered so much choice to the nighttime reveller.

That's the good news. The bad is that the Bangkok nightlife scene has taken a hit since 2001 when the government introduced a Social Order Campaign with confusing Nightlife Zoning laws and draconian policing of entertainment venues. Bent on clamping rampant drug abuse and under-age drinking, the government has designated three nightlife zones: Thanon Silom, Thanon Ratchadaphisek and Royal City Avenue (RCA), where venues with valid dance licences can stay open until 2am. The rest must close at 1am. Of the three, the only zone found in downtown Bangkok is Silom, which means the acclaimed nightlife spots found along Thanon Sukhumvit – like Q Bar, Bed Supperclub and Mystique – all close painfully early at 1am.

The Silom zone includes the famous Patpong red light district and night market as well as numerous pubs and restaurants, but little in the way of dance clubs outside Soi 2 and Soi 4. Thanon Ratchadaphisek has been the traditional stomping ground of huge clubs and even larger massage parlours, visited mainly by Thais and Asian tourists, but recently, a clutch of smaller new bars are attracting young Thais. Of the three zones, it's RCA – long maligned as a tortuous teen hangout – that has the most scope to develop into a mature club scene. The signs are evident that it's at last responding, with venues like Astra and Route 66, offering varied international music styles and brand-name DJs.

Thanks to the Social Order Campaign, be prepared for the occasional police raid when revellers are urine-tested for drugs. During such raids, the police may ask foreigners to show their passports. Many clubs won't let you in without one. To get around the miserably early closing time, do as what most Thais are forced to do: start your evening early, say by 10.30pm, so there is ample time to wind down by the time the clubs close.

Another sign of the drastic changes is that the queen of nighttime activities in Bangkok is shopping. Night markets have sprung up along Thanon Sukhumvit and Thanon Silom. Even that wrinkled old harlot of a street, Patpong, has not been immune to change. Vendors' tables choke the street, drawing more patrons than the bars with counterfeit designer watches, clothing and music.

BARS AND PUBS

Bangkok Bar, 149 Soi Rambuttri. Tel: 0 2629 4443. After recent renovation, this two-floor bar with a stylish DJ booth is a happening place again. DJs are mainly homegrown talent.
Café Democ, 78 Thanon Ratchadamnoen. Tel: 0 2622 2571. Progressive drum 'n' bass, and hip and trip hop is the music of choice here, mixed by local "celebrity" DJs with the occasional international guest spinner.
Distil, State Tower, Thanon Silom. Tel: 0 2624 9555;

Listings

Check the daily newspapers for announcements of concerts, art shows, lectures and other offerings around the city. The Friday morning Bangkok Post and The Nation carry listings for the following week.

www.thedomebkk.com. Rising taller than any of the city's other nightspots, Distil is part of the opulent Dome complex on the 64th floor of State Tower building. Choose your poison from the 2,000-bottle wine cellar, lie back on the outdoor balcony sofa cushions and enjoy the spectacular panorama.
Hu'u, The Ascott, Thanon Sathorn. Tel: 0 2676 6677. This Singapore import is a class act, combining a sophisticated cocktail lounge, restaurant and an art gallery.
Met Bar, Metropolitan Hotel, Thanon Sathorn. Tel: 0 2625 3399. Equalling the panache of London's trendy Met Bar, Bangkok's younger sister at the Metropolitan is one of the capital's most exclusive yet friendly nightspots. The dark, intimate members-only bar has resident and visiting international DJs.
Syn Bar, Nai Lert Park Hotel, 2 Thanon Witthayu. Tel: 0 2253 0123 This former hotel lobby bar has been dramatically transformed into a retro-chic cocktail lounge by a New York designer. The stunning all-female bartenders mix up some devilishly tasty cocktails and flavoured martinis.
V9, Sofitel Silom Hotel, Thanon Silom. Tel: 0 2238 1991. With awesome views from the 37th floor, this stylish wine bar and restaurant is a fine spot to sip great-value wines. There's a wine shop in front, while inside fusion cuisine is served.
Zuk Bar, The Sukhothai Hotel, Thanon Sathorn. Tel: 0 2287 0222. The chic lobby level lounge bar induces relaxation from the moment you recline onto its plush sofas. Overlooking tranquil ponds and embellished with Asian antiques, the DJs here mixes chilled-out grooves.

DANCE CLUBS

Bed Supperclub, 26 Sukhumvit Soi 11. Tel: 0 2651 3537; www.bedsupperclub.com. This striking, elliptically-shaped eatery and lounge bar has diners literally eating off from beds. Laid-back vibes are played by resident DJs, while diners mull over their meal. The other half of the venue operates as a bar/club.
Q Bar, 34 Sukhumvit Soi 11. Tel: 0 2252 3274; www.qbarbangkok.com. Modelled after a New York lounge bar, this stylishly dark and seductive two-floored venue hosts some of the city's coolest dance music. The nightly line-up of mix maestros at the bar is legendary and the drinks list is no less impressive, featuring 50 brands of vodka alone.
Mystique, 71/8 Sukhumvit Soi 31. Tel: 0 2662 2374; www.mystique bangkok.com. This grotto to hedonism deliberately combines kitsch with retro chic. The ground floor is a club with a bar counter framed by a massive fish tank. Level 2 is a bar called Purple Room, while the chill-out roof-top bar looks like a transplant from Morocco.
Narcissus, 112 Sukhumvit Soi 23. Tel: 0 2258 2549; www.narcissus bangkok.com. One of the city's biggest and best clubs with fancy lights, sound system and decor, topped by a glitter globe hanging over the dance floor.

LIVE JAZZ VENUES

Diplomat, Conrad Hotel, 87 Thanon Withayu. Tel: 0 2690 9999. One of the city's best bars, this is a great warm-up spot for the hotel's other hip hang out spot, the 87 Plus club. Sit at the circular bartop in the middle and be mesmerised by seductive jazz singers.
Living Room, Sheraton Grande Sukhumvit, 205 Thanon Sukhumvit. Tel: 0 2653 0333. Top-notch jazz has become synonymous with this open-plan circular bar. Often features respected jazz musicians and singers from overseas.

GAY AND LESBIAN VENUES

Balcony, 86-88 Soi 4 Thanon Silom Tel: 0-2235 5891; www.balconypub. com. Longstanding lively bar with a mixed party crowd who spill out onto the street.

Boy's Bangkok, 894/11-13 Soi Pratuchai, Duangthawee Plaza. Tel: 0-2237 2006. One of the better gay go-go bars on a strip of several such places.

DJ Station, 8/6–8 Silom Soi 2. Tel: 0 2266 4029; www.dj-station.com. Bangkok's most popular gay club, packed throughout the night. The atmosphere is electric and patrons often dress outrageously.

Chiang Mai

Chiang Mai nightlife is centred for the most part around the **Night Bazaar** and near **Tapae Gate**. The number of sex-for-sale bars has multiplied over the years, though most are low key in comparison to what Bangkok has on offer.

Music Clubs and Bars

The normal evening entertainment is to sit in a restaurant or pub and listen to local musicians sing soft tunes. **Riverside Restaurant** on Thanon Charoenrat and **The Cottage** on the Thanon Chiang Mai-Lamphun are two examples of this kind of entertainment. Bars along Thanon Chaiyaphum in the vicinity of Tapae Gate offer live and recorded music. The latter also have bargirls but not in the same numbers as Bangkok or Pattaya.

During the dry season most of Chiang Mai's evenings are spent in outdoor restaurants like **Antique House** (Thanon Charoen Prathet), **The Brasserie** and the **Gallery** (Thanon Charoenrat), or one of the many places in the Night Bazaar offering food, drinks and people watching.

Pattaya

Pattaya's nightlife is still somewhat in the old mould, with bars proliferating in the South Pattaya area. Here, the emphasis is on picking up bargirls and drinking.

There are one or two music clubs where one can sip a beer and listen to 60s rock and roll.

Hotels have lobby bands and bars with lounge singers. Thanon Beach and Thanon Pattaya 2 are lined with beer bars, which differ little from their cousins in South Pattaya.

Phuket

As Phuket has become sophisticated, so has its nightlife. In Patong, **Simon Cabaret** (tel: 0 7634 2114; www.phuket-simon cabaret.com) has evolved into a highly professional showpiece with elaborate stage sets and a few comic laughs. The cast is exclusively, and deceptively, feminine. Shows: 7.30pm and 9.30pm.

The **Safari Pub**, 1 km (½ mile) up the hill from Simon, heats up around 11pm with the live band luring an unlikely mix of cocktail-compromised Thais and tourists to the dance floor. In downtown Patong, the dance scene revolves around the evergreen **Banana disco** on Thanon Beach, and the Thai-oriented **Tin Mine**. The Sports Pub at the Shark shows live sports events via satellite. Dozens of beer bars with hostesses still provide the backbone of Patong's nightlife in and around Soi Bangla. A-go-go thrives at **Extasy**, **Firehouse** and **Rock Hard**. Massage houses are many; **Christin Massage** is the glossiest while, the traditional version is available at **Hutavat** in Thanon Phra Baramee.

In Karon there are beer bars opposite **Crystal Beach Hotel** and massage at the **Blue Moon**. In Kata there are a few beer bars south of the Siam Commercial Bank, but the upscale **Islander Bar** is a better bet.

For live music try Phuket town's **Timber Rock** club in Thanon Yaowarat. Ten-pin bowling at **Pearl Bowl** on Thanon Montri is a tradition. The slick Thai-style coffee shop, **Bua Luang**, on Thanon Pattana, is a Phuket institution.

Molly Malone's is the island's first Irish theme bar with an in-house band. Check it out on Patong Beach.

Culture

Modern pop culture seems to have gained ascendancy over traditional arts, despite government support for Thai arts and performers. Foreign culture is promoted by the respective country cultural organisations, but little is done to attract foreign performers in the manner of, say, Hong Kong's Art Center and the annual Hong Kong Arts Festival.

The many museums in Bangkok and in major towns around the country contain some superb specimens. Exhibitions of modern art are arranged by private gallery owners, foreign cultural centres, or by corporate patrons, usually banks.

Museums

BANGKOK

The National Museum, Thanon Na Phra That. Tel: 0 2224 1333; www.thailandmuseum.com. Open 9am–4pm, Wed–Sun, last ticket sold at 3.30pm, admission 40 baht. Next to Sanam Luang in the heart of the old royal city, the National Museum is a repository of archaeological finds, Buddha images, old royal regalia, ceramics and objets d'art (usually Buddhist) from neighbouring countries. The walls of the **Buddhaisawan Chapel** in the museum grounds are covered in some of the finest Buddhist murals in Thailand.

The National Museum offers free guided tours of Buddhist and other art, and conducts them in a number of languages. The schedule is:

English: Buddhism (Wed); Thai art and culture (Thur)
French: Thai art (Wed)
German: Thai art and culture (Thur)

Spanish: By special arrangement for groups.

Tours start at 9.30am and last about two hours. For information call the museum volunteers at 0 2215 8173. Whatever tour you take, be sure to visit the **Buddhaisawan Chapel** and the **Cremation Chariot Hall** (Hall 17) afterwards.

Almost every urban centre in Thailand has a branch of the National Museum.

CHIANG MAI

The National Museum, near Wat Jet Yot on Highway 11. Tel: 0 5322 1308. Open Wed–Sun 9am–4pm. Collections of Sawankhalok china and Buddha images are highlights. **The Folk Art Museum**, near the junction of Thanon Thiphanet and Thanon Wualai. Open Fri–Wed 10am–4pm. Collection of household items housed in a traditional-style house. **The Tribal Research Center**, on Chiang Mai University campus. Tel: 0 5321 0872. Open Mon–Fri 9am–4pm. A small ethnographical museum with costumes and implements of hill tribes on display. **The Hall of Opium** (Tel: 0 5378 4444-6; fax: 0 5365 2133; www.doitung.org), aptly situated in the middle of the infamous Golden Triangle, is a royally sponsored museum detailing the historic opium trade. (Open Tues–Sun 10am–3.30pm, admission 300 baht). The newly-opened museum cost almost ten million US dollars to complete, and there is no other museum in Southeast Asia like it. Interactive displays and dioramas allow visitors to view a 19th century opium den. There is also an impressive collection of antique opium pipes, lamps and sundry accoutrements on display. The museum is located on the road between Mae Sai and Chiang Saen in Chiang Rai province – just opposite the Anantara Resort and Spa Golden Triangle.

Art Galleries

The National Gallery, 4 Thanon Chao Fa. Tel: 0 2281 2224; www.thailandmuseum.com. Open 9am–4pm, Wed–Sun. To the north of the National Museum in Bangkok, across the approach to the Phra Pinklao Bridge the National Gallery displays works by Thai artists and offers frequent film shows. Exhibitions of paintings, sculpture, ceramics, photographs and weaving are varied and numerous. Check the *Bangkok Post* for details.

Silpakorn University, opposite the Grand Palace on Thanon Na Phralan, is the country's premier fine arts college. It frequently stages exhibitions of students' work. Other promoters of Thai art and photography are the **British Council**, the **Goethe Institut** and **Alliance Française**, all of which sponsor exhibitions.

Concerts

The Fine Arts Department periodically offers concerts of Thai music and dance/drama at the **National Theatre** (Tel: 0 2224 1342, 0 2222 1092). On Saturday afternoons at 2pm, programmes of Thai classical dance are presented at the auditorium of the **Public Relations Building** on Ratchadamnoen Klang Avenue opposite the Royal Hotel.

Concerts of European music and dance are now regular events. The **Bangkok Symphony Orchestra** gives frequent concerts, as do groups from Western countries. See *Bangkok Post's* Sunday magazine for details.

Theatres

The **National Theatre** presents Thai works and, occasionally, big-name foreign ensembles like the New York Philharmonic. For more experimental works, Thai or foreign, look to the **Thailand Cultural Centre** (Tel: 0 2247 0028; fax: 0 2245 7747; www.thaiculturalcenter.com). The centre, which is a gift of the government of Japan, is located on Thanon Ratchadapisek north of Bangkok, tel: 0 2247 0028. Its three stages present everything from pianists to puppets. See the newspapers for announcements of forthcoming performances.

It is also possible to find Chinese opera performed as part of funeral entertainment or during the Vegetarian Festival each September in Chinatown. These performances are normally not announced, but are an unexpected surprise one stumbles across when wandering back alleys. It is hard to miss; the clash of cymbals and drums and the screech of violins identify it.

Likay, the village version of the great *lakhon* and *khon* dance/dramas of the palace, was once staple fare at temple fairs. Alas, most of the fairs have faded away in the city and are found only in rural areas. Even there, *likay* performances are often given second billing to popular movies shown in the open air on big screens. About the only place one can see truncated *likay* performances is at Lak Muang, where successful supplicants pay a troupe to perform for gods of the heavens and angels of the city.

Traditional puppet theatre is best represented by **Joe Louis Theatre** (Suan Lum Night Bazaar, 1875 Thanon Rama IV. Tel: 0 2252 9683; www.joelouistheater. com), which stages two *hun lakhon lek* puppet shows nightly (7.30pm and 9.30pm). *Hun lakhon lek*, a fading art, is inspired by local folk tales and the Ramakien. Three puppeteers move visibly on stage manipulating expressive marionettes.

The nucleus of the Thai contemporary theatre scene, on the other hand, is **Patravadi Theatre** (69/1 Sol Wat Rakhang, Thanon Arun Amarin, Thonburi. Tel: 0 2412 7287; www.patravadi theatre.com). Heading the theatre is Patravadi Medchudhon, who artfully melds traditional and modern dance and drama. Shows are on Saturday and Sunday nights at 7.30pm.

Cinema

Bangkok's movie theatres and multiplexes, usually found in shopping malls, normally show Hollywood blockbusters with Thai subtitles, often not too long after the movie's debut in the States. British and European-based productions are less common. The Thai film industry is currently experiencing a renaissance and locally made films often come with English subtitles these days. Multiplexes in upscale malls are surprisingly plush – you can watch a movie in air-conditioned comfort while reclining in huge lounge chairs. At some theatres the ushers even pass out pillows, blankets and socks – it's like watching the wide screen while flying first class. sTickets cost 500–700 baht (about the same as you pay at home to sit in a cramped cinema). Check the *Bangkok Post* and *The Nation* for daily schedules, or go online for listings at www.movieseer.com, www.chiangmaivista.com and www.majorcineplex.com. Remember to stand when the national anthem is played before each performance.

Libraries

For reading or reference, stop in at one of these libraries. All carry books in English on Thailand.
American University Alumni (AUA), 179 Thanon Ratchadamri. Tel: 0 2252 8170-3; www.auathailand.org. The library, which is sponsored by the US Information Agency, is open to non-members. In Chiang Mai: 24 Thanon Ratchadamnoen. Tel: 0 5321 1973, 5327 8407.
Neilson Hayes, 195 Thanon Suriwong. Tel: 0 2233 1731. Open Tues, Thur–Sat 9.30am–4pm, Wed 9.30am–7pm, Sun 9.30am–2pm; closed Mon. The oldest English-language library in Thailand, with over 20,000 volumes housed in a charming colonial-style building. If you plan to spend some time in Bangkok it's a good library to join – just being able to relax amidst the ornately carved hardwood shelves on leather upholstered chairs is to step back into time. One-day membership is available.
Siam Society, 131 Soi 21 (Soi Asoke), Thanon Sukhumvit. Tel: 0 2661 6470; fax: 0 2258 3491; www.siam-society.org. Open Tues–Sat 9am–5pm.

Bookstores

Bangkok has perhaps the best bookstores in Southeast Asia. If you want to read about something you have encountered in Bangkok or just want a light read for the beach, try one of these bookshops.
Asia Books, tel: 0 2715 9000; fax: 0 2714 2799; www.asiabook.com, with branches at 221 Thanon Sukhumvit (between Soi 15 and 17); Peninsula Plaza (153 Thanon Ratchadamri); Landmark Plaza (138 Thanon Sukhumvit); Thaniya Plaza (next to Soi Patpong 2); Times Square; Central World Plaza (4 Thanon Ratchadamri); Seacon Square (Thanon Si Nakharin); Emporium (Soi 24, Thanon Sukhumvit, 3rd floor); and Siam Discovery Center.
Bookazine branches can be found on Thanon Ploenchit (Sogo Department Store, 3rd Floor); Thanon Silom (CP Tower, 313 Thanon Silom, near Thanon Convent); and Thanon Sukhumvit (Robinson Department Store).
Dasa Book Café at 710/4 Thanon Sukhumvit between Soi 26 and Soi 28 is the perfect place to grab a cup of coffee and a paperback novel. Tel: 0 2661 2993–4; www.dasabookcafe.com.
D.K. Books, branches at Siam Square (Thanon Rama I); Mahboonkrong (opposite Siam Square) and Seacon Square (Thanon Si Nakharin).
Chulalongkorn University (Thanon Phaya Thai, south of Siam Square) also has a good bookshop with some esoteric titles in English.
Kinokuniya (www.kinokuniya.com). A real treat for book lovers with branches at Central World Plaza, 6th Floor, Isetan Department Store, tel: 0 2255 9834 and Emporium, 3rd Floor, tel: 0 2664 8554.

Festivals

What to see

Small temple fairs upcountry are great fun to attend. They are usually held in the evenings during the cool season to raise money for repairs to temple buildings. There are carnival rides, the odd freak show, halls of horror, rumwong dances, food vendors and deafening noise – the one element without which a fair would not be a fair. If you see one in progress, stop, park and enjoy yourself.

The dates for these festivals and fairs change from year to year. Check the exact dates by calling the TAT in Bangkok.

January

New Year's Day is a day of relaxation after the festivities of the night before. It is a public holiday.
Phra Buddha Chinarat Fair is held in late January or early February. Enshrined in Phitsanulok's Wat Phra Si Rattana Mahathat, Phra Buddha Chinarat is one of Thailand's most sacred and delicately cast Buddha images of the Sukhothai style. The fair includes a display of giant birds made from straw, folk performances and various forms of entertainment.
Don Chedi Memorial Fair in Suphanburi (late January) commemorates the decisive battle won by King Naresuan at Don Chedi. The fair features historical exhibitions, entertainment and local handicraft stalls.
Bo Sang Umbrella Fair, in Bo Sang near Chiang Mai, is held in the main street and celebrates the traditional skill of making gaily painted umbrellas and other handicrafts.

February

Flower Festival is held in Chiang Mai during early February. This annual event features flower displays, floral floats, beauty contests and coincides with the period when the province's temperate and tropical flowers are in full bloom.

Dragon and Lion Parade is held annually between January and February in the central Thailand town of Nakhon Sawan, by people of Chinese ancestry. The Dragon and Lion procession is a traditional homage-paying rite to the golden dragon deity in gratitude for his benevolence to human beings. The lively parade includes marching bands, golden dragon and lion dances, and processions of deities.

Chinese New Year is not celebrated with the boisterousness of other Asian countries. The temples are a bit busier with wishes made for good fortune in the coming year, but otherwise there is nothing to mark the period. Shops close and, behind the steel grilles, private family celebrations go on for three or four days.

Magha Puja, a public holiday in Bangkok and a Buddhist holiday on the full moon night of February, marks the spontaneous gathering of 1,200 disciples to hear the Lord Buddha preach. In the evening, Thais gather at temples to hear a sermon by the chief monk of the *wat*. Then, when the moon is rising, they place their hands in a praying position before their faces and clasping candles, incense and flowers, follow the chanting monks around the *bot* of the *wat* three times before placing their candles and incense in trays at the front of the *bot*. It is a most solemn and moving ceremony.

March

Kite flying is not a festival but it would be difficult to convince kite enthusiasts otherwise. They gather at Sanam Luang, in Bangkok, in the afternoons as the brisk winds haul their large kites aloft, filling the sky with bright colours.

Barred Ground Dove Festival. Dove lovers from all over Asia come to Yala for this event. The highlight is a dove-cooing contest involving over 1,400 competitors.

April

Chakri Day on 6 April, celebrates the founding in 1782 of the dynasty that presently rules Thailand. It is celebrated in the palace, but there are no public ceremonies. An official holiday, most Thais celebrate it as a day off from work.

The Phra Chedi Klang Nam Fair is one of the larger temple fairs. It is celebrated at the *wat* on the river's edge at Phrapadaeng, 15 km (9 miles) south of Bangkok, on the Thonburi side of the river.

Songkran is a public holiday that, in the past, was the traditional Thai New Year – until royal decree shifted the official New Year to 1 January. It most closely resembles the Indian festival of Holi which occurs at the same time. Songkran is a time of wild revelry, a chance for the normally placid Thais to let off steam. The central event is the sprinkling of water on one's friends to bless them, but this usually turns into a boisterous throwing of buckets of water on passers-by.

On the whole, the celebration of Songkran in Bangkok seems a little more subdued than in the north, but only because certain areas have become the focus for most of the partying. Curiously, Thanon Khao San has been the most popular Songkran destination in recent years, as many young Thais converge on the backpacker enclave to douse the visitors. Other areas where you're sure to get a good soaking are the Patpong and Nana nightlife districts.

To see Songkran at its most riotous, travel down the western bank of the Chao Phraya River to the town of Phrapadaeng. There, no one is safe, but in the April heat, who cares? Songkran in the north of Thailand, particularly in Chiang Mai, is fervently celebrated over several days and attracts many visitors from Bangkok.

Turtle Releasing Fair. At Nai Yang beach in Phuket, young turtles are released for their journey to the sea. The festival begins early in the morning with alms offered to monks and is accompanied by music, dancing, sports and food.

May

Labour Day is on 1 May.

Coronation Day on 5 May, is a private royal affair and a public holiday.

The Rocket Festival in Yasothon in the northeast of Thailand is held in early May. Well worth the trip to witness the launching of the locally made missiles of all shapes and sizes, some as tall as a person.

The Ploughing Ceremony is a colourful ancient tradition celebrated only in Bangkok. Held at Sanam Luang, it is presided over by King Bhumibol and marks the official start of the rice planting season. Crimson-clad attendants lead bullocks, drawing an old-fashioned plough, around a specially prepared ground. The lord of ceremonies, usually the minister of agriculture, follows behind, scooping rice seed out of baskets held by pretty maidens and sowing it in the furrows left by the plough, all to the accompaniment of blaring conch shells and drums.

Visakha Puja is a public holiday on the full moon night of May that commemorates the birth, enlightenment and death of Buddha. The three things are all said to have happened on the same day. Visakha Puja is celebrated like Magha Puja, with a triple circumambulation around the temple as the moon is rising.

Fruit Fairs. There are annual fairs in Chiang Mai, Rayong, Chanthaburi, Trat and several other locations throughout Thailand to celebrate the harvest of lychees, durian, mangosteen, rambutan, jack fruit and zalacca. Besides stalls selling the produce of the surrounding orchards, there are beauty pageants, cultural shows and local entertainment.

June

Sunthorn Phu Day. This annual celebration in late June commemorates the birth of the Thai poet Sunthorn Phu. The festivities include dramatic performances and puppet shows depicting his literary works, poetry recitals and folk entertainment.

July

Asalaha Puja on the full moon night of July is the third most important Buddhist holiday and marks the occasion when Buddha preached to his first five disciples. It is celebrated on the full moon night in similar manner to Magha Puja and Visakha Puja. It also marks the beginning of the three-month Lenten season. Tradition says that Buddha was approached by farmers who asked that he bar monks from going on their morning alms rounds for a period of three months, because they were trampling on the rice shoots they had just planted. They offered instead to take food to the monks at the temple during this period, a practice which has been followed ever since.

Khao Phansa is celebrated immediately following Asalaha Puja and marks the commencement of the annual three-month Rains Retreat.

Candle Festival takes place during Khao Phansa in the northeast town of Ubon. It celebrates the commencement of Khao Phansa with a lovely spectacle where some beautifully embellished beeswax candles are ceremoniously paraded before being presented to temples.

August

Queen Sirikit marks her birthday (12 August) by religious ceremonies and private celebrations. It is a public holiday. The date is also celebrated as Mothers Day.

September

Moon Festival. On the first day of the eighth lunar month, Chinese place small shrines laden with fruit, incense and candles in front of their houses to honour the moon goddess. It is a lovely festival, the highlight of which is the availability of utterly scrumptious cakes shaped like a full moon. They are specially prepared, often by chefs flown in from Hong Kong, and found no other time of the year.

Phichit Boat Races. A regatta featuring long-boat races. Similar events are held in Phitsanulok and all over Thailand at this time of year. The low-slung, wooden boats are raced with great gusto.

Taan Khuay Salak. A series of races held between mid-September and mid-October on the Nan River in long, narrow "dragon" boats propelled by 50 oarsmen.

October

Chinese Vegetarian Festival, held in mid-October, is a subdued affair in Bangkok by comparison with the firewalkers of Phuket. Enormous amounts of vegetarian food, Chinese operatic performances and elaborate offerings are made at various Chinese temples around the city. A superb photographic opportunity. Only those wearing all-white attire are allowed in the area of the altar, so dress appropriately.

Ok Phansa marks the end of the three-month Lenten season, and the beginning of the Kathin season when Buddhists visit *wat* to present monks with new robes and other necessities. Groups will rent boats or buses and travel long distances to spend a day making gifts to monks of a particular *wat*. If you are invited, by all means go, because it is a day of feasting and fun as well.

Chulalongkorn Day on 23 October honors King Rama V (1868–1910), who led Thailand into the 20th century. On this public holiday, students lay wreaths before his statue in the plaza at the old National Assembly building during an afternoon ceremony.

Lanna Boat Races, this regatta is as exciting as the Phichit Boat Races.

The Buffalo Races held in late October in Chonburi rival the excitement of the Kentucky Derby.

November

Golden Mount Fair, held the first week of November in Bangkok, is one of the noisiest of temple fairs. Carnival rides, food concessions, variety performances and product stalls are the main attractions.

The Little Royal Barge Festival at Wat Nang Chee in Phasi Charoen in early November is a smaller version of the grand Royal Barge procession, but it is marked by more gaiety in small towns.

Loy Krathong, one of the most beautiful festivals anywhere in Asia, is on the full moon night of November. It is said to have been started in Sukhothai in the 13th century. A young queen, Nang Nopamat, is said to have floated a small boat laden with candles and incense downstream past the pavilion where her husband was talking with his friends. Whatever the origins, it has grown to be one of the country's most enchanting festivals, a night when Thais everywhere launch small candle-laden boats into the rivers and canals to ask blessings. The tiny dots of light and shimmering water are mesmerizing.

Long-boat races have become increasingly popular in the past few years, and it is not unusual to open a newspaper during November and find that yet another race is being staged somewhere in Thailand. They are colourful and exciting and provide superb photo opportunities.

The Elephant Round-Up in Surin is held in mid-November and attracts visitors from all over Thailand.

Phra Pathom Chedi Fair at the world's biggest *chedi*, in Nakhon Pathom, is regarded as one of the most exciting temple fairs.

Khon Kaen Silk Fair. Silk weaving demonstrations and a chance to buy lustrous silk in a major centre of production.

River Kwai Bridge Week. A sound-and-light presentation recaptures this dark period of recent history when Asians and Europeans died in their thousands at the hands of the Japanese to build the infamous Death Railway during World War II.

Usually late November or December.

Sunflower Fair. The photogenic sight of Mexican sunflowers in bloom is best seen in the hills of Doi Mae U-Khor, as Mae Hong Son holds a three-day festival of ox-carts decorated with the beautiful flowers. When the flowers fade, the seeds are used to make insecticides.

December

Trooping of the Colours On 3 December, the royal regiments dressed in brilliantly coloured costumes pass in review before the king. Held on the plaza before the old National Assembly building, the Trooping of the Colours is the most impressive of martial ceremonies.
King Bhumibol celebrates his birthday on 5 December with a ceremony at Wat Phra Kaew for invited officials and guests, and with a private party. It is a public holiday as well as Thailand's Fathers Day.
King's Cup Regatta. Long-distance yacht racing from Nai Harn Bay in Phuket with competitors from around the world.
Constitution Day on 10 December is a public holiday in Thailand.
Christmas may soon be an official Thai holiday if the merchants have any say in the matter – that is if endless repetitions of Christmas carols in department stores bludgeon everyone into acceptance.
New Year's Eve on 31 December is a public holiday.

Shopping

General

Whatever part of your budget you have allocated for shopping, double it or regret it. Keep a tight grip on your wallet or you will find yourself being seduced by the low prices and walking off with more than you can possibly carry home. If you cannot resist, see the "Export" section for an inexpensive way to get souvenirs home.

Over the years, there have been two major changes in the shopping picture. First, there have been subtle design alterations and the introduction of new products to make the items more appealing to foreign buyers. The purists may carp, but the changes and the wider range of products have been welcomed by shoppers.

The other change is that while regional products were once found only in the towns that produced them, there has been a homogenisation of distribution, so that it is now possible, for example, to buy Chiang Mai umbrellas in Phuket. The widest range of items are found in Bangkok and Chiang Mai, but if you never have a chance to leave Bangkok, do not despair; nearly everything you might want to buy in provincial towns can be found in the capital.

Export

SHIPPING

Most shops will handle documentation and shipping for your purchases. Alternatively, the **General Post Office** on Thanon Charoen Krung (New Road), near the Oriental Hotel, offers boxes and a packing service for goods sent by sea mail.

Packages can be shipped from most post offices. Post offices in most towns sell cardboard boxes specially created for shipping packages.

Thai Airways in Bangkok also offers a special service called THAIPAC that will air freight your purchases (regardless of your mode of transport or the airline you are using) to the airline's destination closest to your home for 25 percent of the normal rate. For THAIPAC rates, visit their website: www.thaicargo.com/thaipacset.htm. Just take your goods to the airline's office at 485 Thanon Silom. They must fit into a special box and weigh no more than 33 kg (73 lbs) per box. For a small charge, Thai Airways will also handle the documentation and customs clearance.

EXPORT PERMITS

The Fine Arts Department (Tel: 0 2224 4702, 0 2221 7811; fax: 0 2222 0934) prohibits the export of all Thai Buddha images, images of other deities and fragments (hands or heads) of images dating from before the 18th century.

All antiques and art objects, regardless of type or age, must be registered with the Fine Arts Department. The shop will usually do this for you. If you decide to handle it yourself, take the piece to the Fine Arts Department at the National Museum on Thanon Na Phra That, across from Sanam Luang, together with two postcard-sized photos of it. The export fee ranges between 50 and 200 baht depending on the antiquity of the piece.

Fake antiques do not require export permits, but airport customs officials are not art experts and may mistake it for a genuine piece. If it looks authentic, clear it at the Fine Arts Department to avoid problems later.

Complaints

The customer is (nearly) always wrong might be the most candid way of putting it. Except for very large shops, expect that once you have paid for an item and left the store – unless the defect is very glaring and there is no possible way you could have caused it – the moment you walk out the door, that's it. You can report the shop to the Tourist Police, but they are not usually interested. Shop carefully: *caveat emptor.*

Shopping Areas

BANGKOK

Bangkok is a most comfortable place to shop. Shopping venues range from huge air-conditioned malls to tiny hole-in-the-wall shops to crafts sections of large department stores.

Queen Sirikit's Chitralada stores sell the rare crafts she and her organization, SUPPORT, have worked so diligently to preserve by teaching the arts to village women. There are branches at the Grand Palace, in Oriental Plaza and the Hilton International Hotel, and at the airport, as well as in Pattaya.

Note that **Nancy Chandler's Map of Bangkok** (www.nancychandler. net), widely available in bookstores and hotels, is an invaluable reference for serious shoppers. It is not the best map for finding specific street addresses in Bangkok, but for pointing you in the direction of the top shopping areas, restaurants and sights, it is unparalleled.

Central Bangkok

Central World Plaza, 4 Thanon Ratchadamri. The flagships of this huge 8-floor shopping complex are Zen Central and Isetan, two well regarded department stores. Other attractions include a **Duty Free Shop** on the 7th floor (passport and ticket must be presented), many fast-food outlets and bistro-type restaurants, and a wealth of small boutiques selling nearly everything imaginable.

Narayana Phand, the government handicraft centre, 127 Thanon Ratchadamri (across the street from the Central World Plaza), is the very best place to go to see the whole range of Thai crafts, particularly if your time is limited. Wood carvings, bencharong, jewellery, pewter,

ceramics, silk, handmade paper, textiles, and clothing can all be found at reasonable (and fixed) prices here. There is a pleasant restaurant on the second floor. The market in the basement beneath Narayana Phand is the best place in town for inexpensive blue jeans; leather goods, casual jewellery, videos and T-shirts are also available here.

Erawan Bangkok on 494 Thanon Ploenchit is behind the famous Erawan shrine and connected to the Grand Hyatt Erawan. This new boutique mall has both chic shops and eateries and a beauty centre.

Value Added Tax

Value Added Tax (VAT) refunds: Any non-Thai visitor to Thailand is entitled to reclaim the seven percent VAT charged on all goods and services. Some of the conditions are:

The goods must be purchased from stores displaying the "VAT refund for Tourists" sign.

At each point of purchase, ask the sales assistant to complete two refund forms and attach the original tax invoice to the forms.

Before departure at any of the country's four international airports, present your claim at the departure lounge after check-in and passport control.

Amarin Plaza, Thanon Ploenchit (near Erawan Shrine), is the place to go for up-market shoes and jewellery. **Siam Square** at Thanon Rama I, between Thanon Henri Dunant and Thanon Phaya Thai, is home to seven cinemas, several bookstores and innumerable Western and Asian fast-food outlets. It also has many small shops selling clothing, electrical goods and gift items. Investigate the vendors along the central laneways.

Siam Centre, 989 Thanon Rama I, contains several tailors and numerous clothing stores, a video game arcade for kids and home decor stores. Restaurants and sports zone are on the top floor.

Siam Paragon, being constructed next to Siam Centre at Thanon Rama I, is a massive new mall, slated for completion at the end of 2005.

Siam Discovery Centre, 989 Thanon Rama I, is packed with imported brands with prices to match. On the 5th floor is Kids World, a whole floor devoted to youngsters. Grand EGV cinema is on the top floor.

Mahboonkrong at 444 Thanon Phaya Thai is a multi-level shopping complex offering a variety of items including leather goods, clothing, jewellery, audio tapes and CDs at mid-range prices.

Gaysorn Plaza, at the intersection of Thanon Ploenchit and Thanon Ratchadamri, and Peninsula Plaza, 153 Thanon Ratchadamri, are two chic shopping malls with designer fashion outlets and a variety of small boutiques.

Pratunam Market, at the intersection of Thanon Phetburi and Thanon Ratchaprarop, is a huge, bustling warren of stalls which caters less to tourists than to Thais. It is somewhat difficult to locate, but a good place to absorb lots of local colour. There are many street vendors along Thanon Ratchaprarop outside the market.

Playground at 818 Soi Thonglor, Sukhumvit 55 is Bangkok's newest boutique mall, combining art installations with home decor and fashion shops, trendy cafés, and a cooking school.

The Emporium at Soi 24, Thanon Sukhumvit is the mall of choice for many of Thailand's high society with its huge number of designer stores. **H1** on 998 Soi Thonglor, Sukhumvit 55 is a clutch of low-rise trendy shops, restaurants and bars on the road that is becoming Bangkok's home to boutique malls.

Thanon Sukhumvit

There are many craft shops in soi off the Sukhumvit corridor. Among the best for a variety of items are these: **Gifted Hands**, 172/18 Soi 23 (Soi Prasanmit), Thanon Sukhumvit. Tel: 0 2258 4010; fax: 0 2285 4086. Handcrafted silver beads, necklaces, earrings.

L'Arcadia, 12/2 Soi 23 (Soi Prasanmit), Thanon Sukhumvit. Tel:

0 2259 9595; fax: 0 2259 1517; www.larcadia.net. Thai and Burmese wood and lacquer items.
Nandakwang, 108/3 Soi 23 (Soi Prasanmit), Thanon Sukhumvit. Tel: 0 2258 1962, 0 2664 0017; fax: 0 2664 0020. Mon–Sat 9am–4pm, Sun 10am–5pm. Cotton table/bed linens and clothing.
Rasi Sayam, 32 Soi 23 (Soi Prasanmit), Thanon Sukhumvit. Tel: 0 2258 4195; fax: 0 2262 0729; e-mail: rasisayam@rasisayam.com. High-quality handicrafts.
Siamraj Marketing, 160/4-6 Soi 55 (Soi Thong Lo), Thanon Sukhumvit. Tel: 0 2390 1248; fax: 0 2381 2608; e-mail: siamrajhouse@hotmail.com. Silk flowers, bencharong and other ceramic items.
Vilai, 731/1, Soi 55 (Soi Thong Lo), Thanon Sukhumvit. Tel: 0 2391 6106; fax: 0 2382 2236. Excellent fabrics.

Street vendors are common, particularly after dark, along both sides of Thanon Sukhumvit, between Soi 3 and 11. Perhaps the most useful items they sell are suitcases in a variety of sizes, handy to carry all the extra shopping home.

Thanon Charoen Krung
River City, 23 Trok Rongnamkaeng, Thanon Yota (on the river, a little north of the Royal Orchid Sheraton). Tel: 0 2237 0077–8; fax: 0 2237 7600; www.rivercity.co.th. Daily 10am–8pm. Fashionable shopping arcade, the top two floors of which are devoted entirely to antiques. Bangkok is a magnet for antiques and antiquities from as far afield as Nepal. There is also a surprising amount of European antiques on offer here – much of which has come from neighbouring countries (Burma, Cambodia, Laos) that formerly had sizable populations of European colonial masters. Prices can be alarmingly high and the merchants are not fond of bargaining, but it can be done, particularly if you have some time to devote to the endeavour. Keep in mind too that many of the "antiques" to be found here are cleverly aged reproductions.

Oriental Plaza, Soi Oriental, Thanon Charoen Krung (New). Tel: 0 2266 0186; fax: 0 2237 4062, is another stylish shopping complex with a wide variety of top quality merchandise and antiques, but it's proximity to the Oriental Hotel can make for astoundingly high price tags.
Bangrak Market, Thanon Charoen Krung (New), between the Oriental and Shangri-La hotels, something of a contrast to the more sophisticated shopping complexes in the area, sells Indian spices, fresh fruit and cut flowers, and a variety of household goods. Street vendors are common along Thanon Charoen Krung (New Road) between Thanon Silom and Thanon Suriwong.

Thanon Silom
Soi Patpong hosts a bustling **night market** each evening from about 6pm. Provided you aren't bothered by the occasional flash of skin through the open club doors, or by the touts doing their best to lure you inside, it can be an enjoyable experience. Silver jewellery, audio and video tapes, T-shirts, dresses, ties, leather goods and watches are common here. This nightly market has become so popular that the vendors' stands now stretch up and down Thanon Silom and Thanon Surawong for several blocks. The vendors start putting away their wares at around midnight. Bargain for everything.
Soi Lalai Sap, Soi 5, Thanon Silom (beside Bangkok Bank). Vendors offering a variety of inexpensive food, flowers, leather goods, watches and clothing line this small soi on weekdays only, until about 3pm. Interesting shops include:
Jim Thompson's Thai Silk, 9 Thanon Suriwong (near Thanon Rama IV). Tel: 0 2234 4900; www.jimthompson.com. Daily 9am–9pm. Staggering array of silk items; expensive but top quality.
Motif, 296/7 Thanon Silom. Tel: 0 2233 1203; fax: 0 2237 1459; e-mail: motif_marif@hotmail.com. Daily 10am–8pm. Export quality silk and cotton fabrics, handmade paper, paper flowers and a splendid range of cloth items.

Shinawatra Thai, 626 Thanon Rama IV, Bangrak. Tel: 0 2633 1220; fax: 0 2261 6606. Large assortment of silk and cloth items, including table linen, cushion covers and lingerie.
Silom Village Trade Center, 266 Thanon Silom (near Soi 24). www.silomvillage.co.th. An attractive complex of small shops offering a variety of leather goods, wood carvings, handmade paper products, Burmese lacquerware, jewellery and cloth goods. The coffee shop at the entrance is a good place to people-watch.
Thaniya Plaza, Thanon Thaniya, off Thanon Silom. Small shopping complex with boutiques, bookshops, a coffee shop, and one or two small gift shops. Legend on the 3rd floor has a good selection of handicrafts, including celadon, teak and baskets.

Chinatown
Even if you don't have any use for a dozen hand towels, six large rolls of gift wrap or entire bolts of cloth, a stroll down **Sampeng Lane** (Soi Wanit) in the heart of Chinatown is a delightful, if somewhat sense-assaulting, way to pass several hours. There are many small soi leading off Sampeng which are jammed with shops selling fabrics, herbal remedies, toys, clothes, paper items and household goods.

Follow Sampeng Lane up to the canal and cross over into **Pahurat**, an adjoining market with a strong Indian flavour. This is the place to find batik and other textiles, sewing notions and a wide range of spices.

North of Pahurat you will find **Old Siam Plaza**, a market with an old world ambience. The gun shops will likely be of little interest to the average tourist, but there are many handicrafts to be found here, as well as decent restaurants and coffee shops.

Pak Khlong Talad is a huge, crowded riverside market at the northwestern edge of Chinatown. It is at its most atmospheric around 2–3am when masses of fresh flowers and vegetables are unloaded from the boats and made ready for sale the following morning.

Banglamphu Area
Banglamphu Market, a sprawling area beside the river northeast of Sanam Luang, caters more to the budget traveller than to the one with gold cards. This is a good area for inexpensive clothing, and 1960s-inspired jewellery and fashions that seem to be the backpacker's uniform of choice. If you're looking for beaded necklaces and Indian-style cotton outfits, this is the place to find them. Second-hand books as well as many craft shops can be found along Thanon Khao San. Shops offering hair braiding and beading are a common sight in this area. Thai musical instruments can be purchased at **Duriyabanna**, 151 Thanon Tanao, and gold leaf beating takes place at 321 Thanon Phra Sumen (eastern edge of Banglamphu Market, before Thanon Prachatipatai; 9am–3pm, Mon–Fri). There is a bookstore with a good selection of Buddhist books next door.

On the other side of Democracy Monument, the markets at **Tha Phra Chan** and **Wat Ratchanatda** sell love potions and amulets to protect you from every conceivable misfortune. On Friday and Saturday, investigate the night market at **Democracy Monument**, mostly offering second-hand goods without a lot of the traditional tourist fare, but entertaining nevertheless.

Chatuchak Weekend Market
By far the most challenging (and often most rewarding) shopping experience is the huge weekend market at **Chatuchak Park** on Thanon Phaholyothin. Over 8,500 vendors ply their wares here on Saturday and Sunday; it's best to come early to avoid the heat. Antiques, clothing, jewellery, wood carvings, brassware, masks, baskets, handmade paper, and other crafts from around Southeast Asia can be found here, in addition to fruit, vegetables, plants and animals.

Bargaining adds to the fun of a day at Chatuchak, and when energy levels start to flag, there are many food stalls, and even a coffee shop or two, to offer sustenance. If

you're not content just to wander aimlessly through the many alleyways, the aforementioned Nancy Chandler map *(page 387)* is essential to help you find your way to a particular area of the market.

Suan Lum Night Bazaar
Situated on a former military compound just east of Lumphini Park, the "Night Bazaar Suan Lum" as it's known in Thai, is open nightly. This is a great alternative to battling the weekend crowds at Chatuchak Weekend Market during the heat of the day – you'll find many of the same handicrafts for sale here. In front of the market is a large "beer garden" where live bands play on weekends. The market is best between 7pm and midnight.

Department Stores

Finally, no matter which area you find yourself in, most major department stores have special handicrafts sections carrying a wide selection of items. Try **Central** (branches at 1691 Thanon Phaholyothin; 306 Thanon Silom; and 191 Thanon Silom, www.central.co.th), **Robinson** (branches at 1 Thanon Phaholyothin; intersection of Thanon Silom and Thanon Rama IV; and Soi 19, Thanon Sukhumvit, www.robinson. co.th), **Erawan** at Amarin Plaza, **Tokyu** at Mahboonkrong, **Zen Central** at the Central World Plaza, and the **Emporium** department store at Soi 24 Thanon Sukhumvit.

OUTSIDE BANGKOK

Chiang Mai also has air-conditioned department stores that sell household and personal products. Handicrafts can be found at studios along the 9-km (5½-mile) road to Borsang and along Thanon Wua Lai. For fake antiques, you must travel further, to **Baan Tawai** on the highway to Chom Thong. The famous Night Bazaar on Thanon Chang Klan and the vendors along Thanon Tapae are also places to pick up bargains.

Pattaya has malls like Mike's

Shopping Mall, Big C, Royal Garden Shopping Plaza and Thai Pan, but most of the casual items are found on the Thanon Beach. Shops sell a good selection of casual wear.

Phuket offers fewer shopping areas, and most are concentrated on Highway 402 between the airport and Phuket town. Thai Village (2½km; 1½ miles), Native Handicraft Center (8½km; 5 miles), Shinawatra (9km; 5½ miles) and Cheewa (10½km; 6½ miles) offer both local handicrafts and those imported from other regions of Thailand. Thai Village has workshops where you can watch the artisans at work. For casual wear, check the shops and vendors along Patong's Thanon Beach and Soi Bangla, and in Kata and Karon. In Phuket town, browse vendors and shops along Thanon Ranong.

What to Buy

REAL/FAKE ANTIQUES

Wood, bronze, terracotta and stone statues from all regions of Thailand and Burma can be found in

Hill Tribe Crafts

Northern hill tribes produce brightly coloured needlepoint work in a wide variety of geometric and floral patterns. These are sold either as produced, or else incorporated into shirts, coats, bags, pillowcases and other items.

Hill-tribe silver work is valued less for its silver content (which is low) than for the intricate work and imagination that goes into making it. The genre includes necklaces, headdresses, bracelets and rings the women wear on ceremonial occasions. Enhancing their value are the old British Indian rupee coins that decorate the women's elaborate headdresses.

Other hill-tribe items include knives, baskets, pipes and gourd flutes that look and sound like bagpipes.

Bangkok and Chiang Mai. There are religious figures and characters from classical literature, carved wooden angels, mythical animals, temple bargeboards and eave brackets. Note that most fake antiques passed off as real are crafted in Chiang Mai and surrounding villages.

Although the Thai government has banned the export of Buddha images, there are numerous deities and disciples which can be sent abroad. Bronze deer, angels and characters from the Ramakien cast in bronze do not fall under the export ban. It is also possible to buy and export Burmese Buddha images.

Chiang Mai produces beautiful wooden replicas modelled on antique sculptures. Sold as reproductions, with no attempt to pass them off as genuine antiques, they make lovely home decor items. Animals, Buddha's disciples and dozens of items range in size from small to life-sized.

Chiang Mai also produces beautifully crafted wooden furniture. Cabinets, tables, dining room sets, elephant howdah, bedroom sets or simple items like wooden trays are crafted from teak or other woods and carved with intricate designs.

BASKETS

Thailand's abundant bamboo and grasses are transformed into lamps, storage boxes, tables, colourful mats, handbags, letter holders, tissue boxes and slippers. Bamboo and other plants are turned into storage lockers with brass fittings and furniture to fill the entire house.

Yan lipao, a thin, sturdy grass, is woven into delicate patterns to create purses and bags for formal occasions. The bags are durable, retaining their beauty for years.

CERAMICS

Best known among the distinctive Thai ceramics is the jade green celadon, which is distinguished by its finely glazed surface. Statues, lamps, ashtrays and other items are also produced in dark green, brown and cobalt blue hues.

Modelled on its Chinese cousin, blue-and-white porcelain includes pots, lamp bases, household items and figurines. Quality varies according to the skill of the artist, and of the firing and glazing.

Bencharong (meaning five colours) describes a style of porcelain derived from 16th-century Chinese art. Normally reserved for bowls, containers and fine chinaware, its classic pattern features a small religious figure surrounded by intricate floral designs. The whole is rendered in five colours – usually green, blue, yellow, rose and black.

Earthenware includes a wide assortment of pots, planters and dinner sets in a rainbow of colours and designs. Also popular are the big, brown glazed Shanghai jars bearing yellow dragons. Antique stoneware includes the double-fish design plates and bowls originally produced at Sawankhalok, the kilns established near Sukhothai in the 13th century. Some of the best ceramics come from Ratchaburi, southwest of Bangkok. The wide variety makes a special trip there worthwhile.

DECORATIVE ARTS

Lacquerware comes in two styles: the gleaming gold-and-black variety normally seen on temple shutters, and the matte red type with black and/or green details, which originated in northern Thailand and Burma. The lacquerware repertoire includes ornate containers and trays, wooden figurines, woven bamboo baskets and Burmese-inspired Buddhist manuscripts. The pieces may also be bejewelled with tiny glass mosaics and gilded ornaments.

Black lacquer is also the base into which shaped bits of mother-of-pearl are pressed. Scenes from religious or classical literature are rendered on presentation trays, containers and plaques. Beware of craftsmen who take shortcuts by using black paint rather than the traditional seven layers of lacquer. On these items, the surface cracks, often while the item is still on the shelf.

FABRICS AND CLOTHES

Thai silk is perhaps Thailand's best-known craft. Brought to world attention by American entrepreneur Jim Thompson, Thai silk has enjoyed enduring popularity. Sold in a wide variety of colours, it is characterised by the tiny nubs which, like embossings, rise from its surface. Unlike sheer Indian silks and shiny Chinese-patterned silks, Thai silk is a thick cloth that lends itself to clothes (It is most popular as blouses, ties and scarves), curtains and upholstery. It is also used to cover purses, tissue boxes and picture frames. Lengths printed with elephant, bamboo, floral and dozens of other motifs are turned into decorative pillowcases to accent rooms.

Mutmee is a northeastern silk whose colours are sombre and muted. A form of tie-dyed cloth, it is sold in lengths or as finished clothes.

Cotton is popular for shirts and dresses, since it breathes in Thailand's hot, humid air. Although available in lengths, it is generally sold already cut into dresses and shirts. Southern Thailand is a batik centre and offers ready-made clothes and batik paintings.

Burmese in origin and style, kalaga wall hangings depicting gods, kings and mythical animals have gained increasing popularity in the past few years. The figures are stuffed with kapok to make them stand out from the surface in relief.

GEMS AND JEWELLERY

Thailand is one of the world's exporters of cut rubies and sapphires. The rough stones are mostly imported from Cambodia and Burma, as local mines are not able to meet the demand. Visitors should be very wary about buying gems in Thailand however. Unless you happen to be an expert on precious stones, chances are you'll be fleeced.

Thailand is now regarded as the world's leading cutter of gemstones, the "Bangkok cut" rapidly becoming one of the most popular. Thai artisans set the stones in gold and silver to create jewellery and bejewelled containers. Artisans also craft jewellery that satisfies an international clientele. Light green **Burmese jade** (jadeite) is carved into jewellery and art objects. The island of Phuket produces international standard natural, cultured **Mob** (teardrop) and **artificial pearls** (made from pearl dust glued to form a globule). They are sold as individual items or are set into gold jewellery.

Costume jewellery is a major Thai business, and the choice is wide. A related craft which has grown rapidly in the past decade is that of gilding Thai orchids for use as brooches.

METAL ART OBJECTS

Although Thai craftsmen have produced some of Asia's most beautiful Buddha images, modern bronze sculpture tends to be of less exalted subjects and execution. Minor deities, characters from classical literature, deer and abstract figures are cast up to 2 metres (7 ft) tall and are normally clad with a brass skin to make them gleam. Bronze is also cast into handsome cutlery and coated in shiny brass.

Silver and gold are pounded into jewellery items, boxes and other decorative pieces; many are set with gems. To create nielloware boxes and receptacles, a design is incised in silver or gold. The background is cut away and filled with an amalgam of dark metals, leaving the figures to stand in high relief against the black background.

Tin, mined near Phuket, is the prime ingredient in **pewterware**, of which Thailand is a major producer. Items range from clocks and steins to egg cups and figurines.

Steel flatware, hand forged and

hammered, is a popular buy in Thailand. The selection of designs is huge and prices are quite reasonable.

PAINTINGS

Modern Thai artists paint everything from realistic to abstract art, the latter often a weak imitation of Western art. Two areas at which they excel are depictions of everyday village life and of new interpretations of classical Buddhist themes. Artists also work from live sittings or photographs to create superb charcoal or oil portraits. A family photograph from home can be transformed into a painting. The price depends on size: a 40 cm x 60 cm (16" x 24") charcoal portrait costs around 1,000 baht. There are several street-side studios in Bangkok, Phuket and Pattaya that specialize in this art.

THEATRE ART OBJECTS

Papier mâché **khon masks**, like those used in palace dance/drama, are painted and accented with lacquer decorations and gilded to create superb works of art.

Shadow puppets cut from the hides of water buffaloes and displayed against backlit screens in open air theatres tell the Ramakien story. Check to be sure the figure is actually cut from hide and not from a sheet of black plastic. These brightly coloured puppets make excellent wall decorations.

Inspired by the Ramakien, craftsmen have fashioned miniature models of chariots and warriors in gilded wood or glass sculpture. These two materials are also employed to create reproductions of the famous Royal Barges.

UMBRELLAS

Chiang Mai produces lovely umbrellas and fans made from silk or *sa* paper, a fine parchment often confused for rice paper but made from pounded tree bark.

Sport

Participant Sports

Thailand has developed its outdoor sports facilities to a considerable degree and air-conditioned the ones played indoors. Nearly every major hotel has a swimming pool and a fitness centre; some have squash courts and jogging paths.

CANOEING

Canoeing is slowly catching on in Thailand. In the north, trips are available on the Kok river. Try **Track of the Tiger**, 108/2 Thanon Charoenphratet, tel: 0 5381 8641; fax: 0 5381 8221; www.track-of-the-tiger.com, which offers various adventure trips. Several operators in Mae Hong Son also organise canoeing trips.

Sea Canoe, based in Phuket, tel: 0 7625 4505–7; fax: 0 7622 6077; www.johngray-seacanoe.com, pioneered sea-canoeing in the country, notably to the sea caves around the island. Several similar operations have since opened in Phuket and Krabi, mostly notably. **Paddle Asia**, also based in Phuket. Tel: 0 7624 0952; fax: 0 7621 6145; paddleasia.com. Well known for their multi-day trips into Khao Sok National Park.

DEEP SEA FISHING

For deep-sea fishing, go to Phuket or to Bang Saray south of Pattaya. At Bang Saray, marlin, king mackerel, cobia, yellow jack, barracuda, bonito, giant groupers, red snapper, rays and black tip sharks lurk among submerged rocks. Boats, tackle and guides are available for very reasonable fees. There are small hotels in Bang Saray, but most fishermen spend the night in Pattaya and head out early in the morning.

The waters off Phuket offer sailfish, barracuda, albacore, marlin, wahoo, tuna and king mackerel. The fishing around Phi Phi is also supposed to be quite good, and there are a handful of operators on the island who rent boats and equipment.

Some charter operators in Phuket:

Aloha Tour
Tel: 0 7638 1215, 0 7638 1220
Fax: 0 7638 1592
www.thai-boat.com

Andaman Hooker
Tel: 0 7628 2036, 0 1894 7161
www.phuketsportfishing.com

Phuket Big Game Fishing
Tel: 0 7620 2679, 0 1676 2629
www.bluewater-anglers.com

Wahoo Big Game Fishing
Tel: 0 7628 1510
Fax: 0 7628 0775
www.wahoo.ws

FITNESS CENTRES

California WOW Experience, located on Thanon Silom near the Sala Daeng skytrain station. Tel: 0 2631 1112; www.californiawowx.com, open Mon–Sat 6am–midnight, Sun 8am–10pm, is one of the most popular of many to be found in the city. The Asia-wide **Clark Hatch** has a branch in the Thaniya Plaza, off Thanon Silom. Tel: 0 2231 2250;

www.clarkhatchthailand.com, open Mon–Fri 6am–9pm, Sat–Sun 10am–8pm. All the top hotels in Bangkok have well equipped fitness centres.

Outside Bangkok

Most of the major hotels in Chiang Mai, Pattaya and Phuket have fitness centers, and many are open to walk-ins.

Fitness Parks

There is a fitness park in one corner of Bangkok's **Lumphini Park**. In Chiang Mai, the free fitness park on **Thanon Nimmanhaemin**, is open 5am–10pm. In Pattaya, the fitness park is located on the slopes of **Pattaya Hill**; in Phuket, it sits atop **Rang Hill** in the middle of town.

Scuba Diving

Shops in Pattaya and Phuket's Patong beach provide comprehensive courses leading to internationally-recognized PADI or NAUI certification.

Ko Tao

Ko Tao is popular with both experienced and first-time divers; the placid bays and leeward shores are perfect for the beginner. The visibility is usually exceptional in the pristine waters off this tiny island, and sightings of spotted rays, trigger fish, whale sharks and even giant clams are not uncommon. There are over 20 diving schools on Ko Tao with 100 or more professional instructors, including:

Buddha View Dive Resort, Thanon Khao San, Bayon Building. Tel: 0 2629 3824; fax: 0 2629 3981; www.buddhaview-diving.com.

Samui International Diving School/Planet Scuba, Bangkok, tel: 0 2253 8043; www.planet-scuba.com. Contact Samui offices: Tel: 0 7742 2386, 0 7741 3050; fax: 0 7723 1242. (Head office at Malibu Resort Chaweng Beach.)

Ban's Diving Resort, Surat Thani, tel: 0 7745 6061, 0 7745 6466; www.amazingkohtao.com.

Pattaya

Seafari Sports Center on Thanon Beach, tel: 0 3842 9060; fax: 0 3836 1356, and **Mermaid Xtreme Diving**, tel: 0 3842 0411; fax: 0 3836 0095; www.pattaya scubadiving.com, at Soi 6 on the Thanon Beach offer PADI and NAUI courses and diving trips to the outer islands. The water in the bay is murky and visibility is limited.

Phuket

Fantasea, tel/fax: 0 7628 1388, 0 7628 1389; www.fantasea.net, also at www.oceanriver.com, the real thing for serious divers.

South East Asia Liveaboards, tel: 0 7634 0406, 7634 0932; fax: 0 7634 0586; www.sealiveaboards.com.

Santana Diving and Canoeing, Patong Beach, tel: 0 7629 4220; fax: 0 7634 0360; www.santanaphuket.com.

Sea Bees Diving, Thanon Viset, Chalong Bay, tel: 0 7638 1765; fax: 0 7638 0467; www.sea-bees.com.

Marina Divers, 45 Thanon Karon, Karon Beach, tel: 0 7633 0272; fax: 0 7633 0998; www.marinadivers.com.

These, among others, have a good reputation. Shop around and

you can find scuba trips aimed at German, Scandinavian, French, Thai and Japanese customers.

Trips

For beginners, the four-day PADI **Open Water course** costs around 8,500 baht, including classroom theory, shallow water introduction, and four dives, usually in Phi Phi, Shark Point or Raja Island.

Day trips for divers with an Open Water card typically visit **Phi Phi**, **Shark Point** or the two **Raja islands**. Day trips average 2,000–3,000 baht, plus 500 baht for full equipment rental.

There is a trend towards liveaboard trips to the high visibility dive sites at the **Similan** and **Surin** islands, and even into Burma. These places offer a better chance of seeing large turtles, whale sharks, manta rays and the like. Depending on the vessel, which can be basic or luxurious, trips run to 2,500–6,000 baht per person per day. Trips usually last from 2 to 7 days. In Bangkok contact:

Larry's Dive, Soi 22 Thanon Sukhumvit. Tel: 0 2663 5463; www.larrysdive.com. Both run regular trips to various dive sites in Thailand.

GOLF

Thais are great golfing buffs, going so far as to employ some of world golfing's stellar architects to design international-class courses. The best are in Bangkok, Phuket and Pattaya, with other courses in Chiang Mai, Khao Yai and Hua Hin. Greens fees range from 500–1,000 baht per round on weekends, and generally speaking it is not too difficult to reserve a time to play.

Among Bangkok's courses are the **Navathanee Golf Course** (22 M.1, Thanon Sukhapiban 2. Tel: 0 2376 1034–6; fax: 0 2376 1685) designed by Robert Trent Jones Jr. It is open 6am–6pm. The **Army Golf Course** at 459 Thanon Ram Intra, tel: 0 2521 5338; fax: 0 2521 3391, is open 5am–9.30pm. **Krungthep Kreetha Sports Club**, 516 Thanon Krungthepkreetha, Hua Mark, tel: 0 2379 3716-7; fax: 0 2379 3768, is open 5am–5pm.

In Chiang Mai, the **Lanna Golf Course** on Thanon Chotana, tel: 0 5322 1911; fax: 0 5322 1743, is open 6am–6pm.

In Pattaya, try the **Siam Country Club Golf Course**, tel: 0 3824 9381-6; fax: 0 3824 9387; www.siamcountryclub.com, 10 km (6 miles) east of town in rolling hills.

Phuket has excellent, if pricey, golf courses at the **Banyan Tree** (Laguna Phuket Golf Club, tel: 0 7632 4374; fax: 0 7632 4375; www.banyantree.com/phuket/golf. htm), **Blue Canyon Country Club** (tel: 0 7632 8088; fax: 0 7632 8068; www.bluecanyonclub.com), the **Phuket Country Club** (tel: 0 7632 1038–41; 0 7632 1721; www.phuketcountryclub.com) and **Loch Palm Golf Club** (tel: 0 7632 1929–34; fax: 0 7632 1927; www.lochpalm.com).

Many Thai golfers reckon that the best and most convenient golfing is to be found at Hua Hin.

HORSE RIDING

There are no public horse-riding facilities in Bangkok, but in Chiang Mai riding can be arranged through **Travel Shoppe**, tel: 0 5387 4091; horseriding.chiangmaiinfo.com.

In Phuket, ride at **Phuket Bangtao (Laguna) Riding Club** at Laguna Hotel Entrance (Tel: 0 7632 4199; fax: 0 7632 4099; www.phuket-bangtao-horseriding. com). Instructors accompany riders through rice fields and down the beach. Morning rides into the jungle are also offered. During the dry season, owners take riders on 2-hour trips into the hills.

ICE SKATING

One of the more unusual tropical pursuits, ice skating has a certain popularity in Bangkok. Try it at the **World Ice Skating Center**, Central World Plaza, 8th Floor, 4 Thanon Ratchadamri. Tel: 0 2255 9500. Daily 10am–2.45pm, 3.30pm–8.30pm.

In Chiang Mai try **Bully Ice**, Kad Suan Kaew, tel: 0 5322 4444. Daily 10am–1am.

JOGGING

Bangkok has several jogging sites for those wise enough not to challenge the city's traffic for right-of-way. These include Lumphini Park, Queen Sirikit Park at Lad Prao, Benjasiri Park between Soi 22 and 24 Thanon Sukhumvit, and Chatuchak Park. The Ambassador hotel, among others, have jogging paths.

In Chiang Mai, many joggers run up the hill to Doi Suthep and catch a minibus back. In Pattaya, jog up Pattaya Hill. In Phuket, try Rang Hill, a 1½ km (1 mile) jaunt. There is a fitness park at the top.

SNOOKER

Thailand has some excellent snooker players who are now nipping at the heels of world champions.

As a result, parlours have sprung up everywhere in Thailand, as aspiring champions focus their eyes on complex shots and potential riches. In Bangkok, there are numerous snooker parlours around the city. The "Rooks" chain is the most popular, with dozens of establishments around town.

Spectator Sports

Despite the hot climate, Thai men and women are avid sports enthusiasts, playing and watching both their own sports and those adopted from the West according to international rules.

The king of foreign sports is soccer and is played by both sexes. Following a close second is badminton, with basketball, volleyball, rugby, track and field, swimming, marksmanship, boxing, tennis and golf trailing only a short way behind. Check the English-language newspapers for schedules of the latest events.

The principal sports venues in Bangkok are the **National Stadium**, on Thanon Rama I just west of Mahboonkrong Shopping Center; the **Hua Mark Stadium**, east of the city next to Ramkhamhaeng University; and the **Thai-Japanese Sports Center**, at Din Daeng near the northern entrance to the expressway.

In Chiang Mai, games are played at the **Chiang Mai Stadium** and at **Chiang Mai University**; in Phuket, at the **Phuket Stadium** on Thanon Vichaisongkhram.

Thailand has also created a number of unique sports and these are well worth watching, as much for the grace and agility displayed by the players as for the element of fun that pervades every competition.

TAKRAW

With close relatives in the Philippines, Malaysia and Indonesia, Laos and Burma, takraw employs all the limbs except the hands to propel a woven rattan ball (or a more modern plastic ball) over a net or into a hoop. In the net version, two three-player teams face each other across a head-high net, like that used in badminton. As the match heats up, it is not unusual for a player to turn a complete somer-sault to spike a ball across the net.

In the second type, six players form a wide circle around a basket-like net suspended high in the air. Using heads, feet, knees and elbows to keep the ball airborne, they score points by putting it into the net. A team has a set time period in which to score as many points as it can, after which it is the opposing team's turn.

Tournaments are held at the **Thai-Japanese Sports Center** (tel: 0 2465 5325 for dates and times) four times a year; admission is free. Competitions are also held in the northwest corner of Bangkok's **Sanam Luang** during the March–April kite contests. Free admission. During the non-monsoon months, wander into a park or a temple courtyard anywhere in the country late-in the afternoon.

Kite Flying

The heat of March and April is relieved somewhat by breezes that the Thais use to send kites aloft in Sanam Luang in Bangkok and open spaces everywhere.

They have also turned it into a competitive sport, forming teams sponsored by major companies. Two teams vie for trophies. One flies a giant star-shaped male *chula* kite nearly 2 m (6½ ft) high. The opposing teams (there may be more than one) fly the diminutive diamond-shaped female *pakpao* kites. One team tries to snare the other's kite and drag it across a dividing line.

Surprisingly, the odds are even and a tiny female *pakpao* stands a good chance of pulling down a big *chula* male. Teamwork and fast action make for exciting viewing. Competitions at Bangkok's **Sanam Luang** start at 2pm.

THAI BOXING (MUAY THAI)

One of the most exciting and popular Thai sports is Thai boxing. In Bangkok, **Lumphini Boxing Stadium**, on Thanon Rama IV, stages bouts on Tuesday and Friday at 6.30pm and on Saturday at 10am and 5pm. Ticket prices run between 500 and 1,000 baht for ringside seats (depending on the quality of the card), running downwards to 100 baht. The Sunday matinee at 6.30pm is recommended, as it has the cheapest seats.

Note: In October 2005, Lumphini Boxing Stadium is scheduled to move to a new location about 2 km (1 mile) away, at Soi Nang Linchi 3, near the Thai Immigration Department on Thanon Suan Phlu.

Ratchadamnoen Stadium on Ratchadamnoen Nok Avenue offers bouts on Monday, Wednesday, and Thursday at 6.30pm and on Sunday at 6.30pm. Ticket prices are the same as at Lumphini, and, as above, weekend afternoon matinees are the cheapest.

There are also televised bouts on Saturday and Sunday, and at 10.30pm on some week nights. For many visitors this will be sufficient introduction to the sport.

For details of matches, visit www.muaythai2000.com, or www.bestmuaythai.com, which is the website of Suwit Boxing Camp in Phuket.

The Rose Garden and Phuket's **Thai Village** offer short demon-strations of Thai boxing, but these are played more for laughs than for authenticity.

Thai boxing bouts in Chiang Mai can be seen at the Dechanukrau boxing ring, on Thanon Bumrungrat, on the weekends. Bouts are staged each Friday at 8pm at the **Phuket Boxing Stadium** at Saphan Hin (to the right of the tin dredge memorial where Thanon Phuket meets the sea). Most large rural towns have their own boxing gyms and stage weekly bouts by young hopefuls.

Language

Origins and Intonation

For centuries, the Thai language, rather than tripping from foreigners' tongues, has been tripping them up. Its roots go back to the place Thais originated from, in the hills of southern Asia and is overlaid by Indian influences. From the original settlers come the five tones which seem designed to frustrate visitors – one sound with five different tones to mean five different things. So, when you mispronounce, not only are you saying the word incorrectly, chances are you're saying another word entirely. It is not unusual to see a semi-fluent foreigner standing before a Thai running through the scale of tones until suddenly a light of recognition dawns on his companion's face. There are misinformed visitors who will tell you that tones are not important. These people do not communicate with Thais; they communicate at them in a one-sided exchange that frustrates both parties.

Thai Names

From the languages of India have come polysyllabic names and words, the lexicon of literature. Thai names are among the longest in the world. Every Thai first name and surname has a meaning. Thus by learning the meaning of the name of everyone you meet, you would acquire a formal, but quite extensive vocabulary.

There is no universal transliteration system from Thai into English, which is why names and street names can be spelled three different ways. For example, the surname Chumsai is written Chumsai, Jumsai and Xoomsai depending on the family. This confuses even the Thais. If you ask a Thai how you spell something, he may well reply "how do you want to spell it?" Likewise, Bangkok's thoroughfare of Ratchadamnoen is also spelled Rajdamnern and Ratchadamnoen. Ko Samui can be spelled Koh Samui. The spellings will differ from map to map, and book to book.

Phonology

Consonants

The way Thai consonants are written in English often confuses foreigners. An "h" following a letter like "p", and "t" gives the letter a soft sound; without the "h" the sound is more explosive. Thus, "ph" is not pronounced "f" but as a soft "p". Without the "h", the "p" has the sound of a very hard "b". The word Thanon (street) is pronounced "tanon" in the same way as "Thailand" is not meant to sound like "Thighland". Similarly, final letters are often not pronounced as they look. A "j" on the end of a word is pronounced "t"; "l" is pronounced as an "n". To complicate matters further, many words end with "se" or "r" which are not pronounced; for instance Suriwongse, one of Bangkok's main thoroughfares, is simply pronounced "Suriwong."

Vowels

Vowels are pronounced like this:
i as in sip, **ii** as in seep,
e as in bet, **a** as in pun,
aa as in pal, **u** as in pool,
o as in so, **ai** as in pie,
ow as in cow, **aw** as in paw,
iw as in you, **oy** as in toy.

In Thai, the pronouns "I" and "me" use the same word but it is different for males and females. Men use the word phom when referring to themselves; women say chan or diichan. Men use khrap at the end of a sentence when addressing either a male or a

Numbers

1	Nung (l)
2	Song (r)
3	Sam (r)
4	Sii (l)
5	Haa (f)
6	Hok (l)
7	Jet (l)
8	Paet (l)
9	Kow (f)
10	Sip (l)
11	Sip (l) Et (l)
12	Sip (l) Song (r)
13	Sip (l) Sam (r)...
20	Yii (f) Sip (l)
30	Sam (r) Sip (l)...
100	Nung (l) Roi (h)
1,000	Nung (l) Phan (m)

female i.e. pai (m) nai, khrap (h) (where are you going? sir). Women add the word kha to their statements as in pai (m) nai, kha (f). To ask a question, add a high tone mai to the end of the phrase i.e. rao pai (we go) or rao pai mai (h) (shall we go?). To negate a statement, insert a falling tone mai between the subject and the verb i.e. rao pai (we go), rao mai pai (we don't go). "Very" or "much" are indicated by adding maak to the end of a phrase i.e. ron (hot), ron maak (very hot).

Listed below is a small vocabulary intended to get you on your way. The five tones have been indicated by appending letters after them viz. high (h), low (l), middle (m), rising (like asking a question) (r), and falling (like suddenly understanding something as in "ohh, I see") (f).

Useful Phrases

DAYS OF THE WEEK

Monday Wan (m) Jan (m)
Tuesday Wan (m) Angkan (m, m)
Wednesday Wan (m) Phoot (h)
Thursday Wan (m) Pharuhat (m, h, l)
Friday Wan (m) Sook (l)
Saturday Wan (m) Sao (r)
Sunday Wan (m) Athit (m, h)
Today Wan (m) nii (h)
Yesterday Mua (f) waan (m) nii (h)

Tomorrow Phrung (f) nii (h)
When Mua (f) rai (m)

BASICS

Yes Chai (f)
No Mai (f) chai (f)
Hello, goodbye Sawasdee (a man then says "khrap"; a woman says "kha"; thus, sawasdee khrap or sawasdee kha)
How are you? Khun sabai dii, mai (h)
Well, thank you Sabai dii, Khapkhun
Thank you very much Khapkhun Maak
May I take a photo? Thai roop (f) noi, dai (f) mai (h)
Never mind Mai (f) pen rai
I cannot speak Thai Phuut Thai mai (f) dai (f)
I can speak a little Thai Phuut Thai dai (f) nit (h) diew
Where do you live? Khun yoo thii (f) nai (r)
What is this called in Thai? An nii (h), kaw riak aray phasa Thai
I do not feel well Mai (f) sabai

Glossary of Terms

Ao Gulf/bay
Bot central sanctuary in a Thai temple
Khao hill
Khlong canal
Ko Island
Likay traditional folk drama and dance
Muay Thai Thai boxing
Naga Serpent with dragon's head
Phra monk or Buddha image
Sanuk fun or enjoyment
Soi lane or alleyway
Tuk-tuk Three-wheeled open cab
Wai palms-together Thai greeting
Wat temple or monastery

DIRECTIONS AND TRAVEL

Go Pai
Come Maa
Where Thii (f) nai (r)
Right Khwaa (r)
Left Sai (h)

Turn *Leo*
Straight ahead *Trong pai*
Please slow down *Cha cha noi*
Stop here *Yood thii* (f) *nii* (f)
Fast *Raew*
Hotel *Rong raam*
Street *Thanon*
Lane *Soi*
Bridge *Saphan*
Police Station *Sathanii Dtam Ruat*

SHOPPING

Do you have...? *Mii... mai* (h)
How much? *Thao* (f) *rai*
Expensive *Phaeng* (m)
Do you have something cheaper?
Mii arai thii thook (l) *kwa, mai* (h)
Can you lower the price a bit? *Kaw lot noi dai* (f) *mai* (h)
Do you have another colour? *Mii sii uhn mai* (h)
Too big *Yai kern pai*
Too small *Lek kern pai*
Do you have bigger? *Mii arai thii yai kwa mai* (h)
Do you have smaller? *Mii arai thii lek kwa mai* (h)

FOOD

Hot (heat) *Ron* (h)
Hot (spicy) *Phet*
Cold *Yen*
Sweet *Waan* (r)
Sour *Prio* (f)

Further Reading

General

Amranand, Pimsai. **Gardening in Bangkok**. Bangkok: Siam Society. Good work on plants though could do with more photos.
Clutterbuck, Martin R. **The Legend of Siamese Cats**. Bangkok, White Lotus Press, 1998. Breeds and Thai folklore relating to these cats.
Cooper, Robert and Nanthapa. Gerson Ruth. **Traditional Festivals in Thailand**. Oxford University Press, 1996.
Gray, Denis, et al., **National Parks of Thailand**. Bangkok: Industrial Finance Corporation of Thailand, 1994.
Hollinger, Carol. **Mai Pen Rai**. Boston: Houghton Mifflin. Expatriate life in the 1950s. Despite its age, much of this insightful account of Thai culture still holds true today.
Ingram, J.C. **Economic Change in Siam Society, Culture and Environment in Thailand**. Siam Society: Bangkok, 1989.
Sternstein, Larry. **Thailand: The Environment of Modernisation**. Sydney: McGraw-Hill, 1976. Excellent geography text.
Stockmann, Hardy. **Thai Boxing**. Bangkok: D.K. Books, 1979. Excellent, well illustrated book on the basics of Thai boxing.
Warren, William. **The Legendary American**. Boston: Houghton Mifflin. The intriguing story of American Thai silk king Jim Thompson.

Fiction

Burdett, John. **Bangkok 8**. Vintage, 2004. A best-selling story about a half-Thai, half-American policeman who avenges his partner's death.
Cotterill, Colin. **Evil in the Land Without**. Bangkok: Asia Books, 2003. A gripping novel about Detective John Jessel being threatened by a serial killer called "The Paw".

Garland, Alex. **The Beach**. New York: Riverhead Trade, 1998. The beach read that inspired the movie staring Leonardo Dicaprio about a group of backpackers trying to find their own paradise.
Moore, Christopher G. **A Killing Smile**. Bangkok: Heaven Lake Press, 2004. A gripping thriller set in the capital city of Thailand.
Needham, Jake. **The Big Mango**. Bangkok: Asia Books, 1999. An action-adventure story about a search for millions of dollars in cash that went missing during the fall of Saigon in 1975.
Quartermaine, Ian. **Sleepless in Bangkok**. Bangkok: IQ Inc., 2002. A tough and funny erotic thriller, based on actual events, about an ex-SAS security consultant on a covert assignment to Siam.

History

Chakrabongse, Prince Chula. **Lords of Life**. London: Alvin Redman, 1960. A history of the Chakri kings.
Kasetsiri, Charnvit. **The Rise of Ayudhya**. London: East Asian Historical Monographs, 1976. A narration of the history of early Ayutthaya.
Coedes, George. **The Indianized States of Southeast Asia**. Trans. Susan Brown Cousing. Ed. Walter F. Vella. Honolulu: East-West Centre Press, 1968. Well written scholarly work.
Ghosh, Suchita. **Thailand, Tryst with Modernity**. Vikas Publishing House, New Delhi, 1997. 20th century Thai politics.
Hall, D.G.E. **A History of South-east Asia**. 3rd ed. London: Macmillan, 1968. The classic text.
Highham, Charles. **Prehistoric Thailand: from Early Settlement to Sukothai**. River Books, Bangkok, 1998. An overview of Thai history up to 1782.
Hutchinson, E.W. 1688: **Revolution in Siam**. Hong Kong University Press. The events leading to the expulsion of the foreigners from Ayutthaya.
McCoy, Alfred W. **The Politics of Heroin in Southeast Asia**. New York: Harper & Row, 1973. The pioneering

work. Readily found in Bangkok.
Moffat, Abbot Low. Mongkut, *The King of Siam*. Ithaca, New York: Cornell University Press, 1961. Superb history of one of Asia's most interesting 19th century men.
Phongpaichit, Pasuk and Baker, Chris. *Thailand's Boom!* Chiang Mai: Silkworm, 1997. Two academics give a lively, popular account of the forces that fuelled a decade of rapid economic growth. Some portents of the collapse.
Van Beek, Steve. *Bangkok Only Yesterday*. Hong Kong: Hong Kong Publishing, 1982. Anecdotal history of Bangkok illustrated with old photos.
Vella, Walter F. *Chaiyo!* Honolulu: University of Hawaii Press, 1979. The life and times of King Vajiravudh (1910–1925).
Wright, Joseph. *The Balancing Act: A History of Modern Thailand*. Oakland: Pacific Rim Press, 1991. Accessible and detailed history of modern Thailand.
Wyatt, David K. *Thailand: A Short History*. Bangkok/London: ThaiWattana Panich/Yale University Press, 1984. Concise and well written.

Art and Culture

Boynes, Jon *Tiger-men and Tofu Dolls: Tribal spirits in northern Thailand*. Chiang Mai, Silkworm Books, 1997. A study of religion and ethnology in northern Thailand.
Diskul, M.C. Subhadradis. *Art in Thailand: A Brief History*. Bangkok: Silpakorn University, 1970. By the Dean of the Fine Arts University.
Klausner, William J. *Reflections on Thai Culture*. The Siam Society: Bangkok, 1987. Observations of a longtime resident anthropologist.
Rajadhon, Phya Anuman. *Essays on Thai Folklore*. Bangkok: D.K. Books. A description of Thai ceremonies, festivals and rites of passage.
Van Beek, Steve & Tettoni L.I. *The Arts of Thailand*. London: Thames & Hudson, 1991. Lavishly illustrated; includes the minor arts.
Warren, William. *The House on the Klong*. Tokyo: Weatherhill. The story

of the Jim Thompson House.
Wray, Joe, Elizabeth Wray, Clare Rosenfeld and Dorothy Bailey. **Ten Lives of the Buddha; Siamese Temple Paintings and Jataka Tales**. Tokyo: Weatherhill, 1974. Well illustrated, valuable for understanding Thai painting and the Tosachat (Jataka Tales).

People

Aylwen, Axel. *The Falcon of Siam*. London: Methuen, 1988. A fictionalised story of Constant Phaulkon, Greek adventurer in Siam in the late 1600s.
Ekachai, Sanitsuda. *Behind the Smile, Voices of Thailand*. Thailand. Thai Development Support Committee, 1990. Well written and informative portraits of Thai life by local journalist.
Lewis, Paul and Elaine. *Peoples of the Golden Triangle*. London: Thames and Hudson, 1984. Excellent text and photographs of the hill tribes.
Seidenfaden, Erik. *The Thai Peoples*. Bangkok: Siam Society, 1967. Solid work by long time resident.
Skinner, G. William. *Chinese Society in Thailand*. Ithaca, New York: Cornell University Press, 1957. Gives an insight into an important segment of Bangkok's history.

Religion

Bunnag, Jane. *Buddhist Monk, Buddhist Layman*. Cambridge: Cambridge University Press, 1973. Gives an insight into the monastic experience.
Nivat, Prince Dhani. A *History of Buddhism in Siam*. Bangkok: Siam Society, 1965. By one of Thailand's most respected scholars.
Rahula, Walpola. *What the Buddha Taught*. New York: Grove Press, 1974. Comprehensive account of Buddhist doctrine.

Natural History

Gray, Dennis, Collin Piprell and Mark Graham. *National Parks of Thailand*. Bangkok: Industrial

Finance Corp. of Thailand, 1991. Accommodation information is very unreliable. Otherwise, this is a useful survey of the natural assets of many national parks.
Lekagul, Boonsung and Philip D. Round. *A Guide to the Birds of Thailand*. Bangkok: Saha Karn Bhaer, 1991. The standard handbook.
Rabinowitz, Alan. *Chasing the Dragon's Tail: The Struggle to Save Thailand's Wildcats*. New York: Doubleday, 1991. Well told tales from a zoologist.
Stewart-Cox, Belinda and Gerald Cubitt. *Wild Thailand*. Bangkok: Asia Books, 1995. A coffee-table book with a solid text and a sobering tone.

Other Insight Guides

The Insight Guide series covers nearly 200 destinations. These are among the titles on Asian hot spots.

Insight Guide: Bangkok. takes the lid off one of the most exciting cities in the world while titles to **Burma. Indonesia, Laos and Cambodia, Malaysia, Singapore** and **Vietnam** cover the rest of the region.

In Insight's companion *Compact Guide* series, handy-sized books designed as mini-encyclopedias for instant on-the-spot reference, current titles in the Southeast Asia region include **Cambodia, Bali, Thailand, Bangkok** and **Vietnam**.

The *Insight Pocket Guide* series is written by local hosts. The books, many with full-size fold-out maps, take you on specially worked-out tours which help to make the most of a visit when time is limited. Current titles include **Bali, Kuala Lumpur, Sabah, Singapore, Bangkok, Chiang Mai, Phuket, Vietnam** and **Hanoi**.

Insight Guide Fleximaps have a laminated finish for ease of use, informative text and detailed cartography. There are Fleximaps to the following destinations: **Bali, Bangkok, Kuala Lumpur, Phuket, Singapore** and **Thailand**.

ART & PHOTO CREDITS

Cartographic Editor **Zoë Goodwin**
Production **Caroline**
Design Consultants
Klaus Geisler, Graham Mitchener
Picture Research **Hilary Genin**

Index

A
B
C
D
E
G
H
I
J
a
b
c
d
e
f
g
j
k